INVESTMENT
MANAGEMENT

INVESTMENT MANAGEMENT

Edited by

Peter L. Bernstein and
Aswath Damodaran

John Wiley & Sons, Inc.

New York • Chichester • Weinheim • Brisbane • Singapore • Toronto

Library of Congress Cataloging-in-Publication Data:

   Investment management / Peter L. Bernstein, ed., Aswath Damodaran, ed.
       p.   cm.
    Includes index.
    ISBN 0-471-19716-5 (cloth : alk. paper).—ISBN 0-471-19715-7
(paper : alk. paper)
     1. Portfolio management. 2. Investment analysis. I. Bernstein,
Peter L. II. Damodaran, Aswath.
   HG4529.5.I58 1998
   332.6—dc21   97-43844

Printed in the United States of America

10 9 8 7 6 5 4 3 2 1

CONTENTS

PREFACE
Peter L. Bernstein

Once upon a time, Wall Street lived off little homilies, like "Buy low and sell high," "Nothing ventured, nothing gained," "Don't put all your eggs in one basket," or "The bulls get something and the bears get something but the pigs get nothing." Like all sayings that endure, these simple proverbs contain a lot of truth, even if not the whole truth. When wrapped into a body of theory that supports them with logic and a systematic set of principles, these elementary wisdoms pack a great deal of power. Today, Wall Street lives off this body of theory.

Yet, if the theory is so consistent, logical, and powerful, another fabled Wall Street saying comes to mind: "If you're so smart, how come you're not rich?" The answer is disarmingly simple: The essence of investment theory is that being smart is not a sufficient condition for being rich. This book is about the missing ingredients.

Investing is a process of making decisions today to achieve results that will not be known until tomorrow. Nobody knows what tomorrow will bring, because nobody can control everything that is going to happen tomorrow. The overarching reality, the launching pad from which investment theory takes off, is that being wrong on occasion is inescapable, even for people who are very smart. The subject matter of investment theory explains why being wrong is inescapable, and tells how best to manage our affairs in the face of that disagreeable reality.

Because the book is about how to make decisions as well as about the way markets behave, I have selected authors whose understanding of the theoretical side can be matched by firing-line experience of the exhilaration as well as the frustration that all investors encounter. These authors know well how to pick their way between logic and intuition in arriving at investment judgments.

Despite the amorphous future that shapes the outcomes of our bets, investing is always a matter of numbers, which makes it inherently mathematical. Investing is also a matter of dynamic relationships between the prices at which assets trade and variables such as interest rates, inflation, taxes, earnings, and exchange rates—relationships that are shaped by expectations as well as by cool logic. This analysis of systematic relationships is also an inherently mathematical affair. A quick riffle through the pages that follow will reveal that mathematical formulations appear with some frequency throughout most of the chapters.

Even though the authors say in plain English everything that they also express mathematically, the math is indispensable because most of the leading applications of current investment concepts have derived from these equations. Working your way through them is therefore unavoidable if you want to understand what professional investors are up to. In any case, all these forbidding formulations are in reality nothing more than statements of logic and of how one variable responds to changes in other variables. I make a firm promise that, once you get the hang of it, the mathematical passages will not be a chore.

Finally, and perhaps most important, this book presents investing as a *process*. Investing is not a collection of things like stocks and bonds and derivatives, nor is it a set of two separate boxes, one for analyzing markets and another for making decisions. The way investors make decisions is precisely what makes markets behave as they do. The book also ignores conventional but artificial barriers, such as those between domestic investments and investments outside one's home country.

Investing is a seamless procedure that begins with understanding both the role of time and uncertainty and the institutional structure within which we make our decisions. Once aware of where the pitfalls lie and where the solutions may be had, investors must then consider the way their own individual situations will influence the point at which they choose to trade off the inevitable risks against the expected rewards. Not two investors are likely to have identical responses. These are the essential elements of the prelude.

Only after those steps have been taken can we begin to consider how to select the securities that will compose the portfolio and meet the constraints that we have established. We must study both the choices offered on the left side of the investment menu and the prices that appear on the right. The left side offers variety, but the basic principles of valuation are the same whether we choose stocks or bonds, domestic or international, or any of the wide variety of opportunities offered to us.

Now we can approach the interaction between the portfolio and the markets, in order to frame strategies that will minimize risk and maximize the returns we expect. But the risks will always be there, so we must explore the many interesting tools that can help us to control risks we cannot avoid taking. Finally, off and running, we can turn our attention to managing taxes, assessing the portfolio's performance, and evaluating the management structure of the corporations in which we invest.

This view of investing as a process explains the structure of the book's contents. Unlike most books on investing, this one has no separate chapters for each of the different asset classes. International investing is treated right along with domestic, for the issues involved are identical—an asset is an asset is an asset. Foreign exchange fluctuations are a risk in international investing, but managing exchange risk is, in principle, no different from managing the many other kinds of uncertainties the investor must face. Some subjects treated in an early chapter reappear in another, but I purposely let the duplication remain, not just because some ideas bear repeating for better comprehension, but also because only a few cardinal principles run like a thread right through the whole subject of investing, regardless of the particular aspect of it that may be under discussion.

There is a lot to learn here. I envy you the experience.

INVESTMENT MANAGEMENT

INTRODUCTION: THE INVESTMENT PROCESS

Aswath Damodaran

As investors, we would all like to beat the market handily and pick great invest-ments instinctively. However, even when intuition is correct, it is only part of the process of investing. Most investors prefer to focus their energy and efforts on investment philosophies and strategies rather than on the investment pro-cess. Reading about how Peter Lynch picks stocks or what makes Warren Buf-fett a great investor is far more interesting than talking about the steps involved in creating a portfolio or in executing trades. Yet, an understanding of the in-vestment process is critical for every investor, and the functions of the process should be communicated by advisers. The investment process:

1. Outlines the steps in creating a portfolio and emphasizes the sequence of actions involved, from understanding the investor's risk preferences to selecting and allocating assets and then evaluating their performance. By emphasizing the sequence, the process provides an orderly way in which an investor can create a personal portfolio or a portfolio for some-one else.

2. Provides a structure that allows investors to see the sources of the differ-ent investment strategies and philosophies described in the press and in investment newsletters, and to trace them to their common roots.

3. Emphasizes the various components that are needed for an investment strategy to be successful, thereby revealing why some strategies that look good on paper never work for those who use them.

This book talks about how the process of investing is the same, no matter what investment philosophy one might have. The book does not emphasize individual investors or push a particular investment philosophy, nor does it focus heavily on supposed beat-the-market strategies, though the latter are not entirely ignored.

The investment process always starts with understanding the investor's needs and preferences. For a portfolio manager, each investor is a client who has unique needs, a distinctive tax status, and, most importantly, personal risk preferences. For an individual investor constructing a personal portfolio, this first step of understanding one's own needs, financial limitations, and risk preferences is just as important as it is for a portfolio manager.

The next part of the process, the actual construction of the portfolio, has three subparts:

- The decision on how to allocate the portfolio across different asset classes, defined broadly as equities, fixed-income securities, and real assets (such as real estate, commodities, and other assets). The asset allocation decision can also involve investments in domestic assets versus foreign assets, and the supportive and prohibitive factors driving this choice.
- The selection of individual assets within each asset class, to make up a complete portfolio.
- The execution, which includes the putting together of the desired portfolio. Investors may have to trade off transactions cost against transactions speed. The importance of execution can vary, depending on the investment strategies employed.

The final part of the process, and often the most painful one for professional money managers, is performance evaluation. Investing is focused on one objective: Make the most money you can, given the risk constraints on a particular portfolio. Investors are not forgiving of failure, and they are unwilling to accept even the best of excuses; loyalty to money managers is not a common trait among clients. Performance evaluation is equally important to individual investors who construct their own portfolios. The results of one's evaluation should largely determine the individual investor's portfolio strategy in the future.

The investment process is summarized in the chart on the next page. We will refer to this chart as we move through the book.

Our opening chapter provides an overview of investment management as a business. The chapters in Part One deal with the complexities of understanding clients' needs and preferences. We look at not only how to think about or be

The Investment Process

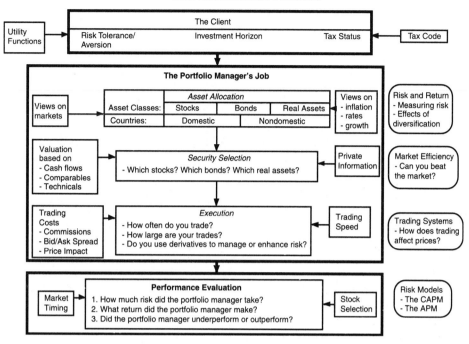

influenced by the risk in investing but also how to measure an investor's willingness to take risk. Part Two probes the asset allocation decision, and Part Three examines different approaches to selecting assets. Part Four looks briefly at the execution decision, and Part Five develops different approaches to evaluating performance. The concluding part looks at trends in corporate governance and how they have impacted portfolio performance.

1 THE INVESTMENT SETTING

Charles D. Ellis

We all make investments whenever we decide to forgo current consumption or pleasure in order to enjoy more consumption in the future. Investing is *not* a smooth, graceful progression to wealth: It is a bumpy road and requires persistence and constancy of purpose. As we shall see, long-term rates of return can be changed greatly by removing a small fraction of the total time that the investor is exposed to the market. Hence, "market timing" is unappealing to long-term investors. As in hunting deer or fishing for rainbow trout, investors have learned the importance of "being there" and using patient persistence—so they are there when opportunity knocks.

TIME

The great power of *time* is that it enables investors to convert *apparent* "uncertainty" into the actuarial "near certainty" that in statistics is called *probability* or *risk*—with all the possible outcomes accurately described in their specific probability of occurrence. It's not that bad things won't happen: They will. But the frequency and magnitude of their occurrence are known and expected—and understood. Over time, history tells us, more good things happen than bad things.[1]

The reason time is so important in investing is simple—and profound. In the short run, the problem with investing appears to be how to deal effectively with those fascinating day-to-day fluctuations and changes in market prices that dominate current "news" reporting. Most professional investors know that such movements are superficial—and ephemeral. For long-term investors, the real problem is the unrelenting destructive power of compounding *inflation.*

Inflation corrodes purchasing power. When average annual inflation is 4 percent, we know from the Rule of 72 that purchasing power is cut in half in just 18 years—and cut in half again in another 18 years.[2] At 6 percent inflation, the investor's purchasing power is halved in just 12 years and halved again in another 12 years. If you retire at 60, by the time you reach 84, the purchasing power of your monthly retirement benefit check will be 75 percent lower than was the purchasing power of your initial check—even though your expenses for health care, groceries, and help around the house may be increasing.

As investing inevitably involves making decisions about the future today, the dominant concern of investors is and should be outpacing the corrosive powers of inflation. But investing is also an opportunity to participate in the long-term growth of the economy and the corporations that make their growth happen. If the investor and the purpose of the fund being invested truly have a long-term horizon, the secret to success is to invest for the maximum long-term return.

Investors with realistically shorter time horizons will need to incorporate into their investment policy equation the terminal date and the risk (or negative utility) of falling short. Examples of shorter periods during which funds will be invested (before being spent on consumption) include funds for a child's education or for buying a family home. For these "purpose" funds, particularly as the intended spending date comes closer, preserving capital will become increasingly important, and ultimately the "end period" will be dominant.

To oversimplify a complex calculation, most investors will find investing for a year or shorter limits them to money market instruments. With a five-year investment period, bonds will suit; with longer periods, stocks will be increasingly dominant.

INVESTING DIFFERS

Investing always involves giving up part of the pleasurable aspects of the present, in the hope and expectation of enhancing the future. When we go to school to improve our abilities and prospects for productive careers, for example, we invest by giving up current income and paying tuition and using our time to study (instead of for pleasure). Much as we may enjoy learning and growing at school and making new friends, any economist would remind us that we are *investing* now—investing in ourselves by enhancing our capabilities to succeed in the future. The magnitude of our investment—tuition and expenses paid—

plus income we could have been earning but have forgone—can be measured rather accurately. Yet the magnitude of our returns on the investment would be hard to measure: We seldom know how *much* our earning power will be increased as a result of our investment in education. Nor do we usually know for exactly how *long* our earning power will continue to produce higher incomes.[3]

Investing in securities is different from real investing in many ways. Two differences are dominant: liquidity and duration. Liquidity determines the investor's ability to sell—or buy—in large volume in a short period of time without causing a significant change in price. The extreme high in liquidity is in the foreign exchange market for major currencies in normal times. A well-known market participant, such as the Bank of England, can buy $100 million in a few seconds and $1 billion in minutes—with no perceptible impact on the rate of exchange with pounds sterling.

In contrast, buying or selling a custom-built private home of an unusual design can take many months, and the bids and offers may cover a 30 percent to 50 percent range. Imagine the impact on the price of insisting on selling such an unusual home quickly—or selling several such unusual houses in rapid succession.

LIQUIDITY

What causes liquidity to be high? Several factors contribute. The first is many active and sizable buyers and sellers or market participants—ideally with a wide variety of different and independent reasons for buying or selling. The second is the existence of information on *price* as well as *value* that is accurate and is both widely and quickly distributed to all active and potentially active market participants. The third is a high degree of confidence among market participants that the market is—and will continue to be—free and fair.

The great thing about liquidity is that it allows us to change our minds. We can correct any errors we might make quickly and easily (or cheaply). Therefore, as our circumstances and objectives change, we can adjust our investments to stay in close harmony with our changing objectives and our changing assets.

Ironically, these advantages are often offset by that all-too-human behavioral reality that investors who know they can "always change their minds" may not subject themselves to the rigorous thinking through of their investment objectives and resources so necessary to developing wise investment objectives and the investment policies by which to achieve them. Every investor should have clearly defined investment goals and clearly delivered investment policies that can realistically be expected to achieve those goals.

There are two great tests of how an investor has thought through and defined investment goals and policies. First, they are in *writing*. If called away, the investor must be willing to give the written statement of investment goals and policies to a competent colleague—or a competent stranger—and entrust *all* specific decision-making on implementation to that colleague for a period of years, knowing that in following the written statement the colleague will be executing an investment program that is well thought out and well matched to the individual's long-term goals and objectives.[4]

The second "all-too-human" reaction to abundantly available liquidity is not doing enough homework on each specific investment decision.

FEWER DECISIONS

One of America's favorite investors, Warren Buffett, advances an engagingly simple device to encourage us to be rigorous about each of our investment decisions: Assume you start out as an investor with a ticket that entitles you to make 20 decisions over your entire career. After each decision you make, your ticket gets punched; 20 punches, and your investing is finished. If we could make only 20 decisions—one decision on average every two years—wouldn't we be more careful about each decision we make? And wouldn't we do our homework quite rigorously before making each decision? It seems reasonable that investors making fewer decisions with greater care would make better decisions.

Liquidity is not always "good," any more than the gift of fire has always been "good" for humanity. But liquidity does increase an investor's freedom of choice—and its value depends on how wisely and well we *use* liquidity.

Time is Archimedes' lever in investing. (The Greek philosopher, Archimedes, is often quoted as saying, "Give me a lever long enough, and a place to stand, and I can move the earth!") In investing, that lever is *time*.

The fundamental nature of investments and the basic character of investing are both changed decisively by time. Consider a choice between two investments:

	Best Return	**Worst Return**	**Difference**
Investment A	Gain over 50%	Loss over 35%	0.85%
Investment B	Gain over 35%	Loss of 20%	55%

Studies have shown that most investors would choose Investment B because they would accept *giving up* 15 percentage points of possible gain to *avoid* 15 percentage points of possible loss—even if the average expected rate of return of A were greater than B. Now consider the following choices for 25-year holding periods—with the same *expected average* rate of return:

	Best Return	**Worst Return**
Investment A	Gain over 11%	Gain of 2½%
Investment B	Gain over 6%	Loss of 1¾%

The choice is easy: Investment A has a higher "best" return and a *gain* instead of a *loss* on the "worst" return. From these choices, an investor will pick Investment A. For investors, both of these, in fact, are *actual,* not hypothetical choices for the period between 1901 and 1990 in the United States. Investment A was in *stocks;* Investment B was in *bonds.* The choice between the two is made even easier when we include the reality that stocks earned an *average* rate of return of 8.3 percent versus only 2.4 percent for bonds.

HOLD TO POLICY

The importance of persistence in investing—holding rigorously to predetermined policy—is made strikingly clear in two illustrations. Take away a few of the biggest days of market gains during the 1980s—and missing out on these biggest days would severely reduce an investor's return. In fact, removing just ten *days* from nine *years* (or 2,250 trading days)—less than ½ percent of the total period—would reduce the investor's average annual rate of return by one-third—from 18 percent to 12 percent. And removing the 30 best days— less than 1½ percent of the total period—would cut the total period return from 18 percent to 5 percent—or by over 70 percent. Here are the data:

	Rate of Return
S&P 500 (1982–1990)	18%
Less 10 biggest days	12%
Less 20 biggest days	8%
Less 30 biggest days	5%

We can learn the same lesson by removing individual *years* from the long, long term. Table 1-1 shows the cumulative returns on $1 invested for the 63-year

TABLE 1-1   Effects of particular years on return

	Cumulative Value of $1
S&P 500 (1928–1990)	$332
Less one year: 1933	215
Less two years: 1933 and 1954	141
Less three years: 1933, 1954, and 1935	96

period from 1928 through 1990. The first cumulative total return on $1 is an enormous $332. But this drops by almost one-third when we remove just the year 1933. And we drop to well under half the total return for the full 63-year period just by deleting two years: 1933 and 1954. When we take out three years, or less than 5% of the full period studied, the total cumulative return is cut by more than two-thirds—from $332 to $96.

Time is the single most important force in investing and the greatest power—for good or for ill. Clients should ask the prospective investment manager, "How do you conceive of and make productive use of time?" A manager who understands the power of time will be able to respond wisely and usefully to this question. Many investment managers, however, will not understand why you are even asking such a question about time.

USING RISK

The primary question to ask an investment manager is, "How do you use risk and riskiness *productively;* how do you make them work *for* you and *for* your clients?" Experienced investors know that they cannot control returns; they can control only the risks that, in turn, drive returns.

Over the long term, higher rates of return are usually associated with increased riskiness—that is, higher rates of price variability and perceived risk. Tversky and Kahneman clarified the elements of risk perception in their study of the behavior of human beings with regard to taking risk. They asked individuals, "Will you take this bet? If you toss a coin and it comes down heads, you win $150; if it comes down tails, you lose $100."

Most people are uncomfortable taking this bet, but many will. The bet takers rightly estimate that it is a good bet for those sums of money. If the terms are greatly increased—to winning $150,000 versus losing $100,000—however, almost no one will take the bet. Even if they know they can take that same bet a thousand times in succession, and within the normal distribution of odds and payouts will thus stand to make considerable money, almost every individual says, "No, I will not do that." The fear of loss is too important to most people—including investment managers—to take that large a risk. We say we will take risk, but as human beings we are afraid of risk, and will avoid it even when we would "in all probability" profit by taking risks of a certain kind.

The second powerful phenomenon Tversky and Kahneman find is the fear of regret, or shame. Fear of having to express regret or to apologize to others—particularly to clients—is a powerful restraining influence on the way most professional investment managers do their work. We do not want to be in the position of apologizing, so we avoid risk. And being human, we avoid risk too much—giving up rather large opportunities for profit in order to avoid rather small risks of loss.

Tversky's and Kahneman's third discovery is the extraordinary capacity of human beings, including investment managers, to exaggerate the *importance of very unusual events* with quite remote possibilities of occurrence. The researchers presented a large number of people the choice between an opportunity to bet $300,000 and be a winner in 2 percent of the cases, or an opportunity to bet $600,000 and be a winner in 1 percent of the cases. The amount of expectable winnings, after adjusting for the probability, is exactly the same; mathematically, the first choice is "worth" $6,000—and so is the second. In the first case, the bettor has a 2 percent chance of winning (2 times out of 100, the bettor will win), and the payoff is $300,000. In the second case, the bettor has a 1 percent chance of winning $600,000. A win is very unlikely in either case, but the choices are mathematically *equal* in expected value or payoff. Nevertheless, the study found that most people prefer the first choice, apparently because the smaller payoff and proportionately larger probability seem less extreme than the second choice's alternatives.

A fourth phenomenon discovered by Tversky and Kahneman is *overreaction to recent information.* This is true for investment managers who know yesterday's events in such detail, have so much information about these events, and are so impressed with the speed with which the information is provided that current information overwhelms other, less immediate information. As a result, recent experiences and statistics have a strong tendency to drive security prices away from their intrinsic values, preserving profitable opportunities for cooler-headed investors who understand this "regression to the mean" applies to investing in the majority of cases.

Managers are hard-pressed to remember the details of what happened a year ago. And like everyone else, they are even less able to recall the events of 10 or 20 or 30 years ago. We remember a lot about what happened yesterday, less about what happened last week, and a good deal less about what happened a month ago; recollection of a year ago is dim; that of a decade ago is very dim indeed.

The reality is that investment managers are working today with investments that will be the dominant part of the portfolio a month from now, or a year from now, and perhaps even ten years from now. As the future unfolds, those investments in the portfolio will have been made a month ago, a year ago, and so on. What we invest in today and what we will hold in the future are extraordinarily connected, so we should always assess risk from a long-term, multiperiod perspective.

DEFINING RISK

Risk means that we do not know what is going to happen, even though we occasionally have a good idea of the range of possibilities that we face. Investors face two distinct kinds of risk, and recognizing the difference between them is critically important.

"Systematic" risk is the risk that none of us can avoid if we are seeking returns higher than we would earn in a money market fund or a savings account. Once we decide to go into the stock market or the bond market, or buy a piece of real estate, or buy a share of a privately owned business, we face the risks that are inherent to those types of investments—such as the vagaries of business activity, inflation, overvaluation, credit crunches, and foreign exchange crises. *These are risks you cannot avoid if you are going to invest at all.*

Investors will refuse to take these risks unless they expect a return greater than the low-risk return of cash or cash substitutes. In general, then, the expected returns on the broad asset classes bear some kind of systematic relationship to the risks as investors perceive them. These higher expected returns are known as "risk premiums." For example, the difference between the expected return on stocks and the expected return on bonds is known as the "equity risk premium"; the difference between the expected return on long-term bonds and 90-day Treasury bills is called the "term premium." When investors are gloomy or frightened by the economic environment, equities will tend to have a higher expected return than times when everyone is optimistic and stocks are priced way up; the equity risk premium, therefore, varies directly with the fear or greed in the marketplace.

What about the investor who decides to put 75 percent of a portfolio in automobile stocks or technology stocks? This investor is taking a risk over and beyond the risk of being in the stock market, because the market as a whole might go up a lot more, or go down a lot less, than these specific choices. This investor, in other words, has taken on "specific" risk in addition to systematic risk. But specific risk is avoidable. The investor can always hold a diversified portfolio with a risk that is no greater than the risk of the market as a whole. Hence, the investor who decides to be a stock-picker cannot expect to be rewarded simply for passing up the opportunity of being diversified and taking on specific risk instead.

We can think of this in another way. No one will go into the stock market unless the stock market appears to offer a return greater than the return to be earned by holding cash. It has to be a positive-sum game, or no one will play, and stock prices will fall until the expected returns are appropriate to the risks involved. Stock-picking is a zero-sum game—if one investor is right to buy

Stock A, the seller has to be wrong. Thus, stock-picking has no inherent reward for investors in the same way that the market as a whole incorporates an expected reward.

One of the real attractions of international investing is that the systematic risk of investing in one market—say, the American market—can be reduced significantly by diversifying the investor's portfolio across many different markets. In other words, the systematic risk facing well-diversified global investors is *less* than the systematic risk they would face if confined to just one national market.

Many investment managers devote their time and energy to seeking out profitable investments from which they hope to earn *more* than the equity premium return offered by the overall market (the increment of expected reward for investing in widely diversified portfolios that are structured to diversify away all specific risk and all extra-market risk). They operate on the belief that they know more than the sellers from whom they buy—and therefore will be able to buy low. Or when they are selling, they will know more than the buyers to whom they sell—and therefore will be able to sell high. This may have been realistic for numerous investors many years ago, but it is a more questionable strategy in today's market where the prices of stocks are set by the trading of sophisticated, informed, professional investors managing the funds of large institutions.

CHANGING MARKETS

If, 50 years ago, 20 percent of the buying and selling of common stocks was by the professionals working at investing institutions—and 80 percent was by individual investors, that ratio is now inverted. Today, 80 percent of the buying and selling is by professionals at institutions. So if Investment Manager A wants to buy low and sell high, she usually is implicitly counting on Investment Manager B—another equally well-informed, ambitious, and rational (or cold-blooded) professional at another institution—to be willing to *buy high* and *sell-low* regularly!

The "classic" (but erroneous) concept of the "typical" investor is a business executive (or lawyer or doctor) who owns six to ten stocks in a portfolio worth $200,000 to $500,000, invests primarily for long-term gain, buys a little more on price weakness, and knows the companies he owns rather well because he reads annual reports carefully and "does his homework" on a regular basis. In truth, this idealized investor is very, very rare.

Today, the typical investor is not an individual. Individual investors account for less than 20 percent of investment activity today; 80 percent of all the buying and selling on the New York Stock Exchange is by institutions. Even among the minority of individual investors, the so-called typical investor is rare. As Table 1-2 indicates:

- The average investor has total holdings of less than $5,000.
- Only 15 percent of all individual investors buy or sell shares in a typical year.
- Fewer than half of all individual share owners have an account with a stockbroker.
- The median investor's annual income is under $30,000.
- The number of substantial individual investors active in the market (including hyperactive traders) is remarkably small; using $50,000 of total purchases and sales as a threshold (which might involve no more than, say, selling 100 shares and buying 100 of a typical $40 stock every other month), the New York Stock Exchange estimates there are fewer than 500,000 active, substantial investors.
- A majority of individual investors have never purchased a share of stock through a stockbroker. Instead, they received their shares as gifts from relatives or through an employer's stock purchase program.

The remarkable way in which trading volume has increased in recent years is documented in data from the *NYSE Fact Book* published by the New York Stock Exchange.

TABLE 1-2 Individual investors: A profile 1952–1980[a]

	1952	1956	1959	1962	1965	1970	1975	1980
Total shareowners	6,490	8,630	12,490	17,010	20,120	30,850	25,270[b]	29,840[c]
NYSE shareowners		6,880	8,510	11,015	12,430	18,290	17,950	23,520
Mutual funds only				2,165	3,205	3,977	2,897	2,200
Unlisted stocks only				2,550	3,180	6,695	3,301	2,900
Median income	$7,100	$6,200	$7,000	$8,600	$9,500	$13,500	$19,000	$27,700
Adult shareowners	6,350	8,280	11,090	16,256	18,490	28,630	23,380	27,560
Male	3,140	4,260	6,350	8,290	9,430	14,290	11,750	14,027
Female	3,210	4,020	5,740	7,970	9,060	14,340	11,630	13,533
Minors				450	1,280	2,221	1,818	2,280
Under $10K income			9,340	10,340	10,080	8,170	3,420	
Over $10K income			2,740	5,920	8,410	20,130	19,970	
Median Age	51	48	49	48	49	48	53	45.5

[a] Data from New York Stock Exchange surveys.
[b] The widely publicized "loss of shareowners" from 1970 to 1975 had almost *no* impact on the number of owners of NYSE-listed stocks. Over 90 percent of the "lost investors" had incomes under $10,000 and owned only OTC stocks and mutual funds, and all had portfolios of less than $20,000. In other words, small speculators attracted by the bull market of the sixties had been shaken out.
[c] Includes 3.1 million shareholders of AT&T, of which one million owned less than 20 shares and another million owned between 20 and 99 shares.

Share volume multiplied four times in the sixties, nearly quadrupled again in the seventies, and more than tripled in the eighties—and kept right on increasing. And block trades of 10,000 shares, which were not even officially counted in the sixties, now represent over half of all trading volume, while turnover grew from just 12 percent in 1960 to 54 percent in 1993—changing the average share holding period from over eight years to shorter than one year.

In the past 25 years, trading volume has increased more than 30 times—greatly increasing liquidity, the ease with which large transactions are accomplished by the market, *and* increasing the speed and intensity with which information—coming from both corporate and market sources—is collected and distributed—and acted upon—by institutional investors (see Table 1-3).

And that profound inversion from 80:20 to 20:80 is not the only major change. Information technology constantly puts into institutional investors' hands extraordinarily large amounts of information provided by corporations and by the thousands of expert industry analysts and economists and portfolio strategists working at dozens of securities firms—all competing with each other to win the institutions' commission business by providing data, interpretation, insight, and recommendations for action. Half of all the trading on the New York Stock Exchange is by the 50 most active institutional investors. All of these institutions are very large in terms of assets managed (some over $100 billion). They are fully staffed with dozens of professionals, have all the latest technology, databases, and communications, receive the most extensive and intensive service by all the best people at all the best and biggest securities dealers, and compete to achieve the best performance all the time. Every investor in the market is competing with these giants all the time.

Two great movements of funds for investment into investing institutions have been evident in the enormous growth of retirement funds—primarily pension funds—and mutual funds. Tables 1-4 and 1-5 show the substantial and

TABLE 1-3 How NYSE trading has grown

	Share Volume[a]	Percent Turnover	Block Trading[b]	Percent of Volume
1950	525	23	—	—
1960	767	12	—	—
1970	2,937	19	—	—
1980	11,352	36	3,311	29
1990	38,664	46	19,682	50
1991	45,266	48	22,474	50
1992	51,376	48	26,069	51
1993	66,923	54	35,959	54

[a] Millions of shares.

[b] 10,000 shares or more in thousands of shares.

TABLE 1-4 Rapid growth of private and public pension funds

	Private Trusteed Corporate and Union		Private[b] Trusteed Pension Assets	Insured (Primarily Group & Other Annuities)[c]	Total[d] Private Pension Plan	State & Local Government	Federal Government	Total	Union Plans	401(k) Plans	Memo		
	Defined Benefit[a]	Defined Contribution[a]									Cumulative Last 4 Years of GIC Issuance	Pension Assets Held in Mutual Funds	IRA Assets
1975	$ 186	$ 74	$ 260	$ 72	$ 332	$ 105	$ 42	$ 479	$ 23	—	—	—	—
1976	216	82	298	89	387	120	46	553	27	—	—	—	—
1977	234	91	325	103	428	133	53	614	30	—	—	—	—
1978	273	105	377	122	499	154	60	713	34	—	—	—	—
1979	320	126	445	144	589	170	68	827	41	—	—	—	—
1980	401	162	564	172	736	198	76	1,010	49	—	—	—	—
1981	444	185	629	200	829	224	86	1,139	57	—	—	—	$ 24
1982	553	236	789	243	1,032	263	98	1,393	73	—	$ 8	—	52
1983	642	281	923	286	1,210	311	112	1,633	80	—	18	—	91
1984	701	344	1,045	314	1,359	357	130	1,846	97	$ 35	30	$ 17	132
1985	826	427	1,253	375	1,628	405	149	2,182	116	50	51	28	200
1986	895	488	1,383	440	1,823	469	170	2,462	132	73	66	40	277
1987	877	525	1,402	497	1,900	517	188	2,605	136	103	84	42	338
1988	912	592	1,504	557	2,061	606	208	2,875	152	141	97	44	391
1989	988	688	1,676	618	2,294	735	229	3,257	170	186	100	59	465
1990	958	710	1,668	685	2,353	752	251	3,355	194	221	117	67	513
1991	1,196	927	2,123	742	2,865	877	276	4,018	238	269	134	86	618
1992	1,260	1,052	2,313	791	3,104	972	304	4,380	256	315	144	103	725
1993E	1,335	1,183	2,518	850	3,368	1,075	345	4,788	280	365	160	120	800
1994E	1,410	1,310	2,720	920	3,640	1,200	380	5,220	305	415	150	135	880
Average Annual Growth Rates													
1975–1984	15.9%	18.6%	16.7%	17.8%	17.0%	14.6%	13.4%	16.2%	17.6%	—	—	—	24.3%
1984–1993E	7.4	14.7	10.2	11.7	10.6	13.0	11.5	11.2	12.5	29.8%	20.7%	24.3%	22.2%

Source: U.S. Department of Labor, Federal Reserve Board, EBRI, Money Market Directory, The GIC Association, and S. C. Bernstein estimates.

[a] Includes insured assets held in private-trusteed accounts.
[b] A benchmark revision by the Federal Reserve Board is forthcoming which will boost this total by about $200 billion.
[c] Excluding GICs held in Defined Contribution plans.
[d] Excluded from this analysis are tax-exempt assets sponsored by endowments and foundations. At the end of 1992 endowment assets totalled $110 billion, while foundation assets totalled $120 billion.

TABLE 1-5 Rapid growth of mutual funds

In $Billions	1978	1994 Estimate
Private Pensions	$332	$3,640
State and Local	105	1,200
Total	$479	$5,220

	Money Market & Short-Term Municipal Bonds	Equities	Fixed Income	Municipal Bonds	Total Long-Term Fixed Income	Total Long-Term Funds	Total Funds	Number of		
								Open-End Mutual Funds	Closed-End Mutual Funds	Total
1978	$ 10.9	$ 36.8	$ 4.7	$ 2.6	$ 7.3	$ 44.2	$ 55.0	505	—	505
1983	179.4	85.8	11.3	14.6	25.9	111.8	291.1	1,026	—	1,026
1988	338.0	216.6	169.0	86.7	255.7	472.3	810.3	2,718	160	2,878
1993E	560.0	780.0	365.0	260.0	625.0	1,405.0	1,965.0	4,450	450	4,900

In $Billions	1978	1993 Estimate
Equity	$37	$ 780
Bonds	7	625
Money Market	11	560
Total	$55	$1,965

Source: Investment Company Institute and S. C. Bernstein estimates.

rapid growth of private and public pension funds since 1975 and of mutual ands since 1978. These two major forces for institutional growth—and others—have tended to concentrate on what have become the largest investing institutions—with increasing numbers of institutions actively managing funds aggregating *over* $100 billion.

EFFICIENT MARKETS

Those few investors like John Neff, Warren Buffett, and Peter Lynch who achieve prominence because they have repeatedly outperformed the overall market give evidence that the market is *not* perfectly efficient. In other words, a few investors appear to have the ability to process information into consistently successful decisions (although even these fabled investors have all had extended dry periods). On the other hand, the reality that institutional investors—as a whole—*underperform* the market in most individual years (and cumulatively over time) gives compelling evidence that the market *is very* efficient, even though not "perfectly" efficient.

The primary reason for overall underperformance is that transaction costs—commissions plus dealer spreads—exceed the average incremental profit of acting on perceived "investment opportunities" or market inefficiencies. Where they apply, capital gains taxes also extract a heavy penalty on returns. The degree to which you do *not* believe Mr. B will *regularly* accommodate Ms. A is the degree to which you *do* believe in the "efficient market." But overreaction to short-term news also results in misvaluations that tend to be corrected over time.

In its strong form, the efficient markets theory posits that all that can be known *is* known—and widely and immediately known.

We can easily identify the *financial* challenges in managing investments. The larger challenge is *human* or *social:* It is managing ourselves and the other people who join with us in managing investments—particularly managing our emotions and our behavior.

Investment professionals need to be fearless at those times when others, with less experience, might feel afraid. And as professionals, they need to avoid overconfidence when things have gone well and look good. They need to keep taking the long-term view, even when short-term demands might otherwise command their attention. In brief, ideally they will manage themselves—and be totally rational at all times.

Investment professionals also need to keep in mind that many of the people who participate in making responsible investment decisions—including some of the most powerful—are not very experienced with investing and its often counterintuitive nature. Most top corporate executives have lived in a real world where smart, hard-working people control the outcomes and make things happen. For them, the world of investing can be very confusing and frustrating, because none of us can control the course of the market—which is why managing risk is so essential. As trustees of their alma mater or of their state's employee pension fund, business executives may care greatly about the fund being discussed, but may not be expert in the real work of investing in securities. Professionals must help "manage the understanding" of these important nonprofessionals, which means educating them in a decision-making environment that is often totally foreign to them.

For example, unlike investing in real assets, when the wise investor usually looks for the *most attractive* prospective choice, in securities investing it may be more astute to look for what *appears* to be the *least attractive* prospective investment, because a consensus based on a dour view often will have caused security prices to be at such very low levels that a regression to the mean could mean a large favorable change in the future outlook—and a correspondingly large favorable increase in securities prices.

UNDERSTANDING POLICY

In managing investors' understanding of investments (and their emotions) at times of severe experience—such as usually prevail near market highs or market lows—two factors are paramount: the setting of investment policy for the long, long term, and the ability to adhere to investment policy throughout whatever positive and negative, if often disconcerting, short-term experiences.

The process of setting long-term investment policy guidelines must recognize the significance of each specific fund's particular circumstance—because fund circumstances differ enormously—in cash flows, available funds, levels of funding, and amounts of reserve money available to cover shortfalls. Because corporations are likewise very different, their pension funds should have very different investment policies. Unfortunately, they are far too often similar.

Large differences exist between companies in the average age of employees, growth in employment, turnover, and size and character of benefits—to say nothing of the riskiness of the business itself. But the pension portfolios meant to provide retirement benefits for company employees usually exhibit few clearly corresponding differences from one company to another. For example, a large corporation's pension fund—in a stable industry with almost no growth and an average worker age of nearly 50—may have a portfolio asset mix essentially identical to that of the portfolio of a young company in a high-technology industry that is growing very rapidly, has an average worker's age of 35, and that anticipates hiring increasing numbers of new people during the next 10, 20, or 30 years.

The first company will soon be paying out large amounts of money in retirement benefits. The second company, in contrast, will be rapidly adding to its pension fund far more in contributions than it will pay out in retiree benefits. Besides this difference in cash flows, the participants' investment interests and concerns are different. The older workers and the younger workers are worried about entirely different things—the older about death and illness, the younger about getting married, educating children, and buying a home. That the asset mix in the pension funds set aside for the needs of those two very different groups of people should be so similar raises questions for all investment professionals.

A striking illustration of the reality that pension funds often do not develop investment policies suited to the particular situation is seen in a comparison of the equity/debt ratios of pension funds in various nations. Here is the proportion of assets invested currently in equities in several major nations:

- Japan—1–5%
- Canada—15–20%
- United States—40–60%
- United Kingdom—70–80%

DEFINED CONTRIBUTION VERSUS DEFINED BENEFIT

The United States has defined-benefit and defined-contribution funds, but the defined-contribution funds are growing more rapidly than defined-benefit funds. Companies are saying to individual employees—as though it were truly good news, "You will be able to control your own financial destiny. You will be in control of your investments for retirement." Some employees will fortunately know what to do and how to do it well, and some others will be lucky and their investments will work out well. Many employees, however, will be disappointed by the long-term results of their actions because they are not well-prepared for the daunting responsibilities of managing risk, time, and investment opportunity. They do not know how to combine those important considerations with a mature understanding of the capital markets into a long-term investment policy for a portfolio that will have a high probability of achieving their objectives for their retirement years. And they would find it very, very difficult to hold onto that long-term policy day after day through the vicissitudes of the capital markets.

For support for this view, consider what individual investors have done thus far with their self-directed investments in 401(k) plans. They have put their retirement money into *savings* rather than *investments*. Most of this retirement money is invested in very short-term investments whose principal characteristic *is safety* from market fluctuations, but *not safety* from the persistent corrosion of purchasing power caused by inflation.

CLIENT–MANAGER

In setting long-term policy for an investment portfolio, the client and the investment manager need to communicate certain information to each other. The client needs to understand the realistic expectations for each type of investment and each asset class—for both the short term and the long term. Clients also need to understand the probable and possible "chaotic events" that occur within the long, long term. They should know what the long-term average rate of return is and what the distribution of events is around the long-term average. In other words, what are the risks; what are the uncertainties; and what are the longer-term average returns achieved in the past? And, most important, how may the future differ from the past?

The client needs to communicate the financial and nonfinancial constraints of the fund for the short, medium, and long term. For example, how much short-run volatility can the fund sustain in the search for higher long-term rates of return? Only the owner of the assets can bring such information to these joint discussions in which investment policy can be resolved. Through communicating the necessary information, the manager and the client *together* can resolve investment policy effectively. This is their most important task and responsibility; when they have completed this task, they should commit their decisions to a written statement.

In most markets around the world, however, most of the decisive work is done by investment managers who are working alone and have none of the client's vital knowledge. Too many clients come to managers and say in almost helpless terms: "You know so much, you are so well-informed, you should decide. Please tell us what we should do."

Investment managers may indeed know much more than a given client about investing and the capital markets. But they know all too little about the unique needs of each client. Relying on a manager's *general* knowledge leads to all clients getting the same Procrustean asset mix in their funds.

The manager's responsibility is not to lead the processes of discovery and decision-making; rather, it is to assure the *implementation* of investment decisions after they have been made. The best procedure is for the client to lead and control the process of discovery and the resolution of policy. The owner of the assets is ultimately responsible for decisions on investment policy, because only the owner knows the economic objectives of the fund and the noneconomic constraints on the fund; in the end, these are the most powerful determinants of investment policy in most organizations. The rest of the factors in the decision are free information widely available in the marketplace.

MEASURING RESULTS

In this regard, performance measurement (as it is usually defined) is of surprisingly little value when used in the way it is usually used—to justify hiring or firing managers. In investment management, *useful* performance measurement of the conventional type—for hiring or firing managers—is virtually impossible in the short run. Over and over again, the record shows how very difficult it is to use performance measurement for even this crudest task. (Those fired all too often go on to outperform those who have been hired as their replacements!) The record suggests that recent years' past performance seldom predict, future performance. Indeed, performance records are so volatile that separating luck from skill is a complex and sometimes impossible task.

Performance measurement is covered in detail in Chapter 13, but a few observations based on long experience are appropriate at this point. The measurement data that *would* be useful in the short run would, like standard cost data in manufacturing, measure the incidence and magnitude of difference between actual results and intended results at the micro level—that is, how well did the manager anticipate optimal weights of individual stocks and industries, portfolio turnover, betas of individual stocks, and estimates of covariance across the portfolio's holdings? These are the structural design elements that can be specified—and therefore measured objectively even in the very short run.

This is not the typical format of performance measurements in today's world. The data coming from the conventional performance measurement tools are *precise* but not necessarily *accurate.* (They may lead to discussions that are *intense,* but not necessarily *useful.*) Moreover, the data either come too late to be used well or, if timely, are not sufficiently reliable or accurate to be converted into useful decisions.

By measuring and reading performance reports, and believing they have learned something from the process, clients may keep themselves from studying the deeper meaning beyond the reports, the substance behind the data. The Greek philosopher, Plato, describes individuals in a dark cave with a small light who are trying to understand reality by studying shadows moving on the wall. Their situation is not unlike investing: Current prices of securities are shadows of reality cast on a cave wall; they are not the real business values. When receiving reports of performance measurement, we should ask: Are we looking at the shadows on the wall, and getting very precise information— about which shadow moves to the left, which to the right; which shadow is darkest, which is lightest; which gains in size, which one seems to get smaller—but *not* gaining an understanding of what is really going on behind the shadows?

The misleading precision of performance measurement data shows up most clearly in one extraordinary characteristic of the investment management industry in the United States, namely, a very high rate of hiring and firing of investment managers. The typical U.S. pension fund will hire one or more investment managers every second or third year—and "performance measurement" is almost always the justification given in these decisions.

Ironically, as we have observed, the manager terminated because the performance data mandate it often "outperforms" the new investment manager who is brought in. Thus, the process of changing investment managers—and selling off one manager's portfolio and then buying another—imposes a cost on pension funds. Those in charge pay little mind, however, because the data clearly say, "For the *past* three years, this manager has failed, and for the *past* three years, this other manager has done very well." The decision-makers might be better off if they were to look behind the data (treating the data as shadows) to examine what is causing the performance to be different, and learn what is temporary and likely to be reversed versus what is enduring and warrants action.

IMPLEMENTING POLICY

When investment policies are being implemented, certain client executives and manager executives play key roles. They do not all have the same purposes and will not behave in the same way, but each has an important role. Investment professionals who understand these roles have a better chance of managing the total implementation process wisely and successfully.

First, the staff for any large fund has clear responsibilities (although those responsibilities may not always be made explicit by their own organizations), which are to clarify the issues, provide clear alternatives to every decision being brought before the decision-making board or committee, and assure that the investment managers follow the established policy of the fund in the particular portfolio they manage, and that all their actions conform to agreed-upon policy and long-term plans.

The senior committee has two responsibilities: formulating policy for the very longest term, and making the final decisions about hiring or terminating any manager who is unwilling or unable to follow that investment policy (and to *keep* managers who, with skill and discipline, *will* follow investment policy—even if current reported "performance" is below conventional standards).

The investment manager's responsibility is to execute exactly what has been planned, and to advise the plan sponsor of the consistent conformance of the portfolio with the intended policy. The investment manager may also be responsible for advising the senior people in the fund about how they might consider a revision in investment policy as the broad character of markets changes.

The most important variable in the whole process is how well we understand ourselves. I do not mean to imply that investing is nothing more than a case in human psychology. Nevertheless, investing involves making decisions whose outcomes we cannot predict. All of us respond in our own way to uncertainty—some of us calmly, some of us foolishly. Until we recognize how we react when things are not going our own way, we will fail at managing the risks that we are inevitably going to face when we put our money on the line.

The key consideration is time. We know a lot less about the distant future than we know about tomorrow, and less even about tomorrow than we know about today. Yet we do know one thing for certain: The capitalist system has tremendous vitality and resilience. Over time, economies will grow. The long term, even if only dimly conceived, is therefore the investor's best friend.

History, in other words, has much to teach us. The philosopher, George Santayana, in summarizing his life's learning, says, "Those who cannot remember the past are condemned to repeat it." Investment professionals have a wonderful opportunity to study and to learn from history. To say that there is nothing new under the sun is not far from wrong. (Almost everything we can do in modern capital markets could be done 400 years ago on an exchange conducted in Amsterdam; there were calls, puts, calls on calls, and puts on puts. The range of investment freedom was wonderfully wide—and it enabled many people to win—or lose—large amounts of money.)

The best and cheapest lessons are those we can learn from someone else's mistakes; we do not have to make *all* the mistakes ourselves in order to begin the learning. As professionals, one of our highest purposes is to *learn how to learn* from history so we do not need to learn the same lessons again and again at our clients' expense—and so we can share our learning with our clients.

PART ONE

UNDERSTANDING THE CLIENT

The investment process starts with the investor. To design the "right" portfolio for any investor, we need to ask about and understand his or her needs and preferences; attitude toward and limit on risk; cash needs; and tax status.

The most critical component of this stage of the process is the risk assessment. Willingness and capacity to bear risk vary widely among investors, and each portfolio should reflect the owner's risk preference. Most people would agree with the basic concept that to earn a higher return, an investor has to be willing to take more risk. To assess risk accurately, however, we need to define risk, and this is where the consensus breaks down. In portfolio theory, risk is generally measured as the deviation of actual returns from expected returns. The several competing financial models of risk all share a common view: Only the risk that an investment adds on to a diversified portfolio is rewarded, not the total risk associated with the investment. This statistical derivation of risk is convenient from the standpoint of developing portfolio theory, but it is unlikely that even the most sophisticated investor thinks of risk in these terms. Most investors think about risk in much more intuitive terms—the likelihood of "losing" on an investment, or the "worst case scenario." Part of the task of a portfolio manager or investor is to convert these intuitive measures of risk into statistical measures that can be used in portfolio design.

The second critical component of this stage of the process is an understanding of the cash needs of the investor. An investor who needs to withdraw cash on a regular basis will have a very different portfolio from someone who does not expect to make periodic withdrawals or someone who expects to add cash to the portfolio over time. In a sense, a need for significant cash withdrawal shortens the expected time horizon for the portfolio.

The third critical component is the tax status of the investor. Investors' tax liabilities vary widely, especially when we consider institutional investors in the mix. At one extreme are pension funds that pay no taxes. At the other extreme are wealthy individual investors who must pay federal, state, and local taxes and are subject to the complexities of the Internal Revenue Code. Regulations mandating different tax rates for capital gains and ordinary income, penalties for improper tax deductions, and schedules for estate taxes drive home the message that portfolio decisions cannot be made without an understanding of the tax law. Yet, a portfolio constructed purely for the purpose of minimizing tax liabilities is likely to be an inferior portfolio. The objectives in portfolio management are: to construct the best possible portfolio for an investor, given his or her tax liabilities and cash needs, and to maximize the after-tax returns realized over time.

This section begins with a review of the models of risk and utility functions, by Mark Kritzman.

This idea is expanded upon in the following chapter by Aswath Damodaran, and is used to explain the differences between the competing models for risk—the capital asset pricing model, the arbitrage pricing model, and other multi-factor model. Roger Clarke's chapter discusses alternative measures of risk in portfolios and the notion of nondiversifiable risks. The final chapter, by Robert Jeffrey, makes the argument that portfolio managers pay too little attention to taxes, and shows the significant impact of taxes on returns.

The Investment Process

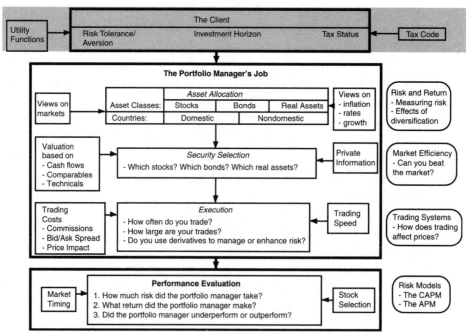

2 RISK AND UTILITY: BASICS

Mark Kritzman

The first task to address in pursuing an investment program is to decide your purpose. Do you want to increase your wealth as quickly as possible, regardless of the risk that typically accompanies aggressive investment strategies, or do you prefer to accumulate wealth gradually, taking comfort in the certitude that your savings will be preserved through volatile markets? Should you frame your investment objectives as absolute goals, or define them in terms of the behavior of some benchmark? Finally, what is the role of your investment horizon in determining your investment objectives?

These questions suggest that the process of setting investment objectives is a process of balancing several competing trade-offs: the trade-off between accumulating wealth and exposure to risk; the trade-off between absolute and relative performance; and the trade-off between near-term goals and distant goals.

To evaluate these trade-offs properly, you must understand several important issues, some of them quite subtle and often the source of some disagreement: the estimation of future value from historical returns; the estimation of return distributions; the notion of utility; the technique for maximizing expected utility; and questions about the role of the investment horizon.

Many of the issues discussed in this chapter are included in Mark Kritzman, *The Portable Financial Analyst: What Practitioners Need to Know* (Chicago: Probus Publishing Company, 1995).

The purpose of this chapter is to offer a clear and intuitive explanation of these issues so that you as an investor will feel confident in evaluating the trade-offs that you face in setting investment objectives.

Before proceeding, I must offer some cautionary notes. Several of the issues I discuss assume implicitly that we estimate future results from past experience. Although it is common to sample the past in order to forecast the future, this approach by itself can be very dangerous. I use this method to illustrate certain points, but I do not endorse it as the only approach, or necessarily the preferred approach, for predicting future results.

Throughout the chapter, I also assume implicitly that investors follow a disciplined and rational process in setting their investment objectives. In fact, however, many investors set unrealistic or inappropriate objectives, because they are driven by emotional considerations such as fear or avarice. Investors who set objectives on the basis of emotional urges often create opportunities for investors who follow a systematic and logical process in setting their objectives.

Finally, to make some concepts as precise as possible, the chapter includes several equations, some of them probably intimidating. Never fear; all the material is covered in the text, and the equations can be safely skipped over without damage to the chapter's message. Those who want to deal with the equations, however, should not ascribe more precision than is warranted to an area dominated by uncertainty.

ESTIMATING AN INVESTMENT'S FUTURE VALUE

One of the first notions we need to address within the context of setting objectives is the notion of *future value*. It refers to the market value of a fund at a future date. Nearly all investors, whether institutional or individual, seek to increase the future value of their assets, because a higher fund value gives them more ability to consume. One of our first priorities, therefore, is to understand how to estimate future value on the basis of prior experience, which raises the issue of the relevance of the arithmetic and geometric average.

Arithmetic and Geometric Average

Suppose we currently have $1 million invested in an S&P 500 index fund, and we want to estimate its value 20 years from now, given its history of annual returns during the past 20 years, assuming we make no additional contributions, do not disburse any of the funds, and pay no taxes. (For the sake of convenience, I ignore the effect of taxes throughout the chapter. The points I make still hold, although the specific values of course change when taxes must be paid. The impact of taxes is discussed in Chapter 14.)

It might seem reasonable to calculate the arithmetic average of the past returns, by summing the annual returns and dividing by 20, and then to assume that the $1 million investment compounds at this return for 20 consecutive years. You will find, however, that this approach will almost certainly produce a higher cumulative growth rate than the growth rate that actually occurred.

Consider, for example, a $100 investment that returns 50 percent in one year followed by a return of −50 percent in the subsequent year. Although the average annual return over the two years is 0 percent, the investment would have grown to only $75 by the end of the second year—a cumulative two-year loss of 25 percent. The first year it increases from $100 to $150 only to decline 50 percent in the second year to $75. The arithmetic average thus overstates the actual terminal value of an investment.

It is the geometric average that yields an investment's terminal value. The geometric average is computed by adding one to the annual return to compute a "wealth relative," multiplying the wealth relatives together, raising the product of the wealth relatives to the power one divided by the number of returns, and then subtracting one.

In the $100 example, we compute the geometric average as $[(1 + 0.5) \times (1 - 0.5)]^{1/2} - 1$, which equals −0.1340. An investment that depreciates 13.4 percent in two consecutive years will yield the same terminal value as an investment that increases 50 percent in the first year and then decreases by 50 percent in the second year, assuming they both have the same initial value.

This example demonstrates that we estimate an investment's terminal value (the value that actually results from a sequence of investment returns) by compounding at the geometric average rather than the arithmetic average.

Expected Future Value

Now consider how to estimate the "expected future value" from a sequence of past returns. The expected value is defined as the probability-weighted outcome, and it is estimated by compounding the arithmetic average of past returns. Suppose, for example, an investment has a 50 percent chance of increasing by 25 percent and a 50 percent chance of decreasing by 5 percent. After one period, there is an equal chance that $100 will grow to $125 or decrease to $95. The probability-weighted value of these two outcomes is $110 ($125 × 0.5 + $95 × 0.5). After two periods, there are four equally likely outcomes. The investment can first increase to $125 and then increase another 25 percent to $156.25. It can increase to $125 and then decrease to $118.75. It can first decrease to $95 and then increase to $118.75. Or finally, it can decrease

FIGURE 2-1   Possible paths of $100 investment

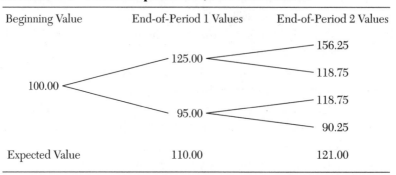

Beginning Value	End-of-Period 1 Values	End-of-Period 2 Values
		156.25
	125.00	118.75
100.00		118.75
	95.00	90.25
Expected Value	110.00	121.00

5 percent to $95 and then decrease another 5 percent to $90.25. Figure 2-1 diagrams these four possible paths.

The expected value after two periods (the probability-weighted value) equals $121.00. This value corresponds precisely to the initial value of $100 compounded for two periods at the arithmetic average of 10 percent. The geometric average of a 25 percent increase followed by a 5 percent decrease or a 5 percent decrease followed by a 25 percent increase equals 8.9725 percent, which when compounded over two periods for this example yields $118.75. The compounded geometric average underestimates the expected value, except in the unusual case in which all of the periodic returns are equal. Paradoxically, here the expected value is higher than the actual value you would achieve if you invested in the returns on which the expected value is based.

The reason for this apparent paradox is quite simple: compounding. A path of high returns raises the expected value more than a path of equal-magnitude low returns lowers it, because of the effect of compounding. A 10 percent return compounded over two periods, for example, produces a 21 percent increase in value, while a −10 percent return compounded over two periods lowers a fund's value by only 19 percent.

By now it should be clear that, if you accept the past as prologue, the compounded arithmetic average of past returns yields a better estimate of a fund's expected future value than does the compounded geometric average of past returns. It is also true, however, that you are more likely to achieve a future value below the expected value than above the expected value. If you want to estimate the probability that a fund's future value will exceed a particular target value, you should base this estimate on the geometric average of past returns. If you compound a fund's initial value at the geometric average, you derive an estimate of the median value. The median splits the distribution of future values in half. The median future value falls below the expected future value, because the (fewer) values above the expected value have a greater impact per outcome than the (more frequent) outcomes that fall below the expected value.

I discuss how and why the geometric average is used to estimate probabilities later in the chapter.

Risk

To estimate the probability of achieving a particular future value, we must first understand how to measure risk. Risk is typically defined as uncertainty. It arises from imperfect knowledge or from incomplete data. Risky events are characterized by random variation. The toss of a coin, for example, is considered a random event, because it is governed by chance. Stock prices, to the extent they are efficiently arrived at, also seem to have a large random component. The influence of chance, however, does not mean we are completely ignorant about the values a random variable can take on. We can examine historical data for clues about the values a random variable may take on in the future.

Table 2-1 shows the yearly returns of the S&P 500 index from 1954 through 1993. We measure the S&P's risk as the dispersion of these returns, which as we will see, enables us to assess the probability that a future value for the S&P will exceed or fall short of a particular threshold.

FREQUENCY DISTRIBUTION

As we discuss earlier, it is appropriate to estimate the expected return from past data on the basis of the arithmetic average, which in the case of our data equals 10 percent. It would be foolish to predict that next year's return will

TABLE 2-1   S&P 500 annual returns

Year	Percent	Year	Percent	Year	Percent	Year	Percent
1954	52.6	1964	16.5	1974	−26.5	1984	6.3
1955	31.6	1965	12.5	1975	37.2	1985	32.2
1956	6.6	1966	−10.1	1976	23.8	1986	18.8
1957	−10.8	1967	24.0	1977	−7.2	1987	5.3
1958	43.4	1968	11.1	1978	6.6	1988	16.6
1959	12.0	1969	−8.5	1979	18.4	1989	31.8
1960	0.5	1970	4.0	1980	32.4	1990	−3.1
1961	24.0	1971	14.3	1981	−4.9	1991	30.6
1962	−8.7	1972	19.0	1982	21.4	1992	7.7
1963	22.8	1973	−14.7	1983	22.5	1993	10.0

Source: Data through 1981 from R. Ibbotson and R. Sinquefield, *Stocks, Bonds, Bills and Inflation: The Past and the Future* (Charlottesville, VA: The Financial Analysts Research Foundation, 1982). Data from 1982 through 1993 was provided by Dimensional Fund Advisors.

TABLE 2-2 Frequency distribution

Range of Return (%)	Frequency	Relative Distribution (%)
−30 to −20	1	2.5
−20 to −10	3	7.5
−10 to 0	5	12.5
0 to 10	8	20.0
10 to 20	9	22.5
20 to 30	6	15.0
30 to 40	6	15.0
40 to 50	1	2.5
50 to 60	1	2.5

equal exactly 10 percent, or any specific value, for that matter. Instead, we should be more confident in asserting that next year's return will fall within a particular *range* of returns. Table 2-2 shows how many of the returns fall within various ranges and reports these amounts as percentages of the total number of returns. Such an arrangement of the data is called a frequency distribution.

If we base our prediction of next year's return on this historical data, we can predict with 22.5 percent confidence that it will fall within the range of 10 percent to 20 percent. Furthermore, we can assert that there is a 22.5 percent chance it will be negative, but only a 10 percent chance that it will fall below −10 percent. We can also assert that we have a 35 percent chance of experiencing a return in excess of 20 percent.

Figure 2-2, which is called a discrete probability distribution, displays this information graphically. It is "discrete" because it covers a finite number of returns.

FIGURE 2-2 Discrete probability distribution

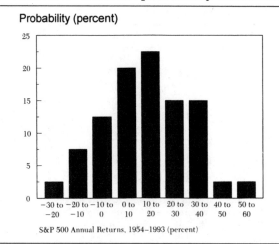

S&P 500 Annual Returns, 1954–1993 (percent)

The Normal Distribution

If we increase the number of returns and assign them to narrower ranges, the distribution will begin to look more and more like the familiar bell-shaped curve known as the normal distribution.

The normal distribution is a *continuous* probability distribution because it assumes an infinite number of observations covering all possible values along a continuous scale. It is appealing for two reasons. First, it is a good approximation of the true distribution of investment returns. Second, an entire distribution can be described by only two values; the mean of the observations and the variance of the observations. The mean is computed as the arithmetic average of the observations. The variance is computed as the average of the squared differences from the mean. We subtract each return from the mean of all the returns, square these differences, sum these squared values, and then divide by the number of returns less 1. We subtract 1 from the number of returns because we use up one degree of freedom when we calculate the mean.

The square root of the variance is called the standard deviation. Typically it is this value rather than the variance that we use to represent risk because it is measured in the same units as the returns themselves.

The Central Limit Theorem

It is worth discussing why many seemingly disparate phenomena conform to a normal distribution. It has to do with one of the most important ideas in statistics: the Central Limit Theorem. This theorem holds that the sum or the average of independent random variables, which themselves may or may not be normally distributed, will approach a normal distribution as the number of random variables increases.

Suppose, for example, that the value of a random variable called X is determined by the toss of a die. There is a one-sixth chance that X will take on the value 1, a one-sixth chance that it will take on the value 2, and a one-sixth chance each that it will take on the values 3, 4, 5, or 6. Because each value is equally likely, the random variable X is uniformly distributed rather than normally distributed. Now consider a second random variable called Y, whose values are determined by the toss of a second die. This random variable is also uniformly distributed. Moreover, it is independent of the random variable X, because the outcome for X does not affect the outcome for Y.

Finally, consider a third random variable, called the average of X and Y. The distribution of this random variable is not uniformly distributed, because there are more ways to experience a value close to 3 or 4 than one close to 1 or 6. For example, the only way that the average of X and Y will equal one is if both X and Y take on the value 1, which, given the independence of X and Y, has a $\frac{1}{36}$ chance of occurring ($\frac{1}{6} \times \frac{1}{6}$).

TABLE 2-3   Demonstration of the central limit theorem

| | Relative Frequencies | | |
Value	X	Y	(X + Y)/2
1.0	1/6	1/6	1/36
1.5	0	0	2/36
2.0	1/6	1/6	3/36
2.5	0	0	4/36
3.0	1/6	1/6	5/36
3.5	0	0	6/36
4.0	1/6	1/6	5/36
4.5	0	0	4/36
5.0	1/6	1/6	3/36
5.5	0	0	2/36
6.0	1/6	1/6	1/36

There are two ways that X and Y can average 1.5: X takes on the value 1 when Y takes on the value 2, which has a $\frac{1}{36}$ chance of occurring, or X takes on the value 2 when Y takes on the value 1, which also has a $\frac{1}{36}$ chance of occurring. Thus there is a $\frac{2}{36}$ chance of at least one of the combinations occurring. There are three ways in which X and Y can average 3; hence the $\frac{3}{36}$ chance of occurring.

Table 2-3 shows the relative frequencies for all three random variables. Table 2-3 shows that, although neither X nor Y is normally distributed, their average begins to approach a normal distribution.

Properties of the Normal Distribution

Now let us review the properties of a normal distribution, which is shown in Figure 2-3. The normal distribution has several important characteristics. First, it is symmetric around its mean; 50 percent of the returns are below the mean return, and 50 percent are above it. Because the normal distribution is symmetric, its mode (the most common observation) and the median (the middle observation) are equal to each other and to the mean. The area enclosed within one standard deviation on either side of the mean encompasses 68 percent of the total area under the curve. The area enclosed within two standard deviations of the mean includes 95 percent of the distribution's total area, and a three-standard deviation band covers 99.7 percent of the area.

It is thus quite easy to estimate the probability of experiencing returns that are greater than or less than one, two, or three standard deviations away from the mean. There is, for example, about a 16 percent probability of experiencing a return less than one standard deviation below the mean and an

FIGURE 2-3   Normal distribution

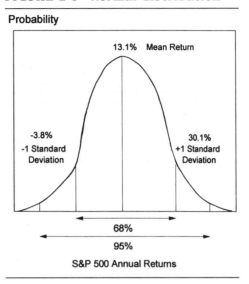

Probability

13.1%   Mean Return

-3.8%
-1 Standard
Deviation

30.1%
+1 Standard
Deviation

68%

95%

S&P 500 Annual Returns

equal chance of experiencing a return greater than the mean plus one standard deviation.

It is more likely, however, that we would be interested in returns that are other than one, two, or three standard deviations from the mean. To determine the probability of achieving these returns, we subtract the mean return from the target return, and divide this quantity by the standard deviation. By standardizing the returns, we rescale the distribution to have a mean of 0 and a standard deviation of 1.

For example, if our target return equals 5 percent, and the distribution of returns has a mean of 8 percent and a standard deviation of 12 percent, then we subtract 8 percent from 5 percent and divide by 12 percent:

$$-0.25 = \frac{0.05 - 0.08}{0.12}$$

This value tells us that 5 percent is 0.25 standard deviations below the mean of 8 percent.

Because the normal distribution is so important in statistical analysis, most statistics books include tables showing the areas under a standardized normal distribution curve that correspond to various standardized values. If you look at such a table, you find that 40.15 percent of the area under a normal distribution with an 8 percent mean and a 12 percent standard deviation is to the left of 5 percent. You thus can conclude that there is about a 60 percent chance of experiencing a return greater than or equal to 5 percent.

Lognormality

The probability estimate in the previous example assumes that returns are normally distributed. Although the Central Limit Theorem implies that the sum of many random variables is normally distributed, you know that the effect of compounding causes investment returns to be skewed rather than symmetric as implied by a normal distribution. Now we come full circle to our earlier discussion of future value. Although we estimate the *expected future value* by compounding at the arithmetic average, it is more convenient to estimate a *probability distribution* by using the geometric average.

Continuous Return

To understand the reasoning behind these different approaches, it is necessary to introduce the notion of a continuous return. Suppose you invest $100 at an annual interest rate of 100 percent. At the end of one year, that is, the initial investment of $100 will grow to $200. If the interest is compounded semiannually, the investment will grow to $150 after six months and then to $225 by year end. Quarterly compounding would produce a year end value of $244.14, and daily compounding would give a final value of $271.46. It would seem as though the more frequently the interest is compounded, the more money you end up with at year end. Yet, no matter how frequently we compound, the $100 will never grow to more than $271.83. When the interest rate equals 100 percent, the limit of the function, $(1 + r/n)^n$ where r equals the annual interest rate, and n equals the frequency of compounding, equals 2.71828. This value is referred to as "e," and it is the base of the natural log.

   We can use this result to convert periodic rates of return into continuous rates of return. A periodic rate of return is computed as the percentage change of an investment from the beginning of the period to the end of the period, assuming there are no contributions or disbursements. A continuous rate of return assumes that the income and growth are compounded instantaneously. Because e raised to the power 1 (the continuous rate of return is our example) yields 1 plus 1.7183 (the periodic rate of return in our example), the natural log of the quantity, 1 plus the periodic rate of return, must equal the corresponding continuous rate of return. For example, e raised to the power 0.0953 equals 1.10. Therefore, the natural log of 1.10 equals 0.0953. Thus $100 invested at 9.53 percent compounded continuously will grow to $110.

   This tangent is relevant because we sum continuous returns to arrive at a cumulative return. Recall the earlier example of an investment that increases 50 percent and then decreases 50 percent. Although these returns sum to 0 percent, the investment actually returns −25 percent over the two periods.

TABLE 2-4   Effect of compounding on return distribution

	Average of 10 Samples (%)	10-Year Cumulative Values of 10 Samples (%)
Mean return	9.56	152.44
Median return	9.89	121.79

The sum of the natural logs of 1 plus these returns equals −0.2877 [ln (1 + 0.5) + ln (1 − 0.5)]. The value e raised to the power −0.2877 equals 0.75, which when we subtract 1 from it equals −0.25 percent, the two-year cumulative return. Because we sum the continuous returns to arrive at the cumulative continuous return, but we multiply the quantities 1 plus the periodic returns to arrive at the cumulative periodic return, it is the continuous returns that are normally distributed. Remember that the Central Limit Theorem provides that the summation of random variables generates a normal distribution.

Table 2-4 demonstrates that the process of compounding causes returns to be lognormally distributed. In a normal distribution, the mean and median are equal. In a lognormal distribution, by contrast, the mean return exceeds the median return.

Table 2-4 reports the results of a simulation in which 10 samples of 100 annual returns are drawn from a population of returns with a normal distribution that has a mean of 10 percent and a standard deviation of 15 percent. As the table reveals, although the average of the means and medians of the 10 samples are both close to 10 percent, the 10-year cumulative mean return is quite a bit higher than the 10-year cumulative median return.

The arithmetic mean of the continuous returns equals the natural log of 1 plus the geometric average of the periodic returns. This explains why we use the geometric average to estimate probability distributions of returns. To estimate the probability of achieving a target future value, we use a particular formula that assumes that the continuous returns are normally distributed and that the periodic returns are lognormally distributed:

$$Z = \frac{\ln (T/B - \ln (1 + R_g)n}{S \times n^{1/2}} \tag{1}$$

where: Z = standardized variable
  T = target value
  B = beginning value
  R_g = geometric average of periodic returns
  n = number of periods
  S = standard deviation of the logarithms of the quantities 1 plus the periodic returns

Suppose, for example, you want to estimate the probability that a $1 million fund will grow to $1.5 million in five years, assuming that the geometric average of past returns equals 11 percent and that the standard deviation of continuous returns equals 13 percent. The standardized value that you look up in the normal distribution table is equal to -0.3227, as shown below:

$$-0.3227 = \frac{\ln(1.5/1.0) - \ln(1.11) \times 5}{0.13 \times 5^{1/2}}$$

If you look up this value in a normal distribution table, you find there is about a 63 percent chance that your investment will grow to $1.5 million by the end of five years.

Summary

It is useful at this point to review the main points discussed so far:

1. To use historical investment returns to estimate the future value of an investment, we must distinguish between whether we are interested in estimating the expected future value or the probability of achieving some target future value.
2. The expected future value is estimated from past returns by compounding at the arithmetic average of past returns.
3. The geometric average of past returns is used to estimate the probability of achieving a target future return, because the natural log of the quantity 1 plus the geometric average is equal to the mean of continuous returns. It is the continuous returns that are normally distributed.
4. The difference between a target return and the mean return is standardized by dividing this difference by the standard deviation. The target return and the standard deviation must be expressed as continuous values. We then use a normal distribution table to find the area under the normal distribution that corresponds to a particular standardized variable.

UTILITY

It should be clear from the explanation of the estimation of expected future value and of the probability of achieving a target future value that you maximize the expected future value by choosing the investment that has the highest expected return. If you want to maximize the probability of achieving a particular target return, however, you must also consider the riskiness of the investment. Probably you are interested not only in the chance of achieving a particular target wealth, but also in the amount by which you could conceivably fall short of this objective. You also may be interested in several target future values. For example, you might want considerable assurance of achieving a modest goal and less assurance of achieving a more ambitious goal.

It is likely the case that you have a range of goals that you endeavor to satisfy. Generally, people do not necessarily seek to maximize the chance of achieving a specific return, or to minimize the chance of suffering a particular loss. Rather they seek to maximize expected utility, where utility is a measure of a degree of satisfaction.

The notion of utility was introduced originally by the famous mathematician, Daniel Bernoulli, in a classic work entitled, "Exposition of a New Theory on the Measurement of Risk," published in 1738.[1] Bernoulli proposes that "the determination of the value of an item must not be based on its price, but rather on the utility it yields. The price of the item is dependent only on the thing itself and is equal for everyone; the utility, however, is dependent on the particular circumstances of the person making the estimate. Thus there is no doubt that a gain of one thousand ducats is more significant to a pauper than to a rich man though both gain the same amount."[2] Today economists refer to Bernoulli's insight as diminishing marginal utility.

Figure 2-4 illustrates this concept. The horizontal axis represents wealth, while the vertical axis represents utility. The curved line measures the relationship between wealth and utility. That it is positively sloped indicates that investors prefer more wealth to less wealth. That the steepness of the slope decreases as wealth increases means that investors derive less and less satisfaction with each incremental unit of wealth. This curvature also implies that investors

FIGURE 2-4   Diminishing marginal utility

Utility (Logarithm of Wealth)

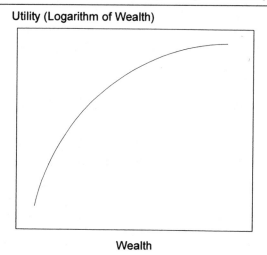

Wealth

FIGURE 2-5 Changes in utility versus changes in wealth

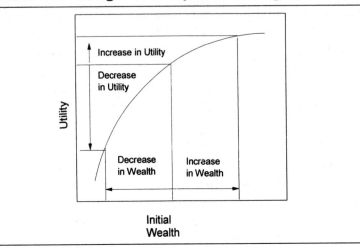

suffer greater disutility from a decline in wealth than the utility that would accrue to an increase in wealth of equal magnitude. Figure 2-5 illustrates this difference.

Specifically, Bernoulli assumes that utility increases by the natural log of the quantity 1 plus the percentage change in wealth. Therefore, if our wealth rises from $100,000 to $150,000, our utility would increase by 0.405465 units [ln (1 + 0.5)]. A subsequent and equal $50,000 increase to $200,000, however, increases our utility by only 0.287682 units [ln (1 + 0.33)].

Risk Aversion

Bernoulli's notion of utility implies that people are risk-averse, which technically means that they will reject a fair game. A fair game is defined as a game in which the expected outcome is equal for both participants. Suppose two participants who each have $100 contribute $50 as a stake in the game. A coin is tossed to determine the winner. The winner ends up with $150, the combined $100 stake in the game and her remaining $50. The loser ends up with $50.

The expected value of the game is $100 (0.5 × $50 + 0.5 × $150), which is exactly the expected value of *not* participating. The expected utility of not participating in the game is less than the utility of not playing. The utility of not playing equals the natural log of $100, which is 4.6052. The expected utility of participating in the game is found by adding the utility of $50 times its probability of occurring to the utility of $150 times its probability of occurring, which equals 4.4613 as shown in Table 2-5.

TABLE 2-5   Expected utility of participating in a fair game

Payoff	Utility of Payoff	Probability of Payoff (%)	Probability-Weighted Payoff
50	3.9120	50	1.9560
150	5.0106	50	2.5053
Expected Utility			4.4613

Bernoulli's definition of utility implies that we prefer a certain prospect to an uncertain prospect of equal expected value, which means we are risk-averse.

Certainty Equivalent

The value of a certain prospect that yields the same utility as the expected utility of an uncertain prospect is called a certainty equivalent. Let us continue with Bernoulli's assumption that utility is equal to the natural log of wealth. Thus we wish to set the natural log of the certain payoff equal to the natural log of the favorable payoff times its probability of occurring plus the natural log of the unfavorable payoff times its probability of occurring, as shown in equation (2):

$$\ln(C) = \ln(F) \times p + \ln(U) \times (1 \times p) \tag{2}$$

where: C = certain payoff
F = favorable payoff
p = probability of favorable payoff
U = unfavorable payoff

We then solve for C as follows:

$$C = e^{[\ln(F) \times p + \ln(U) \times (1 - p)]} \tag{3}$$

The certainty equivalent of the coin tossing game in which each participant starts out with $100 and puts up $50 as a stake equals $86.60:

$$86.60 = e^{[\ln(150) \times 0.5 + \ln(50) \times (1 - 0.5)]}$$

If our utility is equal to the logarithm of wealth, we would be indifferent between a certain $86.60 payoff and a game that offers a 50 percent chance of receiving $150 and an equal chance of receiving $50. The difference between the expected value of the risky prospect and the certain payoff is called the risk premium. To participate in the risky game, we would require an expected risk premium greater than 15.5 percent [(100 − 86.60)/86.6]. If we start out with $1,000, however, the certainty equivalent would equal $998.75, and we would require an expected risk premium of only ⅛ of 1 percent. That is, if we start out with $1,000, we are not nearly as disinclined to lose $50, because this amount represents a smaller fraction of our wealth. If the potential loss is $500, though, we would again require a risk premium in excess of 15 percent to induce us to participate in the risky game.

Risk Preferences

Although Bernoulli's assumption that utility is equal to the natural log of wealth is plausible, it is by no means comprehensive. Some of us are more risk-averse than the risk aversion implied by a log wealth utility function. Our utility function might be better approximated by the negative of the reciprocal of wealth. This function has more curvature than a log wealth utility function. Given this utility function, the certainty equivalent of a risky game with an even chance of generating $150 or $50 equals $75 ($-1/75 = 0.5 \times -1/150 + 0.5 \times -1/50$), which is significantly lower than the $86.60 certainty equivalent associated with the log wealth utility function. Or we might be more tolerant of risk. In fact, some of us might be risk-neutral or even risk-seeking.

Because there are a variety of attitudes toward risk, economists have expanded Bernoulli's insights into a comprehensive theory of risk preference. Economists distinguish among those who are risk-averse, those who are risk-neutral, and those who seek risk. A risk-averse investor will reject a fair game; a risk-neutral investor would be indifferent to a fair game; and a risk-seeking investor would accept a fair game. Economists also characterize risk aversion by whether it increases, remains constant, or decreases as a function of wealth in an absolute sense or as a percentage of wealth. Table 2-6 summarizes these various descriptions of risk aversion.

The log wealth utility function assumes that investors have constant relative risk aversion. As their wealth changes, the percentage that they are willing to allocate to risky assets remains constant. If they have $10,000 and allocate $6,000 to risky assets, they will allocate $60,000 to risky assets should their wealth increase to $100,000.

TABLE 2-6   Risk aversion

	Absolute	**Relative**
Decreasing	Increase risky amount	Increase risky percentage
Constant	Maintain risky amount	Maintain risky percentage
Increasing	Decrease risky amount	Decrease risky percentage

Indifference Curves

It is sometimes useful to represent expected utility as a function of expected return, a risk aversion coefficient, and expected risk measured as variance, as depicted in Equation (4):

$$E(U) = E(r) - \lambda \times \sigma^2 \qquad (4)$$

where: $E(U)$ = expected utility
$E(r)$ = expected return
λ = risk aversion coefficient
σ = standard deviation of returns

If, at the margin, we are willing to give up five units of expected return in order to lower our risk by one unit, an investment with an 8 percent expected return and a 10 percent standard deviation would yield 0.03 units of expected utility $(0.08 - 5 \times 0.10^2)$. We would prefer this investment to an alternative investment that has an expected return of 10 percent and a standard deviation of 12 percent. This latter investment yields only 0.028 units of expected utility $(0.10 - 5 \times 0.12^2)$. Given a risk aversion coefficient of 5, the 2 percent incremental return is not sufficient to compensate for the 2 percent incremental risk.

If instead our risk aversion equals 3, the higher expected return investment would yield expected utility equal to 0.057 units, which exceeds the 0.05 units of expected utility from the investment with the lower expected return; hence we would prefer the investment with the higher expected return.

If we could identify investments that yield the same expected utility, they would form a positively sloped convex curve in dimensions of expected return and standard deviation. For example, assuming a risk aversion coefficient equal to 4, the combinations of expected return and standard deviation in Table 2-7 all yield expected utility of 0.05 units.

TABLE 2-7   Risk–return combinations with equal expected utility (risk aversion coefficient = 4)

Expected Return (%)	Standard Deviation (%)	Expected Utility (%)
6.00	0.00	5.00
8.00	8.66	5.00
10.00	11.18	5.00
12.00	13.23	5.00
14.00	15.00	5.00
16.00	16.58	5.00
18.00	18.03	5.00
20.00	19.56	5.00

FIGURE 2-6   Indifference curves

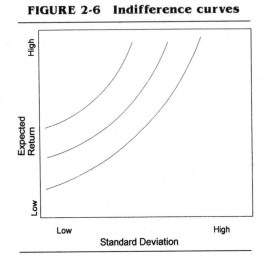

Table 2-7 shows that we are more willing to accept incremental risk at lower levels of expected return in order to raise expected return than we are at higher levels of expected return. By tracing a curve through combinations of expected return and standard deviation that yield the same utility, we can create an indifference curve.

Figure 2-6 depicts three hypothetical indifference curves. We are indifferent among all of the combinations of expected return and risk along a particular indifference curve, because they all yield the same expected utility. We prefer, however, indifference curves that are closer to the upper left corner.

FIGURE 2-7   The optimal portfolio

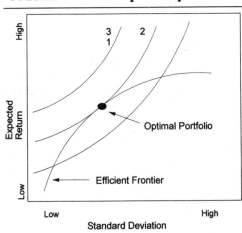

Later in the chapter I describe how to identify combinations of assets that offer the highest expected return for a given level of risk. A continuum of these portfolios plotted in dimensions of expected return and standard deviation constitutes the efficient frontier, which is shown in Figure 2-7. There is on the efficient frontier a unique portfolio that is tangent to one of the indifference curves. It is this portfolio that, subject to the constraints of the efficient frontier, maximizes a particular investor's expected utility—your expected utility. Given the analytical framework I have described, and the assumptions that underlie this framework, this portfolio is optimal in the sense that it matches a person's preference for incurring risk in order to raise expected return with the best available trade-off of risk and return from the capital markets.

IDENTIFYING THE OPTIMAL PORTFOLIO

There is no doubt that investors seek to maximize expected utility. How they describe their particular utility, however, might be considerably more complex than the simple utility functions described earlier. Investors may be concerned with relative performance as well as absolute performance, or they may be sensitive to particular thresholds in their wealth. Moreover, some investors' choices are dictated by behavioral considerations that are difficult to describe in the traditional mean-variance framework. For the time being, it is simplest to continue with the naive assumption that it is possible to measure an investor's willingness to trade off expected return and risk. Later on we deal with some of the complexities mentioned above.

The investor faces the task of constructing a portfolio of assets that maximizes expected utility, which is defined as expected return minus risk aversion times portfolio risk, as shown earlier in Equation (4). Therefore, we need to measure a portfolio's expected return and standard deviation as a function of the expected returns and standard deviations of the component assets.

Let us suppose we want to allocate our portfolio between stocks and bonds. The expected return of a portfolio made up of just stocks and bonds is simply the weighted average of the components, as shown in Equation (5):

$$R_p = (R_s \times W_s) + (R_B \times W_B) \qquad (5)$$

where: R_p = expected return of the portfolio
R_s = expected return of stocks
W_s = percentage of portfolio allocated to stocks
R_B = expected return of bonds
W_B = percentage of portfolio allocated to bonds

A portfolio's risk is a little trickier. Although the standard deviation of returns measures an individual asset's risk, the average of the standard deviations (or variances) of two assets does not accurately measure the risk of the portfolio made up of these two assets. The portfolio's risk depends also on the extent to which the two assets move together—that is, the extent to which their prices react in like fashion to a particular event. The comovement between asset returns is measured by their covariance. It equals the standard deviation of the first asset times the standard deviation of the second asset times the correlation coefficient between the two assets.

The correlation coefficient measures the association between the returns of the two assets. It ranges in value from $+1$ to -1. If one asset's returns are higher than its average return when another asset's returns are higher than *its* average return, for example, the correlation coefficient will be positive. By contrast, if one asset's returns are higher than its average returns when another asset's returns are *lower* than its average return, the correlation coefficient will be negative.

The correlation coefficient, by itself, is an inadequate measure of covariance because it measures only the direction and the degree of association between the returns of two assets. It does not account for the magnitude of variability in the assets' returns. Covariance captures magnitude by multiplying the correlation coefficient by the standard deviation of the assets' returns.

Finally, the portfolio's standard deviation depends on the weightings of the component assets. It equals the square root of the portfolio's variance, which, for a portfolio of two assets, is computed as the variance of the first asset times its weighting squared, plus the variance of the second asset times its weighting squared, plus twice the covariance between the two assets times each asset's weighting, as shown in Equation (6):

$$\sigma_p = (\sigma_S^2 \times W_S^2 + \sigma_B^2 \times W_B^2 + 2 \times \rho \times \sigma_S \times W_S \times \sigma_B \times W_B)^{1/2} \qquad (6)$$

where: σ_S = standard deviation of stocks
σ_B = standard deviation of bonds
ρ = correlation between stocks and bonds

These equations for a portfolio's expected return and standard deviation enable us to rewrite expected utility as follows:

$$E(U) = R_S \times W_S + R_B \times W_B - \\ \lambda (\sigma_S^2 \times W_S^2 + \sigma_B^2 \times W_B^2 + 2 \times \rho \times \sigma_S \times W_S \times \sigma_B \times W_B) \qquad (7)$$

The investor wants to maximize expected utility as a function of exposure to stocks and bonds. Therefore we need to measure how sensitive expected utility is to a small change in its exposure to stocks and to a small change in its exposure to bonds. These sensitivities are called the marginal utility of stocks and the marginal utility of bonds, and they are measured as the partial derivative of expected utility with respect to the stock and bond weightings, respectively, as shown in Equations (8) and (9).

$$\partial E(U)/\partial W_S = R_S - \lambda\ (2 \times \sigma_S^2 W_S + 2 \times \rho \times \sigma_S \times \sigma_B \times W_B) \qquad (8)$$

$$\partial E(U)/\partial W_B = R_B - \lambda\ (2 \times \sigma_B^2 W_B + 2 \times \rho \times \sigma_B \times \sigma_S \times W_S) \qquad (9)$$

The marginal utilities measure how much we can increase or decrease expected utility, starting from the current allocation, by increasing exposure to each asset by one unit. A positive marginal utility indicates that we increase expected utility by increasing exposure to the asset. A negative marginal utility indicates that we decrease expected utility by increasing exposure to the asset. Because we cannot increase the exposure to both assets simultaneously, we increase a portfolio's expected utility by reducing the weight of the asset with the lower marginal utility, even if it is positive, and increasing by the same amount the weight of the asset with the higher marginal utility.[3]

Suppose you estimate the expected return of stocks to equal 12 percent with a 20 percent standard deviation, the expected return of bonds to equal 8 percent with a 10 percent standard deviation, and the correlation between the two assets to equal 50 percent. Also assume that your portfolio is currently allocated 60 percent to stocks and 40 percent to bonds, and that your risk aversion coefficient equals 2.

If you substitute these values into the marginal utility equations, you find that you can increase your expected utility by 0.008 units by increasing the portfolio's exposure to stocks by 1 percent, and that you can improve expected utility by 0.04 units by increasing the portfolio's exposure to bonds by 1 percent. You should therefore shift 1 percent of the portfolio from stocks (which have the lower marginal utility) to bonds (which have the higher marginal utility).

Now we recompute the marginal utilities, given the new allocation of 59 percent stocks and 41 percent bonds. Again, bonds continue to have a higher marginal utility than stocks, so we shift another 1 percent from stocks to bonds. We continue in this fashion until the marginal utilities of the stock and bond allocations are equal to each other. Given your assumptions about returns, standard deviations, and correlation, the marginal utilities are identical to one another when the stock allocation equals one-third, and the bond allocation equals two-thirds. At these allocations, you cannot improve expected utility any farther by shifting the portfolio between stocks and bonds.

By varying the risk aversion values, we can construct the entire efficient frontier of stock and bonds. For each level of risk aversion, there is a portfolio along the efficient frontier that maximizes expected utility; hence it is the optimal portfolio for that degree of risk aversion.

COMPLEX UTILITY FUNCTIONS

In the real world, people's utility functions are not so simple. They take a variety of forms, depending on different preferences.

Relative Performance

Thus far we have assumed implicitly that investors care only about absolute return and absolute risk. It is normal, though, to expect that some of us care about how we perform in a relative sense, such as compared to other investors or to some benchmark. Relative performance is a common standard when agents make investment decisions for others. In the case of pension fund investment, for example, although the legal constituents of pension investment policy are the pension plan participants, and the economic constituents are the corporate shareholders, the pension investment decisions are made by agents, usually corporate officers in the treasurer's department, and their job evaluations often depend on the fund's performance relative to other pension funds or some prespecified benchmark.

One can also conceive of circumstances in which relative performance is relevant even in the absence of "agency" issues. Colleges and universities, for example, compete with one another for faculty, students, and grants. To the extent that one institution's endowment fund performs better than another's, it will improve its competitive position.

In both these situations, the investor is concerned with relative performance. Thus return is measured as the fund's return net of the return of some benchmark, which typically is defined as a combination of market indexes or a universe of competing funds. Risk, within this context, is defined as tracking error, and it is measured by taking the square root of the average of the squared deviations between the fund's returns and the benchmark's returns. This calculation is shown in Equation (10).

$$TE = \sqrt{\frac{\sum_{i=1}^{n}(R_F - R_B)^2}{n}} \qquad (10)$$

where: TE = tracking error
R_F = return of fund
R_B = return of benchmark
n = number of returns

If we are concerned exclusively with relative performance, we would define expected utility as expected relative return less aversion to tracking error times tracking error squared, and we would attempt to maximize this quantity as a function of exposure to the various assets under consideration.

The typical investor is not concerned exclusively with absolute performance or exclusively with relative performance, but rather with both. A recent innovation depicts expected utility as a function of two risk parameters: standard deviation of total returns and tracking error.[4] Expected utility is defined as expected return, minus the quantity of aversion to total risk times standard deviation of total returns squared, minus the quantity of aversion to tracking error times tracking error squared, as shown in Equation (11):

$$E(U) = E(r) - \lambda\sigma^2 - \lambda\, TE^2 \tag{11}$$

where all the terms are defined as before.

This description of expected utility has three dimensions: expected return, absolute risk, and relative risk. It assumes that the investor likes expected return and dislikes both absolute risk and relative risk, assuming that standard deviation and tracking error have positive risk aversion coefficients. Thus the portfolios that maximize expected utility are plotted in three dimensions as an efficient plane rather than an efficient frontier.

In the absence of this framework for maximizing expected utility, many investors follow heuristic procedure, meaning that they impose constraints on asset classes so that the ultimate portfolio does not differ very much in composition from the relevant benchmark. For example, left unconstrained, an optimizer might dictate that a large fraction of the portfolio be allocated to foreign assets or to real estate. Because many investors do not want to perform significantly worse than their peers or some benchmark that may not be heavily invested in foreign assets and real estate, they maximize expected utility subject to the constraints that no more than 10 percent be allocated to foreign assets or real estate, for example.

Although this heuristic approach helps to reduce tracking error, it does so inefficiently and assuming a highly improbable theoretical premise. The assumption is that an investor is completely tolerant of a particular asset up to a specific threshold, and then completely intolerant of that asset beyond that threshold, irrespective of the impact on portfolio risk and tracking error. This approach is inefficient because it is often the case that there is some portfolio with a higher allocation to at least one of the constrained assets that has a higher expected return with a lower standard deviation and with lower tracking error than a portfolio on the efficient frontier that meets all constraints.

Kinked Utility Functions

The utility functions we have described so far assume that the translation formulas of wealth into utility are constant. This does not imply that the relationship between utility and wealth is constant but rather that the formula that we use to translate wealth into utility remains the same. Some investors might be particularly sensitive to sustaining losses that would lower their wealth below some threshold, because below that threshold their life would change qualitatively. The same is true for agents. For example, a pension investment officer might expect smaller and smaller raises as a fund's wealth falls toward a particular value, and expect to be fired if the fund penetrates that value.

To address this circumstance, we can define risk as the square root of the average of the squared deviations below a particular return, as shown in Equation (12):

$$DR = \sqrt{\frac{\sum_{i=1}^{n}(R_D - R_T)^2}{n}} \tag{12}$$

where: DR = downside risk
R_D = returns below target return
R_T = target return
n = number of returns below target return

Given this downside risk criterion, expected utility equals expected return minus the quantity of aversion to downside risk times downside risk squared. This definition of expected utility assumes that we are indifferent to volatility around the expected return but above the target return, which is unlikely. Thus we can again expand our utility function to include multiple risk parameters. For example, we can include a term for standard deviation of returns and another term for deviations below a target return. Moreover, we can create a hybrid utility function that combines symmetric risk and downside risk with absolute risk and relative risk. The definition of expected utility in Equation (13) which has this hybrid characteristic, is probably a realistic description of many investors' attitudes toward risk:

$$E(U) = E(r) - \lambda_T \sigma^2 - \lambda_{DTE} \, DTE^2 \tag{13}$$

where: $E(U)$ = expected utility
λ_T = aversion to standard deviation of total returns
σ = standard deviation of total returns
λ_{DTE} = aversion to downside tracking error
DTE = deviations below benchmark returns

This definition of expected utility implies that we are concerned with the variability of total returns and *also* with the deviations of our relative performance below a target benchmark return. The intuition behind this asymmetric attitude toward relative performance is that we will not be rewarded if we outperform our benchmark but that we will be penalized if we underperform it.

INVESTMENT HORIZON: IS IT RELEVANT?

It is commonly assumed that investors with longer horizons should allocate a larger fraction of their savings to risky assets than investors with shorter horizons. The rationale for this argument is rather simple. If our savings are invested in a risky asset such as stocks, over a short horizon we could lose a substantial part of our savings. Over a long horizon, however, favorable short-term stock returns are likely to offset poor short-term stock returns, so in that case it is more likely that stocks will realize an actual return close to their expected return.

Time Diversification

The notion that above-average returns tend to offset below-average returns over long horizons is called time diversification. If returns are independent from one year to the next, the standard deviation of annualized returns diminishes with time. The distribution of annualized returns consequently converges as the investment horizon increases.

Figure 2-8 shows a 95 percent confidence interval of annualized returns as a function of investment horizon, assuming that the geometric return is 10 percent and the standard deviation of continuous returns equals 15 percent. These confidence intervals assume that the returns are lognormally distributed, as discussed earlier. It is apparent from Figure 2-8 that the distribution of annualized returns converges as the investment horizon lengthens.

The idea of time diversification may be clearer if you think about the probability of losing money as a function of horizon. If we proceed according to Equation (1), with the assumption that the S&P's return equals 10 percent and its standard deviation equals 15 percent, we find there is a 26 percent probability that the S&P 500 will generate a negative return in any one year. Given a ten-year horizon, however, the probability that the S&P 500 will produce a negative return falls to only 2.2 percent. This does not imply that it is

FIGURE 2-8   95% Confidence interval of annualized returns

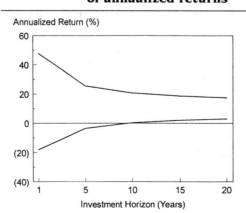

just as improbable to lose money in any one of the ten years; it merely reflects the tendency of above-average returns to cancel out below-average returns.

The original description of time diversification by Peter Bernstein in the *Journal of Portfolio Management* is worth repeating. Investors diversify because they never know which opportunity among the choices they face is the best opportunity. This uncertainty applies to individual securities, asset classes, and time periods in which to invest. Since investors cannot know which period is the best period, they invest through many periods. Hence they are more comfortable investing in risky assets over the long run than over the short run.

Time Diversification Refuted

Several prominent economists, most notably Paul Samuelson,[5] argue that the notion of time diversification is specious, because the relevant metric is terminal wealth, not annualized return. As the investment horizon increases, the dispersion of terminal wealth diverges from the expected terminal wealth.

This result implies that, although we are less likely to lose money over a long horizon than over a short horizon, the magnitude of our potential loss increases with the length of our investment horizon. According to the critics of time diversification, if we elect a riskless investment when we are faced with a short horizon, we should also elect a riskless investment when our horizon is 10 years, 20 years, or any duration.

It may be clearer to explore this idea from the perspective of cross-sectional diversification. Suppose you have an opportunity to invest $10,000 in an oil well, and you decline this offer because you think it is too risky. You are then offered an opportunity to invest in ten independent oil wells, each with the same risk as the one you declined, and each requires a $10,000 investment. It is obviously less likely that you will lose money by investing in ten equally risky but independent oil wells than by investing in just one of these wells. The amount you could conceivably lose, however, is $100,000.

Now consider a third choice. Suppose you have a chance to invest a total of $10,000 in ten equally risky but independent oil wells, so that the investment per well is only $1,000. This investment diversifies the risk across ten oil wells without increasing total exposure beyond the $10,000 exposure of the initial opportunity. Although you might still be opposed to this investment, your opposition to it should be less extreme than it would be to either of the first two choices.

There is a reason you might remain unpersuaded by these arguments. Although it is true that the dispersion of terminal wealth increases with the passage of time, it increases around a higher expected wealth. This point is illustrated by Figure 2-9. The graph compares the expanding dispersion of the

**FIGURE 2-9   95% Confidence interval
of terminal wealth**

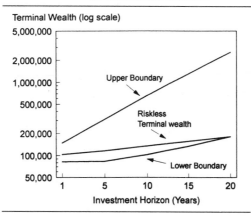

terminal wealth that results from investing $100,000 in the S&P 500, assuming a 10 percent annual return and a 15 percent standard deviation of continuous returns, to the terminal wealth of a $100,000 investment in a Treasury bill with a 3 percent annual yield.

After one year, the terminal wealth of the S&P investment ranges from $81,980 to $147,596 with 95 percent confidence, compared to a certain $103,000 from the Treasury bill investment. If we increase the horizon to 10 years, the spread in the S&P investment's terminal wealth expands from $65,616 to $554,829, but the lower boundary of a 95 percent confidence interval is greater than the initial investment of $100,000. By the end of 20 years, the lower boundary of the 95 percent confidence interval for the S&P investment actually exceeds the terminal wealth of the Treasury bill investment.

This line of reasoning, although ostensibly credible, fails to validate the notion of time diversification. If you compute the lower boundary of the 99 percent confidence interval, you will find that it falls below the terminal value of the Treasury bill investment. In fact, for any horizon, we can widen the confidence interval of a risky investment sufficiently so that its lower boundary of terminal wealth will fall below the terminal wealth of a riskless investment. The growing improbability of a loss is always offset by the magnitude of potential losses.

The mathematical truth that time does not diversify risk can easily be demonstrated by returning to the notion of expected utility. Suppose that our utility is equal to the logarithm of wealth as suggested by Bernoulli. Thus $100 conveys 4.60517 units of utility [$\ln(100.00) = 4.60517$]. Now consider an investment opportunity that has a 50 percent chance of a one-third gain and a 50 percent chance of a one-quarter loss. The expected wealth of this investment after one period equals \$104.17 (133.33 × 0.50 + 75.00 × 0.50). The certainty equivalent of this risky investment is \$100.00, because it too conveys 4.60517 units of expected utility [ln(133.33) × 0.50 = ln(75.00) × 0.50]. Thus, given a log wealth utility function, we are indifferent between holding on to our \$100.00 and investing in this risky asset that has an equal chance of a one-third gain or a one-quarter loss, because both choices convey 4.60517 units of utility.

Now consider investing in this risky asset over two periods, assuming that the same odds of a gain and a loss prevail. There are four possible paths that the investment can take. It could first increase to 133.33, and then increase again to 177.78. It could first increase to 133.33 and then decrease to 100.00. It could decrease to 75.00 and then increase to 100.00. Finally, it could decrease to 75.00 in the first period and then decrease again to 56.25. After two periods the expected terminal wealth equals \$108.51, but the expected utility still equals 4.60517. Thus, not only are we indifferent between a certain \$100.00 and an equal chance of a one-third gain and a one-quarter loss, but we are also indifferent between investing in this risky asset over one period or investing in it over two periods.

If we extend the investment horizon to three periods or four periods or any number of periods, the same mathematical truth prevails. The expected utility will never change. Figure 2-10 shows this result.

Moreover, this result will obtain regardless of our utility function. Consider a function that defines our utility as the negative of the reciprocal of our wealth. This utility function implies that we are more averse to risk than a log wealth investor. We would thus prefer to keep our \$100.00 given a risky alternative that has a 50 percent chance of a one-third gain and a 50 percent chance

FIGURE 2-10   Utility = In (Wealth)

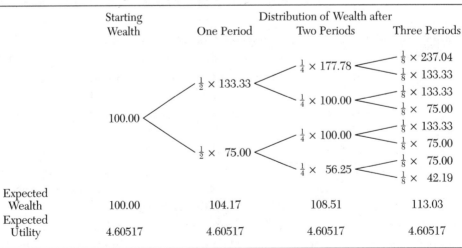

	Starting Wealth	Distribution of Wealth after		
		One Period	Two Periods	Three Periods
	100.00	$\frac{1}{2}$ × 133.33	$\frac{1}{4}$ × 177.78	$\frac{1}{8}$ × 237.04 $\frac{1}{8}$ × 133.33
			$\frac{1}{4}$ × 100.00	$\frac{1}{8}$ × 133.33 $\frac{1}{8}$ × 75.00
		$\frac{1}{2}$ × 75.00	$\frac{1}{4}$ × 100.00	$\frac{1}{8}$ × 133.33 $\frac{1}{8}$ × 75.00
			$\frac{1}{4}$ × 56.25	$\frac{1}{8}$ × 75.00 $\frac{1}{8}$ × 42.19
Expected Wealth	100.00	104.17	108.51	113.03
Expected Utility	4.60517	4.60517	4.60517	4.60517

FIGURE 2-11   Utility = −1/Wealth

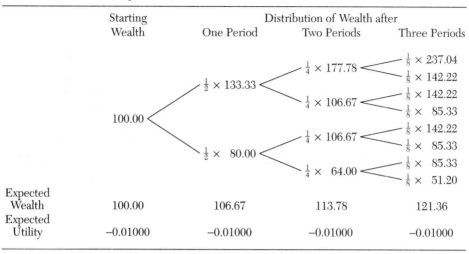

	Starting Wealth	Distribution of Wealth after		
		One Period	Two Periods	Three Periods
Expected Wealth	100.00	106.67	113.78	121.36
Expected Utility	−0.01000	−0.01000	−0.01000	−0.01000

of a one-quarter loss. We would be indifferent, however, between a certain $100.00 and a risky prospect that offers an even chance of a one-third gain and a one-fifth loss. Figure 2-11 reveals the constancy of expected utility as the horizon expands given that our utility equals −1/W.

Time Diversification Resurrected

There remain several valid reasons why you might still condition your risk posture on your horizon, even though we accept the mathematical verity that time does not diversify risk. This result depends on the assumption that returns are independent from one period to the next. In a perfectly efficient market, you would expect investment returns to be serially independent. The historical record, however, is less clear about the serial dependence of stock returns. There is some evidence that U.S. stock returns mean-revert over long intervals, although it would be imprudent to expect this result as an inevitable outcome.[6] If, however, investment returns do tend to revert to their long-run mean return, then it is more likely that an above-average return would be followed by a below-average return than another above-average return. If returns revert to their mean, then the dispersion of terminal wealth increases at a slower rate than implied by a lognormal distribution. And it follows that if we are more averse to risk than a log wealth investor, we will be led to favor risky assets over a long horizon if we are indifferent between a risky and a riskless asset over a short horizon.[7]

   If we assume that the risky asset has a 60 percent chance of reversing direction, and therefore only a 40 percent chance of repeating its prior return,

FIGURE 2-12   Utility = −1/Wealth with mean reversion

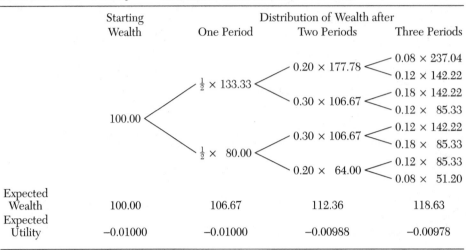

	Starting Wealth	Distribution of Wealth after		
		One Period	Two Periods	Three Periods
Expected Wealth	100.00	100.00	106.67	112.36	118.63
Expected Utility		−0.01000	−0.01000	−0.00988	−0.00978

we find that the expected utility of the risky asset increases as the investment horizon grows. This result is displayed in Figure 2-12.

Investors who have a log wealth utility function would still not be induced to accept more risk over long horizons than short horizons if investment returns mean-revert. This result applies only to investors who are more risk-averse than log wealth investors.

Another valid reason why you might be induced to accept more risk over long horizons is that you would have greater discretion to adjust your consumption and work habits.[8] If a risky investment performs poorly at the beginning of a short horizon, there is little you can do to compensate for the loss in wealth. Over a long horizon, however, you can postpone consumption, and work harder to achieve your financial goals. The argument against time diversification assumes implicitly that your wealth depends only on investment results and not on consumption or work habits.

You might also be willing to change your risk posture as a function of the investment horizon, because your utility function changes abruptly at a particular threshold of wealth. If the date at which this threshold becomes relevant is far into the future, it is less likely that you will penetrate it with a risky investment than if the threshold were to become relevant more imminently.

The bottom line about time diversification is that investors should not change their risk posture depending on investment horizon unless one or more of three circumstances prevail:

1. The investor believes that investment returns mean-revert rather than follow a random walk, and is more risk-averse than a log wealth investor.

2. The investor has the ability to modify consumption and work habits sufficiently to compensate for early investment losses.

3. The investor has a kinked utility function, in that it changes abruptly as a condition of nearness to a particular wealth threshold.

CONCLUSION

Whether or not we realize it, our investment objective is to maximize expected utility. The challenge in setting investment objectives is to express our utility function clearly and concisely so that we can go about the process of selecting an investment strategy that maximizes expected utility.

To achieve the setting of objectives, we must understand many technical issues, some of them quite subtle. To understand and estimate future value, we must first grasp the distinctions among arithmetic, geometric, and continuous returns. Furthermore, we need to understand how risk is measured, and how from this value, together with the mean return, we can infer the entire distribution of returns. One of the subtleties that we must not ignore is the way that compounding introduces skewness in the distribution of periodic returns, causing them to be lognormally distributed.

Next, we need a theoretical framework for describing our attitude toward risk and return. Utility theory provides the theoretical underpinning for balancing our desire to increase future wealth with our aversion to sustaining losses.

We need to understand the process of combining assets to satisfy our investment objectives. To understand this process, we must be familiar with the calculation of return and risk at the portfolio level and the way we identify portfolios that maximize expected utility.

Because risk has several dimensions, we must be prepared to move beyond simple utility functions to more complex variations. For example, we may need to incorporate relative risk as well as absolute risk and deviations below a target return along with total variability.

Finally, we must understand the role that the investment horizon plays in setting our objectives. Surprisingly, it plays no role at all unless specific conditions prevail. Hence, we must understand to what extent these conditions apply to us.

This chapter clarifies these issues and provides a framework in which you will be confident in setting your investment objectives.

3 MODELS OF RISK

Aswath Damodaran

Risk is traditionally viewed as a negative factor in investing. *Merriam-Webster's Collegiate Dictionary,* Tenth Edition, defines the verb *risk* as "to expose to hazard or danger." The Chinese have a better definition: They combine two symbols to represent risk: the symbol for "danger" and the symbol for "opportunity." Every investor and business has to make a tradeoff between the higher rewards that potentially come with opportunity and the higher risk that has to be borne as a consequence of danger. The key goal in finance is to ensure that when an investor is exposed to risk, there will be an "appropriate" reward for taking the risk.

In this chapter, we lay the foundations for analyzing risk in finance, and we present alternative models for measuring risk and converting these risk measurements into "acceptable" hurdle rates.

INGREDIENTS FOR A GOOD RISK AND RETURN MODEL

A number of different risk and return models are presented in this chapter. As a basis for evaluating the relative strengths of these models, we define the characteristics of a good risk and return model as follows:

1. It should provide a measure of risk that applies to all assets and not be asset-specific.

2. It should clearly delineate those types of risk that are rewarded and those that are not, and should give a rationale for the delineation.

3. It should be based on standardized risk measures; (i.e., an investor presented with a risk measure for an individual asset should be able to draw conclusions about whether the asset involves above-average or below-average risk).

4. It should translate the measure of risk into a rate of return that the investor can expect or demand as compensation for bearing the risk.

5. It should work well not only as an explanation of past returns, but also as a prediction of future expected returns.

GENERAL MODELS FOR RISK AND RETURN

To understand how risk is viewed in finance, we will present the analysis in three steps. First, we will define risk in terms of the distribution of actual returns around an expected return. Second, we will differentiate between risk that is specific to one investment or a few investments, and risk that affects a much wider cross section of investments. We will argue that in a market where the marginal investor is well diversified, only the latter risk, called market risk, will be rewarded. Third, we will look at alternative models for measuring market risk and at the expected returns that go with it.

Measuring Risk

Investors who buy assets have a targeted return that they expect to realize over the time that they will hold the asset. The actual return that they make over this holding period may be very different from the expected return; this is where risk comes in. Suppose an investor with a 1-year time horizon buys a 1-year Treasury bill (or any other default-free 1-year bond) with a 5 percent expected return. At the end of the 1-year holding period, the actual return that this investor would have on this investment will always be 5 percent, or the expected return. The return distribution for this investment is shown in Figure 3-1. This is a riskless investment, at least in nominal terms.

In contrast, consider an investor who invests in Disney, the media and entertainment giant. This investor, having done appropriate research, may conclude that a return of 30 percent on Disney can be expected over a 1-year holding period. The actual return over this period will almost certainly *not* be equal to 30 percent; it might be much greater or much lower. The distribution of returns on this investment is illustrated in Figure 3-2.

FIGURE 3-1   Return on a risk-free investment

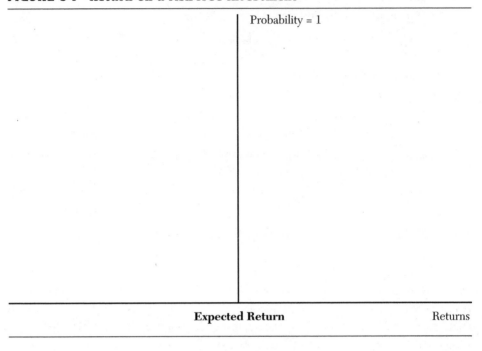

Probability = 1

Expected Return   Returns

FIGURE 3-2   Probability distribution for a risky investment

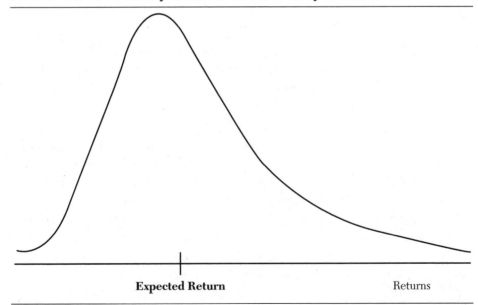

Expected Return   Returns

In addition to the expected return, investors now have to consider the following:

1. The spread of the actual returns around the expected return is captured by the *variance* or *standard deviation* of the distribution; the greater the deviation of the actual returns from expected returns, the greater the variance.

2. The bias toward positive or negative returns is captured by the *skewness* of the distribution. The distribution in Figure 3-2 is said to be "positively" skewed: there is a greater bias toward large positive returns than toward large negative returns.

3. The shape of the tails of the distribution is measured by the *kurtosis* of the distribution; fatter tails lead to higher kurtosis. To investors, the configuration in Figure 3-2 captures the tendency of the price of this investment to jump in either direction.

In the special case where distributions are symmetric and normal, investors do not have to worry about skewness and kurtosis: there is no skewness, and a normal distribution is defined to have a kurtosis of zero. Investments with symmetric returns can be measured on two dimensions: (1) the expected return on the investment comprises the reward, and (2) the variance in anticipated returns comprises the risk.

Figure 3-3 illustrates the return distributions on two investments with symmetric returns. When faced with a choice between two investments with the same standard deviation but different expected returns, an investor will always pick the one with the higher expected return.

Where distributions are neither symmetric nor normal, it is still conceivable, though unlikely, that investors will choose investments on the basis of only the expected return and the variance, if the investors possess utility functions[1] that allow them to do so. More likely preferences, however, are for positive rather than negative skewed distributions, and for distributions with a lower likelihood of jumps (lower kurtosis) rather than a higher likelihood of jumps (higher kurtosis). Investors tend to trade off good moments (higher expected returns and more positive skewness) against bad ones (higher variance and kurtosis). Among the risk and return models that we will be examining, the capital asset pricing model (CAPM) explicitly requires that choices be made only in terms of expected returns and variances. It does ignore the other return moments, but whether these additional moments of the distribution are factors in determining expected returns is not clear.

The return moments encountered in practice are almost always estimated using past returns rather than future returns. The assumption we make when

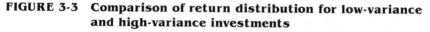

FIGURE 3-3   **Comparison of return distribution for low-variance and high-variance investments**

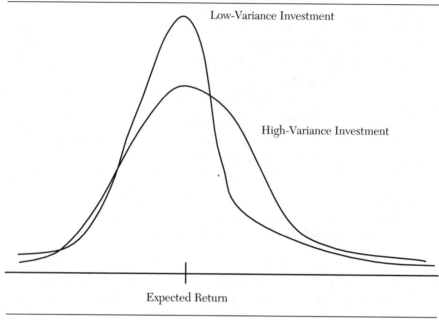

we use historical variances is that past return distributions are good indicators of future return distributions. When this assumption is violated, as happens when the asset's characteristics have changed significantly over time, the historical estimates may not be good measures of risk.

Figure 3-4 shows the monthly returns on an investment in Disney stock for every month from January 1992 to November 1996.

The standard deviation and the variance in these monthly returns were estimated to be:

Standard deviation in monthly returns = 6.14 percent.

Variance in monthly returns = 37.66 percent.

These measures can be annualized[2] fairly simply, as follows:

Annualized standard deviation = 6.14 percent $\times \sqrt{12} = 21.26$ percent.

Annualized variance = 37.66 percent $\times 12 = 452$ percent.

Rewarded and Unrewarded Risk

Risk, as we have defined it, arises from the deviation of actual returns from expected returns. This deviation, however, can have any number of causes, and these causes can be classified into two categories: (1) those that are specific to

FIGURE 3-4   Monthly returns on Disney: 1992–1996

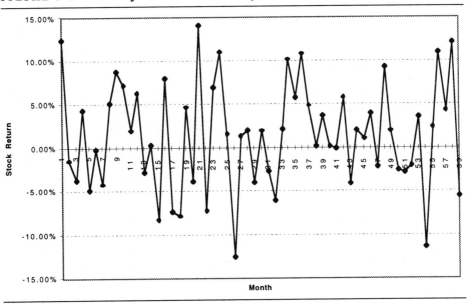

the investment being considered (firm-specific risks) and (2) those that apply across all investments (market risks).

The Components of Risk

The risk that a firm faces when it makes a new investment comes from a number of sources: the project itself, competition, shifts in the industry, international considerations, and macroeconomic factors. Some of this risk will be eliminated by the firm over the course of multiple investments, and some will be absorbed by investors holding diversified portfolios.

Project-specific risk occurs when an individual project has higher or lower cash flows than expected, either because the analyst misestimated the cash flows or because of factors specific to that project. When firms take a large number of similar projects, much of this risk should be diversified and reduced in the normal course of business. For instance, when Disney is producing a new movie, it exposes itself to estimation error; it may underestimate or overestimate the cost and time required to complete the movie, and may also err in its estimates of revenues from both theater receipts and the sale of related merchandise. Because Disney releases several movies each year, some or much of this risk should be diversifiable across the annual production list.

The second source of risk is *competitive risk:* how the earnings and cash flows on a project are affected (positively or negatively) by the actions of competitors. A good project analysis might factor the expected reactions of competitors into estimates of profit margins and growth, but the actual actions taken by competitors may differ from these expectations. This component of risk will usually affect more than one project and is therefore more difficult to diversify away in the firm's normal course of business. Disney, for instance, in its estimate of revenues from its Disney Store division, may err in its assessments of the strength and strategies of competitors such as Warner Brothers Stores and Toys "Я" Us. Disney cannot diversify away much of its competitive risk, but its stockholders can, if they have the capacity and willingness to hold stock in Disney's competitors.[3]

The third source of risk is *industry-specific risk*—those factors that primarily impact the earnings and cash flows of a specific industry. There are three subdivisions within this category:

1. *Technology risk,* which reflects the effects of technologies that change or evolve in ways different from those expected when a project was originally envisaged.
2. *Legal risk,* which reflects the effects of changing laws and regulations.
3. *Commodity risk,* which reflects the effects of price changes in commodities and services that are used or produced disproportionately by a specific industry.

Disney, in assessing the prospects of its broadcasting division (ABC), is likely to be exposed to all three risks: technology risk, because the lines between television entertainment and the Internet are increasingly blurred by companies like Microsoft; legal risk, because of changes in the laws governing broadcast television; and commodity risk, because of changes in the costs of producing new television programs. A firm cannot diversify away its industry-specific risk without diversifying across industries, either with new projects or through acquisitions. The firm's stockholders should be able to diversify away industry-specific risk by holding portfolios of stocks from different industries.

The fourth source of risk is *international risk*. A firm faces this type of risk when the currency in which its earnings are measured (and its stock is priced) differs from the currency of its cash flows, or when it takes projects outside its domestic market. Earnings and cash flows might be different than expected because of exchange rate movements or political conflict. Disney, for instance, was clearly exposed to international risk with its 33 percent stake in EuroDisney, the theme park it developed outside Paris. Some of this risk may be diversified away if the firm, in the normal course of business, takes on projects in different countries (and/or over multiple years) and the respective currencies do not all move in the same direction. Citibank and McDonald's operate in many countries and are much less exposed to international risk than was Wal-Mart in 1994, when its foreign operations were restricted primarily to Mexico. Companies can also reduce their exposure to the exchange rate component of international risk by choosing a financing mix that matches the cash flows projected for overseas ventures—for instance, by borrowing money in Deutsche marks to support projects in Germany. Investors whose portfolios are restricted to domestic investments because of transactions costs or other constraints will be exposed to currency risk and political risk, to the extent that they hold stock in a multinational company. An international investor, with investments in multiple countries and currencies, may be able to diversify away the international risk.

The final source of risk is *market risk*—macroeconomic factors that affect, to varying degrees, essentially all companies and all projects. For example, changes in interest rates affect the value of investments directly, through the discount rates, and indirectly, through the cash flows. Other factors that affect all investments include the term structure (the difference between short- and long-term rates), the risk preferences of investors (as investors become more risk-averse, risky investments lose value), inflation, and economic growth. The expected values of all these variables enter into project analysis, and changes in these variables will affect the value of investments. Firms cannot really diversify away this risk in the normal course of business, though they could conceivably do so by using interest rate or market derivatives. Investors also cannot diversify away this risk by creating portfolios of risky investments (such as stocks), because all risky investments bear some exposure to this risk.

Why Diversification Reduces or Eliminates Firm-Specific Risk

Diversification reduces or, at the extreme, eliminates firm-specific risk for two reasons:

1. Each investment, in a diversified portfolio, is only a small percentage of that portfolio. Thus, any action that increases or reduces the value of only one investment or a small group of investments will have a small impact on the overall portfolio.

2. The effects of firm-specific actions on the prices of individual assets in a portfolio can be either positive or negative for each asset during any period. In large portfolios, this risk will average out to be zero and thus not impact the overall value of the portfolio.

In contrast, the effects of marketwide trends are likely to be in the same direction for most or all of the investments in a portfolio, though some assets may be affected more than others. For instance, other things being equal, an increase in interest rates will lower the value of most assets in a portfolio. Being more diversified does not eliminate this risk, but holding assets in different industries may reduce the impact.

Why the Marginal Investor Is Assumed to be Diversified

The suggestion that diversification reduces an investor's exposure to risk is not often contested. But risk and return models in finance go further. They argue that the marginal investor, who sets prices for investments, is well diversified; thus, the only risk that will be priced is the risk as perceived by that investor. The justification offered is simple. The risk in an investment will always be perceived to be higher for an undiversified investor than for a diversified investor because the latter does not carry any firm-specific risk and the former does. If both investors have the same perceptions about an asset's future earnings and cash flows, the diversified investor will be willing to pay a higher price for that asset because of the perceived risk. Consequently, the asset, over time, will end up being held by diversified investors.

This argument is powerful for stocks and other assets that are traded in small units and are liquid; it is less so for large and illiquid investments. Real estate, in most countries, is still held by investors who are undiversified and have the bulk of their wealth tied up in these investments. The benefits of diversification are strong, however. Securities such as real estate investment trusts (REITs) and mortgage-backed bonds were created to allow investors to invest in real estate and stay diversified at the same time.

Measuring Market Risk

Most risk and return models developed in investments and finance agree on the first two steps of the measurement process: (1) risk comes from the distribution of actual returns around the expected return, and (2) risk should be measured from the perspective of a marginal investor who is well diversified. But the models part ways on how to measure the nondiversifiable or market risk. This section provides a sense of how each of the four basic models—the capital asset pricing model (CAPM), the arbitrage pricing model (APM), multifactor models, and regression models—approaches the issue of measuring market risk.

The Capital Asset Pricing Model (CAPM)

The capital asset pricing model (CAPM) is a simple risk and return model that has been in use longer than the others and is still the standard in most real-world analyses.

1. Assumptions   Diversification is attractive because it reduces the exposure of investors to firm-specific risk; however, most investors limit their diversification by holding only a few assets. Even large mutual funds are reluctant to hold more than a few hundred stocks; many funds hold as few as 10 to 20 stocks. There are two reasons for this reluctance. (1) The marginal benefits of diversification shrink as a portfolio gets more diversified. The twenty-first asset added will generally provide a much smaller reduction in firm-specific risk than the fifth asset added, and it may not cover the marginal costs of diversification, which include transactions and monitoring costs. (2) Many investors (and funds), believing that they can find undervalued assets, choose not to hold any assets that they believe are correctly valued or overvalued.

The CAPM assumes that there are no transactions costs, that all assets are traded, and that investments are infinitely divisible (i.e., investors can buy any fraction of a unit of the asset). It also assumes that there is no private information and that investors therefore cannot find under- or overvalued assets in the marketplace. By making these assumptions, it eliminates the factors that cause investors to stop diversifying. With these assumptions in place, the logical end limit of diversification is to hold every traded asset (stocks, bonds, and real assets included) in one's portfolio, in proportion to their market value.[4] A portfolio that contains every asset traded in the marketplace is called the *market portfolio*.

2. Implications for Investors   If every investor in the market holds the identical market portfolio, how do investors reflect their risk aversion in their investments? In the CAPM, investors adjust for their risk preferences in their allocation decision, where they decide how much to invest in a riskless asset and how much to place in a market portfolio, which contains all traded (risky) assets. Investors who are risk-averse might choose to put much, or even all, of their wealth in the riskless asset. Investors who want to take more risk will invest the bulk of their wealth, or even all of it, in the market portfolio. Those investors who invest all their wealth in the market portfolio and are still desirous of taking on more risk, would do so by borrowing at the riskless rate and investing in the same market portfolio as everyone else.

These results are predicated on two additional assumptions: (1) a riskless asset exists where expected returns are certain; and (2) investors can lend and borrow at one riskless rate to arrive at their optimal allocations. Some variations of the CAPM allow these assumptions to be relaxed and still arrive at conclusions that are consistent with the CAPM.

3. Measuring the Market Risk of an Individual Asset   The risk of any asset to an investor is the risk that the asset adds to the investor's overall portfolio. In the CAPM, where all investors hold the market portfolio, the risk of an individual asset to an investor will be the risk that this asset adds on to the market portfolio. Assets that move more with the market portfolio will tend to be riskier than assets that move less, because the movements that are unrelated to the market portfolio will be eliminated when an asset is added to the portfolio. Statistically, this added risk is measured by the *covariance* of the asset with the market portfolio.

The covariance is a nonstandardized measure of market risk; knowing that the covariance of Disney with the market portfolio is 55 percent does not provide a clue as to whether Disney is riskier or safer than the average asset. The risk measure is therefore standardized by dividing the covariance of each asset within the market portfolio by the variance of the market portfolio, to yield the beta of the asset:

$$\text{Beta of an Asset } i = \frac{\text{Covariance of Asset } i \text{ with the Market Portfolio}}{\text{Variance of the Market Portfolio}}.$$

Because the covariance of the market portfolio with itself is its variance, the beta of the market portfolio—and, by extension, the average asset in it, is one. Assets that are riskier than average (using this measure of risk) will have betas that exceed 1, and assets that are safer than average will have betas that are lower than 1. The riskless asset will have a beta of zero.

4. *Getting Expected Returns*   The fact that every investor holds some combination of a riskless asset and a market portfolio leads to the next conclusion: The expected return on an asset is linearly related to the beta of the asset. In particular, the expected return on an asset can be written as a function of the risk-free rate and the beta of that asset, as follows:

$$\text{Expected Return on Asset } i = \text{Risk-Free Rate} + \text{Beta of Asset } i \times (\text{Risk Premium on Market Portfolio})$$

$$= R_f + \beta_i[E(R_m) - R_f].$$

where: $E(R_i)$ = expected return on asset i.
   R_f = risk-free rate.
   $E(R_m)$ = expected return on market portfolio.
   β_i = beta on asset i.

5. *The CAPM in Practice*   For now, briefly, to use the capital asset pricing model, we need three inputs, each of which is estimated as follows:

1. A riskless asset is an asset for which the investor knows with certainty the expected return for the time horizon of the analysis. Consequently, the riskless rate used will vary, depending on whether the time period for the expected return is 1 year, 5 years, or 10 years.

2. The risk premium is the premium demanded by investors for investing in the market portfolio, which includes all risky assets in the market, instead of investing in a riskless asset. In practice, the premium is often estimated using historical data on the returns on risky assets (usually stocks) and the riskless return.

3. The beta, which we define as the covariance of the asset divided by the variance of market portfolio, can be obtained directly by regressing past returns on the asset against past returns on the market portfolio, or some proxy thereof (usually a stock index). The slope of the regression is the beta.

In summary, in the capital asset pricing model, all of the market risk is captured in one beta, measured relative to a market portfolio, which, at least in theory, should include all assets traded in the marketplace. The assets are held in proportion to their market value.

The Arbitrage Pricing Model (APM)

The restrictive assumptions in the capital asset pricing model, and its dependence on the market portfolio, have long been viewed with skepticism by both academics and practitioners. In the late 1970s, Ross (1976)[5] suggested an alternative model for measuring risk: the arbitrage pricing model (APM).

1. Assumptions   The arbitrage pricing model is built on the simple premise that investors take advantage of arbitrage opportunities. In other words, if two portfolios have the same exposure to risk but offer different expected returns, investors will buy the portfolio that has the higher expected returns, and will, in the process, adjust the expected returns to equilibrium.

Like the CAPM, the APM begins by breaking risk down into firm-specific and market risk components. The firm-specific component covers primarily information on individual assets. The market risk that affects investments originates in unanticipated changes in a number of economic variables, including gross national product, inflation, and interest rates. Incorporating this into the return model above, we have:

$$r = E(R) + m + \varepsilon,$$

where m is the marketwide component of unanticipated risk, and ε is the firm-specific component. Note that this distinction is very similar to the distinction between firm-specific risk and market risk in the CAPM.

2. The Sources of Marketwide Risk   Both the CAPM and the APM distinguish between firm-specific and marketwide risk, but they part ways when it comes to measuring the market risk. The CAPM assumes that the market risk is captured in the market portfolio. The APM sticks with economic fundamentals, allowing for multiple sources of marketwide risk, such as unanticipated changes in gross national product, interest rates, and inflation, and it measures the sensitivity of investments to these changes with factor betas. In general, the market component of unanticipated returns can be decomposed into economic factors:

$$R = R + m + \varepsilon$$
$$= R + (\beta_1 F_1 + \beta_2 F_2 + \dots + \beta_n F_n) + \varepsilon$$

where: β_j = the sensitivity of the investment to unanticipated changes in factor j.
F_j = unanticipated changes in factor j.

3. The Effects of Diversification   The benefits of diversification have been discussed extensively in our treatment of the CAPM. The primary point was that diversification of investments eliminates firm-specific risk. The APM makes the same point and then concludes that the return on a portfolio will not have a firm-specific component of unanticipated returns. The return on a portfolio can be written as the sum of two weighted averages—that of the anticipated returns in the portfolio, and that of the factor betas. We then have:

$$R_p = (w_1 R_1 + w_2 R_2 + K + w_n R_n) + (w_1 \beta_{1,1} + w_2 \beta_{1,2} + K + w_n \beta_{1,n})F_1$$
$$+ (w_1 \beta_{2,1} + w_2 \beta_{2,2} + K + w_n \beta_{2,n})F_2 \dots$$

where: w_j = portfolio weight on asset j.
R_j = expected return on asset j.
$\beta_{i,j}$ = beta on factor i for asset j.

4. Expected Returns and Betas   The fact that the beta of a portfolio is the weighted average of the betas of the assets in the portfolio, in conjunction with the absence of arbitrage, leads to the conclusion that expected returns should be linearly related to betas. To see why, assume that there is only one factor and that there are three portfolios: A, B, and C. Portfolio A has a beta of 2.0 and an expected return of 20 percent, portfolio B has a beta of 1.0 and an expected return of 12 percent, and portfolio C has a beta of 1.5 and an expected return of 14 percent. The investor can put half of the available wealth in portfolio A and half in portfolio B, and will end up with a portfolio that has a beta of 1.5 and an expected return of 16 percent. Consequently, no investor will choose to hold portfolio C until the prices of assets in that portfolio drop and the expected return increases to 16 percent. Using the same rationale, the expected returns on every portfolio should be a linear function of the beta, or there will be an opportunity for arbitrage. This argument can be extended to multiple factors, with the same results. Therefore, the expected return on an asset can be written as:

$$E(R) = R_f + \beta_1\left[E(R_1) - R_f\right] + \beta_2\left[E(R_2) - R_f\right]\mathrm{K} + \beta_n\left[E(R_n) - R_f\right]$$

where: R_f = expected return on a zero beta portfolio.
     $E(R_j)$ = expected return on a portfolio with a factor beta of 1 for factor j and 0 for all other factors.

The terms in the brackets can be considered to be risk premiums for each of the factors in the model.

Note that the CAPM can be regarded as a special case of the APM where there is only one economic factor driving marketwide returns and the market portfolio is the factor:

$$E(R) = R_f + \beta_m(E(R_m) - R_f).$$

5. *The APM in Practice*   The arbitrage pricing model requires estimates of each of the factor betas and factor risk premiums, in addition to the riskless rate. In practice, these are usually estimated using historical data on assets and a "factor analysis." Intuitively, a factor analysis examines the historical data looking for common patterns that affect broad groups of assets (rather than just one sector or a few assets). The factor analysis provides two output measures:

1. It specifies the number of common factors that affected the historical data.
2. It measures the beta of each investment relative to each of the common factors, and provides an estimate of the actual risk premium earned by each factor.

The factor analysis does not, however, identify the factors in economic terms.

In summary, in the arbitrage pricing model, the market risk is measured relative to multiple unspecified macroeconomic factors, and the sensitivity of the investment relative to each factor is measured by a beta. The number of factors, the factor betas, and the factor risk premiums can all be estimated using a factor analysis.

Multifactor Models for Risk and Return

The arbitrage pricing model's failure to identify specifically the factors in the model may be a strength from a statistical standpoint, but it is a clear weakness from an intuitive standpoint. The solution seems simple: Replace the unidentified statistical factors with specific economic factors, and the resultant model should be intuitive while still retaining much of the strength of the APM. That is precisely what multifactor models do.

Deriving a Multifactor Model Multifactor models generally are not based on an extensive economic rationale but are driven by data instead. Once the number of factors has been identified in the arbitrage pricing model, the behavior of the factors over time can be extracted from the data. These factor time series can then be compared to the time series of macroeconomic variables to see whether any of the variables are correlated, over time, with the identified factors.

Chen, Roll, and Ross (1986)[6] suggest that the following macroeconomic variables are highly correlated with the factors that come out of factor analysis: industrial production, changes in default premium, shifts in the term structure, unanticipated inflation, and changes in the real rate of return. These variables can then be correlated with returns to come up with a model of expected returns, and firm-specific betas can be calculated relative to each variable. We then have:

$$E(R) = R_f + \beta_{GNP}(E(R_{GNP}) - R_f) + \beta_i(E(R_i) - R_f)\text{K} + \beta_\delta(E(R_\delta) - R_f)$$

where: β_{GNP} = beta relative to changes in industrial production.
$E(R_{GNP})$ = expected return on a portfolio with a beta of 1 on the industrial production factor and 0 for all other factors.
β_i = beta relative to changes in inflation.
$E(R_i)$ = expected return on a portfolio with a beta of 1 on the inflation factor and 0 for all other factors.

The costs of going from the arbitrage pricing model to a macroeconomic multifactor model can be traced directly to the errors that can be made in identifying the factors. The economic factors in the model can change over time, as will the risk associated with each one. For instance, oil price changes were a significant economic factor driving expected returns in the 1970s but were less significant in other time periods. Using the wrong factor(s) or missing a significant factor in a multifactor model can lead to inferior estimates of expected returns.

In summary, multifactor models, like the APM, assume that market risk can be captured best by using multiple macroeconomic factors and betas relative to each. Unlike the APM, multifactor models do attempt to identify the macroeconomic factors that drive market risk.

Regression Models

All of the models described so far begin by thinking about market risk in broad intuitive terms and then developing economic models that might best explain the market risk. All of them, however, extract their parameters by looking at historical data. A final class of risk and return models starts with the returns and works backward to a risk and return model. These models try to explain differences in returns across long time periods by researching firm characteristics such as size and price multiples. The models are essentially regression models, and the firm characteristics that best explain differences in returns can be viewed as effective proxies for market risk.

Fama and French,[7] in a highly influential study of the CAPM in the early 1990s, noted that actual returns over long time periods have been highly correlated with price–book value ratios and size. They suggested that these measures, and similar ones developed from the data, should be used as proxies for risk, and that the regression coefficients should be used to estimate expected returns on investments. For instance, Fama and French reported the following regression for monthly returns on stocks on the New York Stock Exchange (NYSE), using data from 1963 to 1990:

$$R_t = 1.77\% - 0.11\ln(MV) + 0.35\ln(BV/MV)$$

where: MV = market value of equity.
BV/MV = book value of equity/market value of equity.

The values for market value of equity and book–price ratios for individual firms, when plugged into this regression, should yield expected monthly returns.

In summary, regression models measure market risk by using firm characteristics as proxies for market risk. The firm characteristics are identified by looking at differences in returns on investments over very long time periods, and correlating with identifiable characteristics of these investments.

Testing the CAPM

Does the CAPM work? Is beta a good proxy for risk, and is it correlated with expected returns? The answers to these questions have been debated widely in recent decades. The first tests of the model suggested that betas and returns were positively related, though other measures of risk (such as variance) continued to explain differences in actual returns. This discrepancy was attributed to limitations in the testing techniques. In 1977, Roll, in a seminal critique of the model's tests,[8] suggested that because the market portfolio could never be observed, the CAPM could never be tested, and, therefore, all tests of the CAPM were joint tests of the model and the market portfolio used in the tests. In other words, all that any test of the CAPM could show was that the model worked (or did not work), given the proxy used for the market portfolio. It could therefore be argued that, in any empirical test that claimed to reject the CAPM, the rejection could be of the proxy used for the market portfolio rather

FIGURE 3-5   Returns and betas: The ten worst months between 1926 and 1991

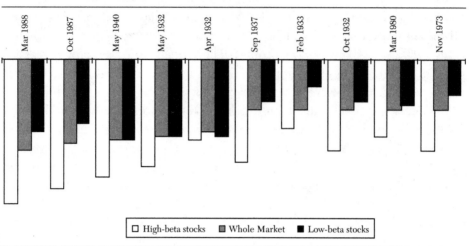

than of the model itself. Roll noted that there was no way to ever prove that the CAPM worked, and thus, no empirical basis for using the model.

In their indictment, Fama and French (1992)[9] examined the relationship between betas and returns between 1963 and 1990 and concluded that there is no relationship between the two. They also noted that two other variables—size and book-to-market value—explain differences in returns across firms much better than beta does, and may in fact be better proxies for risk. These results have been contested on two fronts:

- Amihud, Christensen, and Mendelson[10] used the same data, performed different statistical tests, and showed that betas did, in fact, explain returns during the time period.

- Chan and Lakonishok[11] looked at a much longer time series of returns, from 1926 to 1991, and found that the positive relationship between betas and returns broke down only in the period after 1982. They attributed this breakdown to indexing, which, they argued, has led the larger, lower-beta stocks in the S&P 500 to outperform smaller, higher-beta stocks. They also found that betas are a useful guide to risk in extreme market conditions. The riskiest firms (the 10 percent with the highest betas) performed far worse than the market as a whole, in the ten worst months for the market between 1926 and 1991 (see Figure 3-5).

A Comparative Analysis of Risk and Return Models

All the risk and return models described in this chapter have common characteristics. They all assume that only marketwide risk is rewarded, and they derive the expected return as a function of measures of this risk. The CAPM makes the most assumptions but arrives at the simplest model, with only one factor driving risk and requiring estimation. The APM makes fewer assumptions but arrives at a more complicated model, at least in terms of the parameters that require estimation. The CAPM can be considered a specialized case of the APM where there is only one underlying factor and it is completely measured by the market index. In general, the CAPM has the advantage of being simpler to estimate and to use, but it will underperform the richer APM when a company is sensitive to economic factors not well represented in the market index. For instance, oil companies, which derive most of their risk from oil price movements, tend to have low CAPM betas. Using the APM, where one of the factors may be capturing oil and other commodity price movements, will yield a better estimate of the risk and the higher expected return for these firms.[12]

The biggest intuitive block in using the APM is its failure to identify specifically the factors that drive expected returns. This omission may preserve the flexibility of the model and reduce statistical problems in testing, but it makes it difficult to understand what the APM beta coefficients for a firm mean, and how they will change as the firm changes (or restructures).

The initial tests of the APM and the multifactor models suggested that they might provide more explanation of the differences in past returns, but a distinction has to be drawn between the use of these models to explain differences in past returns and to predict expected returns for the future. The models competing against the CAPM clearly do a much better job of explaining past returns; they do not constrain themselves to one factor, as the CAPM does. The extension to multiple factors becomes more of a problem when we try to project expected returns into the future: the betas and premiums of each of these factors have to be estimated. Because the factor premiums and betas are themselves volatile, the estimation error may wipe out the benefits that could be gained by moving from the CAPM to more complex models. The regression models that were offered as alternatives are even more exposed to this problem; the variables (such as size) that work best as proxies for market risk in one period may not be the ones that work in the next period.

Ultimately, the survival of the CAPM as the default model for risk in real-world applications is testament both to its intuitive appeal and to the failure of more complex models to deliver significant improvement in expected returns. We would argue that a judicious use of the CAPM (without an overreliance on historical data), in conjunction with the accumulated evidence[13] presented by those who have developed the alternatives to the CAPM, is still the most effective way of dealing with risk in modern finance.

Models of Default Risk

When an investor lends to an individual or a firm, there is a possibility that the borrower may default on interest and principal payments on the amount borrowed. This possibility of default is called the *default risk*. Generally speaking, borrowers with higher default risk should pay higher interest rates than borrowers with lower default risk. This section examines the measurement of default risk and the relationship of default risk to interest rates on borrowing.

In contrast to the general risk and return models described above, which focus on market risk, models of default risk examine the consequences of firm-specific default risk for expected returns. The rationale for diversification can be used to explain why firm-specific risk will not be priced into expected returns, but the same rationale does not apply for securities that have limited upside potential and much greater downside potential from firm-specific events. For instance, corporate bonds benefit only marginally from firm-specific events that increase the value of a firm and make it safer, but they bear the risk of any firm-specific events that lower the value of the firm and increase the probability of default. Consequently, the expected return on a corporate bond is likely to reflect the firm-specific default risk of the firm issuing the bond.

A General Model of Default Risk

The default risk of a firm is a broad function of two variables: (1) the firm's capacity to generate cash flows from operations and (2) its financial obligations, including interest and principal payments.[14] All else being equal:

- Firms that generate high cash flows relative to their financial obligations have lower default risk than firms that generate low cash flows relative to their financial obligations. Thus, firms with significant assets (assets that generate high cash flows) will have lower default risk than will firms without significant assets.
- The more stability there is in a firm's cash flows, the lower is that firm's default risk. Firms that operate in predictable and stable businesses will have lower default risk than will otherwise similar firms that operate in cyclical and/or volatile businesses.

Most models of default risk (1) use financial ratios to measure the cash flow coverage (i.e., the magnitude of cash flows relative to obligations) and (2) control for industry effects, to capture the variability in cash flows.

Bond Ratings and Interest Rates

The most widely used measure of a firm's default risk is its bond rating, which is generally assigned by an independent rating agency, using a mix of private and public information.

The Rating Process   The process of rating a bond (shown in Figure 3-6) starts when the issuing company requests a rating from a rating agency. The rating agency then collects information from publicly available sources, such

FIGURE 3-6   Standard & Poor's rating process

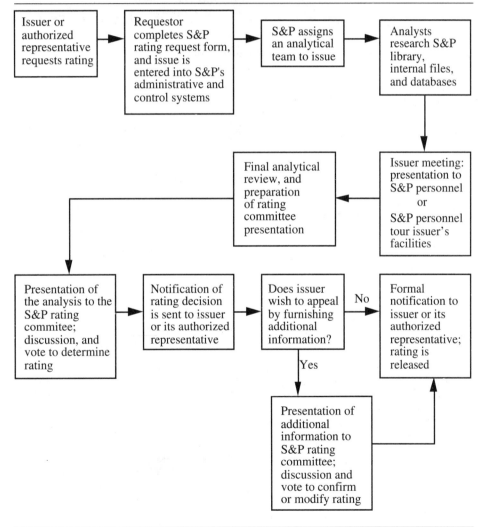

as financial statements, and from the company itself, and makes a decision on the rating. If it disagrees with the rating, the company is given an opportunity to present additional information.

Description of Bond Ratings   The two major agencies rating corporate bonds are Standard & Poor's (S&P) and Moody's. The ratings assigned by the two agencies are fairly similar, but there are some differences. Table 3-1 describes the bond ratings assigned by the two agencies. In financial markets, bonds with ratings of BBB or higher (Standard & Poor's) are considered "investment grade."

Determinants of Bond Ratings   The bond ratings assigned by rating agencies are primarily based on publicly available information, although private information conveyed by the firm to the rating agency does play a role. The rating that is assigned to a company's bonds will depend, in large part, on financial

TABLE 3-1   Index of bond ratings

Standard & Poor's		Moody's	
AAA	The highest debt rating assigned. The borrower's capacity to repay debt is extremely strong.	Aaa	Judged to be of the best quality, with a small degree of risk.
AA	Capacity to repay is strong and differs from the highest quality only by a small amount.	Aa	High quality, but rated lower than Aaa because margin of protection may not be as large or because of other elements of long-term risk.
A	Has strong capacity to repay; borrower is susceptible to adverse effects of changes in circumstances and economic conditions.	A	Bonds possess favorable investment attributes but may be susceptible to risk in the future.
BBB	Has adequate capacity to repay, but adverse economic conditions or circumstances are more likely to lead to risk.	Baa	Neither highly protected nor poorly secured; adequate payment capacity.
BB,B, CCC, CC	Regarded as predominantly speculative; BB is the least speculative and CC is the most.	Ba	Judged to have some speculative risk.
D	In default, or payments are in arrears.	B	Generally lacking characteristics of a desirable investment; probability of payment small.
		Caa	Poor standing and perhaps in default.
		Ca	Very speculative; often in default.

ratios that measure the capacity of the company to meet debt payments and to generate stable and predictable cash flows. Table 3-2 summarizes some of the key ratios that are used to measure default risk. There is a strong relationship between the bond rating a company receives and its performance on these financial ratios. Table 3-3 provides a summary of the median financial ratios, from 1990 to 1992, for different S&P ratings classes for manufacturing firms. Note that the Pretax Interest Coverage ratio and the EBITDA Interest coverage ratio are stated in terms of times interest earned, whereas the rest of the ratios are stated as percentages.

Not surprisingly, firms that (1) generate income and cash flows that are significantly higher than debt payments, (2) are profitable, and (3) have low debt ratios are more likely to be highly rated than are firms that do not have these characteristics. Some individual firms' ratings are not consistent with their financial ratios, however, because the rating agencies do bring subjective judgments into the final mix. Thus, a firm that performs poorly on financial ratios but is expected to improve its performance dramatically over the next period may receive a higher rating than is justified by its current financials. For most firms, however, the financial ratios should provide a reasonable basis for guessing at the bond rating.

TABLE 3-2   Financial ratios used to measure default risk

Ratio	Description
Pretax interest coverage	(Pretax income from continuing operations + Interest expense)/Gross interest
EBITDA interest coverage	EBITDA/Gross interest
Funds from operations/Total debt	(Net income from continuing operations + Depreciation)/Total debt
Free operating cash flow/Total debt	(Funds from operations – Capital expenditures – Change in working capital)/Total debt
Pretax return on permanent capital	(Pretax income from continuing operations + Interest expense)/ (Average of beginning of the year and end of the year of long- and short-term debt, minority interest, and shareholders' equity)
Operating income/ Sales (%)	= (Sales – COGS (before depreciation) – Selling expenses – Administrative expenses – R&D expenses)/Sales
Long-term debt/ Capital	= Long-term debt/(Long-term debt + Equity)
Total debt/ Capitalization	= Total debt/(Total debt + Equity)

TABLE 3-3   Financial ratios for bond ratings: 1990–1992

Ratio	AAA	AA	A	BBB	BB	B	CCC
Pretax interest coverage	17.65%	7.62%	4.14%	2.49%	1.50%	0.92%	0.68%
EBITDA interest coverage	21.03	10.52	6.17	4.24	2.60	1.87	1.16
Funds from operations/ Total debt (%)	120.1	65.3	37.0	26.3	15.5	9.8	5.5
Free operating cash flow/Total debt (%)	42.3	28.0	13.6	6.1	3.2	1.6	0.80
Pretax return on permanent capital (%)	31.9	20.6	15.6	10.9	10.9	6.9	4.6
Operating income/ Sales (%)	22.2	16.3	15.1	12.6	12.7	11.9	12.1
Long-term debt/ Capital	12.5	23.3	34.7	43.8	59.3	59.9	69.3
Total debt/ Capitalization	21.9	32.7	40.3	48.8	66.2	71.5	71.2

Bond Ratings and Interest Rates   The yield on a corporate bond should be a function of its default risk, which is measured by its rating. If the rating is a good measure of the default risk, higher-rated bonds should be priced to yield lower interest rates than would lower-rated bonds. This "default spread" will vary according to the maturity of the bond and can change from period to period, depending on economic conditions.

CONCLUSION

The notion that risk is a negative factor and needs to be rewarded is not contestable, although the precise model for estimating risk and reward is still a subject of debate. For equity investments, all the models of risk and return that are widely used measure risk in terms of nondiversifiable risk; the CAPM measures it with just one "market" factor, whereas the APM and multifactor models use several factors. For debt investments, where the holders have limited upside potential and significant downside risk, models of default risk are used to obtain estimates of appropriate returns.

4 ALTERNATIVE MEASURES OF RISK

Roger G. Clarke

One of the most common ways to describe investment risk is to relate it to the uncertainty or the volatility of potential returns from an investment over time. For example, an investment whose returns could range between 4 and 6 percent is less volatile than an investment whose returns could range between negative 20 and positive 40 percent. The source of the uncertainty and the degree of its impact depend on the type of investment. The most common sources of investment risk are financial exposure to changes in interest rates, and to equity markets, inflation, foreign exchange rates, credit quality, and commodity prices. Effective risk management requires identification of the risk, estimating its magnitude, deciding how much risk will be assumed and building structures to reduce unwanted risk. This chapter describes the most commonly used measures of risk.

Effective risk management requires a decision as to how much of the risk should be hedged and at what cost. Analytical tools are required if one wants to be most precise about measuring risk. As a result, we frequently resort to mathematical expressions to capture the central concepts. Understanding these concepts is critical if the investor wants to apply risk management techniques in practice. In fact, the rigor of the mathematics makes the subject easier to understand and apply, not more difficult. For readers who are less comfortable with the algebra, explanations follow each important mathematical expression.

COMMONLY USED MEASURES OF RISK

The primary building block for discussing risk is the concept of a probability distribution of prices or returns. To illustrate this concept, Figure 4-1 is a bar graph of the return possibilities for an investment. Suppose the investor purchases a security for $100. At the end of a year, the security could take on one of three values: $90, $100, or $120. The probability of each price occurring is given by the height of the bar in Figure 4-1. The *mean return* on the investment of $100 is calculated by multiplying the probability of each occurrence by the corresponding percentage return. Equation (1) shows the mathematical equivalent of the concept, indicating that the expected return is equal to the sum of the possible individual returns times the probability of each occurring:

$$E(R) = p_1 R_1 + p_2 R_2 + \cdots + p_n R_n$$
$$= \sum_{i=1}^{n} p_i R_i$$

(1)

where $E(R)$ equals the expected or mean return, and R_i represents the specific return outcome with probability p_i.[1] Table 4-1 shows that the mean return in the simple example illustrated in Figure 4-1 is equal to 4.0 percent.

Standard Deviation (Variance)

One measure of risk is the *variance* of the probability distribution. The variance is calculated by squaring the deviation of each occurrence from the mean and multiplying each value by its associated probability. The sum of

FIGURE 4-1   Probability of security price at year end

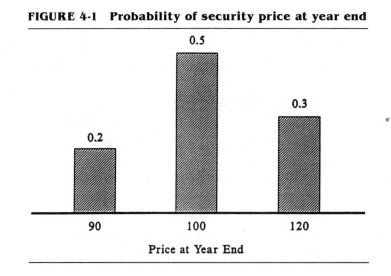

Price at Year End

TABLE 4-1   Expected return and risk for a simple investment

Price at Year End	Percentage Return on Original Investment	Probability	Probability-Weighted Return	Differential Return from the Mean	Probability-Weighted Differential Return Squared
90	−10.0	0.2	−2.0	−14.0	39.2
100	0.0	0.5	0.0	−4.0	8.0
120	20.0	0.3	6.0	16.0	76.8
Totals		1.0	4.0		124.0

Notes: Mean return = 4.0%, Variance = 124.0%, Standard deviation = $\sqrt{124.0}$ = 11.1%

these values is equal to the variance of the distribution, while the square root of the variance is referred to as the *standard deviation.* Equation (2) shows that the standard deviation is calculated by first summing the probability-weighted squared deviations of each outcome versus the mean and taking the square root of the sum:

$$\sigma = \sqrt{p_1[R_1 - E(R)]^2 + p_2[R_2 - E(R)]^2 + \cdots + p_n[R_n - E(R)]^2}$$

$$= \sqrt{\sum_{i-1}^{n} p_i[R_i - E(R)]^2}$$

(2)

Table 4-1 shows that the variance is equal to 124.0 (last column), while the standard deviation is equal to 11.1 percent. The variance or standard deviation is a common measure of risk and represents the variability of the returns around the mean. The higher the level of standard deviation, the more variability there is in the probability distribution.

A more complete probability distribution is shown in Figure 4-2 with its mean and standard deviation. If the distribution is normally distributed (producing the common bell-shaped curve), about two-thirds of the area will fall between plus and minus one standard deviation from the mean. The shaded area in Figure 4-2 represents the probability of returns falling within the delineated range of returns.

Other things being equal, most investors prefer less volatile returns to more volatile returns. Other things, however, are usually not equal, which is when the deficiencies of standard deviation as a risk measure begin to become apparent. The first thing to note about the calculation of standard deviation is that the deviations above and below the mean return are given weights equal to their respective probability of occurring, yet most investors are more averse to negative deviations of the same probability than they are

FIGURE 4-2   Normal probability distribution

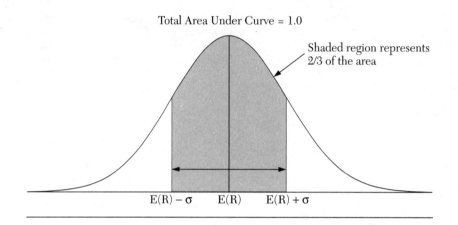

Total Area Under Curve = 1.0

Shaded region represents
2/3 of the area

E(R) − σ   E(R)   E(R) + σ

pleased with positive deviations of the same magnitude. Research in an area called prospect theory indicates that investors treat absolute gains and losses quite differently. [For example, see Kahneman and Tversky (1979).] Consequently, if two investments have the same absolute deviations about the mean (giving the same standard deviation), but one has more negative returns, investors often view the distribution with the lower mean as more risky.

Second, standard deviation as a measure of risk tends to work better when the probability distribution of returns is symmetric. If one distribution is skewed to one side or the other, while another is symmetric around the mean, both might have the same standard deviation but be perceived as having quite different risk. This phenomenon is illustrated in Figure 4-3. Both distributions have identical means and variances. The variances are identical, because the two distributions are mirror images of each other rotated around the mean. One of the important differences between the two is that the distribution skewed to the left (B) is characterized by less likely but larger losses and more likely but smaller gains than the distribution skewed to the right (A). Our intuitive notion of risk is often related to the possibility of "bad surprises." The "bad surprises" in A are more likely but smaller and limited in magnitude while the "bad surprises" in B are less likely but potentially much larger in magnitude. A risk-averse investor would generally prefer A to B on these grounds, although they have the same standard deviation.

The conceptual underpinning for the use of standard deviation (or variance) as a measure of risk is related to the theory of utility functions. Expected utility is a concept developed by Daniel Bernoulli, a famous Swiss mathematician in the 1700s, to explain the "St. Petersburg Paradox." Bernoulli

**FIGURE 4-3   Skewed probability distributions:
Equal means and variances but
different downside risk**

(A) Skewed to the right:

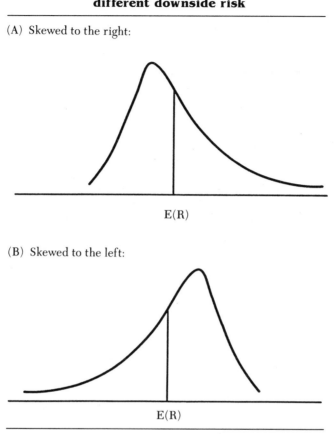

E(R)

(B) Skewed to the left:

E(R)

noted that a particular coin toss game led to an infinite expected payoff, but participants were willing to pay only a modest fee to play. He resolved the paradox by noting that participants do not assign the same value to each dollar of payoff. Larger payoffs resulting in more wealth are appreciated less and less, so that at the margin players exhibit decreasing marginal utility as the payoff increases. The particular function that assigns a value to each level of payoff is referred to as the investor's *utility function*. Von Neumann and Morgenstern applied this approach to investment theory in 1944 in a volume that formed the basis for Markowitz's article in 1952 on how to form an efficient portfolio of securities using expected return and variance.

Consider an unspecified function, $U(R)$, which represents the utility of investment returns to a particular investor. Mathematicians have shown that the value of a particular function when its random input is close to its mean can be approximated by terms related to the expected value of the random input (called a Taylor series expansion). As a result, the expected utility of investment returns can be written as the desirability of the expected random return plus the rate of change in the utility of returns times the variance of returns plus some smaller size terms as shown in Equation (3).

$$E[U(R)] = U[E(R)] + U''[E(R)]\sigma^2 / 2 + \text{Higher-Order Terms} \qquad (3)$$

The term $U''[E(R)]$ represents the rate of change in the utility of investment returns when returns are about average. In mathematical terms, $U''[E(R)]$ represents the second derivative of $U(R)$ with respect to R.

If the returns are normally distributed, the higher-order terms are identically zero and the expected utility is

$$E[U(R)] = U[E(R)] + U''[E(R)]\sigma^2 / 2 \qquad (4)$$

Equation (4) indicates that the expected utility of an investment's returns is equal to the utility of the expected return plus a term related to the variance of returns.[2] It suggests that the investor would be concerned with only the mean and the variance of the investment return. It is this analysis that in part laid the foundation for the use of variance as a measure of risk in analyzing investment returns.

Equation (4) also serves to point out the weaknesses in using variance as a complete measure of risk. Students of mathematics know that a Taylor series expansion is only approximately true in the neighborhood of the expansion point (in our case, the mean return), and it is not in the neighborhood of the mean where investors' questions about risk usually lie. Investors are often concerned about downside returns, which may lie distant from the mean. Thus, investors are usually concerned about returns in a region where the expansion in Equation (4) is known to be less accurate. Using variance as the only measure of risk under these circumstances can lead to difficulties.

Furthermore, when returns are not normally distributed (because of the use of options or nonlinear trading strategies, for example), the higher-order terms in Equation (4) are nonzero, and overlooking this can distort the assessment of risk. Bookstaber and Clarke (1985) present examples where "if one used standard deviation or variance as a proxy for risk, it would appear that covered call writing is preferable [for reducing risk] to buying puts," and where "buying puts [for reducing risk] is inferior to the stock-only portfolio." Yet the purchase of puts eliminates most of the undesirable downside risk, while the sale of call options eliminates the *desirable* upside potential. Bookstaber and Clarke conclude that "variance is not a suitable proxy for risk in these cases because options strategies reduce variance asymmetrically." The asymmetric shape of the probability distribution distorts the conclusions that come from using variance as the only measure of risk.

In summary, variance or standard deviation is a commonly used measure of risk, but it can lead to misleading results under some circumstances:

1. The probability distribution of returns is not symmetric. This could be inherent in the asset itself or could be induced by the use of options or nonlinear trading rules in the portfolio.

2. A significant portion of the distribution lies in a range yielding negative returns. Investors often prefer to value gains differently from losses. This asymmetry is not reflected in the equal weighting treatment implicit in calculating standard deviation.

Tracking Error

A modification of variance or standard deviation as a measure of risk is the calculation of tracking error relative to an underlying benchmark. *Tracking error* is defined as the standard deviation of the difference in return between the investment and a specified benchmark or target position as shown in Equation (5). The differential return is defined as

$$\Delta R = R - B \tag{5}$$

where B represents the benchmark or target return. The tracking error is sometimes used as a measure of risk when the investor is interested in seeing how closely a position tracks a particular desired result. In actuality, the variance of the total return can be thought of as a special case of the *tracking error* that results when the benchmark is equal to the expected return of the investment. In the example in Table 4-1, the tracking error relative to the mean return is 11.1 percent, while it rises to 11.8 percent if zero is used as the target return.

In the more general case, the tracking error is calculated relative to a risky benchmark or index and represents how closely the investment tracks the desired result. Tracking error typically suffers from the same drawbacks as the normal variance, however. The tracking error calculation will treat deviations above the benchmark no differently from deviations below the benchmark return. If the consequences of deviations on the downside are more serious than the benefits of deviations on the upside, tracking error will not give a complete measure of risk.

Individual Security Risk Relative to a Market Index

Related to the notion of tracking error is the concept of expressing risk relative to a broad market index. We will illustrate this concept for typical equity and fixed income securities. It is common to express the risk of a stock relative to the broad market. This relationship is often described by the single index model that relates the return on a stock to the return on a market index:

$$R_i = \beta_i R_m + e_i \tag{6}$$

where: R_i = the return on stock i
β_i = the sensitivity of stock i to the market index (beta)
R_m = the return on the market index
e_i = the stock's residual return unaccounted for by the return on the market

It is typically assumed that the market return is uncorrelated with the stock's residual return e_i so that the variance of the return on the stock is related to the variance of the market and the firm's residual risk:

$$\sigma_R^2 = \beta_i^2 \sigma_m^2 + \sigma_e^2 \tag{7}$$

The first term in Equation (7) is often called the *systematic risk* of the stock while the second term is called the *unsystematic* or *residual risk*. Beta captures the component of the firm's risk which is correlated with broad market movements. This relative risk measure along with the residual risk are often estimated by regressing the stock's return on the market index return. As such, the estimated beta of the security is equal to the covariance of the security with the market index divided by the variance of the market:

$$\beta_i = \frac{\text{covariance}\left(R_i, R_m\right)}{\sigma_m^2} = \frac{P_{Rm}\sigma_R}{\sigma_m} \tag{8}$$

where P_{Rm} represents the correlation coefficient between the return on the stock and the market index. Stocks with a beta close to one have systematic risk approximately equal to the market while stocks with a beta greater than or less than one have systematic risk greater than or less than the market.

The tracking error of a security relative to the market index can be found by noting that the differential return between the stock and the market index is:

$$R_i - R_m = \left(\beta_i - 1\right)R_m + e_i \tag{9}$$

Taking the variance of both sides of Equation (9) allows us to express the tracking error as:

$$\text{Tracking Error for Stock } i = \left[\left(\beta_i - 1\right)^2 \sigma_m^2 + \sigma_e^2\right]^{1/2} \tag{10}$$

The market index itself would have a beta of one with no residual risk resulting in zero tracking error. Individual securities would have tracking error greater than the firm's residual risk for any beta different than one.

To illustrate the relationship between the risk of an individual stock and the broad market, consider a stock with beta equal to 1.1 and residual volatility of 25.0 percent. If the volatility of the market is 15.0 percent, the volatility of the stock using Equation (7) would be:

$$\sigma_R^2 = \beta_i^2 \sigma_m^2 + \sigma_e^2$$
$$= (1.1)^2 (0.15)^2 + (0.25)^2$$
$$= 0.0897$$
$$\sigma_R = 29.95 \text{ percent}$$

The tracking error of the stock relative to the market using Equation (10) is:

$$\text{Tracking Error} = \left[(1.1 - 1.0)^2 (0.15)^2 + (0.25)^2 \right]^{1/2}$$
$$= 25.04 \text{ percent}$$

Because the beta of the stock is close to that of the market, most of the tracking error of the stock relative to the market comes from the stock's residual volatility. As a result the tracking error is close to the residual volatility of the security itself.

With respect to the risk of fixed income securities, it is common to refer to the security's modified duration. Modified duration is related to the maturity of the security and is generally expressed in years. The duration of a typical fixed income security is less than or equal to the maturity of the security itself. As a first-order approximation the short-term return on a fixed income security due to a change in its yield to maturity is related to the modified duration of the security by the expression:

$$\frac{\Delta P_i}{P_i} = -D_i^{\circ} \Delta y_i \qquad (11)$$

where P_i represents the price of the security, D_i° represents the modified duration and y_i represents the yield to maturity for security i.

If the change in the yield to maturity of a particular security i is related to the change in a key market interest rate in a linear fashion, we can write the change in yield to maturity as:

$$\Delta y_i = \beta_i \Delta r + e_i \qquad (12)$$

where: β_i = the sensitivity of the security's yield to the market interest rate (yield beta)

r = the market interest rate

e_i = the residual change in yield unaccounted for by the market rate.

Substituting the yield beta relationship into Equation (11) gives the return on the security equal to:

$$\frac{\Delta P_i}{P_i} = -D_i^* \left(\beta_i \, \Delta r + e_i \right)$$

(13)

Taking the variance of both sides of Equation (13) relates the variance of return on the security to its duration, yield beta, market interest rate volatility and residual yield volatility as:

$$\sigma_R^2 = D_i^{*2} \left(\beta_i^2 \sigma_{\Delta r}^2 + \sigma_e^2 \right)$$

(14)

The security's yield beta and residual yield volatility are often estimated by regressing the security's change in yield against the change in market interest rates giving a yield beta equal to:

$$\beta_i = \frac{\text{covariance} \left(\Delta y_i, \Delta r \right)}{\sigma_{\Delta r}^2} = \frac{P_{\Delta y \Delta r} \sigma_{\Delta y}}{\sigma_{\Delta r}}$$

(15)

where $P_{\Delta y \Delta r}$ represents the correlation coefficient between the change in the security's yield to maturity and the change in market interest rates.

If the modified duration of the market index is represented as D_i^* the difference in return between the security and the market index can be approximated as:

$$\frac{\Delta P_i}{P_i} - \frac{\Delta P_I}{P_I} = -\left(D_i^* \, \Delta y_i - D_I^* \, \Delta r \right)$$

$$= -\left[D_i^* e_i + \left(D_i^* \beta_i - D_I^* \right) \Delta r \right]$$

(16)

Taking the variance of both sides of Equation (16) allows us to express the tracking error of a fixed income security as:

$$\begin{array}{c} \text{Tracking Error for Fixed} \\ \text{Income Security } i \end{array} = \left[D_i^{*2} \sigma_e^2 + \left(D_i^* \beta_i - D_I \right)^2 \sigma_{\Delta r}^2 \right]^{1/2}$$

(17)

A security with a duration similar to the market index and a yield beta equal to one will have tracking error equal to the duration adjusted residual yield volatility. Securities with yield betas and market durations different than the market index will have tracking error greater than the duration adjusted residual yield volatility.

To illustrate the relationship between the risk of an individual bond and the broad market, consider a bond with a modified duration of 6.0 years, a yield beta of 0.9 and residual yield volatility of 1.1 percent. If the yield volatility of the market is 2.0 percent, and the market has a duration of 6.2 years, the volatility of the market using Equation (14) would be:

$$\sigma_I^2 = D_i^{\circ 2}\sigma_{\Delta r}^2$$
$$= (6.2)^2(0.02)^2$$
$$= 0.0154$$
$$\sigma_R = 12.4 \text{ percent}$$

This compares to the volatility of the individual bond of:

$$\sigma_R^2 = D_i^{\circ 2}\left(\beta_i^2\sigma_{\Delta r}^2 + \sigma_e^2\right)$$
$$= (6.0)^2\left((0.9)^2(0.02)^2 + (0.011)^2\right)$$
$$= 0.016$$
$$\sigma_R = 12.66 \text{ percent}$$

The tracking error for the bond relative to the market index with a modified duration of 6.2 years using Equation (17) is:

$$\text{Tracking Error} = \left[(6.0)^2(0.011)^2 + \left((6.0)(0.9) - 6.2\right)^2(0.02)^2\right]^{1/2}$$
$$= 6.79 \text{ percent}$$

The bond has a relatively high tracking error with respect to the market because it has a low yield beta. As market rates fluctuate, the yield on the bond will change somewhat less and introduce tracking error relative to the market as a whole.

Probability of Shortfall

Another measure of risk proposed by Balzer (1994) among others is the probability of shortfall. The *probability of shortfall* measures the chance that returns from the investment may fall below some reference point. The reference point is often set at zero, but it could be set at any other meaningful level to reflect the minimum acceptable return. This measure of risk is captured in Equation (18):

$$\text{Shortfall Probability} = \text{Probability } (R < B) \tag{18}$$

where R = return on the investment and B = benchmark or reference return.

In the case of the simple example in Table 4-1, the probability of shortfall below a return of 0 percent would be 20 percent. Figure 4-4 illustrates the probability of shortfall using a more general probability distribution. The

FIGURE 4-4   Shortfall probability

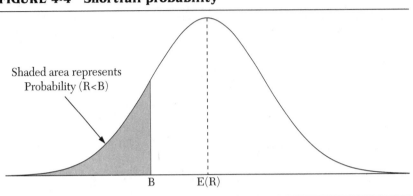

shaded area to the left of the benchmark return represents the probability of shortfall. The benchmark return could also represent a risky asset or index return. In this case the probability distribution would represent the distribution of tracking error relative to the index instead of the distribution of total return.

The risk measure in Equation (18) gives the probability that an undesirable event might occur, but gives no hint as to how severe it might be. For example, an investor might have two possible investment choices. In one case, the investor has a 10 percent probability of losing 20 percent, while in the other case, the investor has a 10 percent chance of losing 100 percent. The probability of shortfall ranks each investment as equivalent from a risk perspective, but most investors would clearly not be indifferent between the two. The second investment presents a much more serious loss if it does occur, even though the probability of losing is the same. Hence, even though the probability of shortfall may be of considerable interest, it is insufficient as a measure of risk.

Expected Shortfall

An alternative to the probability of shortfall is the *expected shortfall*. This measure incorporates not only the probability of shortfall but also the magnitude of the potential shortfall if it does occur. Equation (19) represents this notion, measuring the expected shortfall as the difference between the actual return and the benchmark over the range of returns when there is a shortfall:

$$\text{Expected Shortfall} = E[R - B], \text{ over the range where } R - B < 0 \qquad (19)$$

In the simple example in Table 4-1, the expected shortfall below a zero percent return is −2 percent. The expected shortfall represents the magnitude of the shortfall times the probability of it occurring. This measure is influenced by the entire downside portion of the probability distribution and is a more complete measure of downside risk than just the probability of shortfall itself.

A major problem with the expected shortfall measure is that it treats a large probability of a small shortfall as equivalent to a small probability of a large shortfall. We argued earlier, however, that investors tend to view losses differently from gains. The expected shortfall measure has drawbacks if investors view the consequences of large losses per unit differently from small losses. This is often the case. Consider that most people insure their houses but do not insure many minor items that may have a higher probability of loss than the house.

Lower Partial Moments and Semivariance

Another class of risk measures is termed *lower partial moments* by Harlow (1991). The term *partial* is used to reflect the fact that the measures relate to only one side of the return distribution relative to a target level. *Lower* indicates that the side of interest is the downside, where most investors are the most sensitive to volatility. The lower partial moments defined by Harlow can also be expanded to incorporate a risky benchmark as the target return in place of a fixed target return. This more general formulation allows these risk measures to incorporate the tracking error concept as well as the standard interpretation below a fixed return. A set of *"relative"* lower partial moments can be defined as the expected value of the differential return raised to the power of n:

$$RLPM_n = E[(R - B)^n], \text{ over the range where } R < B$$
$$= 0, \text{ over the range where } R \geq B \tag{20}$$

where n represents the order or ranking of the relative lower partial moment.

This concept captures several of the measures referred to earlier. If $n = 0$, the relative lower partial moment is equivalent to the probability of shortfall in Equation (18). If $n = 1$, the relative lower partial moment is equal to the expected shortfall in Equation (19). Finally, if $n = 2$, the lower partial is equal to the relative lower partial variance. A special case of the lower partial variance when the benchmark is equal to the expected return of the distribution is termed the *semivariance* by Markowitz. The term *relative semivariance* (*relative semideviation* is the square root of the relative variance) is sometimes used in place of the term lower partial moment variance when the target return is not the mean of the distribution. In the example in Table 4-1, the *semideviation* is equal to 6.9 percent (calculated relative to the mean return), while the semideviation calculated relative to a zero percent return is 4.5 percent.

Relative semivariance avoids many of the shortcomings that plague other measures of risk. It is an asymmetric measure that focuses on the downside of the probability distribution and avoids penalizing outperformance. It is a relatively complete measure in that it uses all values of the shortfall with their associated probabilities. It is also nonlinear, in the sense that it penalizes larger values more than smaller values because of the squaring of the tracking errors in the calculation. This is more consistent with observed investor behavior, because most investors perceive infrequent but large losses as more risky than more frequent but small losses.

Nevertheless, there are some disadvantages in using relative semivariance as a measure of risk. Most are not so much conceptual as operational in nature. The first is a general lack of understanding of relative semivariance as a measure of risk. Variance and standard deviation are more well-known and more integrated into the theoretical structure of investment decision-making. Consequently, using semivariance as a measure of risk generally requires some additional education for the user. Second, mathematical optimizers used by most practitioners to make tradeoffs between risk and return are generally not set up to construct portfolios of securities using semivariance as a measure of risk. This makes it more difficult to use relative semivariance as a practical tool without some changes in software. Third, there is no clear way to choose the target or benchmark return that is "best" to use in calculating the relative semivariance. A different benchmark will produce a different set of trade-offs between risk and return. Risk can be measured relative to any benchmark, but there are few guidelines in deciding which benchmark to use. Finally, the analytics for mixing individual securities in a portfolio are more difficult using relative semivariance than they are for using variance as a measure of risk. That is, the interactions of securities are not easily decomposed into the individual securities risk measures as in the case of the calculation of variance. As a result, the portfolio has to be treated as a whole rather than building up the risk measures from its individual parts.

PORTFOLIO MATHEMATICS

Investors are often interested in the characteristics of a portfolio of securities. Here we describe how the expected return and variance of a portfolio can be built up from the individual expected returns and variances of the securities in the portfolio. The expected return on a portfolio of securities is just the weighted average of the expected returns on the individual securities, where the weights are equal to the proportion each security represents of the portfolio value. For example, the expected return of a portfolio is:

$$E(R) = w_1 E(R_1) + w_2 E(R_2) + \cdots + w_n E(R_n) \qquad (21)$$
$$= \sum_{i-1}^{n} w_i E(R_i)$$

where w_i represents the weight of security i in the portfolio, and $E(R_i)$ represents the expected return to security i.

The variance of the portfolio is also a function of the variances of the individual securities in the portfolio. The portfolio variance is equal to:

$$\sigma_R^2 = \sum_{i=1}^{n} w_i^2 \sigma_i^2 + \sum_{i=1}^{n}\sum_{j=1}^{n} w_i w_j C_{ij} \qquad (22)$$

where σ_i^2 represents the variance of security i, and C_{ij} represents the covariance between security i and security j. The *covariance* is a measure of how much two securities move together (covary) in their return patterns. Two securities that move in the same direction on average (positive correlation) will have a positive covariance, while two securities that move in opposite directions on average (negative correlation) will have a negative covariance. The covariance between two securities can be written as the product of their respective standard deviations times the *correlation coefficient* between the two (ρ_{ij}):

$$C_{ij} = \rho_{ij} \sigma_i \sigma_j \qquad (23)$$

Two securities that are perfectly positively correlated will have a correlation coefficient of 1.0, while two securities that are perfectly negatively correlated will have a correlation coefficient of -1.0. Lack of correlation between the two would give a correlation coefficient of zero.

For a simple two-asset portfolio, Equations (21) and (22) representing the expected return and variance can be written as:

$$E(R) = w_1 E(R_1) + w_2 E(R_2) \qquad (24)$$

$$\sigma_R^2 = w_1^2 \sigma_1^2 + w_2^2 \sigma_2^2 + 2 w_1 w_2 C_{12} \qquad (25)$$

Notice that the expected return on the portfolio in Equation (24) is just a weighted average of the individual expected returns. The variance of the portfolio in Equation (25), however, contains a cross-product term that can either increase or decrease the portfolio variance depending on how the securities move together (correlation).

It is instructive to see how the correlation between two securities has an impact on the standard deviation of the portfolio return. Consider the trade-off between expected return and risk in Figure 4-5 using two different securities with different expected returns and different standard deviations. Figure 4-5 shows the trade-off between expected portfolio return and risk that is possible by varying the weights of the two securities in the portfolio.

The solid curved line in Figure 4-5 represents the possible trade-off between risk and expected return assuming a correlation between the two

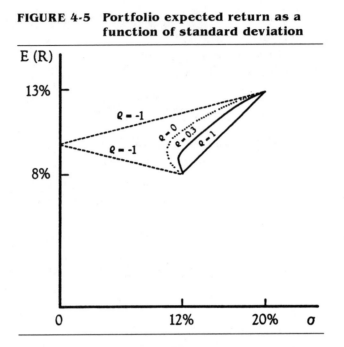

FIGURE 4-5   Portfolio expected return as a function of standard deviation

securities of 0.3. The trade-off curve shows the combination of expected return and standard deviation of all the portfolios that can be constructed from the two available assets as their relative weights change. Second, the line farthest to the right shows the trade-off when the securities are perfectly positively correlated ($\rho_{12} = 1.0$). Diversification results in more risk reduction when the securities are less than perfectly correlated, because the trade-off moves to the northwest, giving lower risk for the same expected return. Finally, when the two securities are perfectly negatively correlated ($\rho_{12} = -1.0$), the trade-off is linear again. This affords a perfect hedging opportunity and maximizes the effects of diversification between the two securities for risk reduction by reducing the risk to zero. The negative correlation between the two securities allows the complete hedging of the price impact of one security with the other.

To summarize, the expected return for a portfolio is a linear combination of the expected returns from the individual securities, but this is not true for the standard deviation of the portfolio. There are natural benefits from diversification in reducing risk when the correlation is less than perfectly positive. The less positive the correlation is, the more reduction in risk that can be achieved. In the extreme case of perfect negative correlation, it is possible to hedge all of the risk away and achieve a zero-risk portfolio, because the gains from one security will perfectly offset the losses from another.

It is also possible to show the relationship between the characteristics of the individual securities and the differential return of the portfolio. In general, the expected relative return of a portfolio compared to its benchmark can be written as a linear combination of the expected returns for each security and the deviation of the portfolio from the respective benchmark weights:

$$E(\Delta R) = \Delta w_1 E(R_1) + \Delta w_2 E(R_2) + \cdots + \Delta w_n E(R_n) \qquad (26)$$

$$= \sum_{i=1}^{n} \Delta w_i E(R_i)$$

where Δw_i is equal to the difference between the portfolio weight in asset i and the benchmark weight.

The tracking error is also a function of the variances and covariances of the individual securities and their respective deviations from benchmark weights. Equation (27) shows that the tracking error is equal to the weighted individual asset variances plus cross-product terms that capture the covariances between assets:

$$\sigma_{\Delta R}^2 = \sum_{i=1}^{n} \Delta w_i^2 \sigma_i^2 + \sum_{i=1}^{n} \sum_{j=1}^{n} \Delta w_i \Delta w_j C_{ij} \qquad (27)$$

In the event that the benchmark return is a constant target return, the benchmark weights in each asset are zero ($\Delta w_i = w_i$) so that the tracking error would be equal to the standard deviation of the underlying portfolio. The expected relative return would be equal to the expected portfolio return minus the constant target return.

Unfortunately, the other measures of risk that involve just the downside of the probability distribution cannot be built up so easily from the characteristics of the individual securities. The probability of shortfall, the expected shortfall, and the relative semideviation all require a knowledge of the joint probability distribution of all of the securities together. These typically become empirical questions, and are not as analytically tractable. This makes optimization procedures for constructing the lowest-risk combinations of assets in a portfolio more difficult, and the trade-off between risk and return is not conveniently handled by most conventional optimizers without a set of empirical relationships to estimate the joint probability distribution.

One of the attractions of using variance as a measure of risk is that it simplifies the portfolio mathematics considerably. Portfolio risk is made up of the risk components of the individual securities plus the correlations between each pair as shown in Equations (22) and (27). We noted earlier that if probability distributions of returns are normally distributed, the use of variance has a conceptual foundation. Normal distributions also have the nice feature that the sum of security returns in a portfolio preserves the normal distribution for the portfolio of securities. Many other return distributions are not so easy to work with analytically. Downside risk measures capture more specific measures of risk, but are not as convenient to estimate or to derive analytical solutions for.

As a result modern portfolio theory typically uses variance as the most convenient measure of risk.

CONCLUSION

There is no one accepted way of thinking about risk, even among sophisticated investors. The statistical approach to thinking about risk begins with probability distributions of prices and returns on an asset or portfolio, and measures the *standard deviation or variance* around the expected return. An alternative statistical approach, used to measured portfolio risk, is to measure the difference between actual returns on a portfolio and the returns on a pre-specified benchmark—this is called the *tracking error*. Both these approaches weigh returns which are higher than expected the same as they weigh returns which are lower than expected. For most investors, however, it is downside risk which is of concern. The downside risk can be measured purely in terms of the *probability that the actual return will be lower* than the benchmark return, or can be weighted by the *magnitude of the shortfall*. In fact, these approaches can be extended to looking at only the variance in returns which are lower than the mean, which is called the *semi-variance.*

The advantage of focusing on standard deviation or variance (in total returns or in deviations from a benchmark) as opposed to some of the "downside only" alternatives specified above is that the variance of a portfolio of assets can be estimated from the variances of the individual assets in that portfolio and the covariance between these assets. This allows us then to consider optimization strategies, where the weights of the individual assets are varied and portfolio variance and returns are computed.

REFERENCES

Balzer, L. "Measuring Investment Risk: A Review." *Journal of Investing* (Fall 1994), pp. 47–58.

Bookstaber, R., and R. Clarke. "Problems in Evaluating the Performance of Portfolios with Options." *Financial Analysts Journal* (January/February 1985), pp. 48–62.

Harlow, V. "Asset Allocation in a Downside-Risk Framework." *Financial Analysts Journal* (September/October 1991), pp. 28–40.

Kahneman, D., and A. Tversky. "Prospect Theory: An Analysis of Decision Making Under Risk." *Econometrica*, 1979, 47, pp. 263–291.

Markowitz, H. "Portfolio Selection." *Journal of Finance* (March 1952), pp. 77–91.

5 TAX CONSIDERATIONS IN INVESTING
Robert H. Jeffrey

For many years, the primary investment tax concern for informed investors has been capital gains, whose effective rate since 1986 has been in the vicinity of 34 percent depending on the taxpayer residence. At the time of this writing, the Congress is debating the possibility of a much lower rate on capital gains, conceivably as low as 14 percent at the federal level, which would produce an effective combined rate of perhaps 20 percent. Should capital gains rates be reduced to this extent, either directly, by permitting costs to be indexed for inflation, or by some other means, many of the examples in this chapter would be dated, and several of the author's conclusions would be overstated.

The reader, however, is advised to bear two points in mind: one, that "what goes down can also go up," especially in the case of tax rates; and, two, that a 20 percent effective capital gains tax is still a very material consideration. The problems and opportunities suggested in this chapter to control investment-related taxes and thereby increase wealth may turn out to be temporarily overstated, but the lessons remain pertinent.

In the second edition of his excellent book *Investment Policy: How to Win the Loser's Game*, Charles Ellis adds a chapter for "The Individual Investor" with some advice on taxes:

1. Don't do anything in investing for "tax reasons."
2. Tax shelters are poor investments.
3. Tax loss selling is primarily a way for brokers to increase commissions.

99

Two of these three comments, the first and the third, are substantially wrong. I make this blunt observation with complete appreciation that Ellis is one of the keenest observers of the investment management process and that his book, with this exception, provides an exceptionally good foundation for a sound investment philosophy. Tax shelters are often poor investments, because the more obvious tax advantages usually dominate the less obvious investment considerations (not to mention that the promotors typically take too much of the pie). But to suggest that one "should not do anything in investing for tax reasons," including collecting rebates of taxes already paid, which is what tax loss selling is mostly about, will be costly advice to any investor who heeds it.

I begin with this reference to Ellis to draw attention to two important but little-understood realities confronting investors and students of investing. The first is that *taxes are simply another item of expense,* which, like salaries and fees and commissions, should be evaluated and managed to insure that they are always adding value. As Ellis (1983) says in an earlier writing, "The investing game includes, after all, *all* transaction costs." For taxable investors, taxes are often the most important of these transaction costs, and this is the primary thrust of this chapter.

The proverbial assertion linking the inevitability of death and taxes is a gross misstatement as applied to investment-related taxes, and in particular those on capital gains. Capital gains taxes are typically not inevitable in any given period, and they are controllable to a far greater extent than is generally recognized. Therefore, to disregard taxes, or to assume that taxable and nontaxable portfolios can be managed properly in the same way is simply not to be a responsible investor.

Responsible investors do not buy an index fund, for example, with an expense ratio of 60 basis points when they can obtain an identical product elsewhere for 20 or 10. And they typically do not pay full-service brokerage commissions merely to execute orders. By the same token, to replace a highly appreciated stock without considering how long it will take the new stock to "make back" the tax expense of the trade, which can be as much as 25 percent to 40 percent, is being just as irresponsible. In a market that is presumed to be highly efficient, the "alpha" required to select a replacement stock that will grow fast enough to recover the tax loss in a reasonable time is very significant, and the empirical evidence strongly suggests that most managers' alphas are not big enough to offset the taxes their trading begets. ("Alpha" is a term borrowed from modern portfolio theory jargon that refers to the differential return of an actively managed portfolio relative to a passive or unmanaged market portfolio. Said more simply, "alpha" is the skill that money managers— for a fee—hopefully bring to the client's party.)

The second little-understood reality confronting investors is that so few people in the money management business understand and articulate the first reality, that is, that taxes *are* a very important item of expense. This tax-free mentality is the result of the fact that the largest customers in the industry have historically been tax-exempt pension funds and endowments. Furthermore, because active managers are in the business of selling alpha, which is diminished by taxes, and brokers are compensated by commissions on the trades that generate the taxes, there is little economic incentive on the "sell side" of Wall Street to highlight tax considerations. And the fact is that adding the new dimension of taxes into the portfolio management equation does make the job more difficult. Witness the comment of an executive of a major mutual fund house: "To force portfolio managers to think about the tax consequences of their actions would 'shackle' their investment styles."[1] Because of these real-world pressures, taxable investors must be continually alert when considering investment advice to insure that it is their economic interests that are being served, and not the convenience of the advisors.

In very recent years, there has been increased interest in investment-related taxes. This is due in part to the rising importance of the so-called high-net worth individuals market that developed in the 1980s. Public interest is also beginning to extend beyond just the very wealthy sector, as evidenced by *Morningstar Mutual Funds'* decision in 1993 to begin reporting tax-adjusted returns, and the recent introduction by Schwab and Vanguard of "tax-managed" index funds explicitly designed to minimize taxes. The money management industry's incentive to serve taxable clients has probably also been enhanced by growing pressure on fees for active management in the traditional tax-exempt markets and the increasing use of low-fee passive management products. Finally, the arrival on the scene of federally mandated Nuclear Decommissioning Trusts (NDTs), which are taxable entities that will eventually have very large asset pools, has also attracted the industry's attention. But the fact remains that most of the industry still has a tax-free mentality, and thus the vast majority of taxable investors must, by and large, still fend for themselves.

The reader should understand that, just as this book is about investing, this chapter is about tax considerations in investing, and not about taxes *per se.* More particularly, except in limited contexts, there is intentionally no discussion of estate taxes or of tax-*motivated* investments such as shelters or offshore funds. These are not unimportant matters, but because of their complexity and because their considerations typically relate more to taxes than to investing, they are not discussed here.

Because of the primary focus on capital gains taxes, the illustrations in the chapter are equity-oriented. Unless otherwise noted, all the figures and examples reflect the same set of assumptions, which are noted in the sidebar.

ASSUMPTIONS

Beginning Market ($100)

Beginning Cost/Market (100 percent). Because of capital gains taxes, a "virgin" portfolio with no embedded unrealized gains will have a higher return, given the same turnover, than a mature portfolio with a low cost-to-market ratio, i.e., with large unrealized gains.

Total Return (9 percent). The total return assumptions for each asset class should always reflect an underlying assumption for *Inflation* (4 percent).

Yield (3 percent) and *Appreciation* (6 percent). The yield assumption obviously has an important bearing on dividend taxes, as has the appreciation assumption on capital gains taxes.

Dividend Tax Rate (45 percent) and *Capital Gains Tax Rate* (34 percent). The tax rate assumptions should relate to individuals or corporations, as the case may be, and should always reflect state and local rates as well as federal.

Spending Rate "Spending" is the amount consumed or withdrawn from the fund each year. It is assumed to start at 3 percent of the original principal and to grow thereafter at the assumed annual inflation rate of 4 percent. The ratio of spending-to-principal will vary to the extent that principal and/or the income stream grows more or less slowly than inflation. In a taxable portfolio, the growth of the fund is adversely affected as the spending rate increases, because the higher cash withdrawals require increased dividends and/or realized gains, both of which are taxable.

Turnover Rates (Ranging from zero to 100 percent). Note that the assumed turnover rate applies throughout the entire period in question and not just to a single year. *The turnover assumption is the biggest single determinant of after-tax performance in a taxable portfolio.*

While the assumptions are intended to be generally reasonable for owners who tend to spend all or most of their investment income, their primary purpose is to provide a simplified mathematical means of illustrating various points. The data for the exhibits are derived using the spreadsheet in the Appendix. Interested readers are encouraged to construct their own spreadsheets using assumptions and asset mixes appropriate to their own particular circumstances.

CAPITAL GAINS TAXES ARE THE BIG PROBLEM

Taxes on dividends and interest are not inconsequential concerns, but, with two principal exceptions, investors have only limited ability to do much to control them. The first exception, which for many owners is not a viable option, is to minimize the portfolio's income by buying low or zero yielding stocks. (Buying bonds with artificially low or zero coupons does not accomplish the same purpose, because the Internal Revenue Service taxes the imputed income.) The second exception is employing tax-exempt fixed-income securities, i.e., municipals. Given a choice between taxable and non-taxable fixed-income instruments of the same yield, quality, duration, call protection, and so on, the taxable investor should obviously choose the one with the higher after-tax return, which is usually the tax-exempt.[2] But too often tax-averse investors assume that, because of the tax exemption, municipals may also be substituted for equities. This decision can prove to be a very expensive mistake for the long-term investor, whose portfolio should typically have a high equity content. In this limited but very important sense, Ellis's admonition against letting "tax reasons" dominate investment decisions is eminently sound.

Except in the case of high-yielding preferreds and utility stocks, the dominant tax problem in owning equities is typically not the taxes on the income, but rather on the capital gains, and the problem grows with the age of the portfolio. As Figure 5-1 illustrates, the capital gains tax costs on a moderately mature, ten-year-old equity portfolio easily outweigh the taxes on dividends at all except the very lowest turnover levels. The explanation for the nonlinear shapes of these curves is discussed shortly, but in the meantime the reader should remember that the turnover rates on the horizontal axis in Figure 5-1 pertain to the entire ten-year period and not just the tenth year in which the tax costs are being measured.

FIGURE 5-1   Dividend and capital gains taxes at various levels of turnover

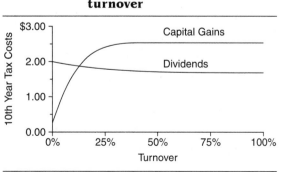

The dominance of the capital gains tax impact is true even though the tax rates on capital gains for individuals (unlike corporations) are almost always lower than rates on dividends and interest.[3] What investors too often forget is that the high tax rate on income applies to only a small percentage of the portfolio, i.e., to its yield, while the lower rate on capital gains applies, depending on the turnover, to the accumulated appreciation on the entire portfolio. A simple case in point can be made using the assumptions in the Appendix: at 100 percent turnover, the annual capital gains tax would be $2.04 ($100 × 6% appreciation × 34% tax); whereas the dividend tax would be only $1.35 ($100 × 3% yield × 45% tax). But by focusing on the lower rates rather than the actual tax costs, investors too often conclude that "capital gains are good." A cynic might suggest that in taxing gains at lower rates the Treasury has intentionally designed a ploy to increase tax revenue. (Those in Washington who contend that lower capital gains tax rates would actually enhance tax revenue are implicitly making this argument.[4])

The hockey stick shape of the capital gains tax curve in Figure 5-1 illustrates the surprising fact that the marginal impact of increases in turnover is the most severe at the outset, and declines progressively and rapidly thereafter to a point—about 25 percent—where further increases in turnover have little additional effect on taxes. At just 5 percent turnover, about 40 percent of the maximum capital gains tax at 100 percent turnover has already been incurred. The impact increases to 65 percent of the maximum at 10 percent turnover, and to 95 percent at 25 percent turnover. At 25 percent, which is exceptionally low by current portfolio management standards, the tax damage is virtually complete.[5] The capital gains tax cost at this point, incidentally, is $2.40, which represents 180 basis points of negative return! (From the Appendix: $2.40 divided by the tenth-year beginning market value of $133.35 equals 0.018.) Unless the trading decisions are very inspired, it is obvious from Figure 5-1 that taxable investors should strive to keep turnover at the very lowest possible levels. (The counterproblems inherent in a strict buy-and-hold strategy will be discussed in due course.)

The surprising—but critical from an economic standpoint—shape of the capital gains tax curve in Figure 5-1 is a complex phenomenon that results from two different but interrelated causes. The first, and probably the least understood, is that the capital gains tax bite is a function of holding period rather than turnover. The holding period in years is the reciprocal of the annual turnover rate (e.g., 1/1% = 100, 1/5% = 20), but, as shown in Figure 5-2, the relationship is nonlinear, to say the least. The fact that nearly all the tax damage has been done when turnover reaches 25 percent is a reflection of the fact that, as turnover increases from 1 percent to 25 percent, holding period drops precipitously from a hundred years to four. And most of that fall—from

FIGURE 5-2   Shape of capital gains tax curve

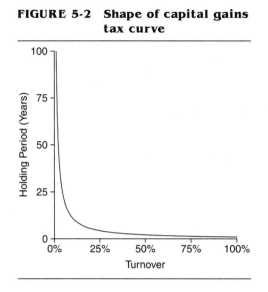

a hundred years to ten—occurs when turnover is only 10 percent. The reason the capital gains tax curve is almost flat in the 25 percent to 100 percent turnover range is because holding period now is changing only slightly, from four years to one.

MAXIMIZING UNREALIZED GAINS IS CRITICAL

The second factor contributing to the hockey stick shape of the capital gains tax curve relates to the impact of turnover on the portfolio's cost basis, and thus on its unrealized—and therefore untaxed—capital gain. The horn-like pattern in Figure 5-3 illustrates the direct relationship between a portfolio's unrealized gain and its market value, and how both are diminished as turnover increases. (The question of what happens when the unrealized gains are realized is addressed later.)

The nonlinear decline of the market value line as turnover increases in Figure 5-3 is a reflection of the hockey stick shape of the capital gains tax curve in Figure 5-1. Because the marginal tax impact is the greatest at the lowest turnover levels, the negative effect on portfolio principal is likewise the greatest. This phenomenon also explains the downward slope of the dividend tax curve in Figure 5-1, because, as capital gains taxes erode the dividend-producing assets, the dividend income declines accordingly, and thus so do the dividend taxes.

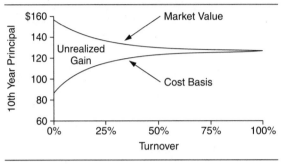

FIGURE 5-3   Effect of turnover on cost and market value

The lower curve in Figure 5-3 depicting cost basis appears to be the mirror image of the upper curve depicting market value, but there are actually very different factors involved. The downward slope of the market value curve is solely the result of the erosion of principal from the turnover-generated taxes, as evidenced by the fact that the line is flat if the capital gains tax rate is set to zero. The upward-sloping cost curve is a function of both the turnover and the appreciation rates. In an appreciating market, the cost basis increases as turnover increases, because earlier low-cost purchases are being exchanged for new purchases at higher costs. But the rate of increase slows as turnover rises, making the line nonlinear, because the compounding of the appreciation diminishes as the holding period gets shorter.

The explanation for the cost basis being lower than the starting asset value of $100 in the low-turnover range is that assets are being liquidated to cover the shortfall between the after-tax dividend income and the withdrawals for spending.[6] If the spending rate in the Appendix were set to zero, the cost basis curve in Figure 5-3 would commence at $100.

The significance of Figure 5-3, however, is not in the complex derivation of the two curves, but rather in illustrating that long-term principal growth varies so directly with the size of the portfolio's unrealized capital gains. The dramatic effect on principal growth of maximizing unrealized gains by minimizing turnover shows up even more clearly in Figure 5-4, where the vertical axis is on a logarithmic scale to depict relative growth rates.[7]

In the tenth year from the portfolio's inception, the terminal values on the 5 percent and 100 percent turnover curves (the upper and the lower lines in Figure 5-4) are $152 and $127, respectively, a difference of about 20 percent or 1.8 percent per year compounded $[(152 \div 127)^{(1/10)}]$. In the 25th year, the terminal values are $264 and $159, which is a 66 percent difference or 2.0

FIGURE 5-4   After-tax growth of $100 at various levels of turnover

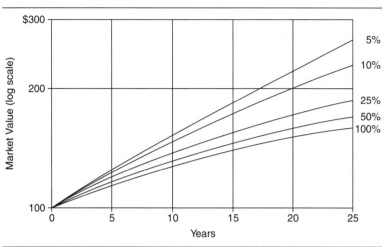

percent per year compounded. The differences between the compound returns on the 10 percent and 50 percent turnover curves (the second and fourth lines) are 1.0 percent in the tenth year and 1.2 percent in the 25th year. In a marketplace that is generally assumed to be highly efficient, frictional losses of this magnitude are by no means trivial, and few managers beat the market consistently by margins large enough to offset this much shrinkage. But might these losses be overstated?

"SOONER OR LATER, CAPITAL GAINS TAXES MUST BE PAID": FACT OR FICTION?

You may have recognized that the examples thus far do not reflect the shrinkage that occurs when all the unrealized gains are finally realized and the deferred taxes are paid.[8] One might thus wonder if the substantial advantages of low turnover cited here do not disappear—or substantially disappear—when this ultimate liquidation occurs. The financial impact of realizing the deferred gains is examined shortly, but the more important point to consider is the inevitability of the "ultimate liquidation," which is the basis of the oft-cited contention that "sooner or later, capital gains taxes must be paid."

In a *Journal of Portfolio Management* article, Roger Hertog and Mark Gordon (1994) summarize the active management community's predictable view that turnover is not as expensive as commentators such as this writer and others contend:

> The first thing to emphasize is that most investments have finite lives. Sooner or later, people need to spend from their portfolios, and when you recognize that capital gains taxes must be paid tomorrow if not today, the after-tax alpha bogey under most normal turnover rates becomes quite reasonable (Hertog and Gordon (1994, p. 93); emphases added).[9]

It is important to understand that two quite different points are made in this short statement, and the points relate to two very separate and distinct aspects of portfolio management. The first, that "most investments have finite lives," is indisputable as a practical matter. A strict buy-and-hold policy, if pursued long enough, will ultimately result in a dead portfolio. The second point, however, that "sooner or later, people need to spend from their portfolios," relates to an entirely different issue. While all well-managed portfolios require some turnover to deal with matured or maturing holdings, *the turnover required to meet the owners' spending needs varies with each owner's particular circumstances.* Because spending requirements are so highly personal and so unique to each situation, determining what that spending requirement shall be is an *undelegatable* responsibility of the owner. (Note that for this reason the illustrations in this chapter intentionally include a spending assumption, i.e., 3 percent of beginning assets growing at a 4 percent inflation rate.) The spending requirement has a material effect on the portfolio's long-term performance, and owners must understand that this factor is totally beyond the domain of any professional advisors they may retain.

Turnover is actually an inappropriate term to use in the spending context, because the word tends to imply that something is being replaced (i.e., "turned over") as distinct from being spent or consumed (i.e., "turned out"). The more descriptive term for the latter would seem to be liquidation. When the turnover-doesn't-matter advocates argue that "capital gains taxes must be paid tomorrow if not today," they are essentially saying that *all* taxable investors will need to liquidate their *entire* portfolios in *short* periods of time. But such an all-encompassing normative statement simply is not realistic in the vast majority of cases.

Some portfolios with modest spending requirements funded from current operations (i.e., from after-tax income supplemented perhaps by modest realized gains) are likely to continue indefinitely, and, under present law, will get a stepped-up cost basis at the owner's death, which eliminates the deferred capital gains tax problem entirely. Other portfolios may be slowly liquidated over time by the realization of larger interim sales, but the effective life of the portfolio may still be very long. The point is that, whether the sales activity in the portfolio is to maintain its long-term vitality, and/or to meet the owner's interim spending requirements, the substantial economic benefits of maximizing unrealized gains by minimizing turnover and postponing taxes are achievable in a great many situations.

THE "INTEREST-FREE LOAN FROM THE TREASURY" ARGUMENT

Those who contend that "sooner or later, capital gains taxes must be paid" often remark that the deferred taxes on unrealized gains are just "an interest-free loan from the Treasury." Unfortunately, this is a misleading and potentially costly analogy. Given that one party's liability is another's asset, the analogy implies that the liability provision for possible future taxes is already an asset of the Treasury, which has somehow benevolently agreed to forgo the interest thereon. But the scenario is not realistic, because in most cases the so-called loan becomes due only at the "borrower's" option, i.e., if and when the tax-payer opts to liquidate the unrealized gain. The truth is that an interest-free loan in this context is not a liability, but rather an extraordinarily valuable asset. Too many taxable investors, not to mention their advisors, too often over-look this immensely important distinction.

THE TAX COSTS OF FINAL LIQUIDATION

While total liquidation of unrealized gains would seem to be far from the general case, for the sake of completeness, Figure 5-5 illustrates the impact of liquidating the entire portfolio at the end of the tenth year under various turnover assumptions. The monetizing of the deferred tax liability does indeed wipe out much of the dramatic benefit of low turnover (e.g., 141 basis points of annual return at 5 percent turnover, 111 at 10 percent, 56 at 25 percent, and 21 at 50 percent). But even after liquidation, low turnover still has some reward. Compared to 100 percent annual turnover, there are 45 basis points of

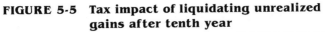

FIGURE 5-5   Tax impact of liquidating unrealized gains after tenth year

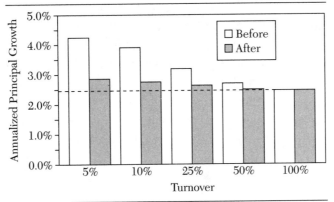

added return per year at 5 percent turnover, 38 at 10 percent, 23 at 25 percent, and 10 at 50 percent. While still significant in a business where success is measured in basis points, the after-tax alpha bogeys required at least to cover the turnover-generated tax expense are now down to levels that might appear attainable from active management.[10]

CONCLUSION

Until very recently, almost no one in the money management community has recognized that taxes *are* as important as any other item of portfolio management expense, and that to a considerable extent taxes are controllable and not inevitable. And very few people realize that most of the tax damage actually occurs in the very lowest turnover range. This lack of awareness of the impact of taxes arose for four basic reasons.

One, most money managers cater to tax-free clients, who have no reason to be concerned with the problem. Two, managing a portfolio with just 5 percent to 10 percent turnover, which is about as much activity as a taxable portfolio can tolerate, is not an easy job, and the lack of trading activity makes it more difficult for managers to justify large fees. Three, owner-clients fail to recognize that most active investment strategies have not demonstrated that their alphas are large enough to offset the tax costs occasioned by their trading activity. And, finally, the clients who have the tax problem have not adequately understood their own economics and the economics of the efficient markets in which they trade, and thus they have not demanded investment products tailored to their needs and not to the needs of other clients for whom taxes are not a problem.

Although this chapter begins by taking issue with Charles Ellis's "don't do anything in investing for tax reasons" advice, it ends in complete agreement with a different observation in the same book: "Clients . . . all too often delegate or more accurately abdicate to their investment managers responsibilities which they can and should keep for themselves" (p. 2).

One of the most important of these undelegatable responsibilities is overseeing the management of the tax expense. It is the owner of the portfolio who has to pay the taxes. It is the owner of the portfolio who has the best overview from which to manage the tax-saving strategies, especially when multiple managers are involved. And it is the owner of the portfolio who must, in the last analysis, set the turnover constraints, because managing a portfolio with minimal turnover is much more difficult than managing an unconstrained, nontaxable portfolio. As Ellis says so well, *"Clients*—not their portfolio managers—have the most important job in successful investment management" (p. 91). Nowhere is this more true than in the case of taxable investors.

REFERENCES

Ellis, Charles D. "Conceptualizing Portfolio Management," Chapter 2, in *Managing Investment Portfolios*, John L. Maginn and Donald L. Tuttle, editors. Boston, MA: Warren, Gorham & Lamont, 1983.

Hertog, Roger, and Mark R. Gordon, "'Is Your Alpha Big Enough To Cover Its Taxes?': Comment." *Journal of Portfolio Management*, Summer 1994, pp. 93–95.

"Magellan and Taxes," *Morningstar Mutual Funds*. Chicago, IL: December 23, 1994.

PART TWO

THE ASSET ALLOCATION DECISION

In 1986, a group of researchers* raised the shackles of many active portfolio managers by estimating that as much as 93.6 percent of the variation in the quarterly performance of professionally managed portfolios could be explained by the mix of stocks, bonds, and cash contained in the portfolios. This statistic is open to question, but there can be no denying the importance of the asset allocation decision to overall portfolio returns. The researchers looked at the allocation across financial assets alone. We extend the asset allocation decision to include real assets such as real estate and, in the most general case, human capital.

The asset allocation decision follows logically from the client assessment in the previous section. Having understood the risk preferences, cash needs, and tax status of the investor, the portfolio manager has to decide on a mix of assets that will maximize the after-tax returns without violating the risk and cash flow constraints. We term this the *passive approach* to asset allocation; the investor's characteristics determine the right mix for the portfolio. For the ingredients of the mix, we draw on the lessons of diversification. Asset classes tend to be influenced differently by macroeconomic events such as recessions or changes in inflation; they do not move in tandem. Diversifying across asset classes should then yield better tradeoffs between risk and return than investing solely in one

---

* Brinson, G., L. R. Hood, and G. Beebower, 1986, "Determinants of Portfolio Performance," *Financial Analysis Journal*, 42, 39–44.

risk class. The same effect might then be expected from expanding portfolios to include both domestic and foreign assets.

In decisions on asset allocation, however, there is an active component that leads portfolio managers to deviate from the passive mix defined above; that component is *market timing*. To the extent that portfolio managers believe that they can time markets—that is, determine which markets are likely to go up more, or less, than expected—they will alter the passive mixes accordingly. A portfolio manager who believes that the stock market is overvalued and is ripe for a correction, while real estate is undervalued, may reduce the proportion of the portfolio that is allocated to equities and increase the proportion allocated to real estate. In spite of their protestations to the contrary, most portfolio managers engage in some market timing, and the high profile of market strategists at all of the major investment firms suggests that asset allocation is an important decision. The reason is very simple: A successful market timer earns tremendous returns.

Its appeal to investors notwithstanding, market timing has been, over the history of the market, mostly an elusive dream. There have been far fewer successful market timers than successful stock selectors, and even the few successes that can be attributed to market timing can be equally attributable to luck. It is far more difficult to gain a differential advantage at market timing

The Investment Process

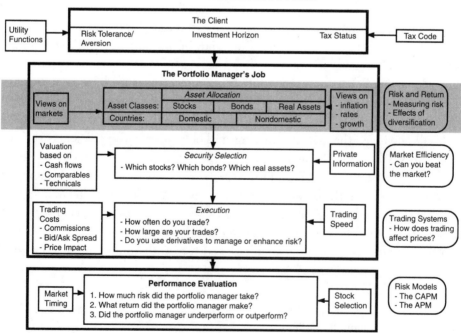

than at stock selection. For instance, it is unlikely that one can acquire an informational advantage over other investors at timing markets, but it is still possible, with sufficient research and private information, to gain an informational advantage at picking stocks. Market timers contend that they can take existing information and use it more creatively or in better models to arrive at predictions for markets, but such approaches can be easily imitated, and imitation is the kiss of death for successful investment strategies.

In the first chapter in this section, Gary Brinson examines extensively the payoff to asset allocation, looking at the benefits of diversification both across asset classes and by inclusion of nondomestic markets. This is followed by a chapter by Robert Arnott, which explores the complexities of the asset allocation decision. It notes the variety of motives behind asset allocation and some of the more common errors made at this stage of the investment process.

6 GLOBAL MANAGEMENT AND ASSET ALLOCATION

Gary P. Brinson

Modern portfolio theory tries to explain the basic balance of the desire for maximum investment returns with the disinclination toward undue risks. Although the notion of a trade-off between returns and risks is simple enough, some of the investment implications of modern portfolio theory may be less than obvious. This chapter presents a process for considering the implications of investment policy, focusing on the issue of global asset allocation. A key conclusion is that failure to take advantage of the increasingly diverse array of global assets will condemn investors to fear unnecessary risks for the returns that they achieve.

The fundamental asset allocation decision—the asset classes to include in the portfolio and their normal weights—is one of the most important in the entire investment process.[1] While active shifting of the asset weights, the selection of specific securities, and the choice of investment manager matter, the relative performance of various portfolios is generally governed by their asset allocation structures.

A substantial portion of the return from a U.S. stock mix, for example, will reflect movements in the U.S. equity market in general, and a U.S. bond mix will produce returns that are highly correlated with the U.S. fixed-income market. As a result, the risks and returns from a portfolio with a 50–50 allocation between U.S. stocks and bonds will be less like a portfolio with a 75–25 allocation than will two investment portfolios with the same allocation but different mixes within the asset classes. In other words, the long-term performance of two managers, or at investment mixes within the same class, is likely to be more highly correlated than are the returns from two different asset classes.

The significance of asset allocation is increasingly obvious as investors expand their horizons to consider a broader range of assets, especially in the markets of other countries. Although investors in a few countries, such as the U.K. and the Netherlands, have held a considerable portion of funds overseas for a long time, only recently have investors in most other countries added significant holdings of foreign investments to their portfolios.

As the investment universe expands, the complexity of the allocation decision grows, to include choices not just between domestic and foreign assets but about considerations of currency risks as well. Global asset markets offer significant opportunities, both to improve investment returns and to manage risks, but the ability to take advantage of those opportunities over the long term requires a consistent and rigorous approach to asset allocation.

Table 6-1 and Figure 6-1 provide an estimate of the size and composition of the investable capital market as of the end of 1996. This is an estimate of the "market portfolio" in today's practical terms. The evidence shows that the global arena is huge and diverse. While the assets of countries such as the United States and Japan account for significant portions of the global market, they do not dominate.

Given this increasingly diverse set of asset classes, a global portfolio should either deliver more return over the long term than a strictly domestic portfolio for a similar amount of risk, or provide similar returns but at a reduced risk

TABLE 6-1   Global investable capital market (December 31, 1996, billions of U.S.$)

	Capitalization	% of Market
U.S. equity	7,915.3	17.5
Japan equity	3,071.0	6.8
Other equities	6,484.5	14.4
Emerging markets equities	684.0	1.5
U.S. bonds	9,200.0	20.4
Dollar bonds	725.0	1.6
High yield bonds	385.3	0.9
Japan bonds	4,017.5	8.9
Non-U.S. bonds	8,524.9	18.9
Emerging markets bonds	598.6	1.3
Venture capital	42.7	0.1
U.S. real estate	1,732.7	3.8
Cash equivalents	1,804.5	4.0
Total	45,186.0	

Source: Brinson Partners.

FIGURE 6-1   Global investable capital market (December 31, 1996)

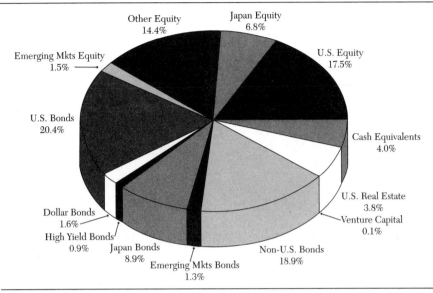

Source: Brinson Partners.

level. The potential power of global diversification can be seen using a simple example of a U.S. investor who maintained a fixed 60–40 allocation between U.S. stocks and bonds for the 25 years ending June 30, 1997. There is no active management in this portfolio, as the investments are held in the form of a Wilshire 5000 equity index fund and a Salomon Brothers Broad Investment Grade bond index fund. The average annual return of this passive portfolio is 11.7 percent, with an annualized volatility of 11.7 percent.

If 15 percent is moved from the investor's domestic equity holdings into an index of non-U.S. equities, and 10 percent shifted from domestic bonds to an index of non-U.S. bonds, the volatility of the portfolio would drop to 11.2 percent, with no attempt to reduce currency risk through currency hedging. Nor does this reduction in volatility come at the expense of a lower return; the annualized return on this passive global asset allocation portfolio is higher, at 11.9 percent.

Figure 6-2 shows the cumulative returns from the major U.S. asset classes between December 31, 1969, and June 30, 1997. Over this period, cash was clearly the least volatile of the series, but also had one of the lowest cumulative returns. Although real estate appears to show extremely low volatility as well, this is an artifact of the way in which real estate prices are reported. Typical real estate indexes reflect appraisal prices, which tend to be much smoother than the prices from actual market transactions. The result is a substantial downward bias in the historical measures of the volatility of real estate returns.

FIGURE 6-2   Wealth indexes U.S. capital markets

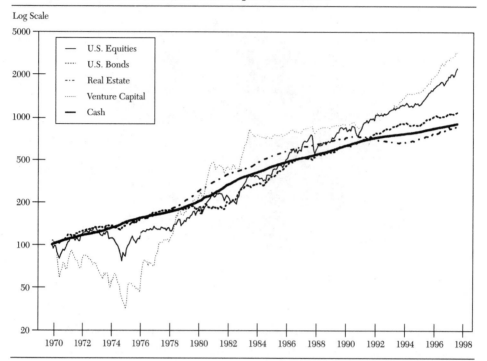

**FIGURE 6-3   Wealth indexes U.S. and non-U.S. equities
(December 31, 1969 = 100)**

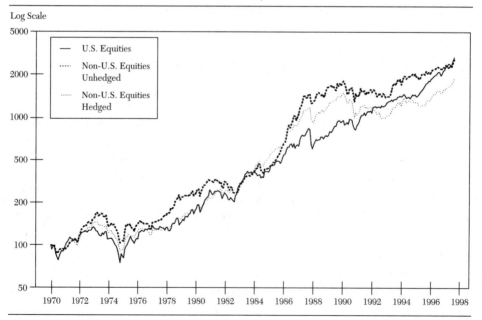

At the other end of the spectrum is venture capital, with both the highest volatility and the highest return over the period. Equities generated the second largest return and also experienced the second greatest level of volatility. Bonds fell between equities and cash in both volatility and return.

The U.S. equity market is compared to an index of non-U.S. equities in Figure 6-3, with the non-U.S. index reported in both unhedged and hedged dollar terms. The unhedged returns reflect both the performance of the various equity markets and changes in the associated dollar exchange rates. The hedged returns, on the other hand, eliminate the exchange rate effects and give an unambiguous picture of the *market* returns that were actually available to an investor in non-U.S.equities. On an unhedged basis, the cumulative dollar return from non-U.S. equities was approximately the same as the U.S. equity return.

In Figure 6-3 and Table 6-2 you can see that U.S. equities substantially outperformed the hedged non-U.S. equity index for the period as a whole. Note also that the volatility of the hedged non-U.S. series is somewhat less than that of the unhedged index. That difference reflects the volatility of exchange rates.

Figure 6-4 shows the differences in hedged and unhedged dollar returns from non-U.S. bonds compared to U.S. bonds. The 170-basis point unhedged return differential with U.S. bonds is larger than that of stock returns. Note also that hedged non-U.S. bonds produced both lower returns and lower volatility than unhedged non-U.S. bonds. The behavior of hedged bonds is more highly correlated with U.S. bonds than unhedged bonds, yet displays important differences in return patterns.

TABLE 6-2   Asset class returns and standard deviations (December 31, 1969 through June 30, 1997)

	Return	Volatility
Equities		
U.S. equity	12.6	17.5
Non-U.S. equities—unhedged	12.4	17.6
Non-U.S. equities—hedged	11.1	15.9
Bonds		
U.S.bonds	9.3	7.2
Non-U.S. bonds—unhedged	11.0	11.7
Non-U.S. bonds—hedged	9.8	5.7
Other		
Real estate	8.3	3.2
Venture capital	13.8	29.6
Cash equivalents	8.5	1.7

Note: Standard deviations are annualized on the basis of continuously compounded quarterly rates of return. Returns are annual geometric averages.

**FIGURE 6-4   Wealth indexes U.S. and non-U.S. bonds
(December 31, 1969 = 100)**

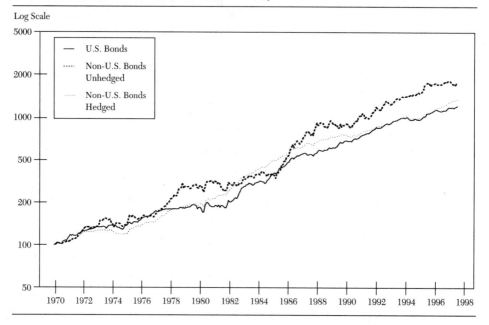

It is interesting to examine how the global market has changed over time. Fifty years ago, in the aftermath of World War II, the United States was arguably the entire world investable capital market. As markets have developed in other countries in the intervening years, however, today's definition of the "market portfolio" includes new entrants. Most recently, the market has grown to include a number of smaller or emerging equity and debt markets. This expanded investment universe has been aided by the development of market indexes by a number of investment banking and consulting organizations.

As financial markets have developed in other countries, the U.S. share of the world capital market has declined substantially. The investable capital market at the start of the 1970s is given in Figure 6-5. The share of U.S. assets in the global market declined from a high of over 70 percent at that time to less than 50 percent in the mid 1990s. The decline in the U.S. share is largely a reflection of growing markets in other parts of the word, not of differences in rates of return.

THE MARKET PORTFOLIO

Theoretically, a strict interpretation of the capital asset pricing model requires that all risky assets be included in the market portfolio. Thus, the market

FIGURE 6-5   Global investable capital market (December 31, 1969)

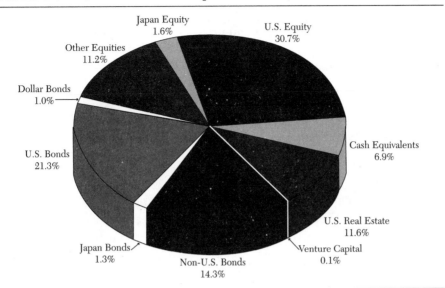

Source: Brinson Partners.

should entail all forms in which wealth is held: stocks, bonds, real estate, privately owned capital, and even human capital such as education and training. Obviously, it is impossible to enumerate all possible assets, and it is even less likely that an investor could estimate measures of the return distribution of each asset in order to determine the characteristics of the market portfolio.[2]

For our purposes here, we will trim the list of global market assets shown in Table 6-1 to focus on global stocks and bonds. This narrower definition of the global market has no effect, however, on the analytical framework that is presented, and is not meant to diminish the significance of real estate and venture capital in a fully diversified global portfolio.[3]

For most of the chapter, we define "the market" as the global assets listed in Table 6-3. Of course, some investors face substantial restrictions on the nature of their investments. Japanese pensions, for example, are restricted by law to a maximum investment of 30 percent of assets in foreign (non-Japanese) equities, and many institutions must hold a minimum of 50 percent in Japanese government bonds. Proposals to ease these restrictions are included in the "Big Bary" legislation. In a similar example, Canadian retirement funds are limited to a maximum foreign investment of 20 percent. Similarly, the South Korean authorities currently restrict foreign ownership of equity interests in Korean companies to a maximum of 23 percent. This is scheduled to be increased to 26 percent or more shortly.

Restraints (of the Japanese type) on permissible investments cause investors to face a narrower set of opportunities. As a result, it is logical that

TABLE 6-3 Market portfolio (December 31, 1996, Billions of U.S. $)

	Capitalization	Percent of Market
U.S. equity	7,915.3	19.0
Non-U.S. equities	10,239.5	24.6
U.S. bonds	10,310.3	24.8
Non-U.S. bonds	13,141.0	31.6
Total	41,606.0	100.0

Source: Brinson Partners.

these investors employ a more narrowly defined market portfolio against which to evaluate their investment alternatives. The implications of using a restricted market proxy when the true market is much larger can be very significant, however.

THE TREATMENT OF CURRENCIES

As the portfolio allocation decision moves from the domestic to the global arena, investors must manage exchange rate exposure. Separation of the currency decision from the asset or market allocation decision allows investors to consider foreign asset return and risks in exactly the same way they evaluate domestic assets. The market allocation involves risk premiums, with no currency effects showing up in those premiums.[4]

Currency movements are an issue in global investing because investors ultimately consume the returns they earn in their home or base currency. A retirement plan with current and future beneficiaries who are exclusively residents of Britain, for example, has sterling liabilities. In making payments to the plan's participants, the pension administrators must look through the yen returns that are earned in the Tokyo market, and convert those returns into pounds sterling. Changes in exchange rates will affect the amount of sterling that will be realized from the yen investment. A depreciation of sterling relative to yen means that each yen earned can be exchanged for more sterling, enhancing the plan's return. Sterling appreciation, however, would have a negative effect.

In many cases, currency volatility can be eliminated by hedging: using currency forwards, futures, options, or swaps. Such instruments do not exist for all currencies, but where they do, currency exposures can be managed. Whether the investor chooses to make explicit currency decisions or not, currency risks are avoidable. An investor who ignores the currency exposures that result from purchases of assets denominated in a foreign currency makes as much of a bet on exchange rates as a foreign exchange speculator. Therefore, the effects of the asset or market decision should be separated from the currency effects.

The importance of this distinction between market and currency decisions can be illustrated by considering the hedged returns from foreign assets. While we take the perspective of a U.S. dollar-based investor, the framework is directly applicable to any other base currency.

The impact of hedging a foreign investment into the dollar is equal to the relative short-term interest rates in the United States and in the foreign country.[5]

$$\text{Hedging Impact} = C_i - C_\$$$

where C is the cash rate or short-term interest rate, i represents the foreign country or currency, and $\$$ is the base currency.

The hedged return of the foreign asset in U.S. dollars is then:

$$\text{Hedged Return} = R_i - (C_i - C_\$)$$

where R_i is the return on the asset in the local currency.

Because the CAPM requires that the market decision be viewed from the perspective of relative risk premiums, the premium on the hedged return is calculated by subtracting the risk-free rate, which is equivalent to the domestic cash rate of the investor, denominated here in dollars($C_\$$):

$$\text{Hedged Return Premium} = RP_i = R_i - (C_i - C_\$) - C_\$$$

This can be simplified to:

$$RP_i = R_i - C_i$$

which is exactly equal to the foreign local-currency risk premium, that is, the asset return in local currency minus the associated local cash return. Notice that even though this analysis is originally framed in terms of a dollar-based investor, the dollar has dropped out of the market return that is required for making asset allocation decisions. Analogously, because the investor's base currency drops out of the asset analysis, risk premiums will be the same for all investors, regardless of where they live, where they conduct business, or their specific home currency.[6]

While investing in global markets raises the issue of currency risk, the analysis of the pure market returns from foreign assets proceeds on the same terms as for domestic assets. The relevant global variable is the local risk premium in each market, just as it is for U.S. assets, and the analysis is independent of the associated currencies.

The exception is in areas where no practical forward exchange market exists (i.e., where currencies cannot be hedged). In this case, as in many of the emerging markets, the market and currency effects are inseparable. Investment in the market means an equal exposure to the currency in these cases. Thus, the total (market plus currency) risks and returns must be evaluated.

Is the separate treatment of the currency and the asset all that important? Table 6-4 shows equity and bond market returns for several countries for the ten-year period ending June 30, 1997. In each of these countries, the cash return represents a significant portion of the local currency return.

Figures 6-6a–c present the same information, except that the markets are ranked according to their local currency returns. In Figure 6-6a, the U.S. and the U.K. had the highest local-currency equity returns over the ten-year period. When the return on cash is taken into account in computing the premiums produced by those markets, the United States remains the top-ranked market but the U.K. falls below Germany. In Australia, the return to holding cash actually exceeded the return to the equity market, giving a negative return premium and dropping that market's ranking below Canada.

TABLE 6-4   Global market returns (June 30, 1987 through June 30, 1997)

Market	Local-Currency Return	+	Dollar Exchange Rate Return	= Dollar = Return	Local-Currency Return Premium	+	Cash Return in Dollars
Equity Markets							
Australia	8.51		0.39	8.90	−1.34		10.24
Canada	7.99		−0.35	7.64	−0.17		7.47
Germany	9.61		0.47	10.07	3.33		6.74
Japan	−1.63		2.49	0.86	−5.44		6.30
United Kingdom	10.73		0.30	11.03	1.62		9.41
United States	13.95		0.00	13.95	7.83		6.12
Global Equity Index	8.62		0.78	9.40	2.567		6.84
Bond Markets							
Australia	12.39		0.39	12.78	2.54		10.24
Canada	10.24		−0.35	9.88	2.41		7.47
Germany	7.12		0.47	7.58	0.85		6.74
Japan	5.93		2.49	8.42	2.12		6.30
United Kingdom	9.92		0.30	10.23	0.82		9.41
United States	8.12		0.00	8.12	2.00		6.12
Global Bond Index	8.31		0.20	8.51	2.02		6.49

Sources: MSCI, Salomon Brothers, and Brinson Partners.

Note: Continuously compounded annual rates of return. The local currency returns for the global equity index are based on the full set of markets that are contained in the MSCI World Equity Index, and the global bond index reflects the performance of the full set of markets in the Salomon Brothers World Government Bond Index. Cash returns reflect the performance of the respective three-month Eurodeposits.

FIGURE 6-6a **Local-Currency Equity Returns (top) and Equity Return Premiums (bottom) June 30, 1987 to June 30, 1997**

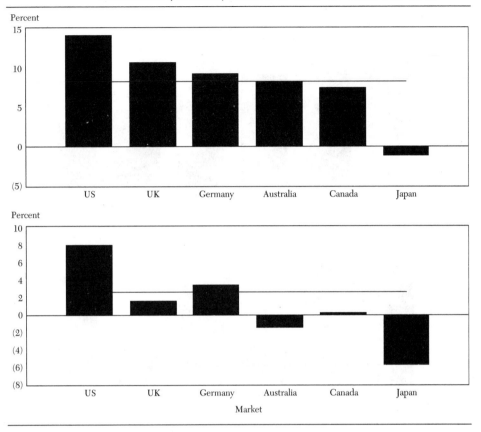

In the bond market returns shown in Figure 6-6b we see similar results. Although the Japanese bond market showed the lowest local-currency return, its return in excess of cash was better than the U.K., Germany, and United States. U.K. bond returns, third highest of the six markets in local-currency terms, actually produced the smallest *excess* returns.

Finally, Figure 6-6c shows the returns earned by a U.S. dollar-based investor from exchange rate changes and from holding cash in the various countries. Investments in Australian and U.K. cash earn the greatest dollar returns because of favorable yields on their cash. Although Japan had the strongest exchange rate gain, invesors in yen would have earned below-average returns because of that country's poor yields.

In terms of asset management, these facts indicate that the investor would have earned the greatest returns by being in the U.S. equity and Australian bond markets, but hedging the U.S. dollar exposure to obtain exposure to the Australian dollar and to a lesser extent the U.K. pound. This strategy would produce better returns than holding unhedged U.S. equities, even though that

FIGURE 6-6b   Local-Currency Bond Returns (top) and Bond Return Premiums (bottom) June 30, 1987 to June 30, 1997

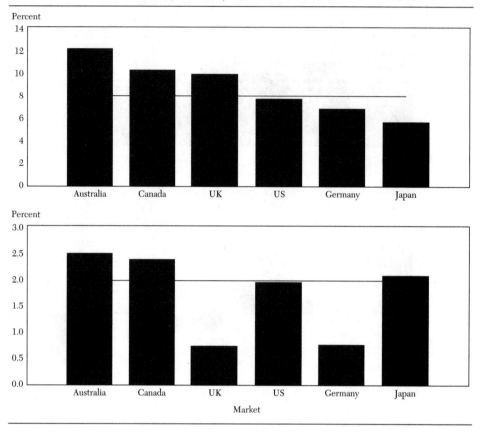

market produced the best local returns. This can also be seen in the middle column of Table 6-4, which shows that the dollar returns of those two assets are below the returns to other assets.

When investors measure performance against unhedged benchmarks, currencies also become an issue. Although the asset decisions may be made in a fully-hedged framework, there may be currency exposures from those foreign assets left unhedged. Thus, the manager's performance can be quite different from the benchmark performance due to the different currency weights. And whether the benchmark is hedged or unhedged, the manager may be able to make active currency bets away from the policy weights given to the currencies in the benchmark. In any event, it is critical to understand the relative contribution of market versus currency returns to the performance of a global portfolio. Market and currency risks are distinctly different from each other, and failure to account for them separately in the analysis can confound understanding of investment performance and lead to unexpected results.

**FIGURE 6-6c   Annual Rate of Change of Dollar Exchange Rate (top)
and Cash Returns in U.S. Dollars (bottom) June 30,
1987 to June 30, 1997**

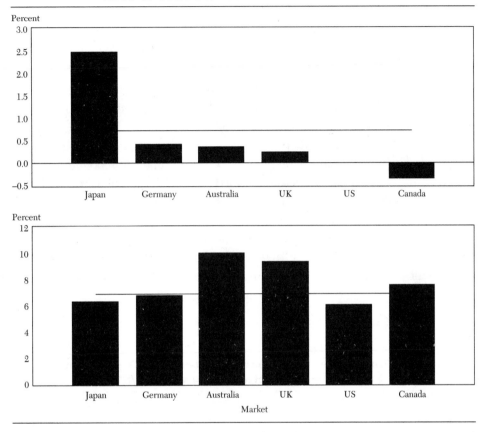

THE NATURE OF MARKET RISKS AND RETURNS

We have said that investors should evaluate assets in terms of the compensation they provide relative to the risk they create. We have also determined that the currency decision is separable from the asset decision in the major global markets and, more importantly, that asset decisions should be evaluated in local risk premium terms in those markets. In our discussion of optimal portfolio construction, all returns are assumed to be in local-currency risk premium terms. The most important result of this framework is that asset risk premiums are the same for all investors, regardless of domicile. A local-currency risk premium is the same for all foreign and domestic investors, and the asset class analysis is the same for everyone. The currencies are dealt with in a separate but parallel fashion.

The Market Portfolio

An index representing the efficient market portfolio is necessary for measuring all the asset classes' betas and thus their risk premiums; it is also needed to estimate the risk and return characteristics of the overall investment market. We assume that the market portfolio in Table 6-3 is as close to efficient as possible; in fact, a true efficient portfolio is unobservable.[7]

To construct the global investment market portfolio, assets are weighted by their capitalization relative to the market value of the investable market. That is, to create an index of capital market risk premiums, we take the premium earned in each asset class and country, weight it according to its global capitalization, and aggregate the results. The U.S. equity market accounted for approximately 19.0 percent of the global portfolio at the start of 1997, so if U.S. equities earned excess returns of 2 percent in 1997, their contribution to the global investment market premium would be about 38 basis points.

This procedure is repeated for all the assets included in our definition of the global investment market, resulting in the historical risk premium series for the market portfolio shown in Figure 6-7. The data displayed here are quarterly risk premiums in percentage terms.

FIGURE 6-7   Global investment market historical risk premium (Quarterly excess returns, ending 6/30/97)

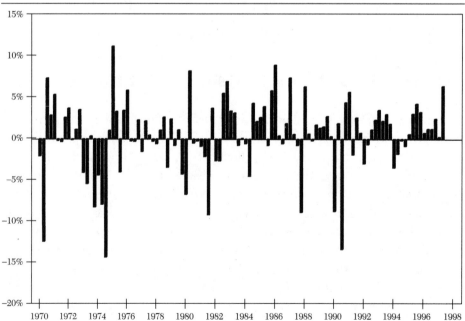

There are several interesting features of the behavior of the risk premium. First, there is a positive reward for assuming risk; the periods in which risky assets outperform cash returns outweigh the periods in which risky assets perform less well.

Second, one striking feature of risk premiums is the tendency for negative returns to be larger in magnitude than positive returns. Interestingly, for several reasons the fourth quarter of 1987 is not extraordinarily bad in comparison to other poor quarters. Because the investment market for our purposes is defined to include bonds as well as stocks, some of the adverse equity market movement is offset by the relatively good performance of fixed-income.[8] In addition, a good deal of October 1987 poor performance was erased during November, so that performance measured over the entire quarter is not as bad.

The last feature to note is the pattern of returns. There are long periods in which the risk premium tends to be in one direction , either positive or negative. Following the first oil price shock late in 1973, most countries experienced accelerating inflation that adversely affected both equities and fixed-income securities. The cluster of negative risk premiums kept many investments purchased at the start of the 1970s underwater until the early 1980s. In the 1980s, the story was reversed. Risk premiums tended to be positive much more often than negative, and many times we find runs of good returns persisting for three and four quarters in a row. Good and bad outcomes can persist for long periods, and depend heavily on events that cannot for the most part be anticipated.

Because theory tells us that risk premiums are the compensation for risk taken, the next step must be to examine the market risk. Because the volatility of the global investment market is *systematic risk,* all individual assets will be priced relative to it in equilibrium. Unfortunately, market volatility is not very stable over time. Figure 6-8 shows the two-year annualized rolling standard deviation of the market's risk premium. Although the average level was around 9 percent, there is clearly a lot of variation, with substantial movements between roughly 2½ percent and 17½ percent.[9] In large part, the increases in volatility correspond closely to the occurrences of large negative risk premiums in Figure 6-7.

Most significantly, there is no apparent trend in the volatility of the global market over the period, despite a substantial expansion of the global market and fundamental changes in structure. On balance, the discipline of an increasingly global market overwhelms the short-term disruptions of forces such as the highly volatile emerging markets and the explosive growth of investment technology and derivative securities. With this history as a guide, an investor might estimate the equilibrium level of risk in the market as a whole to lie somewhere in the range of 7½ percent to 10 percent, with extended periods in which volatility will drop below or rise above those boundaries.

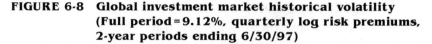

**FIGURE 6-8   Global investment market historical volatility
(Full period = 9.12%, quarterly log risk premiums,
2-year periods ending 6/30/97)**

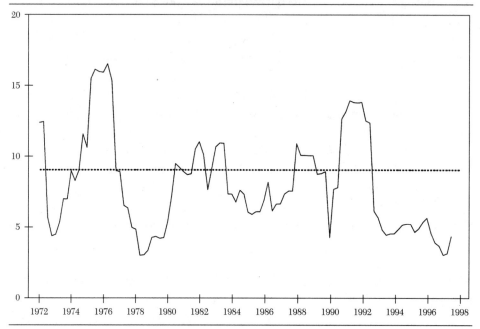

There is a further observation to make about the volatility chart. Because we show two-year rolling periods, any spike in the risk premium, either positive or negative, necessarily persists in the data for two years. Consider the third quarter of 1990, for example. The rather large negative return in that quarter causes the volatility to spike well above 10 percent, and to remain there for eight quarters. When that observation drops out of the rolling period, the risk drops back into low single-digits. Whenever historical data is used to estimate long-term risks, care must be taken to identify the effect of a single unusual event.

Some Risk and Return Observations

Because the global capital market is an aggregate of many asset classes, the behavior of some asset classes is likely to be very similar to that of the market, especially for heavily weighted assets such as the U.S. equity market. Figures 6-9 and 6-10 show historical equity and bond risk premiums in the United States for the same period shown in Figure 6-7. The U.S. equity risk premium went through an extremely poor period around the time of the first OPEC oil price shock in 1973. The bond market also had a string of poor performances at the same time, but even more noticeable is the rash of negative quarters

FIGURE 6-9   U.S. equity risk premium
(Quarterly excess returns, ending 6/30/97)

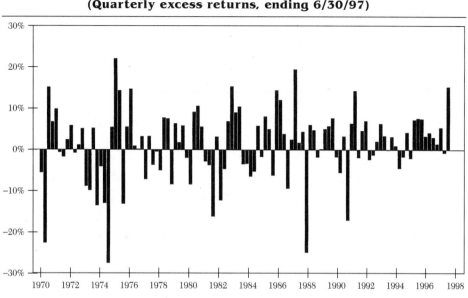

FIGURE 6-10   U.S. bond risk premium
(Quarterly excess returns, ending 6/30/97)

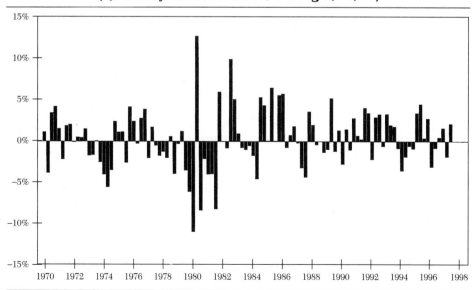

that coincides roughly with the start of the decade of the 1980s. This is often attributed to the second bout of oil price-induced inflation in 1979 and the subsequent Fed change to a policy of money supply targeting.

U.S. stocks constitute a large share of the global investment portfolio. Therefore it is not surprising that the volatility of the overall market in Figure 6-8 shows some resemblance to the historical volatility of the U.S. equity market shown in Figure 6-11.

Non-U.S. equity markets exhibit behavior very similar to the U.S. market. Risk premiums in the non-U.S. markets, shown in Figure 6-12, also were largely negative at the time of the 1973 oil shock and consistently positive in the mid-1980s. These observations seem to point to a conclusion that the investment universe or market for capital is indeed global, as shocks in equity markets are felt across many countries. In fact, at this aggregated level, the behavior of non-U.S. equities may be highly influenced by movements in the Japanese market, which represents a great proportion of the capitalization.

As in the case of risk premiums, the volatility of non-U.S. equities, *when the markets are aggregated,* is also very much like volatility in the United States. The pattern in Figure 6-13 for the non-U.S. markets is similar to that in Figure 6-11 for the U.S. market. In determining risk assumptions, investors should

**FIGURE 6-11   U.S. equity risk premium historical volatility
(Full period = 17.60%, quarterly log risk premiums,
2-year periods ending 6/30/97)**

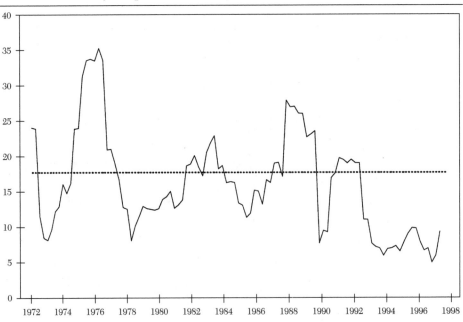

**FIGURE 6-12   Non-U.S. equity risk premium
(Quarterly excess returns, ending 6/30/97)**

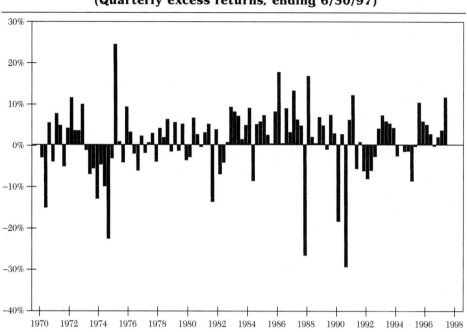

**FIGURE 6-13   Non-U.S. equity risk premium historical volatility
(Full period = 16.02%, quarterly log risk premiums,
2-year periods ending 6/30/97)**

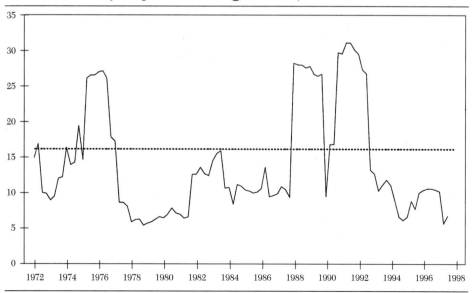

keep in mind that, although day-to-day changes in various stock markets may not be highly correlated, there are global events that may cause volatility to change in a similar way across markets.[10]

Comparison of Figures 6-14a–c reveals the effect of global events in the recent past. Although the Japanese market represents a substantial share of apparent market capitalization, the pattern of volatility across equity markets is quite similar.

Germany, Japan, and the U.K. all experienced some increase in volatility in 1974, with the U.K. showing the largest jump by far. Then the period from 1978 to 1986 is rather quiescent. All three countries show contemporaneous shocks to the equity markets at the end of 1987 and again at the end of 1990. For Japan, the latter event is the huge market correction that occurred when the asset price "bubble" burst. Nevertheless, the timing and direction of the volatility change is identical across all three countries.

The United States also experiences the same increases during those times (see Figure 6-10). In effect, although the Japanese market may skew the level of the non-U.S. equity volatility results because of its large weight, the pattern and timing of shocks cut across boundaries.

Behavior in the bond markets is a somewhat different story. The large negative risk premiums in the United States, attributable to a change in policy by the Fed at the start of the 1980s, show up very clearly in the bond market

FIGURE 6-14a   German equity risk premium historical volatility (Full period = 19.45%, quarterly log risk premiums, 2-year periods ending 6/30/97)

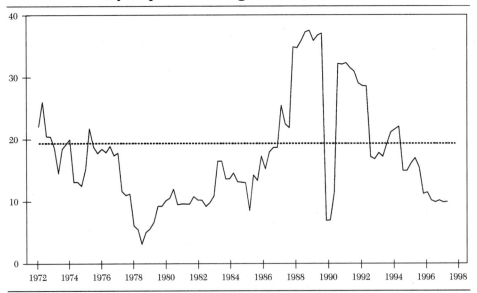

FIGURE 6-14b   **Japanese equity risk premium historical volatility (Full period = 21.36%, quarterly log risk premiums, 2-year periods ending 6/30/97)**

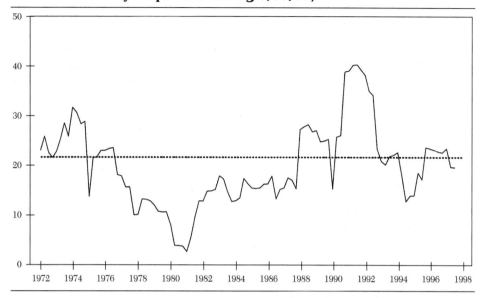

FIGURE 6-14c   **U.K. equity risk premium historical volatility (Full period = 21.29%, quarterly log risk premiums, 2-year periods ending 6/30/97)**

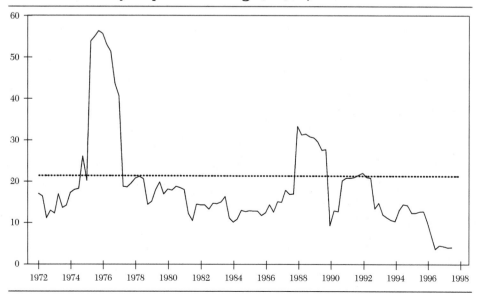

volatility shown in Figure 6-15. At the start of the decade, volatility shot up from low single-digit levels to over 15 percent. As returns returned to more "normal" levels, volatility slowly diminished toward its prior levels. What is interesting is the duration of the shift; it took almost a decade for volatility to dampen.

In contrast to equities where U.S. and non-U.S. markets seemed to have quite a bit in common, the U.S. bond market appears to have been affected by different disturbances from those in non-U.S. bond markets. Figures 6-16 and 6-17 show non-U.S. bonds' risk premiums and volatility. It is clear that the U.S. monetary policy regime change was mostly a domestic phenomenon; non-U.S. bonds do show an increase in volatility in 1980, but the level reached in no greater than during other higher-volatility periods. In fact, it would appear as though non-U.S. bond markets have more in common with U.S. and non-U.S. *equity* markets (Figures 6-10 and 6-12).

On an individual basis, bond market volatility is less congruent across countries than is equity market volatility. Figures 6-18a–c show the volatility in the German, Japanese, and U.K. bond markets. The shock experienced in the U.S. bond market in 1980 was transmitted to the German and Japanese markets as well. It is not obvious that volatility in the U.K. was affected, however, and in Japan the rise is no greater than during other periods of increased volatility. In

**FIGURE 6-15   U.S. bonds risk premium historical volatility
(Full period = 6.91%, quarterly log risk premiums,
2-year periods ending 6/30/97)**

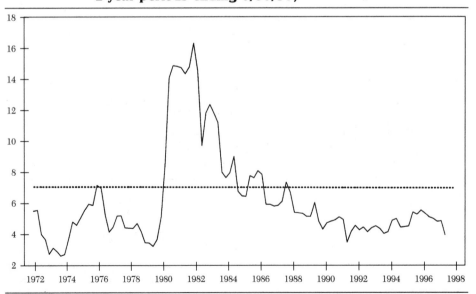

FIGURE 6-16   Non-U.S. bond risk premium
(Quarterly returns, ending 6/30/97)

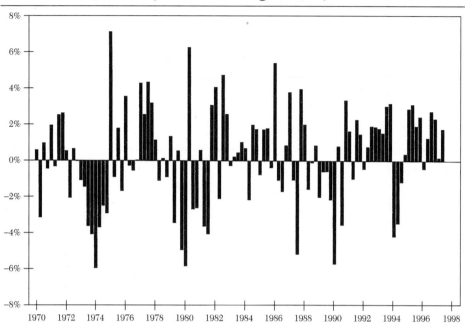

addition, the Japanese bond market appears to have been affected by the same shocks in 1987 and 1990 that occurred in the equity markets.

Because the data on the U.S. markets start much earlier than for other countries, we can check whether the behavior of the U.S. bond market is indeed unusual. Figure 6-19 shows U.S. bond market risk premiums beginning in 1926. Clearly, the 1980s were unprecedented in the magnitude of risk premiums and volatility delivered by bonds.[11]

Again, we may need to stress that these results are not due to any currency translation effect. Recall that this exercise is done in local-currency risk premiums, so there is not currency effect at all.

Thus far, we have focused on historical volatility as a *measure of risk*. It is important to realize that risk is a forward-looking concept, and volatility is a historical statistic. An investor uses volatility information as one part of a larger risk analysis framework.

For U.S. bonds, for instance, an empirical analysis of the historical data might suggest starting with a figure toward the lower end of the recent historical range, given the exceptional nature of the high-volatility 1980s. The investor would combine this information with an analysis of fundamental factors affecting U.S. fixed-income risk, such as government and central bank policy

**FIGURE 6-17   Non-U.S. bonds historical volatility
(Full period = 5.15%, quarterly log risk premiums,
2-year periods ending 6/30/97)**

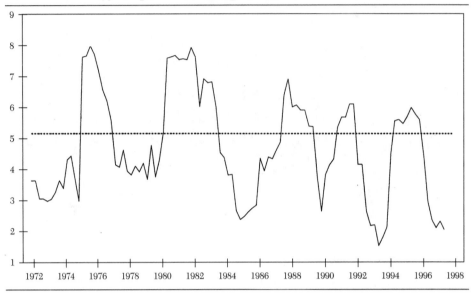

uncertainty, to arrive at a final risk estimate for the asset class. The analysis would be similar for other assets and other countries.

Historical Correlations

The pricing of an asset is not exclusively related to the asset's volatility. In the CAPM framework, the asset's risk premium is a function of its beta, which is a function of its comovement with the market portfolio. To set the risk premium for an asset class, we need to estimate this correlation.

Because the U.S. equity market represents a large part of the global market, we would expect the correlation between the two to be relatively high. Figure 6-20a shows that this is in fact the case, although there has been an apparent decline over the years as other markets have increased in weight. The correlation of non-U.S. equities and the global market is also relatively high, but it too demonstrates periods of reduced correlation. In Figure 6-20b, the recent past is one such instance of lower correlation, although unless there is some fundamental change in market relationships, this would not be expected to persist.

Historically, bond markets have tended to be somewhat less correlated with the global investment market. Figures 6-20c and 6-20d show the global market's correlation with U.S. and non-U.S. bonds. The U.S. bond market was averaging a

**FIGURE 6-18a   German bonds risk premium historical volatility
(Full period = 4.67%, quarterly log risk premiums,
2-year periods ending 6/30/97)**

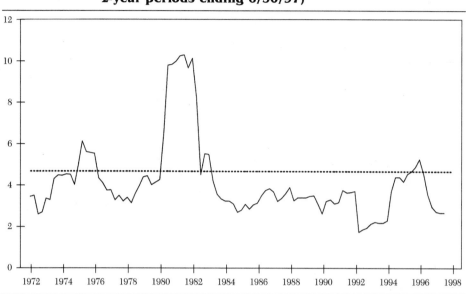

**FIGURE 6-18b   Japanese bonds risk premium historical volatility
(Full period = 5.07%, quarterly log risk premiums,
2-year periods ending 6/30/97)**

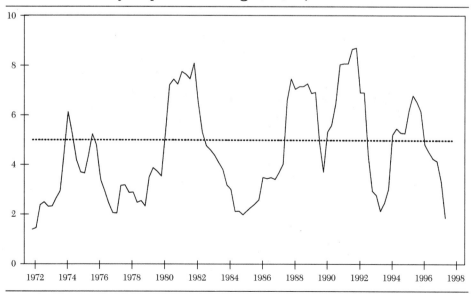

FIGURE 6-18c   U.K. bonds risk premium historical volatility (Full period = 9.41%, quarterly log risk premiums, 2-year periods ending 6/30/97)

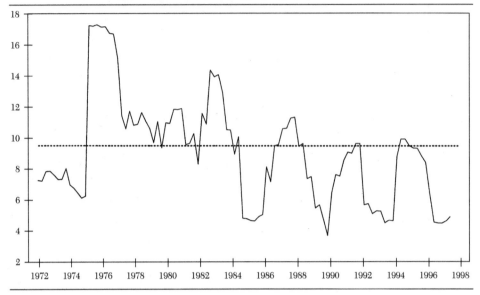

FIGURE 6-19   U.S. bonds risk premiums (Quarterly log risk premiums, 2-year periods ending 6/30/97)

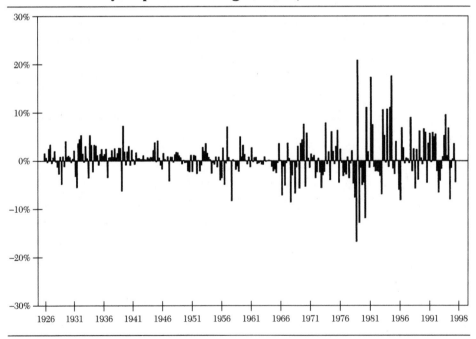

Source: Ibbotson Associates.

FIGURE 6-20a   U.S. equities and global market portfolio historical correlation (Full period = 0.90%, periods ending 6/30/97)

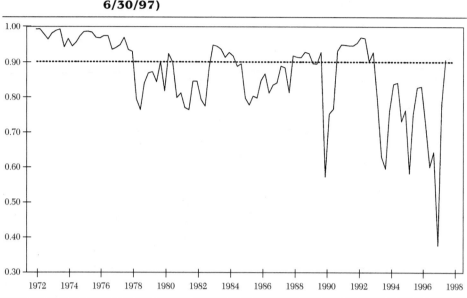

Note: Trailing two-year correlations, based on quarterly log excess returns.

FIGURE 6-20b   Non-U.S. equities and global market portfolio historical correlation (Full period = 0.86%, periods ending 6/30/97)

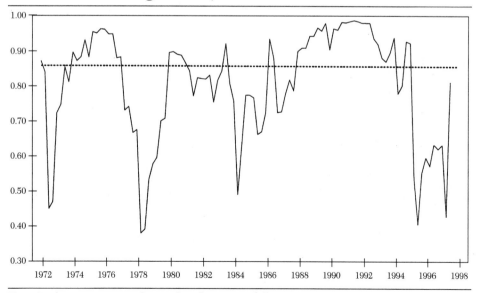

Note: Trailing two-year correlations, based on quarterly log excess returns.

FIGURE 6-20c   **U.S. bonds and global market portfolio historical correlation (Full period = 0.61%, periods ending 6/30/97)**

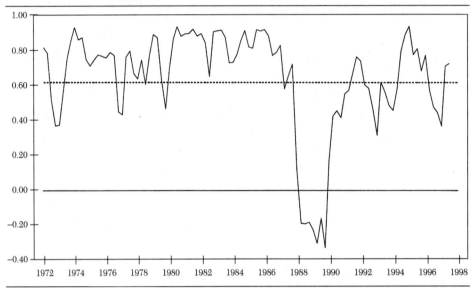

Note: Trailing two-year correlations, based on quarterly log excess returns.

FIGURE 6-20d   **Non-U.S. bonds and global market portfolio historical correlation (Full period = 0.62%, periods ending 6/30/97)**

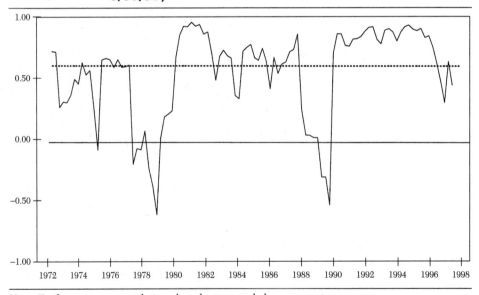

Note: Trailing two-year correlations, based on quarterly log excess returns.

correlation of 0.70 until equity markets crashed in the last quarter of 1987. After the effects of this event worked their way through the series, the correlation increased toward its previous range. The stock market crash affected the non-U.S. bond correlation as well. Here too, the correlation jumps back to its prior path after the event drops out of the rolling period.

Correlations among asset classes are also important in determining an optimal asset allocation. While correlations of assets with the global investment market are used in setting the equilibrium risk premiums, their correlations with each other are used in deciding on the optimal or policy weights given to each asset class. Toward that end, we look at a few examples of asset class correlations.

As we saw in the volatility charts, U.S. and non-U.S. equities seem to behave similarly. This is confirmed in Figure 6-21a. Although the correlation bounces around a lot, it is rarely negative, and is usually between 0.35 and 0.95. The events in 1987 and 1990 that caused the increased volatilities were global in nature, driving the correlation toward 1.0.

An interesting feature of Figure 6-21a is an indication that correlation has not been trending higher. Growing integration of economies and financial markets does not mean that movements in the markets have become more similar, only that flows of capital have become less restricted.

FIGURE 6-21a   U.S. equities and non-U.S. equities historical correlation (Full period = 0.75%, periods ending 6/30/97)

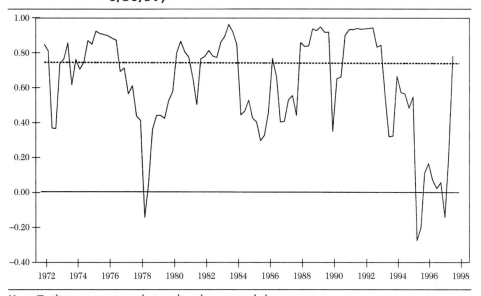

Note: Trailing two-year correlations, based on quarterly log excess returns.

FIGURE 6-21b   U.S. bonds and non-U.S. bonds historical correlation (Full period = 0.63%, periods ending 6/30/97)

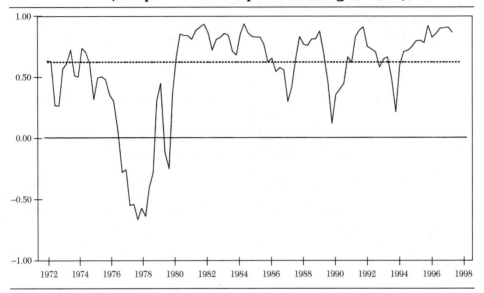

Note: Trailing two-year correlations, based on quarterly log excess returns.

FIGURE 6-21c   U.S. equities and U.S. bonds historical correlation (Full period = 0.43%, periods ending 6/30/97)

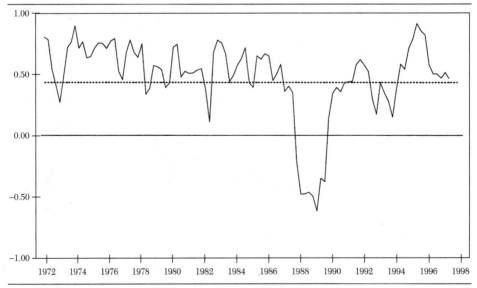

Note: Trailing two-year correlations, based on quarterly log excess returns.

FIGURE 6-21d   Non-U.S. equities and non-U.S. bonds historical correlation (Full period = 0.39%, periods ending 6/30/97)

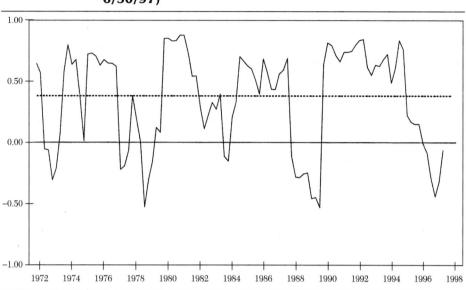

Note: Trailing two-year correlations, based on quarterly log excess returns.

A slightly weaker global scenario is evident in Figure 6-21b, which shows the correlation between U.S. and non-U.S. bond markets. Here, the correlation becomes negative in the late 1970s, much like what happened in the equity markets. The bond market effect, however, is much more pronounced and lasted considerably longer.

Because both equity and bond markets decoupled from the U.S., we can assume that the "event" is likely a U.S. domestic factor. The Federal Reserve did not handle the 1973 oil price shock as effectively as other central banks. As a result, inflation in the U.S. persisted for some time, really curbed only in 1980, by the change to a monetary aggregate target.

Figures 6-21c and 6-21d provide another illustration of the global nature of the 1987 stock market crash. There are clear significant drops in both the correlation between U.S. stocks and bonds and the correlation between non-U.S. stocks and non-U.S. bonds.

We have dealt so far only with fairly broad classifications of assets, and investors are likely interested in more specifically defined asset classes. High-yield bonds, for instance, have characteristics of both equities and fixed-income; they usually have some sort of equity "kicker" or warrant provisions, besides paying interest. Consequently, in the case of high-yield bonds, it is reasonable to set the correlation with another asset at a level between the correlation estimated for equities and that estimated for a straight bond index.

ASSET ALLOCATION: THE PURPOSE BEHIND SETTING ASSET RISKS AND RETURNS

Estimates of equilibrium or long-term risks allow investors to determine equilibrium risk premiums and thus the asset allocation policy or benchmark for the portfolio. A consistent equilibrium structure is a standard against which expected risks and returns can be evaluated consistently. Deviations of asset prices from their equilibrium or sustainable levels offer opportunities or present excessive risks that the asset allocation process should be able to handle, enhancing the risk–reward position of the portfolio if it is to be actively managed.

Segmented/Segmented Approach

Decades ago, investors viewed the investment universe as a single domestic asset class. For example, there were U.S. bond investors and U.S. equity investors, and the two infrequently overlapped. Portfolios also tended to be almost entirely domestic assets. From a global perspective, that environment might be called "segmented/segmented," as there is little crossover from one country to another or across assets within a country.

The "segmented/segmented" condition is mostly irrelevant to our discussion, because if this is truly the way the world works there are no allocation choices to make. Investors would be restricted to investing solely in a single domestic asset class. The reasons might be legal restrictions, or institutional or cultural attachment to one type of asset. For these investors, the primary measure of risk would be the total risk of the asset, that is, its volatility. In such a world, assets with similar risks may be priced differently due to differences in the price of risk across countries and asset classes.

In fact, in a segmented world, the market can be defined by the level of risk and by the amount of return provided to investors. We can think of the reward, or risk premium, that an investor receives as the *price* of risk multiplied by the *amount* of risk. Risks differ in different asset classes, so even if investors in different asset classes require the same compensation per unit of risk, their rewards will differ. For instance, if investors view the stock market and the bond market in a country as segmented not only from other countries' markets but also from one another, a bond investor is likely to be receiving lower returns than a stock investor, simply because of bonds' lower risk.

There may be markets where pricing is set on a segmented basis. If the globally oriented investor can discover such situations, there may be profit opportunities, for reasons discussed below.

Integrated/Segmented Approach

As investors broaden their investment outlooks, the usual path is to look first at other domestic asset classes as alternative investments. Most often this occurs before investors expand their universe to include foreign assets. This approach might be called "integrated/segmented," because while there is integration within the domestic market, there is still segmentation of markets by country. By "integration," we mean simply that capital can flow freely between asset classes in response to perceived differences in returns and risks.

In an integrated/segmented approach, investors look at the domestic assets available to them in terms of their relative returns and risks. They want to combine these assets in such a way as to deliver the portfolio with the highest returns at the desired level of risk. In this case, however, the investment market is not global but is instead domestic.

We demonstrate the asset allocation process using the integrated/segmented approach from a U.S. investor's perspective. Extension to a globally integrated framework is straightforward and is handled in the next section.

We know that asset allocation based on the capital asset pricing model requires estimates for risk premiums, volatility, and correlations for all asset classes. These are the inputs into a mathematical optimization that finds the portfolio that delivers the highest return for a given level of risk, or, equivalently, the lowest risk for a given level of return.

In practice, the risk level for a portfolio will be a function of the characteristics of the investor's liabilities and tolerance for risk. For instance, an overfunded pension plan with a relatively old work force or a large number of retirees would be likely to have less tolerance for short-term volatility than would a plan whose participants are generally much younger. Its liability stream will be accelerating over the near term as more workers reach retirement. An underfunded plan covering a young work force would be likely to maintain a more risky policy stance. Over time, taking on more risk should enable the plan to enjoy greater returns.

For the purposes of illustration, our investor is assumed to want a portfolio risk level equivalent to a standard deviation of 10 percent. We start by assuming that the investor is U.S.-based and that the asset classes under consideration include equities, fixed-income, and high-yield bonds. The first step is to construct the correlation matrix of the assets in the universe.[12] From studying historical data, such as that presented in Figure 6-21c, and analyzing the current and future economic environment, our investor might estimate the correlations:

	Equities	High-Yield Bonds	Fixed-Income
Equities	1.00		
High-Yield Bonds	0.75	1.00	
Fixed-Income	0.45	0.60	1.00

Next, the investor must develop estimates of the asset classes' risks. From Figure 6-13, and an expectation that in equilibrium the likelihood of major shocks is small, equity risk is assumed to be 16.5 percent. The investor also discounts the possibility that the Federal Reserve will create disturbances to the bond market, so estimates 6 percent for bond equilibrium risk, which is closer to the volatility experienced in a more "normal" period like the 1970s. Finally, the high-yield risk estimate is determined to fall between the equity and bond risks, with a value of 10 percent.

The remaining values to be estimated are the risk premiums on the three asset classes. These are forecasts not of market direction or prices, but rather expectations of what premiums the assets must offer in order for them to be attractive to investors. Remember that if an asset is highly correlated to the market, it has considerable nondiversifiable risk, and therefore must offer more compensation.

Returns are highly volatile, so historical data on risk premiums are of little use in estimating expected returns. Moreover, the process outlined here is aimed at determining equilibrium estimates of the risk premiums, not forecasting the returns to be delivered by a given market in the near term. Rather than estimating returns directly, we use the correlation to the market to derive asset risk premiums in the U.S. domestic capital market.

For any asset, the risk premium is the reward received for taking risk, or, in other words, the amount of risk times some "price of risk." The riskiness of an asset is determined by its beta. Beta describes how volatile the asset is relative to the market, so the asset's risk measure is the product of its beta and the market portfolio's risk:

$$\text{Risk of Asset } i = \beta_i \times \sigma_m$$

where $\beta = \rho_{im} \times \sigma_i/\sigma_m$.

We can also express this relationship in terms of the asset's risk and its correlation to the market. The variables in the equation can be rearranged to yield:

$$\text{Risk} = \sigma_i \times \rho_{im}$$

The asset volatility estimates are given above, but the correlations with the *domestic* market portfolio still need to be determined. This process is similar to our earlier examination of asset class correlations with the global investment portfolio. It could yield the values:

Equities	0.95%
High-Yield Bonds	0.82%
Fixed-Income	0.71%

The price of risk, also known as the Sharpe ratio, is the premium the market demands as compensation per unit of risk.[13] The total premium paid to the asset class should be the Sharpe ratio multiplied by the amount of risk. Therefore, given an assumption about the Sharpe ratio, the risk premium on an asset will be:

$$\text{Risk Premium} = \text{Sharpe Ratio} \times \sigma_i \times \rho_{im} \tag{1}$$

In this market, the investor believes that the Sharpe ratio is 25 basis points, resulting in the estimates for equilibrium risk premiums:[14]

Equities	3.92%
High-Yield Bonds	2.05%
Fixed-Income	1.07%

All the inputs needed to find the optimal portfolio have now been estimated: the risk premiums, the risk levels, and the asset class correlations. Any standard portfolio optimization program should be able to take these inputs and produce an efficient frontier. Combining the frontier and the riskless asset produces a market portfolio containing the three asset classes in the proportions:

Equities	43%
High-Yield Bonds	4%
Fixed-Income	53%

This portfolio has an expected risk of 9.33 percent and excess return of 2.34 percent. The relative proportions invested in cash and in the risky assets will then depend on the investor's risk tolerance.

For example, if the investor's desired risk level corresponds to an overall portfolio standard deviation of 10 percent, more than 100 percent of the investor's funds must be placed in the risky assets. At a 10 percent risk level, borrowing would amount to about 7 percent of assets, so 107 percent would be placed in the risky portfolio. The investor's combined position will have an expected risk premium of 2.50 percent, which is equal to the price of risk (Sharpe ratio) times the total risk of 10 percent.

Note that the actual expected return on the portfolio will be the risk-free rate augmented by the 2½ percent risk premium because all the asset returns are in *risk premium* terms.[15] Other desired risk levels will have different proportions of the risky asset and borrowing/lending, with high-risk portfolios more heavily leveraged, and low-risk portfolios having positive cash positions.

Diversification across asset classes has given the investor a portfolio with a better risk–return profile than any of the asset classes taken individually. Remember that a combination of less than perfectly correlated assets will have better risk–reward profile than the individual assets. In this case, the "risk" is the total risk of each of the assets or portfolio, not the beta. The expected reward per unit of total risk for each of the assets is:

Equities	0.24%
High-Yield Bonds	0.21%
Fixed-Income	0.18%

while the efficient portfolio's ratio is 0.25. This can perhaps be illustrated better by showing that an equity-only investor, in taking 65 percent more risk than the portfolio, will receive less than 65 percent in additional premium. The risk of equities is estimated to be 16.5 percent, while the portfolio's risk is 10 percent, and the risk premiums on equities and the portfolio are 3.92 and 2.50, respectively, a difference of 57 percent. Another way to say this is that an efficient portfolio's risk is always lower than any single asset's for a given level of expected return.

One unpleasant characteristic of optimization is its sensitivity to modest changes in the assumptions. This points out the need for consistency across assets in the equilibrium risk-setting exercise. The equilibrium portfolio will be quite different, if there are even small variations in the input estimates.

For example, using the numbers above, except for increasing the correlation between high-yield bonds and other fixed-income from 0.60 to 0.75 (which is the same as high-yield bonds' correlation to equity), causes a dramatic shift out of the high-yield asset class. The portfolio's asset allocation becomes:

Equities	45%
High-Yield Bonds	0%
Fixed-Income	55%

High-yield bonds lose their attractiveness; at a higher correlation to equities, they do not offer sufficient diversification benefit for inclusion in the optimal portfolio. The optimization in effect finds that bonds and equities alone can be combined to produce an efficient portfolio.

This sensitivity to changes in the inputs shows that investors need to pursue an asset allocation *strategy*. When market conditions differ from equilibrium, the portfolio's short-run optimal asset allocation will differ from the long-run or policy allocation. Obviously, the situation we describe for high-yield bonds, when one asset class receives no weight, cannot persist. The price of such an asset must fall in order to increase the premium offered going forward, so that investors will be induced to include it in their portfolios. By constantly reviewing the pricing in markets, the investor can develop expectations for asset class risks and returns. The risks and returns currently offered by the market can be much different from those expected to occur in equilibrium.

For instance, if pricing is such that the investor believes the equity market offers a premium of 3.75 percent rather than the 3.56 percent we determined above, the portfolio would be structured with a higher-than-policy weight in equities because of the favorable risk–reward trade-off. Conversely, if the investor anticipates an increase in the risk of the stock market, the risk premium will have to increase to compensate for this change. The new equilibrium asset allocation might have a greater allocation to equities because of the anticipated higher equilibrium risk level, but the investor would *reduce* equity holdings in the short run. This would be necessary because the assets must decline in price in order to offer higher returns in the future.

These short-run active changes in allocation occur in the context of the long-run policy levels determined in the framework of capital market equilibrium. It is the deviations from equilibrium that offer the investor an opportunity to profit from active strategic changes in asset allocation.

Integrated/Integrated Approach

A domestic-only investable universe is unrealistic for many investors. Expanding the market portfolio to encompass a global market, we now assume that the investor is not restricted by barriers, and can invest anywhere. The market portfolio is essentially the global investment market.

Extension to a globally integrated strategy has implications for risks and rewards. We examine them as we include other assets.

For the sake of simplicity, we initially assume that the U.S.-based investor views some of the available foreign assets in aggregation; equities are broken down into Japanese, U.K., and all other non-U.S. groups, and bonds are categorized as either Japanese or all other non-U.S. Now the investment universe has eight major asset classes: four categories of stocks, three groups of bonds, and the U.S. high-yield market.

Because the market portfolio now comprises more than just domestic assets, the correlations of the asset classes with the market will change. Usually this change will decrease correlations, because the domestic assets are obviously highly correlated with a domestic-only market (i.e., they're highly correlated with themselves) but less correlated with a market in which they represent a smaller share.

Given the information in Figures 6-20a–d, and analysis of the degree to which markets are similar, the investor assigns these correlations of the asset classes with the global investment market:

U.S. Equities	0.91%
High-Yield Bonds	0.82%
U.S. Bonds	0.67%
Japanese Equities	0.69%
U.K. Equities	0.71%
Other Equities	0.80%
Japanese Bonds	0.61%
Other Bonds	0.61%

For this U.S.-based investor, the equity and bond markets are no longer as highly correlated with the market portfolio, because there are foreign assets included in the market that are not included in the domestic market portfolio.

The volatilities of the U.S. assets do not change. Because of the inclusion of smaller, less-diversified markets, foreign equities are assumed to have a somewhat higher level of risk than U.S. equities. Foreign bonds are assumed to have slightly higher risk too, because the group includes a number of countries with moderate inflation uncertainty. The risk assumptions are:

U.S. Equities	16.5%
High-Yield Bonds	10.0%
U.S. Bonds	6.0%
Japanese Equities	21.0%
U.K. Equities	18.5%
Other Equities	20.0%
Japanese Bonds	6.5%
Other Bonds	5.5%

The other set of variables to be estimated is the correlations between asset classes. Here too, the assumptions for U.S. assets do not change because of the addition of other assets. Correlation estimates appear in Table 6-5.

Again, it is important that correlation estimates be consistent across the asset classes. Apparent inconsistencies, such as estimating non-U.S. bonds to be more highly correlated to U.S. equities than are U.S. bonds, should be investigated, because they have enormous potential for distorting the output of the optimization. More important than the distortions is the fact that these inconsistencies raise questions about the investor's equilibrium assumptions.

TABLE 6-5   Global asset correlations

	U.S. Equity	High-Yield	U.S. Bonds	Japanese Equity	U.K. Equity	Other Equities	Japanese Bond	Other Bonds
U.S. equity	1.00							
High-yield bonds	0.75	1.00						
U.S. bonds	0.45	0.60	1.00					
Japanese equity	0.65	0.50	0.35	1.00				
U.K. equity	0.70	0.60	0.40	0.45	1.00			
Other equities	0.70	0.65	0.40	0.35	0.45	1.00		
Japanese bonds	0.40	0.45	0.55	0.50	0.30	0.40	1.00	
Other bonds	0.35	0.45	0.55	0.25	0.30	0.45	0.60	1.00

It is difficult conceptually to justify an equilibrium in which the proposed asset class relationships are not consistent and result in extreme values for asset weights.

Some Implications of Globalization

With the risks and correlations with the global investment market, we can calculate the equilibrium risk premiums using Equation (1). The Sharpe ratio, or price of risk, is assumed not to change; its value is still 0.25. The resulting risk premium values are given in the first column of Table 6-6. The risk premiums for the segmented/segmented case using the U.S. data are from the previous calculations.

Note that the premiums on the U.S. assets decline when the market is defined as fully integrated rather than fully segmented. U.S. equities lose about 9 percent of their reward, while U.S. bonds drop 33 percent.

Premiums also declined as the market expanded from Integrated/Segmented to fully integrated. For example, the U.S. equity risk premium falls from 3.92 percent to 3.76 percent and the risk premium on U.S. bonds declines

TABLE 6-6   Global asset risk premiums

	Integrated/Integrated (%)	Segmented/Segmented (%)
U.S. equity	3.76	4.13
High-yield bonds	2.04	2.50
U.S. bonds	1.00	1.50
Japanese equity	3.61	5.25
U.K. equity	3.27	4.63
Other equities	4.00	5.00
Japanese bonds	1.00	1.63
Other bonds	0.84	1.38

from 1.07 percent to 1.00 percent. This is a direct result of decreased correlations with the broadened market portfolio. The drop in correlations is equivalent to a decline in the systematic risk of an asset class; its comovement with the market is less and therefore its beta is reduced. Because systematic risk is reduced, in equilibrium there is less compensation for holding an asset.

Conceptually, what happens is that global investors bid up the prices of the assets, reducing the risk premiums, because these investors see that the assets offer greater premiums compared to similarly risky assets (when priced by segmented investors). Thus, one of the major implications of a broadening of the market portfolio is that most narrowly defined asset classes will have lower expected returns in equilibrium.

Another implication is that failure to adjust to shifts in the market portfolio has negative consequences. A fundamental change in the composition of the market is a source of nonsystematic risk, resulting, for example, from greater willingness of investors across the world to hold more broadly diversified portfolios of global assets. Investors with broader global portfolios will not demand as much compensation from individual assets, because of their lower correlation with their expanded portfolios. Instead, they will bid up asset prices, taking advantage of the enhanced diversification opportunities of the global market, until the risk premium is reduced commensurate with the decline in market risk.

While some investors may choose not to participate in the "globalization" process, their portfolios will be affected nevertheless. A portion of their portfolio risk, once unavoidable, would become diversifiable. In not adjusting their portfolios, they are now taking avoidable risk. The globalization process of the other investors will drive asset prices and returns to levels that do not provide compensation for those new nonsystematic risks.

Overall, equilibrium risk premiums for specific assets are likely to decline as the investment market becomes more global, even if the volatility of the individual assets is unaffected.[16] Broader diversification of assets within the portfolio is the only way for investors to avoid the resulting increase in nonsystematic risks.

Because narrowly defined assets will not earn the returns they did prior to the globalization of the investment universe, investing in single-asset portfolios becomes increasingly undesirable—not in the sense that the total volatility of the asset class has changed, but instead that the *portion* of the risk that is compensated will decline. Therefore, the risk-adjusted and total returns are reduced. The investor is taking on an increased amount of nonsystematic risk, which is risk that can be eliminated by diversification, therefore not compensated.

With the correlations, volatilities, and risk premium assumptions for the integrated framework, an optimal portfolio can be calculated. The optimal portfolio includes the asset classes in the proportions:

U.S. Equities	20%
High-Yield Bonds	2%
U.S. Bonds	24%
Japanese Equities	7%
U.K. Equities	5%
Other Equities	11%
Japanese Bonds	6%
Other Bonds	25%

Because of inclusion of many assets with less-than-perfect correlations, the global market portfolio in this case has lower total risk (8.6 percent) than does the U.S.-only portfolio in the segmented case. Assuming that the investor wishes to maintain the same risk level (10 percent), the amount of leverage required rises to 15.7 percent.

By combining the efficient portfolio and borrowing in these proportions, the investor's overall position is expected to earn a risk premium of 2.50 percent. The return on this optimal portfolio appears the same as the return to the domestic portfolio (recall that its expected premium is 2.50 percent also), but this is not actually the case.

If the investment universe is truly integrated, then risk premiums will be set by global investors. As a result, the return on the domestic portfolio will be determined by the global premiums, not the premium that the domestic investor is anticipating. Since each of the domestic asset classes earns a lower risk premium in an integrated equilibrium, the premium on the portfolio comprising the three domestic assets in their integrated/segmented proportions drops to 2.41 percent.

Investors who act as if the capital market consists solely of the domestic market will earn lower returns for the same amount of market risk than will global investors. In the case outlined above, the return to a domestic portfolio is lower than the return to a global portfolio. These investors err in assigning too great a correlation between the asset classes and the markets, because of misspecification of the market portfolio.

If there are markets in which the risk premiums are in fact set on the margin by local investors who view their universe in a segmented framework, these assets may offer abnormally attractive returns. If so, the assets will be attractive to a global investor because of their favorable risk–reward characteristics. The global investor will be able to capitalize on these above-market returns, that is, earn a free lunch, by combining the assets into a global portfolio. These investors will exploit the fact that the assets provide better returns than do other assets contributing the same amount of risk to the portfolio.

It may also be that investors who are restricted to domestic assets for cultural or psychological reasons do not demand as large a risk premium as global investors. In the context of the CAPM, this is equivalent to saying that the Sharpe ratio of the investors in that market is lower than the Sharpe ratio of global investors in general. This is often a statement made about the Japanese bond market; Japanese pension funds invest heavily in their domestic bond market for institutional reasons, and do not require the rates of return that foreigners do. If this is the case, then foreigners will find little reason to invest in this market since it will offer a much lower premium than is required and available elsewhere for similar risk.

The globalization of the market can also have a significant impact on overall market returns. As the "market" portfolio is broadened by the availability of new asset classes with low correlation to the existing market, its total risk my decline. If this occurs, the level of systematic risk in the market can decrease, bringing the aggregate risk premium down.

In the eight-asset global portfolio developed above, the investor is obviously taking some currency risk, whichever country is the home market. If the investor is U.S.-based, 54 percent of the assets are not dollar-denominated. If the investor is Japanese, the foreign component of the portfolio is almost 90 percent. Here currency hedging comes into play. Active currency management can be used to eliminate undesirable currency exposures that are introduced by the asset positions. In effect, the exposure would be hedged into currencies that are relatively undervalued.

For example, a U.S. dollar-based investor might hold the portfolio above, yet not want to have any yen exposure. Instead, the investor may believe that the U.S. dollar and British sterling are undervalued. The 13 percent exposure to the yen attributable to the Japanese stock and bond positions could be partially hedged into U.S. dollars and partially cross-hedged into sterling.

The Aggregation Issue

In our examples, we aggregate assets into relatively broad classes. Aggregation allows the optimization inputs to be kept to a manageable number. Generally, assets that are assumed to have similar characteristics can be grouped together. For example, in practice fixed-income assets might be grouped into North American, Japanese, European, and other categories for the optimization.

Theoretically, the investor could run an optimization on the universe with no aggregation at all, and put assets into the program at the security level. The variance–covariance matrix (the correlations and volatilities) required to proceed in this manner quickly becomes unwieldy. The number of covariances and variances to be estimated is equal to n(n + 1)/2, so for a model with 1,000 securities the investor would need to estimate over one-half million parameters.

As the number of assets increases, the investor increasingly runs the risk of creating inconsistent risk or correlation measures. If so, some narrowly defined assets might look attractive on a risk-adjusted basis, and the optimizer will put a large amount of weight on them. Although aggregation into broad classes does not eliminate this problem, the interactions among and the consistency of a small number of risk and return assumptions are much easier to handle.

Aggregation of assets can cause problems as well as minimize them. The disadvantage of aggregating assets is the reverse of the problem with disaggregation: an aggregate asset class may, in its diversified mix, have risk and return characteristics that mask a truly attractive asset.

For example, U.K. bonds may be exceptionally attractive and thus deserve a substantial overweight. When they are combined with other bond markets in an aggregate European bond category, however, unattractive German, French, and Italian markets may cause the entire asset class to be underweighted—and the investor misses an opportunity in the U.K. market.

FURTHER IMPLICATIONS

Approaching the investment decision from a global point of view also has interesting implications related to the choice of benchmark and the portfolio's risk characteristics and to emerging markets and "non-traditional" assets.

Benchmarks

Choice of a benchmark for a portfolio is usually an implicit choice of risk level. Unless the investor is primarily interested in the specific risk characteristics of a particular benchmark, the asset class that the benchmark represents is irrelevant, in the sense that the investor can obtain such a level of risk in any number of assets.[17] Because of this, the investor can choose a diversified, efficient portfolio from the global universe, then adjust the risk characteristics through borrowing or lending to match the desired risk level.

Restricting the asset class to be the same as the benchmark asset class would almost certainly be inefficient, because it would entail assuming a large amount of nonsystematic risk in an integrated world. For example, a pension fund sponsor willing to assume risks equivalent to a 60–40 split between domestic equity and domestic fixed-income could diversify into foreign equities and bonds.

Holding total risk constant, this diversification would reduce the amount of nonsystematic risk in the plan and increase the systematic risk, which should increase the risk premium. If expansion into foreign assets increases the total risk of the plan beyond the characteristics of the benchmark, a portion of the assets would be allocated to cash equivalents.

The benchmark issue also can be examined in terms of the *alpha*, or excess return over the benchmark, produced by a manager. We make the case here that asset allocation decisions should be made on a global basis. This does not preclude making decisions *within* any market, even markets for which no funds have been allocated. Most traditional asset classes can be swapped into another form, usually a short-term Eurodeposit return. Thus, it is possible to hire managers to capture alpha within asset classes, and, through the use of swaps or futures, add the excess returns to the portfolio. In effect, the asset allocation decision is separated from the individual asset selection decisions.

Overall portfolio performance evaluation must take risk into consideration. Any asset allocation or manager returns must be decomposed into changes attributable to the risk taken and the excess return produced. Because increasing the systematic risk of a portfolio should be rewarded with a larger premium, a manager should not be credited for producing above-benchmark returns if high returns are simply the result of assuming more risk than the benchmark.

"Nontraditional" Assets

An enormous amount of money has flowed into emerging markets, ostensibly because of the higher returns in these countries. Investors assume that the growth prospects and high risk in emerging markets will deliver higher returns than in developed markets. From a global CAPM perspective, this movement is somewhat problematical.

Emerging markets have relatively low correlations with the global investment market; therefore most of their risk is nonsystematic. Because the systematic share of the total risk is small, in aggregate the compensation paid to investments in these markets in equilibrium could be quite small, because most of the risk can be diversified away. Yet, because the total risk in these markets can be extraordinarily high, their low correlations with the market may be outweighed by their risk, thus producing large premiums.

It could instead be that these markets are truly segmented from the global capital market, and investors can actually earn above-normal returns. Pricing in these markets may indeed be set on a segmented basis, which would offer a "free lunch" to investors holding a diversified portfolio of emerging markets.

A final alternative explains at least some of the good emerging markets returns: they are attributable to the increase in prices resulting from a move from higher segmented returns to lower integrated returns. If so, the premiums available in these markets in the future will not be nearly as high as those produced in the past.

Some investors might claim that emerging markets investments provide high returns because there is compensation paid for risk factors not captured in a global CAPM. There are models that attempt to price risk factors ex post, but there is little theoretical justification for additional factors entering into an ex ante framework that would explain these results.

Another nontraditional asset class worth noting in this framework is venture capital or private equity. Returns data on venture capital are notoriously bad, because they are not subject to mark-to-market conventions, and there is no completely satisfactory way to handle the effects of the timing of cash flows.

Yet venture investments are primarily equity or equity-related, usually with some warrants or conversion features on debt securities. The ultimate exit from a venture capital investment is also usually sensitive to equity market conditions, depending either on an initial public offering or sale to another company. A case could thus be made that the true underlying correlation of venture capital to the equity market is very high, and so too its correlation to the global investment market. Therefore the systematic risk component should be large, leading one to expect that compensation to the asset class should be high.

CONCLUSION

We have used a CAPM framework to present the issues involved in building and managing a diversified portfolio of global assets. The process of asset allocation and structuring of portfolios depends on the risks and returns offered by an asset relative to those available from all available traded assets. We have demonstrated the mechanics of estimating risks and risk premiums and the optimization process discussed. The sensitivity of optimization to small changes in the inputs remains an important issue, and investors should be aware of these effects on their equilibrium asset allocation.

Several strong implications emerge from looking at the world as a global market. One conclusion is that investors who define their investment universe narrowly are likely to be compensated less for the same level of risk than those who are willing to use the broad range of opportunities in the world. Another is that risk premiums, even for investors with a globally defined universe, are likely to decline as the market portfolio expands to embrace new assets.

7 ACTIVE ASSET ALLOCATION

Robert Arnott

In theory, the asset allocation decision is driven by investor risk preferences, on the one hand, and the statistical imperatives of diversification, on the other. While these are undoubtedly critical components of asset allocation, it is a far more complex decision in practice. In part, the complexity arises because of the different motivations for asset allocation, ranging from the desire to alter the return distribution of the portfolio to the desire to time markets. In this chapter, we will consider the different categories of asset allocation and the motivations of each. We will also consider some common errors made by portfolio managers on this critical component of portfolio management, including the temptation to tinker with allocation mixes and the effect of holding large cash reserves.

THE MANY DIMENSIONS OF ASSET ALLOCATION

It is often said that asset allocation is the most important decision that an investment manager or fund sponsor faces. It is the conventional wisdom, and is demonstrated in academic journals, that asset allocation has more influence on aggregate portfolio returns than any other single decision. Yet, like the blind men disagreeing on the nature of an elephant, different people use the term "asset allocation" for different purposes. It is interesting to note that many of the most costly and flagrant errors in institutional asset management are made at the asset allocation level, either by investors who are ill-positioned for a turbulent market or by clients chasing the most successful recent strategies.

If asset allocation for a portfolio is not managed as a deliberate strategy, then it is presumably drifting on autopilot, driven by the whims of the markets. This is an often overlooked fact of portfolio management: If we don't consciously manage assets on a disciplined basis, the capital markets will do it for us. The markets will assure that we are overexposed to an asset class at market highs and underexposed at market lows. This same problem afflicts smaller asset management decisions such as stock selection.

One of the challenges in asset allocation is that the asset allocation decision is *not* one decision. Much of the mystique that surrounds asset allocation stems directly from the fact that it can mean different things to different people in different contexts.

Asset allocation can be divided into three largely independent categories: *policy* asset allocation, *tactical* asset allocation, and *dynamic* strategies for asset allocation (mechanistic strategies designed to reshape the return distribution). Some observers of the capital markets would add another category, *strategic* asset allocation, which is longer-term than tactical asset allocation and shorter-term than policy asset allocation. While there are many variants on each of the three types of asset allocation, each deserves a brief overview.

Semantics can create needless complexity in understanding tactical asset allocation issues; the same terms are often used for different concepts. While "dynamic asset allocation" most often refers to a mechanistic strategy such as portfolio insurance, it can also describe tactical asset allocation. The label "strategic asset allocation" has been applied to the long-term policy decision, to intermediate-term efforts to position a portfolio to benefit from major market moves, and to some of the most aggressive short-term tactical strategies. Even "normal asset allocation" or "policy asset allocation" convey an image of stability that is not consistent with the real world: As investor risk tolerance changes, or as long-term goals change, the normal policy asset allocation may change. It is critical in any discussions of asset allocation to know what *element* of the asset allocation decision is the subject at hand.

There is no element in investment management that has a greater impact on long-term portfolio returns than the policy asset allocation decision. This decision must be made with all of the skill and wisdom that we can assemble. History suggests that, with courage and patience, active asset allocation may offer opportunities to add measurably to portfolio returns. To do so, the active shifts in asset mix must be handled in a contrarian fashion. Those who lack the courage, discipline, patience, or will required to stay the course with a tactical asset allocation process are probably better served by adopting a rigorous discipline of rebalancing and equitizing of cash reserves.

Dynamic asset allocation, the label often used for mechanistic insurance strategies designed to protect against adverse markets, is generally intended not to enhance portfolio returns, but for "insurance" purposes. As with automobile insurance or a homeowners' insurance policy, it entails a relatively predictable long-term cost. The good thing about these kinds of strategies is that the cost can be softened by a more aggressive normal asset allocation policy (e.g., larger average exposure to stocks over time). Dynamic strategies should not be undertaken without a careful assessment of the long-term costs of the "insurance." Just as an individual or a corporation may often choose to self-insure, thereby cutting costs, so too an institutional investor may be well-advised to follow a similar policy: The long-term costs of forfeiting 100 to 200 basis points per annum with insurance strategies can be immense, particularly with compounding.

For each element of the asset allocation decision, there is no "right answer" that is applicable for everyone. Some investors should bear the risk of an aggressive asset mix policy, coupled with a tactical asset allocation discipline. Others may find that they lack the courage to "stay the course" when such a discipline produces disappointing short-term results. Our discussion provides only a set of issues and considerations that may be useful for investors to choose their own "right answer."

POLICY ASSET ALLOCATION

Many organizations invest significant time and expense to evaluate and select an appropriate long-term asset allocation, ideally predicated on meeting the obligations served by the portfolio at the lowest possible long-term cost to the investor (or owner of the assets), consistent with that investor's tolerance for risk. This deliberate long-term normal asset mix is often called the "policy asset allocation." After this asset mix has been established, the portfolio is typically allowed to drift with the movements of the capital markets. This sort of drifting mix is a costly problem: It moves the portfolio away from the intended policy mix, and it tends to erode long-term investment returns, as we shall demonstrate.

While one might assume that this kind of drifting result is less time-consuming than engaging in a deliberate process for rebalancing the asset allocations, it ultimately imposes a significant drain on the time of the investment officer and the investment committee of the board. This is because a drifting mix must eventually be corrected; correcting the asset allocation after it has drifted far from the intended policy requires a careful decision as to changes in the allocation of assets among asset classes and managers.

The investments and markets that offer the best prospects for long-term returns typically tend to be inherently risky, while those that offer the greatest safety tend to offer only modest return prospects. Policy asset allocation, the central decision of portfolio management, is a balancing act, weighing this quest for improved returns against the avoidance of risk.

Even within this simple definition of policy asset allocation, there are many nuances an investor must consider. To be sure, policy asset allocation is the balancing of risk and reward in choosing a normal asset mix for the long term. But which risks should be avoided, and how do we quantify this risk–reward trade-off? Suppose a corporation has a "downsizing" program, with large lump-sum payoffs expected over the coming year. For this investor, with a relatively short investment horizon and a need to avoid volatility that could deplete fund reserves, the relevant definition of risk is very different from a long-horizon investor, with prospective obligations that stretch over the next century (as is the case for many endowments and foundations). The same holds true for an endowment at a university that has chosen to embark on a major building program. It is not unusual that the lowest-risk strategy for a short-horizon investor may be very different from that of a long-horizon investor.

Does the suitable policy mix shift with changed investor circumstances, or as the duration or maturity of the obligations served by the portfolio changes? Of course. These are the kind of questions that can and must be addressed in assessing the policy asset allocation decision.

Understanding Risk

One of the most important rules in asset management is to always operate within the risk tolerance of the client. If we abide by this rule, then our clients will show due patience when, as inevitably must occur, our investment strategies are temporarily out of step. If we exceed the risk tolerance of our clients, then the clients' patience will expire before a normal dry spell runs its course.

Of course, this rule does not apply only to the asset managers who have explicit client relationships. It is as true for the client as it is for the asset manager. Indeed, even if the "client" is ourselves, investing our own money, the same rule applies. If investors invest in a fashion that exceeds their own risk tolerance, so that when things go awry (as they inevitably will from time to time) they must abandon their strategy, they have done themselves a disservice by engaging in the strategy in the first place.

If we seek not to exceed the risk tolerance of our customers, then we must understand their risk tolerance. This is a multifaceted puzzle. As we shall see, there is no single measure of risk. In essence, risk might be defined *as vulnerability to any unpleasant consequence* of our investment process. It probably includes any failure to educate the client or ourselves as to the patterns of risk and reward associated with our chosen strategies.

The most important part of educating and knowing the client is a recognition of which consequences are truly unpleasant, because these are the consequences that may force a change in strategy. Such consequences may be *objective* if, for example, they force a change in long-term spending plans. Or they may be *subjective* if, for example, they result in a loss of wealth or pension surplus that exceeds the client's tolerance for loss. Education can be an important part of the process in helping the client to understand which risks do not have objective consequences and therefore should be tolerated by the patient investor.

This distinction between objective and subjective consequences is important in the fiduciary's relationship with the client, because clients who react (or overreact) to subjective consequences do their own wealth a disservice. For example, consider investors for the long term (such as a pension fund, a college endowment, or a wealthy family) that spend less than the contributions to the portfolio plus the income generated by the portfolio. Volatility matters only to spenders. If the market falls by 50 percent (a severe bear market, by any definition), and if the portfolio generates the same real dividend payment as before the drop, the long-term investor should, quite literally, not care a whit! Few investors can be so dispassionate or objective in the face of a 50 percent loss in wealth. But it is an important fiduciary responsibility to help a client understand that only objective consequences should matter.

Balancing the conflicting pressures of different definitions of risk requires that we understand our client. Once we do, we can better understand which measures of risk are most important. Portfolio volatility often matters (even if only as a subjective consequence): If a portfolio is volatile, it can suffer a drop in value that exceeds the risk tolerance of our "customer." The mismatch between assets and the obligations that they serve (surplus volatility) matters; a high volatility in surplus creates a serious risk that the surplus could disappear. This is a risk that most investment committees would find distasteful, to say the least.

Even time horizon does not fully define risk. For most investors, there are actually several definitions of risk that merit consideration in establishing an appropriate policy asset allocation. Most institutional investors need to be concerned with volatility of assets and volatility of liabilities, as well as volatility of the surplus (the difference between assets and liabilities). For pension portfolios, volatility of the expense ratio or contribution rate for funding the pension plan, as well as a handful of other factors, may apply.

Under current pension accounting guidelines for U.S.-based corporations, risk also can be defined in terms of shortfall. After all, upside risk is a risk that no one fears, but downside risk is avoided. Notably in pension management, there is a need to avoid any net, new, unfunded liability. If pension assets fall below actuarial liabilities, the fund faces (1) increased cash contributions to the pension fund, (2) increased pension expense on the earnings statement, (3) increased Pension Benefit Guarantee Corporation insurance premiums, and (4) a new liability on the balance sheet. No pension officer would willingly be responsible for a new liability appearing on the balance sheet!

The same holds true for an individual who spends from the investment portfolio. If the portfolio value falls without real portfolio dividends or income falling, no harm is done, unless the investor is spending more than the portfolio income. If the portfolio's ability to generate real spending power falls, then material harm is done to the investor.

Risk can certainly also include the consequences of accepting too little risk. The long-term business consequence of pursuing an overly conservative strategy that moderates portfolio volatility can sharply reduce long-term rewards. For the individual, this can mean portfolio income that fails to keep pace with ordinary inflation; for the corporation, this can mean increased long-term pension cost.

One risk that is difficult to quantify, but that is far more important than most investors realize is "maverick risk"—the risk of straying too far from the actions of our peers. Whether we like it or not, we are in a horse race. If our investment strategies lead to results that lag those of other investors, our judgment is naturally called into question—even if only by ourselves! This can happen even when portfolio volatility works to our benefit, delivering good returns, and surplus volatility similarly accrues to our client's benefit. For the corporate investor (such as a pension portfolio), maverick risk matters for a very important business reason: If our results fall short of those of the competition, we lose clients. By the same token, if our clients earn results inferior to *their competitors,* their cost of doing business will rise relative to their competition. This means that, in the short run, their competitive position is damaged.

More fundamentally, risk could be viewed as the likelihood of "doing something wrong." Each element of risk is a two-edged sword. Each has a direct linkage with the relative importance of long-term and short-term business opportunity for our client. Those who are willing to bear short-term risk and who bear that risk with intelligence should find that their long-term competitive position improves with the improved long-term investment returns. To achieve this happy end, they must tolerate a risk that their competitive position can temporarily deteriorate if short-term investment results are poor.

If clients are willing to bear "maverick risk," they create an opportunity to outstrip the investment results of their competitors; this improves their own competitive position by reducing their cost of doing business. A willingness to bear surplus volatility might give a client an opportunity to choose higher-returning asset classes, which will boost long-term returns and lower long-term business costs (e.g., pension costs). The same, naturally, holds true for a tolerance for portfolio volatility. The two-edged sword can also cut us. A willingness to bear risks that can deliver higher returns also introduces a risk of lower returns.

Many corporations, university endowments, foundations, and other institutional investors behave as though a dollar made in the investment portfolio is worth far less than a dollar made in incremental operating earnings or a dollar saved in operating expense. This is patently false: A dollar is a dollar is a dollar. Indeed, when tax consequences are considered, a dollar earned in a tax-exempt pension, endowment, or foundation portfolio is more valuable than a dollar of taxable earnings. Improved investment returns mean reduced future costs.

Accordingly, the quest for investment portfolio returns should be as important to most institutional investors as the quest for operating profits or reduced operating expense. For the individual investor, an increase in the income that a portfolio generates is as valuable as a salary raise or a cut in living expenses. Few investors, however, behave as if investment gains are as important as other gains. The accounting and actuarial smoothing that makes pension volatility tolerable also makes pension gain easy to ignore. The same holds true for the formulas that many university endowments and foundations use in managing their spending. Pensions, endowments, and foundation portfolios are real money, however, with a direct bearing on the long-term competitiveness, and in many instances even viability, of the institution.

Managing the Policy Mix

The asset allocation decision cannot be avoided. If investors choose not to make a conscious asset allocation decision, the capital markets will do it for them. Unfortunately, the markets will assure that the investor is overexposed at market highs and underinvested at market lows. Most institutional investors follow a policy of permitting asset allocation to drift with the whims of the capital markets, sometimes within well-established but relatively broad bands. Others will consciously choose to reassess the asset mix after markets have made a major move. Neither approach is particularly defensible for the long-term investor.

If markets are efficient, then a recent market rally certainly does not increase the likelihood of improved future returns; so, how do we justify allowing exposure to a market to rise during a market rally? If markets are inefficient, and one can add value with active asset allocation, it makes sense to assume that, after a market rally, a market is priced to provide *lower prospective rates of return,* and therefore should account for a *smaller* fraction of the portfolio than it did before the rally. A drifting mix is not consistent with either an efficient market or an inefficient market!

By the same token, the investors who reexamine asset mix after any major market move are most unlikely to "do the right thing." When markets have plunged, most investors will be tempted to bail out and lick their wounds. When markets have soared, human nature encourages us to take a view that we should not get off until the ride is over. Indeed, often investors will throw more money into markets that have been recently successful, rather than paring back on these holdings. But how can we know when the ride is over? Objective measures of value can help, but they often suggest buying when most investors are fearful and selling when most investors are satisfied, so they are easy to second-guess and overrule.

For those who favor the view that markets are efficient, a simple process of rebalancing to a static asset mix can reverse the damage done by a drifting mix or by ad hoc committee decisions. A simple mechanistic rebalancing strategy actually solves two problems at once. First, it means that the effort invested in choosing the appropriate long-term normal policy mix has not gone to waste. It does so by assuring that the normal mix is maintained in a disciplined fashion. Second, history suggests that rebalancing can add modest value.[1] To be sure, a simple mechanistic rebalancing strategy will not add value in every year or even in every market cycle. Over the long run, however, it appears to add measurably to risk-adjusted returns. With compounding, even modest incremental returns can translate into significant increases in wealth.

A systematic process of rebalancing merits consideration for many reasons. It does not require that an investor believe in "market timing." While an investment committee may tend to frown on active management of the asset mix, it is far easier to persuade a committee to engage in simple rebalancing. This can be an effective way to steer an investment committee away from the ad hoc market timing that has plagued institutional investors for many years. A simple rebalancing strategy is easy to effect, and need not disrupt the ongoing asset management activities of portfolio managers. A rebalancing strategy will return control of the asset mix, the most important investment decision in investment management, to the owner of the assets.

Suppose we believe that the markets are *not* efficient. This implies that we *can* add value with a careful and deliberate choice of the "best" available investment market. Here, once again, a drifting mix or ad hoc committee decisions make no sense. A willingness to engage in active management of asset allocation should necessarily mean moving money into the markets that are priced to offer the best *prospective* rates of return. Because prospective returns fall with a risking market, or rise with a falling market (in much the same way that prospective bond yields fall with rising bond prices and rise with falling prices), this sort of strategy should, over time, tend to put more investment capital into the recently unsuccessful markets rather than chasing the recently successful markets. This is an uncomfortable process, yet it is one that might reasonably be expected to improve investment performance.

The Temptation to Tinker

One of the biggest challenges in managing institutional assets is committee-based pressure to shift money out of recently disappointing markets and into recently successful markets. One of the easiest ways to convince an investment committee not to engage in these ad hoc asset allocation asset mix shifts is to persuade the committee to adopt a long-term policy asset mix and to engage in systematic rebalancing to that mix. In other words, rebalancing can be an easy way to convince a pension committee not to disrupt the long-term asset allocation policy that has been so carefully established.

Can value be added by ad hoc shifts in asset allocation? Possibly, but history suggests that most investors are not particularly successful with their asset allocation decisions. In 1986 and again in 1991, Brinson, Hood, and Beebower looked at the ten-year results of many of the largest U.S. pension funds and the costs that ad hoc shifts place on plan performance. In 1986, they found that the typical pension sponsor forfeited 66 basis points per annum, largely through sloppy ad hoc shifts in asset mix. In a 1992 update, they find a still-significant 26-basis point forfeiture. In both cases, this is a huge difference. After ten years, a $1 billion portfolio, growing at 10 percent per annum, would be worth at least $100 million more without these ad hoc shifts in asset mix.

In the 1986 study, the sponsor benefiting the most from asset allocation shifts adds just 25 basis points per annum, while the most notably unsuccessful gives up an astounding 268 basis points. The 1992 study finds as wide a range, with the best adding 86 basis points and the worst forfeiting 181 basis points. These findings are detailed in Table 7-1.

While a disciplined framework for rebalancing does not necessarily add value in every quarter, year, or even market cycle, institutional investors who embrace it for the long run appear to garner well-earned rewards. When a committee subscribes to a systematic process of rebalancing, it can derive comfort by, as a group, reaffirming its long-term investment policy on a consistent basis. The uneasy decision to buy a market that has plunged is replaced with the satisfying decision to adhere to a discipline, *which accomplishes the same end.* Once committed to the principle of rebalancing, it is reasonable to expect that such investors will stay the course.

TABLE 7-1   Annualized 10-year returns of 91 large U.S. pension plans (%)

	Average Return	Minimum Return	Maximum Return	Standard Deviation
1974 to 1983 Findings[a]				
Portfolio Total Returns:				
Policy Mix	10.11	9.47	10.57	0.22
Policy Mix and Timing	9.44	7.25	10.34	0.52
Policy Mix and Selection	9.75	7.17	13.31	1.33
Actual Portfolio	9.01	5.85	13.40	1.43
Differential Active Returns:				
Timing Only	(0.66)	(2.68)	0.25	0.49
Security Selection	(0.36)	(2.90)	3.60	1.36
Other	(0.07)	(1.17)	2.57	0.45
Total Active Return:	**(1.10)**	**(4.17)[b]**	**3.69[c]**	**1.45[c]**
1977 to 1987 Findings[b]				
Portfolio Total Returns:				
Policy Mix	13.49	12.43	14.56	0.49
Policy Mix and Timing	13.23	11.26	15.09	0.68
Policy Mix and Selection	13.75	10.52	19.32	1.66
Actual Portfolio	13.41	10.34	19.95	1.75
Differential Active Returns:				
Timing Only	(0.26)	(1.81)	0.86	0.47
Security Selection	0.26	(3.32)	6.12	1.52
Other	(0.07)	(3.50)	1.33	0.80
Total Active Return:	**(0.08)**	**(3.43)[c]**	**6.73[c]**	**1.67[c]**

[a] Gary Brinson, "Determinants of Portfolio Returns," *Financial Analysts Journal,* July/August 1986.
[b] Gary Brinson, "Determinants of Portfolio Returns II," *Financial Analysts Journal,* May/June 1991.
[c] Column not additive.

Over the 25 years of 1970 through 1994, simple rebalancing produced an average annual return of 10.31 percent, 26 basis points per year over the results for a drifting asset mix, as shown in Table 7-2. Portfolio volatility slightly increases; the cause is rebalancing into the declining markets, which tend to be more volatile. Systematic rebalancing does appear to enhance performance, particularly on a risk-adjusted basis. Its most valuable attribute, however, is not necessarily the added return, but the added control that it gives over the asset mix of a portfolio and the disciplined basis it provides for resisting the temptation to bail out of a falling market.

A disciplined framework for rebalancing does not add value at all times. Rebalancing into a plunging market is not profitable until that market eventually turns. The incremental return is earned with a turnover of less than 1 percent per month. Maintaining a policy mix on a consistent basis is supremely boring, but makes sense. A belief in market timing is not necessary; indeed, rebalancing is the sensible response to a view that markets are efficient.

TABLE 7-2 Value added by rebalancing versus a drifting mix

	Drifting Mix Return	Rebalancing Return	Value Added
Results for January 1970 to December 1994			
Average Return	10.05	10.31	0.26
Maximum Return	31.37	31.49	2.17
75th Percentile	19.98	20.35	0.60
Median	11.93	11.19	0.32
25th Percentile	1.54	2.76	−0.05
Minimum Return	−10.69	−11.91	−1.65
Standard Deviation	±10.98	±11.01	±0.91
Transactions Average	**0.81% turnover/month**		
Summary of Annual Returns			
1970	8.10	8.32	0.22
1971	13.79	14.04	0.26
1972	12.19	12.15	−0.03
1973	−8.21	−7.83	0.38
1974	−10.69	−11.91	−1.22
1975	20.63	22.81	2.17
1976	19.98	20.35	0.37
1977	−3.99	−4.08	−0.09
1978	2.44	2.76	0.32
1979	8.43	8.21	−0.22
1980	15.28	13.63	−1.65
1981	−2.13	−1.40	0.73
1982	29.86	30.94	1.08
1983	11.93	11.19	−0.74
1984	10.29	10.90	0.60
1985	31.37	31.49	0.12
1986	21.43	21.77	0.34
1987	1.54	2.77	1.24
1988	13.11	12.88	−0.23
1989	25.15	25.93	0.78
1990	1.24	1.76	0.53
1991	24.98	26.54	1.57
1992	7.86	8.01	0.14
1993	14.01	14.58	0.56
1994	−3.48	−3.53	−0.05

Careless Cash

The second element of policy asset allocation management that deserves particular attention is the large cash reserves typical of many institutional portfolios. Most institutional investors maintain idle cash reserves in upmarkets and down, whether or not they believe cash is an appropriate current investment. Idle cash reserves pose two problems. First, they offer the lowest long-term rewards of any major asset class. The second, and more subtle, problem is idle cash reserves do not bear any resemblance to the obligations that are served by most institutional portfolios.

For most investors, cash is actually a very high-risk investment. In a pension portfolio, for example, a sharp drop in interest rates reduces the income on cash reserves, causes the fund to miss the bond and stock market rallies that typically accompany plunging short rates, and sharply *increases* the net present value of future pension obligations, even as performance is held back. For the individual investor, it means that the income for the portfolio falls, forcing the investor to adopt an (often irreversible) pattern of spending from the portfolio itself. This latter problem, while subtle, also afflicts university endowments, foundations, insurance companies, and mutual funds.

Historically, the long-term rate of return on cash has been less than stock and bond returns by roughly 6.6 percent and 1.7 percent per year, respectively.[2] This means that a 60–40 stock–bond asset allocation should outperform cash by over 400 basis points per year. This, in turn, means that a modest 10 percent cash reserve costs the long-term investor 40 basis points, compounded annually.

Even this example understates the damage of cash reserves. According to Federal Reserve data, anywhere from 11 percent to 15 percent of U.S. corporate pension assets over the past two decades have been held in cash equivalents. This means that many institutional investors have forfeited as much as 60 basis points a year because of the cost of excessive idle cash reserves alone. If U.S. pensions, endowments, and foundations had invested their assets and held no idle cash reserves over the past two decades, their aggregate value would be over $200 billion higher than today's combined value. For individual investors, there are no good overall data, but the picture is undoubtedly far worse. Interestingly, this incremental return from a fully invested portfolio, with no idle cash reserves, would have come in the context of a better match between the assets and the obligations served by those assets.

Few investment officers will acknowledge holding cash reserves above 10 percent, yet Federal Reserve data suggest that the average is typically higher than this. The problem here is a simple one. Many investors think of cash as being the explicit cash reserves of a portfolio. Yet, their equity managers hold idle cash reserves, waiting to pounce on equity investment opportunities; the same holds true for the bond managers. Some cash is often contributed to a portfolio and languishes in cash equivalents, pending a deliberate allocation to investment managers. Most institutions also maintain a modest deliberate cash reserve to serve near-term obligations. It is this *combination* that represents a large allocation and a correspondingly large drain on long-term investment results.

One counterargument often heard is that cash reserves are necessary. Stock and bond managers need cash to take advantage of opportunities in their respective markets, and it is true that cash is often needed for near-term

obligations. Yet a portfolio can easily be invested in a fashion that offers the return of a fully invested fund: futures and options can be used to invest idle cash
reserves synthetically. In so doing, a portfolio can always be fully invested,
even though there is idle cash in the portfolio.

A further distinction can be made between *tactical* cash reserves and the
cash reserves that result from simple slippage. If an investor has a deliberate and
disciplined basis for believing that stock and bond returns will be poor, then
cash may be the best-performing asset class. On the other hand, a less-than-full
investment stance is not justified if one is neutral or bullish on the markets, but
most portfolios have some modest cash reserves *at all times,* even when the investor is bullish. Unless we choose to adopt a tactical framework for asset allocation, and unless that tactical framework suggests that stock and bond markets are
vulnerable, the institutional investor has a responsibility to put idle cash reserves
to work. Curiously, this is more the exception than the rule.

The cost of these careless pockets of idle cash reserves to the institutional investing community are immense. Table 7-3 compares the rewards of a
disciplined rebalancing against the rewards for a portfolio with a drifting mix
with 10 percent of the portfolio in idle cash reserves. Cash reserves in the
typical institutional portfolio are larger than this, so the numbers actually un-
derstate the damage. Even so, in this example, an investor with 10 percent
idle cash reserves and with a drifting asset mix realizes returns that are some
51 basis points per annum less than those provided by disciplined rebalancing. History suggests that the average investor actually does moderately
worse than this.

While rebalancing and the full investment of all idle cash reserves
demonstrably improve long-term returns, it is at the cost of somewhat higher
volatility. In 1973 and 1974, rebalancing would have caused the investment of
more and more in a plunging stock market; while the process would have left us
richer after the 1975 and 1976 market recovery, it would not be without pain.
By the same token, investing idle cash reserves in a 1973 or a 1974 bear market
would hurt returns over the longer run, even though cash was actually the most
profitable place to invest during 1973 and 1974. The combination of rebalancing and synthetic investment of idle cash reserves cost an investor 308 basis
points in 1974, a painful shortfall. In 1975 and 1976, however, it left the investor exceptionally well-positioned, with a resulting 696 basis points of outperformance over the two years due to a hefty stock exposure at an important
stock market bottom.

In short, rebalancing and equitizing cash reserves disciplines make a great
deal of sense for the patient long-term investor. They make sense because they
provide an easy, systematic framework for imposing a "buy low, sell high" discipline on a portfolio and because they can give the investment committee the
confidence to stay the course in uncomfortable markets.

TABLE 7-3   Value added by rebalancing versus a drifting mix with 10 percent cash

	Drifting Mix Return	Rebalancing Return	Value Added
Results for January 1970 to December 1994			
Average Return	9.80	10.31	0.51
Maximum Return	29.09	31.49	3.91
75th Percentile	18.46	20.35	1.60
Median	11.41	11.19	0.51
25th Percentile	1.92	2.76	−0.42
Minimum Return	−8.83	−11.91	−3.08
Standard Deviation	±9.92	±11.01	±1.44
Transactions Average	0.85% turnover/month		
Summary of Annual Returns			
1970	7.93	8.32	0.39
1971	12.86	14.04	1.19
1972	11.41	12.15	0.75
1973	−6.89	−7.83	0.94
1974	−8.83	−11.91	−3.08
1975	18.89	22.81	3.91
1976	18.46	20.35	1.90
1977	−3.16	−4.08	−0.92
1978	2.91	2.76	−0.15
1979	8.58	8.21	−0.37
1980	14.87	13.63	−1.24
1981	−0.53	−1.40	−0.87
1982	27.77	30.94	3.18
1983	11.61	11.19	−0.42
1984	10.23	10.90	0.67
1985	29.09	31.49	2.40
1986	20.17	21.77	1.60
1987	1.92	2.77	0.85
1988	12.55	12.88	0.33
1989	23.70	25.93	2.23
1990	1.75	1.76	0.01
1991	23.25	26.54	3.30
1992	7.50	8.01	0.51
1993	13.11	14.58	1.47
1994	−2.86	−3.53	−0.67

TACTICAL ASSET ALLOCATION

Once the policy asset allocation has been carefully crafted, once rebalancing and cash equitization are in place to arrest the costly slippage that plagues so many institutional investors, the investor can turn to active asset allocation, although once again, things are not as simple as they may seem. Active asset allocation can include portfolio insurance and surplus insurance strategies that reduce exposure (hence risk) in plunging markets, but do so at the cost of leaving an investor sharply underinvested at a market bottom. Alternatively, tactical asset allocation may merit consideration. While portfolio insurance and surplus insurance strategies are not intended to add value, tactical asset allocation seeks to add value by opportunistically shifting the portfolio asset mix in response to changing market and economic conditions.

Tactical asset allocation describes any active strategies, typically quantitative and value-oriented by design, that seek to enhance portfolio returns by shifting the asset allocation among the various major markets in response to changing market and economic conditions. Tactical asset allocation (TAA) tends to refer to disciplined processes for evaluating respective rates of return on various asset classes and establishing an asset allocation response intended to invest in markets that are *objectively* priced to offer higher rewards. Not surprisingly, different managers of TAA strategies apply different investment horizons, different decision rules, and different approaches to implementation. These merit a brief review.

Tactical asset allocation can refer to an intermediate-term process, with an investment horizon of one to three years, or a short-term process, with an emphasis on opportunities that may be rewarded in less than a year. There are tactical processes that seek to measure the relative attractiveness of the major markets and that seek to profit from long-term cycles in the stock and bond markets. Other approaches are more short-term in nature, designed to capture movements in the markets that are triggered by shifts in monetary policy or in investor sentiment. There are several shared attributes of most or all tactical asset allocation processes.

- They tend to be objective, quantitative processes, based on analytic tools, such as regression analysis or optimization. Many investors would characterize approaches that rely on subjective judgment, even in part, as conventional balanced management, not tactical asset allocation. It is important to note that spreads in expected returns can be used to make asset allocation decisions without computers, but the quantitative method does impose a discipline that requires a willingness to buy when market conditions are frightening and to sell when "all is well."

- They tend to be dominated by value measures, driven primarily by objective measures of prospective rates of return within an asset class. We know the yield on cash; we know the yield to maturity on long-term bonds. And the prospective returns on stocks can be estimated based on the earnings yield for the stock market (the reciprocal of the price/earnings ratio) or based on a dividend discount model return estimate for the stock market. Objective measures of prospective reward lead inevitably to a value-oriented process.

- Tactical asset allocation processes will usually prompt buying after a market declines and selling after a market rises, unless conditions in other markets change sharply at the same time. They are therefore inherently contrarian. By objectively measuring which asset classes are offering the greatest prospective rates of return, tactical asset allocation disciplines measure which asset classes are out of favor, and steer investment into the unloved asset classes. As noted previously, out-of-favor markets are priced to reflect the fact that investors demand a premium reward for any such investment.

- Tactical asset allocation processes tend to rely on a "return to equilibrium." Suppose that stock earnings yields are 1 percent higher than normal relative to bond yields. We can expect to garner 1 percent more excess return (over and above bond yields) than might have been the norm historically. Second, if markets return to their normal relationship, this can occur through a 1 percent drop in stock earnings yields (a substantial stock market rally) or a 1 percent rise in bond yields (a disappointing slump in bond returns). Either scenario produces excess returns for stocks that far exceed the 1 percent excess risk premium over bonds. This tendency for markets to return to equilibrium is the principal profit mechanism in tactical asset allocation.

While the general principles are the same for most tactical asset allocation processes, their structure and implementation cover a wide spectrum. Some are simple objective comparisons of prospective rates of return, even a simple one-variable stocks versus bonds decision (e.g., if P/E times bond yield exceeds 120 percent, buy bonds; if less than 80 percent, buy stocks). Others seek to enhance the timeliness of these value-driven decisions by incorporating sentiment measures or gauges of macroeconomic conditions; some even include technical measures. We believe that the more elaborate approaches are often superior to purely value-driven models, because, much as an undervalued stock can become more undervalued, so too an undervalued asset class can grow more undervalued. The investor who buys an asset the instant it becomes undervalued will typically earn less than the investor who buys an undervalued asset at a time when market or economic conditions will permit a return to fair value.

The empirical evidence suggests that simple quantitative measures of market attractiveness have impressive potential. Table 7-4 indicates that stock excess returns (stock market returns less cash returns) are strongly correlated with several simple objective measures of the equity risk premium. Table 7-5

TABLE 7-4   Risk premium and market performance

	1 Mo. ER − BR	12 Mo. ER − BR	1 Mo. ER − CR	12 Mo. ER − CR	1 Mo. BR − CR	12 Mo. BR − CR
Stage 1: EX	0.21^b	0.47^b	0.16^a	0.24^a	−0.08	$−0.39^b$
	(3.1)	(7.4)	(2.3)	(3.4)	(−1.2)	(−6.0)
Stage 1: BX	0.14^a	0.04	0.22^a	0.20^a	0.17^a	0.34^a
	(2.0)	(0.1)	(3.2)	(2.7)	(2.5)	(5.1)
Stage 1 Prediction	**0.25^b**	**0.48^b**	**0.27^b**	**0.31^b**	**0.20^b**	**0.53^b**
	(3.6)	**(7.4)**	**(3.9)**	**(4.4)**	**(2.8)**	**(8.5)**

Source: Robert D. Arnott and James N. von Germeten, "Systematic Asset Allocation," *Financial Analysts Journal,* November/December 1983.

Note: T-statistics in parentheses.
[a] Significant at 95 percent level.
[b] Significant at 99.9 percent level.
EX = Equity Risk Premium   (Expected Equity Return − Expected Bond Return)
BX = Bond Risk Premium   (Expected Bond Return − Expected Cash Return)
ER = Equity Return
BR = Bond Return
CR = Cash Return

TABLE 7-5   Comparative tests: Equity risk premium and equity excess returns (1960–1986)

	Test 1	Test 2	Test 3	Test 4	Test 5
Constant term	−0.47	−3.39	−0.34	−0.08	−0.58
Coefficients for Equity Risk Premium:					
Earnings yield	0.48				
Less Treasury bill yield[a]	(4.4)				
Dividend yield[b]		1.88			
		(4.91)			
Treasury bill yield		−0.57			
		(−0.51)			
Constant-growth DDM			(−0.05)		
Less Treasury bill yield[c]			(−0.7)		
Smoothed earnings yield				0.52	
Less Treasury bill yield[a]				(4.7)	
CPI-normalized earnings yield					0.63
Less Treasury bill yield[d]					(5.2)
Correlation with subsequent equity risk returns	0.24	0.29	0.04	0.26	0.29
T-statistic	(4.4)	(4.7)	(−0.7)	(4.7)	(5.2)

Source: R. D. Arnott and E. H. Sorensen, "The Risk Premium and Stock Market Performance," *Salomon Brothers,* September 1987.

Note: T-statistics in parentheses.
[a] Five-year average S&P 500 earnings / S&P 500 price.
[b] Trailing four quarters dividend / S&P 500 price.
[c] Dividend yield plus five-year annualized dividend growth rate; test spans 1964–1986.
[d] Eight-year average real S&P 500 earnings / real S&P 500 price.

shows an updated study of risk premium. This study shows that the simpler measures of equity risk premium actually work even better than the rather complicated methods summarized in Table 7-4 (which is based on dividend discount model rates of return). The historical evidence is no assurance of future success of these risk premium relationships, but their demonstrated long-term effectiveness is rather persuasive.

The Theoretic Foundations for Tactical Asset Allocation

If tactical asset allocation offers the hope of improved long-term rewards, with no corresponding increase in systematic risk or portfolio volatility, it might seem that we are violating basic finance theory. After all, those who believe in efficient markets have long suggested that the linkage between risk and reward is inviolate.

The answer to this puzzle can be found in utility theory. The linkage between risk and reward is not inviolate if a higher-return strategy has lower "utility" than a more comfortable but less rewarding strategy. Let's examine how this can work.

As the market rises, so too does the wealth in a portfolio. It is easy to forget that this increase in wealth is accompanied by a drop in *prospective* returns. Different investors will exhibit different responses to changes in wealth, as shown for investment cases A–D in Figure 7-1. The appropriate asset allocation response to changes in wealth, hence the recent market movements, will differ for each of these investors.

FIGURE 7-1   Risk tolerance and return prospects: Asset allocation response

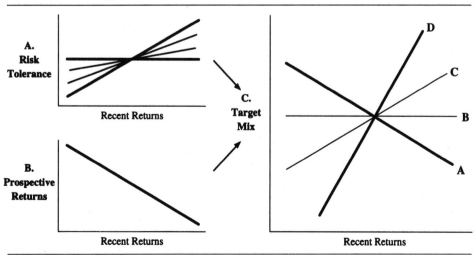

A. Some investors are blissfully unaffected by shifts in wealth. As their wealth goes up or down, their tolerance for risk does not change. These are the *true* long-term investors. If a market has gone up, the prospective returns will have dropped. If the long-term investors' risk tolerance does not change, they will respond to the *reduced* prospective returns by moving to a more defensive posture, all things being equal.

    These investors are natural candidates for tactical asset allocation. The improved return prospects that come with a newly fallen market increase the prospective rates of return; in the absence of a change in risk tolerance, the investor should take advantage of the opportunity and buy. This is what tactical asset allocation often dictates.

B. Other investors are mildly sensitive to recent changes in wealth. As their wealth rises, so too does their tolerance for prospective investment risk. Likewise, a market drop reduces their tolerance for risk, but only slightly. For these investors, the newly improved return prospects of a recently fallen market are only barely large enough to justify a return to a static mix. These are the natural candidates for a simple, mechanistic rebalancing strategy.

C. Yet another class of investors shows somewhat more sensitivity to recent market behavior. Their increased tolerance for risk rises in a rising market barely enough to induce acceptance of their newly increased exposure to that market. The "optimal" strategy for these risk-sensitive investors is to permit their asset allocation to drift with the whims of the capital markets. As the market falls, so too does their tolerance for risk, in parallel with the falling market, so that no trades or changes in asset allocation are indicated.

D. Finally, we have investors who react sharply to recent market behavior. If the market soars, so does their tolerance for risk; if the market plunges, so goes their tolerance for risk. These investors may actually sell as a market falls, reducing exposure sharply as a market approaches bottom. These investors are the natural candidates for a portfolio insurance strategy that will sell after a market decline or buy after a market rally in a disciplined fashion.

In effect, we have natural candidates for portfolio insurance or surplus insurance, for a drifting asset mix, for simple rebalancing to a static mix, and for tactical asset allocation. Just as portfolio insurance is not right for everyone, the same can be said for tactical asset allocation. This holds true for the simple reason that an improvement in long-term returns does not mean an improvement in the "utility" for all investors; utility reflects the natural human desire for both *return and comfort.*

In this context, one could have four different strategies for asset allocation management, with very different rates of return, all maximizing utility (or comfort) to some class of investors. The returns for the patient, long-term investor, using tactical asset allocation, exceed those of the rebalancing investor, which exceed those of the drifting mix investor, which exceed those of the insurance-oriented investor. The investor with the patience and risk tolerance to follow a less-conventional and less-comfortable approach earns rewards at the expense of the investor with a shorter investment horizon and an intolerance for the losses that accompany market declines. While most investors behave as if they have the risk tolerance of investor C or investor D, objectively, most investment portfolios are intended to serve long-term needs, meaning that the more appropriate risk tolerance is that exhibited by investors A or B.

Tactical asset allocation has improved long-term returns without increasing overall average portfolio risk during its two decades. This does not hold true in every year or every quarter, but over market cycles the pattern has been persistent. Yet tactical asset allocation clearly does not offer the long-sought "free lunch": It succeeds because total return and investor utility are not one and the same thing. When wealth is declining, most investors seek the solace of lower risk, hence lower exposure to risky markets. Tactical asset allocation potentially enhances long-run returns without increasing portfolio risk, but at a cost of lower comfort, hence lower utility, for many investors.

This framework is an important addition to our understanding of asset allocation management. It provides an *equilibrium* framework in which tactical asset allocation can and should improve investment returns without increasing risk. The improvement in returns can come without a corresponding increase in portfolio risk only if tactical asset allocation is an uncomfortable strategy that many investors find unacceptable. We already know this to be true. Few investors rushed to buy stocks after the disastrous 1973–1974 bear market, after the 1987 stock market crash, or even after the modest Kuwait bear market in 1990.

CONCLUSION

It is uncontestable that a good asset allocation mix can add significantly to the overall returns on a portfolio, but asset allocation can take a number of different forms. In this chapter, we have considered two of those forms. The first is policy asset allocation, where the allocation mix is tailored to the specific characteristics of the investor, including his or her risk preferences and cash needs. In coming up with this mix, there are two dangers that portfolio managers must avoid. The first is the temptation to react to the past and move assets from markets that have underperformed to markets that have done well. Doing so, more often than not, causes the returns on the portfolio to decrease rather than to increase. The second is the tendency to let cash accumulate, which creates a significant long-term drag on returns.

The second approach is tactical asset allocation, where the portfolio manager allocates more to undervalued markets and less to overvalued markets. The payoff to successful tactical asset allocation can be immense, but there are costs that have to be weighed in the balance. While tactical asset allocation is not for all investors, there are some investors who will gain from employing it in their portfolios.

PART THREE

THE ASSET SELECTION DECISION

As investors, we would all love to have the capacity to time markets well, because we would then be largely relieved of the responsibility of having to pick individual investments well. Given the difficulties of market timing, however, we have to make wise choices within each asset class to earn the excess returns we seek so avidly.

As with asset allocation, asset selection can follow a passive or an active route. A passive asset selector either picks investments randomly within each asset class or follows a strategy of diversifying fully across the investments within each class. In the latter strategy, called *indexing*, the investment in each asset is in proportion to its market value. When passive asset selection is combined with passive asset allocation, the objective is no longer beating the market, but earning a return commensurate with the risk involved. This strategy may not be particularly exciting or ego gratifying, but it is the least costly in terms of transactions costs, investor time, and, often, taxes.

Active asset allocation involves picking, within each asset class, the individual assets that are likely to outperform the rest of that asset class; that is, one buys undervalued assets and sells overvalued assets. As with market timing, asset selectors subscribe to very different approaches to finding these misvalued assets. Technical analysts rely on charts and indicators (price and volume) to find these assets; fundamental analysts rely on publicly available information to arrive at their choices. Even among fundamental analysts there are wide differences. Some use full-fledged financial valuation models to find under- and overvalued assets. Others use multiples and comparables to do the same search, or they rely on more qualitative criteria to create their portfolios. The evidence on whether either technical or fundamental analysis is rewarding

183

is mixed. Dozens of individual strategies seem to beat the market on paper, but the investors who use these strategies do not seem to earn the same excess returns. This variance may be partially attributed to the failure of these investors to adopt the strategies in a disciplined manner, but, more likely, it reflects the difficulties and costs associated with putting the strategies into practice.

Evidence suggests that one final approach to asset selection yields the surest excess returns: the use of private information to pick assets. The irony, of course, is that this is precisely the type of trading that insider trading laws are designed to stop. The fine line between private and inside information notwithstanding, investors and portfolio managers continue to search for information that will give them a differential advantage in the market.

In the first chapter in this section, we examine all of the asset selection approaches and the empirical evidence on the efficacy of each. The second chapter, by Robert Arnott, focuses on the question of whether markets are inefficient enough to allow active portfolio managers to make excess returns.

The Investment Process

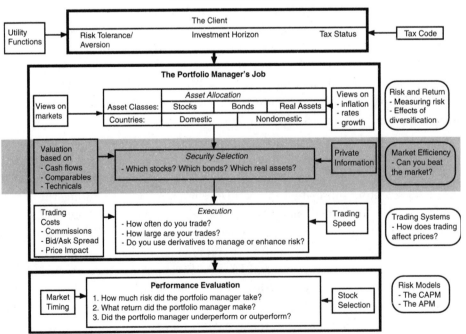

8 ASSET SELECTION: STRATEGIES AND EVIDENCE

Aswath Damodaran

An investor, having decided on the proportions of the portfolio that are to be invested in stocks, bonds, and real assets, has to decide on exactly what stocks will be held in the stock portion of the portfolio, what bonds in the bond portion, and what real assets in the real assets portion. This asset selection decision, like the asset allocation decision, can be *active*—the investor attempts to buy undervalued assets in each asset class (or sell overvalued ones)—or *passive*—the investor invests across assets in an asset class, without attempting to make judgments on under- or overvaluation. In this chapter, we examine not only this fundamental choice but also a whole range of active asset selection strategies and the evidence for whether they, in fact, deliver superior returns. We also examine passive asset selection.

ACTIVE ASSET SELECTION

Every investor fervently hopes to "beat the market," and active asset selection plays to this hope. As attested to by the success of investment newsletters and advice books, investors use hundreds of investment strategies to select what they hope will be the best-performing assets in any asset class. Active asset selection strategies can be classified fairly broadly into four groups:

1. *Intrinsic valuation models* use financial information on an asset in valuation models to find out whether the asset is under- or overvalued.

2. *Relative valuation models* attempt to find assets that are undervalued relative to comparable assets or use investment screens to accomplish the same purpose.

3. *Technical analysis models* use price and volume information on assets to detect trends in prices.

4. *Private information models* attempt to get more or better information on an asset than is available to other investors in the asset.

INTRINSIC VALUATION MODELS

In intrinsic valuation, the value of any asset is viewed as a function of the cash flows generated by that asset, the life of the asset, the expected growth in the cash flows, and the riskiness associated with the cash flows. Building on one of the first principles in finance, the value of an asset can be viewed as the present value of the expected cash flows on that asset.

Basics of Intrinsic Valuation

Three inputs are required to value any asset in this model: (1) the *expected cash flow,* (2) the *timing* of the cash flow, and (3) the *discount rate* that is appropriate, given the riskiness of these cash flows.

At the most general level, the cash flow on an investment can be either a residual cash flow on that investment, the amount left over after other claim holders (such as creditors who financed the asset) have been paid off, in which case it is called a *cash flow to equity;* or a cumulative cash flow to all claim holders, in which case it is called a *cash flow to the firm.* The discount rate should be defined consistently. If the cash flows are only to the equity investors, the discount rate is the rate that equity investors would need to make, given the risk in the investment; this is termed the *cost of equity.* Riskier equity leads to higher costs of equity. If the cash flows are to all claim holders, the discount rate has to be an average of the rates demanded by all of the claim holders, weighted by the proportion of the value held by each; this is the *cost of capital.*

The Continuum of Risk

The model is generic enough to apply to any kind of asset. The simplest asset, from a valuation perspective, is a default-free zero-coupon bond, which has only one cash flow that occurs at maturity and a discount rate that is the riskless rate corresponding to that maturity. The value of this bond can be written as the present value of a single cash flow discounted back at the riskless rate:

$$\text{Value of Zero-Coupon Bond} = \frac{\text{Face Value of Bond}}{(1+r)^t}$$

where r is the market interest rate on the zero-coupon bond and t is the maturity of the zero-coupon bond. Because the cash flow on this bond is fixed, the value of the bond will vary inversely with the discount rate.

One step up the chain of complexity is a default-free coupon bond, which has fixed cash flows (coupons) that occur at regular intervals (say, semiannually) and a final cash flow (face value) at maturity. This bond can be viewed as a collection of zero-coupon bonds, and each can be valued using the riskless rate that applies when the cash flow comes due:

$$\text{Value of Coupon Bond} = \sum_{t=1}^{t=N} \frac{\text{Coupon}}{(1+r_t)^t} + \frac{\text{Face Value of the Bond}}{(1+r_N)^N}$$

where r_t is the interest rate that corresponds to a t-period zero-coupon bond, and the bond has a life of N periods. It is possible to arrive at the same value by using some weighted average of the year-specific riskless rates used above. This rate is called the *yield to maturity:*

$$\text{Value of Coupon Bond} = \sum_{t=1}^{t=N} \frac{\text{Coupon}}{(1+r)^t} + \frac{\text{Face Value of the Bond}}{(1+r)^N}$$

where r is the yield to maturity on the bond. As with the zero-coupon bond, the default-free coupon bond should have a value that varies inversely with the yield to maturity. Because the coupon bond has cash flows that occur earlier in time (the coupons), it should be less sensitive to a given change in interest rates than the zero-coupon bond.

The next step in terms of risk is default risk, which exists when entities other than the government[1] issue securities. The basic structure of the valuation remains the same (i.e., expected cash flows are discounted at a discount rate), but the discount rate used for a bond with default risk is higher than the rate for a default-free bond. Furthermore, as the default risk increases, so will the discount rate:

$$\text{Value of Corporate Coupon Bond} = \sum_{t=1}^{t=N} \frac{\text{Coupon}}{(1+r_c)^t} + \frac{\text{Face Value of the Bond}}{(1+r_c)^N}$$

where r_c is the market interest rate on bonds with similar default risk. (This analysis can be done in terms of year-specific zero-coupon rates, as was done with the government bond.) The default risk of borrowing entities is often measured by independent agencies, which then assign bond ratings that attempt to reflect the risk. To the degree that these ratings are accurate, bonds in the same rating class should be priced to yield the same rate of return. Because the ratings are discrete[2] and ratings agencies sometimes lag the markets, it is common in financial markets to see bonds with the same rating priced to yield slightly different returns.

In a corporate bond, the risk comes from the fact that promised cash flows might not be delivered. In equity investments, the cash flows are residual, and the risk arises from the volatility of these expected cash flows. In the continuum of risk, equity investments should be riskier than bonds issued by the same entities because the priority of claims favors the bondholders. The value of an equity investment follows the same discounted cash flow principles, however. Thus, the value of the equity investment in an asset in a fixed life of N years—say, an office building—can be written as follows:

$$\text{Value of Equity in Finite-Life Asset} = \sum_{t=1}^{t=N} \frac{E(FCFE_t)}{(1+k_e)^N}$$
$$+ \frac{\text{Value of Equity in Asset at End of Life}}{(1+k_e)^N}$$

where $E(FCFE_t)$ is the expected cash flow to equity investors after making debt payments in period t; k_e is the rate of return that the equity investor in this asset would demand, given the riskiness of the cash flows, and the value of the equity at the end of the asset's life is the value of the asset net of the debt outstanding on it. The value of the entire asset, not just the equity in it, can also be estimated by using the cumulated cash flows to all claim holders on the assets (cash flow to the firm) and discounting at the weighted average of their required rates of return (cost of capital):

$$\text{Value of Finite-Life Asset} = \sum_{t=1}^{t=N} \frac{E(FCFF)}{(1+k_c)^t} + \frac{\text{Value of Asset at End of Life}}{(1+k_c)^N}$$

where $E(FCFF_t)$ is the expected cash flow on the asset prior to payments to any of the claim holders, and k_c is the cost of capital. Note, however, that the value of the equity can be obtained by subtracting the value of the nonequity claims (such as debt) from this value.

Equity investments in entities with infinite lives can be assessed as the present value of the cash flows over the perpetuity:

$$\text{Value of Equity in Infinite-Life Asset} = \sum_{t=1}^{t=\infty} \frac{E(FCFE_t)}{(1+k_e)^t}.$$

Practically speaking, cash flows cannot be estimated forever, but valuation models draw on a present-value relationship that proves useful in getting closure in these models. The present value of a cash flow growing at a constant rate forever can be written in terms of the expected cash flow next period, the discount rate, and the expected growth rate:

$$\text{Present Value of Cash Flow growing at constant rate forever} = \frac{E(CF_1)}{r - g},$$

where CF_1 is the cash flow one period from now, r is the discount rate, and g is the growth rate forever. Thus, the value of the equity investment in a firm growing at a constant rate forever (called a stable growth rate) can be assessed using this model:

$$\text{Value of Equity in Infinite-Life Asset with stable growth} = \frac{E(FCFE_1)}{k_e - g_n},$$

where g_n is the expected growth rate in cash flows to equity forever. Note that because the growth rate has to be sustainable forever, it cannot exceed the growth rate of the economy in which the firm operates, and this constraint will always ensure that the growth rate will be less than the cost of equity (which has incorporated into it a riskless rate). The value of the asset (rather than just the equity in it) can be estimated using the same approach:

$$\text{Value of Infinite-Life Asset with stable growth} = \frac{E(FCFF_1)}{kc - g_n},$$

where g_n is the growth rate in cash flows to the asset forever. In the more general framework, where the asset is a business that may be growing currently at a rate far greater than the stable growth rate, the model described above is used to get the terminal value at the end of the period of high growth:

$$\begin{matrix} \text{Value of Equity in} \\ \text{high-growth business} \end{matrix} = \sum_{t=1}^{t=N} \frac{E(FCFE_t)}{(1+k_e)^t} + \frac{\text{Terminal Value of Equity}_N}{(1+k_e)^N},$$

where the high growth is expected to last N periods, and the terminal value of equity at the end of N periods is estimated using the constant-growth model described above. The value of the entire business can be estimated as well:

$$\text{Value of high-growth business} = \sum_{t=1}^{t=N} \frac{E(FCFF_t)}{(1+k_c)^t} + \frac{\text{Terminal Value of Business}_N}{(1+k_c)^N}.$$

The approach is general enough to apply to all firms, ranging from stable firms with large earnings and cash flows, to high-growth firms that might have negative cash flows currently but are expected to have positive cash flows in the future, or to troubled firms that may be losing money currently but are expected to turn around in the future.

Inputs to Valuation

In this section, we examine in more detail the process by which we estimate the inputs to discounted cash flow models—the cash flows themselves, the growth rate in these cash flows, and the discount rates.

Cash Flows

There are two basic cash flows that investors can choose to discount: (1) cash flows to equity investments or (2) cash flows to the firm. In the strictest sense, the only cash flow an equity investor gets out of a publicly traded firm is the dividend; models that use the dividends as cash flows are called *dividend discount models*. A broader definition of cash flows to equity would be the cash flows left over after the cash flow claims of nonequity investors in the firm have been met (interest and principal payments to debt holders, and preferred dividends) and reinvestment. Through reinvestment, enough cash flows back into the firm to sustain the projected growth in cash flows. This is called the free cash flow to equity (FCFE), and models that use these cash flows are called *FCFE discount models*. (See Figure 8-1.)

The cash flow to the firm, or the cumulative cash flow to all claim holders in the firm, is obtained by adding the free cash flows to equity to the cash flows to debt and preferred stock. A far simpler method is to estimate the cash flow prior to debt payment by subtracting from the after-tax operating income the net investment needed to sustain growth. This cash flow is called the free cash flow to the firm (FCFF), and the models that use these cash flows are called *FCFF models*. (See Figure 8-2.)

Expected Growth

Although the expected growth rate is an input in most valuation models, it is itself an output of two variables that are determined by the firm being valued: (1) how much of the earnings are reinvested back into the firm and (2) how well those earnings are reinvested. In the equity valuation model, this expected growth rate is a product of the retention ratio (i.e., the proportion of net income not paid out to stockholders) and the return on equity on the projects undertaken with that money. In the firm valuation model, the expected growth rate is a product of the reinvestment rate (the proportion of after-tax operating

FIGURE 8-1   Estimating free cash flow to equity for a firm: General Electric

General Electric (GE) reported net income of $6,777 million in 1995. In the same year, it had capital expenditures of $6,447 million and depreciation of $3,594 million. Noncash working capital increased by $125 million during the year and was $1.5 billion at year-end. The year-end market value of equity at GE, obtained by multiplying the number of shares outstanding (1,651 million) by the share price ($92.375), was $152 billion. Outstanding debt was $115 billion. Analysts were estimating that earnings would grow 10 percent in 1996. If we assume that capital expenditure, depreciation, and working capital all grow at the same rate as earnings, and that GE maintains its market value debt ratio at 1995 levels, the free cash flow to equity in 1996 can be estimated as follows:

	1995	1996 (Est.)
Net Income	$6,777	$7,455
Less: (Net Capital Expenditures) (1 - Debt Ratio)	1,624	1,787
(Change in Working Capital) (1 - Debt Ratio)	71	85
Free Cash Flow to Equity	5,082	5,583
Information Used:		
Net Capital Expenditures	$2,853	$3,138
Change in Working Capital	125	150
Debt Ratio	43.07%	43.07%

The difference between capital expenditures and depreciation is referred to as net capital expenditures. When added to the change in noncash working capital, it provides a measure of how much GE has available to reinvest, to create future growth. We look at only the equity portion of this investment by netting out the debt portion.

FIGURE 8-2   Estimating free cash flow to the firm: General Electric

Continuing with the example of General Electric, for which we estimated free cash flows to equity in 1996, a similar estimate can be made of cash flows to the firm, using the same inputs as for the free cash flows to equity. The additional information that is provided is that GE had earnings before interest and taxes (EBIT) of $16.339 billion in 1995 and expected these earnings to grow 10 percent in 1996. The free cash flow to the firm can then be estimated as follows:

	1995	1996 (Est.)
EBIT (1 - Tax Rate)	$10,457	$11,503
Less: Net Capital Expenditures	2,853	3,138
Change in Working Capital	125	150
Free Cash Flow to the Firm	7,479	8,214
Information Used:		
Tax Rate	36%	36%
Net Capital Expenditures	$2,853	$3,138
Change in Working Capital	125	150

Unlike the calculation of free cash flow to equity in Figure 8-1, the entire amount of net capital expenditures and working capital change is subtracted from after-tax operating income to arrive at the free cash flow to the firm.

FIGURE 8-3   Estimating expected growth in earnings per share (EPS) and after-tax operating income: General Electric

---

The expected growth in earnings per share at General Electric (GE) can be estimated using the retention ratio (the percentage of net income reinvested in the company) and the expected return on equity. If we assume that the 1995 estimates for these numbers hold, then:

Retention ratio = 58%.
Return on equity = 23.4%.
Expected growth rate in earnings per share = (0.58) (0.234) = 13.57%.

The expected growth rate in operating income is a little more involved. It requires an estimation of the reinvestment rate, which in 1995 was:

Reinvestment rate   = (Net capital expenditures + Change in WC)/ EBIT (1–t)
                    = (2853+125)/10,457 = 28.48%.
Return on capital = EBIT (1–t)/ Average BV of capital = 10,457/83,408 = 12.54%.
Expected growth rate in operating income = (.2848) (12.54%) = 3.57%.

Leverage allows the growth rate in earnings per share to be so much greater than the growth rate in operating income. We are implicitly assuming that the current returns on book value of equity and capital are good measures of what GE will make in the future. To the degree that this is not true, estimates of returns on equity and capital on future projects have to be used instead.

---

income that goes into net new investments) and the return on capital earned on these investments. (See Figure 8-3.)

Discount Rates

In Chapter Three, a number of risk and return models were introduced. These models, such as the capital asset pricing model (CAPM) and the arbitrage pricing model (APM), look different in their final forms and make different assumptions, they agree on these fundamental principles:

1. The risk in an investment that should drive discount rates is the *nondiversifiable or market risk*. In the CAPM, this market risk is measured using the beta of the asset relative to a portfolio that includes all assets traded in that market (the *market portfolio*). In the APM, the market risk is measured relative to multiple macroeconomic factors, and each asset has a beta relative to each factor.

2. The average of the beta(s) in the CAPM/APM across all assets is 1.

3. The expected return on any investment can be obtained by adding to the riskless rate the product of the beta and the risk premium on the market portfolio in the CAPM, and the sum of the products of the betas and the risk premiums relative to each macroeconomic factor in the APM. This expected return, for an equity investment, is the *cost of equity*.

FIGURE 8-4   Estimating costs of equity and capital: General Electric

In 1995, General Electric's equity had a beta of 1.15 and its debt was AAA-rated. Given the long-term government bond rate of 7 percent at that time, the cost of equity and the cost of capital can be estimated as follows.

The cost of equity is estimated using the long-term bond rate, the beta, and a risk premium for stocks over bonds of 5.5 percent, based on historical data:

Cost of equity = 7% + 1.15 (5.5%) = 13.33%.

The cost of debt is obtained by adding a default premium of 0.30 percent to the long-term government bond rate, based on the AAA-rating, and adjusting for the tax benefits of debt, based on the marginal corporate tax rate of 36 percent.

After-tax cost of debt = 7.30% (1–.36) = 4.67%.

Finally, the market values of debt and equity are obtained:

Market value of equity = 1,651 million shares ° $92.375 = $152 billion.
Market value of debt = $115 billion.
Cost of capital = 13.33% (152/(152+115)) + 4.67% (115/(115+152)) = 9.60%.

(As a contrast, the book value of equity was only $32 billion, which would have yielded a cost of capital of around 7.5 percent.)

The *cost of capital* can be obtained by taking an average of the cost of equity, estimated as above, and the after-tax cost of borrowing, weighted by market value. Book value weights are sometimes used, but doing so violates a basic principle of valuation, which is: At a fair value,[3] one should be indifferent between buying and selling. (See Figure 8-4.)

Limitations of Discounted Cash Flow (DCF) Valuation

For several reasons, portfolio managers may desist from using discounted cash flow valuation:

1. Discounted cash flow valuation is the most information-intensive of the valuation approaches, which may make it unsuitable for portfolio managers who have to pick from large universes of assets.

2. It requires inputs for many years into the future, and the inherent uncertainty in these estimates leads some to conclude that valuation is not a particularly productive exercise. (I would argue otherwise. Not doing a discounted cash flow valuation does not make the uncertainty go away; it just sweeps it under the carpet.)

3. It is likely to reveal the analysts' biases. Because the value can be moved around by changing one of two inputs in the process, it is not unusual to see valuations change to reflect the strong prior view that the analyst

might have. (Here again, I would argue that discounted cash flow valuation is not unique. All valuation approaches will be colored by the analysts' biases. In fact, by forcing analysts to be explicit about their assumptions, discounted cash flow valuation may be more successful than other approaches in revealing these biases to outsiders.)

Usage and Empirical Evidence

The usage of discounted cash flow models among portfolio managers seems to be fairly limited. A survey of practitioners[4] reported that few portfolio managers used discounted cash flow valuation as their primary tool for picking undervalued assets. One reason may be the difficulty of applying time and information-intensive valuation techniques to large universes of stocks. Another may be the failure of the model to consider market moods and perceptions, which some contrarians may view as a strength, but which may still lead the analyst to find all stocks in some sectors to be overvalued. For a portfolio manager who has to be invested in equities, this may not be a practical solution. Finally, investment success with discounted cash flow valuation requires more than skill at valuation; other investors must come to the same realization and adjust the price toward the value. If the analysts' predictions of earnings and cash flows are on the mark, this will happen eventually, but it might not happen in the near future. Portfolio managers, who are often evaluated on a short-term basis, may not have the luxury of time as an ally.

Relatively few studies have examined whether asset selection using discounted cash flow valuation yields excess returns. Part of the reason for the paucity of studies is that any test of whether DCF valuation pays off requires that large numbers of assets must be valued using discounted cash flow valuation at points in time, and the excess returns in the following periods must be correlated with these valuations. A study in the *Financial Analysts Journal*[5] noted that using the dividend discount model allowed investors to earn excess returns, but the stocks that emerged as undervalued in these models tended to be stocks with low price–earnings ratios and high dividend yields, which, as we will see in the next section, are correlated with excess returns.

RELATIVE VALUATION

In intrinsic valuation, the objective is to find assets that are priced below what they should be, given their cash flow, growth, and risk characteristics. In relative valuation, the philosophical focus is on finding assets that are cheap or expensive relative to how "similar" assets are being priced by the market right now. It is therefore entirely possible that an asset that is expensive on an intrinsic value basis may be cheap on a relative basis.

Standardized Values and Multiples

To compare the valuations of "similar" assets in the market, we need to standardize the values in some way. They can be standardized relative to: the earnings that they generate, the book value or replacement value of the assets themselves, or the revenues that they generate. Each approach is used widely and has strong adherents.

Earnings Multiples

One of the more intuitive ways to think of the value of any asset is as a multiple of the earnings it generates. When buying a stock, it is common to look at the price paid as a multiple of the earnings per share generated by the company. This *price–earnings ratio* can be estimated using current earnings per share (called a trailing PE) or expected earnings per share in the next year (called a forward PE). When buying a business (as opposed to just equity in the business), it is common to examine the value of the business as a multiple of the operating income (or EBIT) or the operating cash flow (EBITDA). A lower multiple is better than a higher one, but these multiples will be affected by the growth potential and the risk of the business being acquired.

Book Value or Replacement Value Multiples

Markets provide one estimate of the value of a business; accountants often provide a very different estimate of the same variable. This latter estimate, called the *book value*, is driven by accounting rules and is heavily influenced by what was paid originally for each asset, and any accounting adjustments (such as depreciation) made since. Investors often look at the relationship between the price they pay for a stock and the book value of their equity (or net worth) as a measure of how over- or undervalued a stock is; the price–book value ratio that emerges can vary widely across sectors, depending on the growth potential and the quality of the investments in each sector. When valuing businesses, this ratio is estimated using the value of the firm and the book value of *all* assets (rather than just the equity). For those who believe that book value is not a good measure of the true value of the assets, an alternative is to use the replacement cost of the assets; the ratio of the value of the firm to replacement cost is called *Tobin's Q*.

Revenue Multiples

Earnings and book value are accounting measures, and they are affected by accounting rules and principles. An alternative approach, which is far less affected by these factors, is to look at the relationship between the value of an asset and the revenues it generates. For equity investors, this ratio is the *price–sales ratio:* the market value per share is divided by the revenues generated per share. This ratio can be modified as the *value–sales ratio,* where the numerator becomes the total value of the firm. This ratio, again, varies widely across sectors, largely as a function of the profit margins in each sector. The advantage of these multiples, however, is that comparison of firms in different markets becomes far easier, even when different accounting systems have been implemented.

The Fundamentals behind Multiples

One reason commonly given for using relative valuation is that it requires far fewer assumptions than does discounted cash flow valuation. In my view, this is a misconception. The difference between discounted cash flow valuation and relative valuation is that analysts' assumptions have to be made explicit in the former and they can remain implicit in the latter. It is important that we know what variables drive multiples; these are the variables we have to control for when comparing these multiples across firms.

To "look under the hood" of equity and firm value multiples, we will go back to fairly simple discounted cash flow models for equity and firm value, and use them to derive our multiples. Thus, the simplest discounted cash flow model for equity—a stable growth dividend discount model—would suggest that the value of equity is:

$$\text{Value of Equity} = P_0 = \frac{DPS_1}{k_e - g_n},$$

where DPS_1 is the expected dividend in the next year, k_e is the cost of equity, and g_n is the expected stable growth rate. Dividing both sides by the earnings, we obtain the discounted cash flow model for the price–earnings ratio (PE) for a stable growth firm:

$$\frac{P_0}{EPS_0} = PE = \frac{\text{Payout Ratio} * (1 + g_n)}{k_e - g_n}.$$

Dividing both sides by the book value of equity, we can estimate the price/book value ratio (PBV) for a stable growth firm:

$$\frac{P_0}{BV_0} = PBV = \frac{\text{ROE} \degree \text{Payout Ratio} \degree (1 + g_n)}{k_e - g_n}.$$

where ROE is the return on equity. Dividing by the sales per share, the price–sales ratio (PS) for a stable growth firm can be estimated as a function of its profit margin, payout ratio, profit margin, and expected growth:

$$\frac{P_0}{\text{Sales}_0} = PS = \frac{\text{Profit Margin} \degree \text{Payout Ratio} \degree (1 + g_n)}{k_e - g_n}.$$

We can do a similar analysis from the perspective of firm valuation. The value of a firm in stable growth can be written as:

$$\text{Value of Firm} = V_0 = \frac{FCFF_1}{k_c - g_n}.$$

Dividing both sides by the expected free cash flow to the firm yields the value/FCFF multiple for a stable growth firm:

$$\frac{V_0}{FCFF_1} = \frac{1}{k_c - g_n}.$$

Because the free cash flow of the firm is the after-tax operating income netted against the net capital expenditures and working capital needs of the firm, the multiples of EBIT, after-tax EBIT and EBITDA, can also be similarly estimated. The value/EBITDA multiple, for instance, can be written as follows:

$$\frac{\text{Value}}{\text{EBITDA}} = \frac{(1-t)}{k_c - g} + \frac{\text{Depr}\,(t)\,/\,\text{EBITDA}}{k_c - g} - \frac{\text{CEx/EBITDA}}{k_c - g} - \frac{\Delta\,\text{Working Capital/EBITDA}}{k_c - g}.$$

The point of this analysis is not to suggest that we go back to using discounted cash flow valuation, but that we get a sense of the variables that may cause these multiples to vary across firms in the same sector. An analyst who is blind to these variables might conclude that a stock with a PE of 8 is cheaper than one with a PE of 12, when the true reason may be that the latter has higher expected growth. Or, a stock with a P/BV ratio of 0.7 may seem cheaper than one with a P/BV ratio of 1.5, when the true reason may be that the latter has a much higher return on equity. Table 8-1 lists the multiples that are widely used and the variables that drive them. The variable that is, in my view, most significant for each multiple is set in bold type. I call it the *companion variable* for this multiple; it is the one variable I would need to know in order to use this multiple to find under- or overvalued assets.

TABLE 8-1   Multiples and companion variables (bold type)

Multiple	Determining Variables
Price/earnings ratio	**Growth,** Payout, Risk
Price/book value ratio	Growth, Payout, Risk, **ROE**
Price/sales ratio	Growth, Payout, Risk, **Net Margin**
Value/EBIT Value/EBIT $(1 - t)$ Value/EBITDA	Growth, **Net Capital Expenditure Needs,** Leverage, Risk
Value/sales	Growth, Net Capital Expenditure Needs, Leverage, Risk, **Operating Margin**
Value/book capital	Growth, Leverage, Risk and **ROC**

The Use of Comparables

Most analysts who use multiples use them in conjunction with "comparable" firms, to form conclusions about whether firms are fairly valued or not. At the risk of being simplistic, the analysis begins with two decisions: (1) the multiple that will be used in the analysis, and (2) the group of firms that will comprise the comparable firms. The multiple is computed for each of the comparable firms, and then an average is calculated. To evaluate an individual firm, the analyst compares its multiple to the average; if it is significantly different, the analyst makes a subjective judgment on whether the firm's individual characteristics (growth, risk, and so on) may explain the difference. Thus, a firm may have a PE ratio of 22 in a sector where the average PE is only 15, but the analyst may conclude that this difference can be justified by the fact that the firm has higher growth potential than the average firm in the sector. If, in the analyst's judgment, the difference on the multiple cannot be explained by the fundamentals, the firm will be viewed as overvalued (if its multiple is higher than the average) or undervalued (if its multiple is lower than the average).

Choosing Comparables

The heart of this process is the selection of the firms that comprise comparable firms. From a valuation perspective, a comparable firm is one with similar cash flows, growth potential, and risk. If life were simple, the value of a firm would be analyzed by looking at how an exactly identical firm—in terms of risk, growth, and cash flows—is priced. In most analyses, however, a comparable firm is defined to be one in the same business as the firm being analyzed. If there are enough firms in the sector to allow for it, this list will be pruned further, using other criteria; for instance, only firms of similar size may be considered. Implicitly, the assumption here is that firms in the same sector have similar risk, growth, and cash flow profiles, and therefore can be compared with much more legitimacy. This approach becomes more difficult to apply under two conditions:

1. When there are relatively few firms in a sector. In most markets outside the United States, the number of publicly traded firms in a particular sector, especially if it is defined narrowly, is small.
2. When the differences in risk, growth, and cash flow profiles across firms within a sector are large. Thus, hundreds of computer software companies are listed in the United States, but there are wide differences across these firms.

The tradeoff is simple. Defining a sector more broadly increases the number of firms that enter the comparable firms list, but it results in a more diverse group.

Controlling for Differences across Firms

Because it is impossible to find firms that are identical to the one being valued, we have to find ways of controlling for differences across firms in relevant ways. The advantage of the discounted cash flow models introduced in the prior section is that they give a clear idea of the fundamental determinants of each multiple, and therefore of what we should be controlling for. The process of controlling for the variables can range from very simple approaches, such as modifying the multiples to take into account the differences on one key variable, to more complex approaches that allow for differences on more than one variable.

Let us start with the simple approaches. Here, the basic multiple is modified to take into account the most important variable determining that multiple. Thus, the PE ratio is divided by the expected growth rate in EPS for a company, to come up with a growth-adjusted PE ratio. Similarly, the PBV ratio is divided by the ROE to come up with a value ratio, and the price sales ratio is divided by the net margin. These modified ratios are then compared across companies in a sector. Implicitly, it is assumed that these firms are comparable on all the other dimensions of value, besides the one being controlled for. (See Figure 8-5.)

When firms vary on more than one dimension, it becomes difficult to modify the multiples to take into account the differences across firms. It is, however, feasible to run regressions of the multiples against the variables and then use these regressions to get predicted values for each firm. This approach works reasonably well when the number of comparable firms is large and the

FIGURE 8-5 **Comparing PE ratios and growth rates across firms: Software companies**

Listed here are the PE ratios and expected analysts' consensus on growth rates over 5 years for a selected list of software companies.

Company	PE	Expected Growth Rate	PE/Expected Growth (PEG)
Acclaim Entertainment	13.70	23.60%	0.58
Activision	75.20	40.00	1.88
Broderbund	32.30	26.00	1.24
Davidson Associates	44.30	33.80	1.31
Edmark	88.70	37.50	2.37
Electronic Arts	33.50	22.00	1.52
The Learning Co.	33.50	28.80	1.16
Maxis	73.20	30.00	2.44
Minnesota Educational	69.20	28.30	2.45
Sierra On-Line	43.80	32.00	1.37

Although comparisons on the PE ratio alone do not factor in the differences in expected growth, the PEG ratio in the last column can be viewed as a growth-adjusted PE ratio, and, by this measure, Acclaim Entertainment is the cheapest company in this group and Minnesota Educational is the most expensive. This conclusion holds only if these firms are of equivalent risk, however.

relationship between the multiple and variable is strong. When these conditions do not hold, a few outliers can cause the coefficients to change dramatically and make the predictions much less reliable. (See Figure 8-6.) Both approaches described above assume that the relationship between a multiple and the variables driving value is linear. Because this is not necessarily true, it is possible to run nonlinear versions of these regressions.

Expanding the Comparable Firm Universe

Searching for comparable firms within the sector in which a firm operates is fairly restrictive, especially when there are relatively few firms in the sector or when a firm operates in more than one sector. When the definition of a comparable firm is not "one that is in the same business" but "one that has the same growth, risk, and cash flow characteristics as the firm being analyzed," it is unclear why we have to stay sector-specific. A software firm should be comparable to an automobile firm, if we can control for differences in the fundamentals.

The regression approach that we introduced in the previous section allows us to control for differences on those variables that we believe cause differences in multiples across firms. Using the minimalist version of the regression

FIGURE 8-6   PBV ratios and ROE: The oil sector

Price/Book Value ratios of oil companies and reports on their returns on equity and expected growth rates are detailed here.

Company Name	P/BV	ROE	Expected Growth
Total ADR B	0.90	4.10	9.50%
Giant Industries	1.10	7.20	7.81
Royal Dutch Petroleum ADR	1.10	12.30	5.50
Tesoro Petroleum	1.10	5.20	8.00
Petrobras	1.15	3.37	15
YPF ADR	1.60	13.40	12.50
Ashland	1.70	10.60	7
Quaker State	1.70	4.40	17
Coastal	1.80	9.40	12
Elf Aquitaine ADR	1.90	6.20	12
Holly	2.00	20.00	4
Ultramar Diamond Shamrock	2.00	9.90	8
Witco	2.00	10.40	14
World Fuel Services	2.00	17.20	10
Elcor	2.10	10.10	15
Imperial Oil	2.20	8.60	16
Repsol ADR	2.20	17.40	14
Shell Transport & Trading ADR	2.40	10.50	10
Amoco	2.60	17.30	6
Phillips Petroleum	2.60	14.70	7.50
ENI SpA ADR	2.80	18.30	10
Mapco	2.80	16.20	12
Texaco	2.90	15.70	12.50
British Petroleum ADR	3.20	19.60	8
Tosco	3.50	13.70	14

Because these firms differ on both growth and return on equity, we ran a regression of PBV ratios on both variables:

$$PBV = -0.11 + 11.22 \, (ROE) + 7.87 \, (\text{Expected Growth}) \qquad R^2 = 60.88\%$$
$$\quad\;\; (5.79) \qquad\quad (2.83)$$

The numbers in parentheses are t-statistics, and they suggest that the relationship between PBV ratios and both variables in the regression is statistically significant. R^2 indicates the percentage of the differences in PBV ratios that is explained by the independent variables. Finally, the regression itself can be used to get predicted PBV ratios for the companies in the list. Thus, the predicted PBV ratio for Repsol ADR would be:

$$\text{Predicted PBV}_{\text{Repsol}} = -0.11 + 11.22 \, (.1740) + 7.87 \, (.14) = 2.94.$$

The actual PBV ratio for Repsol was 2.20, which would suggest that the stock was undervalued by roughly 25 percent.

equations here, we should be able to regress PE, PBV, and PS ratios against the variables that should affect them:

$$PE = a + b \text{ (Growth)} + c \text{ (Payout ratios)} + d \text{ (Risk)}.$$
$$PBV = a + b \text{ (Growth)} + c \text{ (Payout ratios)} + d \text{ (Risk)} + e \text{ (ROE)}.$$
$$PS = a + b \text{ (Growth)} + c \text{ (Payout ratios)} + d \text{ (Risk)} + e \text{ (Margin)}.$$

It is, however, possible that the proxies that we use for risk (beta), growth (expected growth rate), and cash flow (payout) may be imperfect and that the relationship may not be linear. To deal with these limitations, we can add more variables to the regression—e.g., the size of the firm may operate as a good proxy for risk—and use transformations of the variables to allow for nonlinear relationships.

We ran these regressions for PE, PBV, and PS ratios across publicly listed firms in the United States in March 1997 twice: once, observing individual firms, and then with the firms aggregated into sectors (which reduces the noise in the estimates). The sample, which had 4,527 firms, yielded the regressions reported in Table 8-2. These regressions can then be used to get predicted PE,

TABLE 8-2   Regressions of multiples on fundamentals: Marketwide

Individual Firms (Approximately 1,400 Firms)

PE = 11.07 + 27.82 g + 0.7328 Payout + 2.9465 Beta   ($R^2 = 0.0957$)
   (9.29) (10.27)   (0.85)   (2.98)

PBV = −1.50 + 6.51 g + 0.61 Payout + 0.3292 Beta + 16.54 ROE   ($R^2 = 0.67$)
   (6.67) (11.71) (3.96)   (1.80)   (50.93)

PS = −1.44 + 7.55 g − 0.22 Payout − 0.2166 Beta + 30.86 MGN   ($R^2 = 0.72$)
   (6.96) (16.31) (1.52)   (1.28)   (53.14)

Aggregated Regression (89 Industries)

PE = 22.73 + 45.01 g − 9.28 Payout − 7.4870 Beta   ($R^2 = 0.3847$)
   (6.35) (3.00) (1.69)   (1.69)

PBV = −0.35 + 6.32 g − 0.06 Payout + 0.1666 Beta + 11.60 ROE   ($R^2 = 0.53$)
   (0.50) (3.54) (0.11)   (0.33)   (9.10)

PS = 0.02 + 5.76 g − 0.82 Payout − 0.6755 Beta + 20.76 MGN   ($R^2 = 0.61$)
   (0.04) (3.74) (1.69)   (1.60)   (11.21)

(t − statistics are in parentheses.)
    g = Expected growth in earnings over the next 5 years.
    PE = Price/Current EPS: Companies with negative earnings were eliminated from the sample.
    PBV = Price/Book Value per share: Companies with negative BV were eliminated.
    PS = Price/Sales per share.
  Payout = DPS/EPS: From the most recent year; if negative, it is set to 100 percent.
    Beta = Betas based on 5 years of monthly data.
  MGN = Net Income/Sales.
  ROE = Net Income/BV of Equity.

PBV, and PS ratios for each firm, which, in turn, can be compared to the actual multiples to find under- and overvalued firms.

The first advantage of this approach over the "subjective" comparison across firms in the same sector, as described in the previous section, is that it does quantify, based on actual market data, the degree to which higher growth or risk should affect the multiples. It is true that these estimate are noisy, but this noise is a reflection of the reality that many analysts choose not to face when they make subjective judgments. The second advantage is that, by looking at all firms in the universe, this approach allows analysts operating in sectors that have relatively few firms to make more powerful comparisons. Finally, the approach gets analysts past the tunnel vision induced by comparing firms within a sector, when the entire sector may be under- and overvalued.

Screening for Value

For as long as they have been investing, investors have used multiples of one kind or another to find misvalued assets in markets. Portfolio managers, who have to pick from very large universes of assets, often use simple screens to prune the universe down to a manageable portfolio. For instance, a portfolio manager may screen 4,500 stocks for those with PE ratios less than 12, market capitalization less than $2 billion, and institutional holdings less than 25 percent, to arrive at a portfolio of perhaps 150 stocks. If this is still too large a portfolio, the screens can be made tighter. As data on the financial details of firms have become more accessible, screens have become easier to use. The key decisions then involve which screens to use and what priority to assign to them (primarily or secondary).

A large body of literature has looked at inefficiencies in financial markets that can be of use in making these decisions. Before presenting this evidence, here are some important caveats:

1. To test whether a screen works, we have to compare the actual returns obtained from a portfolio, using the screen, with the expected returns on that portfolio. To get the expected returns on a portfolio, we need to measure the risk on that portfolio and come up with the return we should have made, given that risk. Though there are risk and return models that are used in these studies, there is no consensus on the right model for risk, and significant noise in estimation is present within each of these models. Thus, what a study calls an "excess return" from a screen may really be the result of the use of the wrong model for risk and return.

2. Measuring actual returns is not as simple as it sounds. Most studies assume that you can buy at a price listed on a database (a closing price or a trading

price) and sell later at another listed price, but there are three potential pitfalls. First, it might not be possible to execute an order (buy or sell) at the listed price; this will be the case, for instance, when a strategy requires short selling and there are practical and institutional restrictions on short selling. Second, even if it is possible to execute, there might be a price impact that reduces the return; buying the asset might push up the price of the asset, and selling it may push it down, resulting in much lower returns in practice. Third, there are transactions costs—brokerage fees, and, more importantly, the bid–ask spread—that may also reduce the returns.

3. Even if the actual returns, measured correctly, are greater than the expected returns, and are commensurate with the risk, the strategy itself might not make money in practice because it can be imitated by others at little cost. Thus, the excess returns that inspired the strategy may be short-lived.

These three factors may explain a major contradiction in empirical analyses of investment strategies. Literally dozens of strategies, at least in the empirical studies that test them, seem to create excess returns for investors. There are, however, very few active investors who make excess returns, often using these same strategies. It is difficult and daunting to list all of the empirical irregularities that investigators have found in asset returns, but we will summarize some of the key results in two groups:

- The primary inefficiencies that have been uncovered over time in financial markets;
- The secondary inefficiencies that also seem to create excess returns, though the magnitude may be smaller and the results more contested.

Primary Inefficiencies

Looking at the cross section of empirical studies of investment strategies, four strong "anomalies" seem to have persisted over time:

1. Small companies (measured in terms of market capitalization) seem to earn higher returns, after adjusting for risk, than larger companies.
2. Low price–earnings ratio stocks seem to earn excess returns relative to high price–earnings ratio stocks after adjusting for risk.
3. Low price–book value stocks seem to provide a much better tradeoff between risk and returns than high price–book value stocks.
4. Low price–sales ratio stocks seem to be much better investments, when returns and risk are considered, than high price–sales ratio stocks.

The Size Effect   Studies have consistently found that smaller firms (in terms of market value of equity) earn higher returns than larger firms of equivalent risk, where risk is defined in terms of the market beta. Figure 8-7 summarizes returns for stocks in ten market value classes, for the period from 1927 to 1983.

The size of the small-firm premium, while it has varied across time, has been generally positive. Figure 8-8 summarizes small stock premiums from 1926 to 1990.

The small-firm effect was strongest between 1974 and 1983. Professor Jeremy Siegel[6] has argued in recent years that there is no small-firm effect if this period is not considered. To us, though, this applies selective logic, since it throws out one set of outliers while preserving the other, which, in the case of small stocks, would be the most recent decade (1986–1996).

The small-firm premium uncovered in these studies has led to several possible explanations:

1. *The transactions cost of investing in small stocks is significantly higher than the transactions cost of investing in larger stocks, and the premiums are estimated prior to these costs.* While this is generally true, the differential transactions costs are unlikely to explain the magnitude of the premium across time, and are likely to become even less critical for longer investment horizons. The difficulties of replicating the small-firm premiums that are observed in the studies in real time are illustrated in Figure 8-9, which compares the returns on a hypothetical small-firm portfolio (CRSP Small Stocks) with the

FIGURE 8-7   Annual returns by size class: 1927–1983

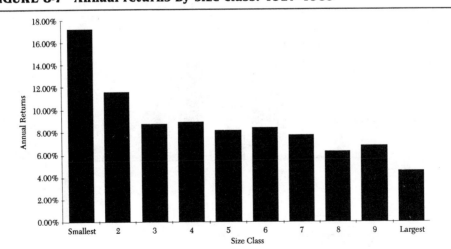

FIGURE 8-8   Small stock premiums from 1926 to 1990

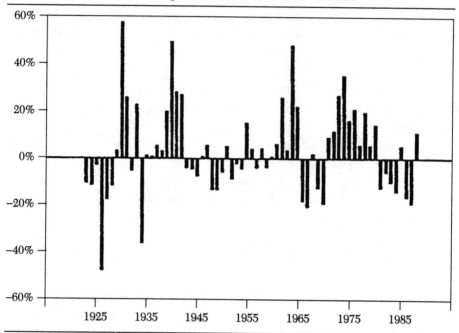

Source: *Stocks, Bonds, Bills, and Inflation 1991 Yearbook™*, Ibbotson Associates, Inc., Chicago (annually updates work by Roger G. Ibbotson and Rex A. Sinquefield).

FIGURE 8-9   Returns on CRSP small stocks versus DFA small stock fund

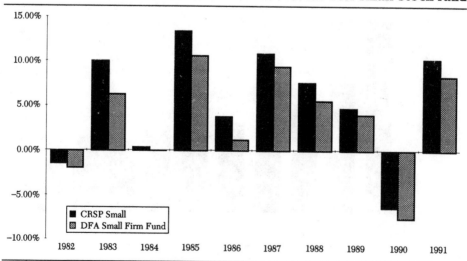

actual returns on a small-firm mutual fund (DFA Small Stock Fund), which passively invests in small stocks.

2. *The capital asset pricing model (CAPM) may not be the right model for risk, and betas may underestimate the true risk of small stocks. Thus, the small firm premium may really be a measure of the failure of beta to capture risk.* The additional risk associated with small stocks may come from several sources. First, the estimation risk associated with estimates of beta for small firms is much greater than the estimation risk associated with beta estimates for larger firms. The small-firm premium may be a reward for this additional estimation risk. Second, there may be additional risk in investing in small stocks because far less information is available on them. In fact, studies indicate that stocks that are neglected by analysts and institutional investors earn an excess return that parallels the small-firm premium.

There is evidence of a small-firm premium in markets outside the United States as well. Dimson and Marsh (1988)[7] examined stocks in the United Kingdom from 1955 to 1984 and found that the annual returns on small stocks exceeded those on large stocks by 7 percent annually over the period. Bergstrom, Frashure, and Chisholm (1991)[8] report a large size effect for French stocks (small stocks made 32.3 percent per year between 1975 and 1989, and large stocks made 23.5 percent a year), and a much smaller size effect in Germany. Hamao (1989)[9] reports a small-firm premium of 5.1 percent for Japanese stocks between 1971 and 1988.

Low Price–Earnings Ratio Stocks Investors have long argued that stocks with low price–earnings ratios are more likely to be undervalued and to earn excess returns. For instance, Ben Graham and Dodd,[10] in their investment classic *Security Analysis,* use low price–earnings ratios as a screen for finding undervalued stocks. Studies that have looked at the relationship between PE ratios and excess returns confirm these priors. Figure 8-10 summarizes annual returns by PE ratio classes of stocks from 1967 to 1988. Firms in the lowest PE ratio class earned an average return of 16.26 percent during the period; firms in the highest PE ratio class earned an average return of only 6.64 percent.

The excess returns earned by low PE ratio stocks persist in other international markets. Table 8-3 summarizes the results of studies that examined this phenomenon in markets outside the United States.

The excess returns earned by low price–earnings ratio stocks are difficult to justify by using a variation of the argument used for small stocks—that the risk of low PE ratio stocks is understated in the CAPM. Low PE ratio firms generally are characterized by low growth, large size, and stable businesses, all of which should work toward reducing their risk rather than increasing it. The

FIGURE 8-10 Annual returns by PE ratio class

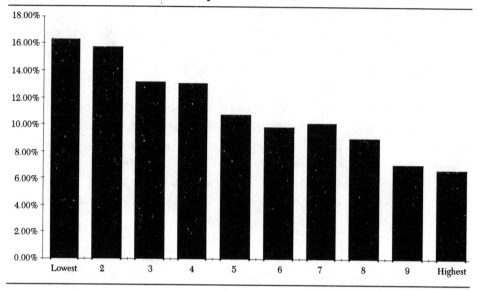

only explanation that can be given for this phenomenon, which is consistent with an efficient market, is that low PE ratio stocks generate large dividend yields, which would have created a larger tax burden in those years when dividends were taxed at higher rates.

Low Price–Book Value Ratio Stocks   Another statistic that is widely used by investors is the price–book value ratio. A low price–book value ratio has been considered a reliable indicator of undervaluation in firms. In studies that parallel

TABLE 8-3   Excess returns on low P/E ratio stocks by country: 1989–1994

Country	Annual Premium Earned by Lowest P/E Stocks (Bottom Quintile)
Australia	3.03%
France	6.40
Germany	1.06
Hong Kong	6.60
Italy	14.16
Japan	7.30
Switzerland	9.02
U.K.	2.40

Annual premium = Premium earned over an index of equally weighted stocks in that market between January 1, 1989, and December 31, 1994. These numbers were obtained from a Merrill Lynch Survey of Proprietary Indices.

those done on price–earnings ratios, a negative relationship has been found be-tween returns and price–book value ratios; that is, low price–book value ratio stocks earn higher returns than high price–book value ratio stocks.

Rosenberg, Reid, and Lanstein[11] (1985) found that the average returns on U.S. stocks are positively related to the ratio of a firm's book value to its mar-ket value. Between 1973 and 1984, the strategy of picking stocks with high book–price ratios (low price–book values) yielded an excess return of 36 basis points a month. Fama and French (1992),[12] in examining the cross section of expected stock returns between 1963 and 1990, established that the positive relationship between book–price ratios and average returns persists in both univariate and multivariate tests, and is even stronger than the size effect in explaining returns. They classified firms into twelve portfolios, on the basis of their book–price ratios. Firms in the lowest book–price (higher P/BV) class earned an average monthly return of 0.30 percent; firms in the highest book–price (lowest P/BV) class earned an average monthly return of 1.83 per-cent for the period from 1963 to 1990.

Chan, Hamao, and Lakonishok (1991)[13] found that the book–market ratio has a strong role in explaining the cross section of average returns on Japanese stocks. Capaul, Rowley, and Sharpe[14] (1993) extended the analysis of price–book value ratios across other international markets, and concluded that value stocks (stocks with low price–book value ratios) earned excess returns in every market that they analyzed, between 1981 and 1992. Their annualized esti-mates of the return differential earned by stocks with low price–book value ratios, over the market index, were as follows:

Country	Added Return to Low P/BV Portfolio
France	3.26%
Germany	1.39
Switzerland	1.17
United Kingdom	1.09
Japan	3.43
United States	1.06
Europe	1.30
Global	1.88

A caveat is in order. Fama and French (1992) point out that low price–book value ratios may operate as a measure of risk because firms with prices well below book value are more likely to be in trouble and go out of business. Investors therefore have to evaluate for themselves whether the additional returns made by such firms justify the additional risk taken on by investing in them.

Low Price–Sales Ratio Stocks   Screening stocks on the basis of price–sales multiples has been incorporated by some investors into their investment strategies. In recent years, evidence has been accumulating that this strategy may yield excess returns to investors. In a direct test of the price–sales ratio, Senchack and Martin[15] (1987) compared the performance of low price–sales ratio portfolios with low price–earnings ratio portfolios, and concluded that the low price–sales ratio portfolio outperformed the market but not the low price–earnings ratio portfolio. They also found that the low price–earnings ratio strategy earned more consistent returns than the low price–sales ratio strategy, and that the low price–sales ratio strategy was more biased toward picking smaller firms. Jacobs and Levy (1988)[16] tested the value of low price–sales ratios (standardized by the price–sales ratio of the industries in which the firms operated) as part of a general effort to disentangle the forces influencing equity returns. They concluded that low price–sales ratios, by themselves, yielded an excess return of 0.17 percent a month between 1978 and 1986, which was statistically significant. Even when other factors were thrown into the analysis,[17] the price–sales ratios remained a significant factor in explaining excess returns (together with price–earnings ratio and size).

The significance of profit margins in explaining price–sales ratios suggests that screening on the basis of both price–sales ratios and profit margins should be more successful at identifying undervalued securities. To test this proposition, the stocks on the New York Stock Exchange were screened on the basis of price–sales ratios and profit margins to create "undervalued" portfolios (price–sales ratios in the lowest quartile, and profit margins in the highest quartile) and "overvalued" portfolios (price–sales ratios in the highest quartile, and profit margins in the lowest quartile) at the end of each year from 1981 to 1990. The returns on these portfolios are summarized in Table 8-4.

TABLE 8-4   Returns on undervalued and overvalued portfolios

Year	Undervalued Portfolio	Overvalued Portfolio	S&P 500
1982	50.34%	17.72%	40.35%
1983	31.04	6.18	0.68
1984	12.33	−25.81	15.43
1985	53.75	28.21	30.97
1986	27.54	3.48	24.44
1987	−2.28	8.63	−2.69
1988	24.96	16.24	9.67
1989	16.64	17.00	18.11
1990	−30.35	−17.46	6.18
1991	91.20	55.13	31.74
1982–1991	23.76	15.48	17.49

During the period, the undervalued portfolios outperformed the overvalued portfolios in six out of the ten years. They earned an average of 8.28 percent more per year than the S&P 500.

Secondary Inefficiencies

In addition to these primary inefficiencies, researchers have uncovered a number of other factors that are correlated with returns. Three points are worth making about these findings:

1. Some of these factors are highly correlated with the four primary inefficiencies listed earlier. For instance, the finding that stocks that are followed by relatively few analysts do better than those followed by a host of analysts is closely related to the size effect; small firms tend to be followed by fewer analysts.
2. Given the volume of data on stock returns that we have accumulated over time, it is not surprising that we have found a number of variables that are correlated with returns.
3. The findings on some of these factors seem to be sensitive to how the test is set up and which period is examined.

Usage   Far more analysts use relative valuation, especially in equity research and portfolio management, than use discounted cash flow valuation, partly because of the ease with which relative valuation can be used to find under- or overvalued assets in large universes. Another reason for equity research analysts' attachment to multiples can be traced to the fact that they are asked to find the most undervalued securities in the sectors that they follow, not to make fundamental judgments about whether their sector itself is over- or undervalued. Similarly, investors who invest with equity money managers expect them to invest in the stocks that are most undervalued in a market, and not to pass judgment on whether the market itself is under- or overvalued. Finally, some analysts think that using multiples relieves them of the responsibility of making assumptions about variables such as net capital expenditures and growth in future years.

Limitations of Relative Valuation   The strengths of relative valuation are also its weaknesses. Relative valuation allows analysts and money managers to find undervalued assets with ease in any market, but it may also blind them to significant misvaluation in a sector or in the entire market. To provide an illustration, it would be possible, using multiples and comparables, to find "undervalued" stocks in a sector that is itself overvalued by 40 or 50 percent. Even if the relative valuation is done with care, all that this "undervaluation" implies is that, if there is a price correction in the sector, the undervalued stock will lose less in value than the comparable firms. Because the better choice for the investor would have to been to avoid the sector all together, relative valuation can lead to returns that are lower than would have been obtained by using intrinsic valuation models. Even when relative valuation is done on a marketwide basis, there is a risk that the entire market is priced too high, relative to its fundamentals, and an intrinsic valuation model may have exposed this undervaluation and allowed the investor to steer clear of the market.

Technical Analysis Models

Technical analysis refers to the use of price charts, trading volume, and other indicators based on market activity, to find under- and overvalued assets. Technical analysis is widely used by investors, but its value has been challenged not only by academics who have looked at the performance of some technical indicators but also by practitioners who use multiples or fundamentals. This "voodoo investing," they say, has no basis in either theory or evidence. In this section, we take a much more sympathetic view of technical analysis. It has many weaknesses, but some of its strengths may account for the following it has among investors.

Basis for Approach   To understand the basis for technical analysis, we went back to one of its early proponents. Levy (1967)[18] argued for technical analysis, noting that market value is determined by supply and demand, and that each is governed by both rational and irrational factors. The irrational factors cause stock prices to move in trends that persist over appreciable lengths of time, and the purpose of technical indicators is to detect shifts in these trends. Thus, all technical indicators are built on the assumption that markets are irrational and that technical indicators give early signals of these irrationalities, which can offer an advantage.

Historians who have examined the behavior of financial markets over time have challenged the assumption of a rationality that underlies much of efficient market theory. They point to the frequency which with speculative bubbles have formed in financial markets, as investors buy into fads or get-rich-quick schemes, and the crashes when these bubbles have burst. They suggest that there is nothing to prevent the recurrence of this phenomenon in today's financial markets because of evidence, in the literature, of irrationality on the part of market players in general.

Most experimental studies suggest that traders are rational, but examples of irrational behavior are included in some of these studies. In an experiment at the University of Arizona, traders were told that a payout would be declared after each trading day, determined randomly from four possibilities: zero, 8 cents, 28 cents, or 60 cents. The average payout was 24 cents. Thus, the share's expected value on the first trading day of a 15-day experiment was $3.60 (24°15); on the second day, it was $3.36, and so on. The traders were allowed to trade each day. The results of 60 such daily experiments are summarized in Figure 8-11.

There is clear evidence that a "speculative bubble" formed during periods 3 through 5, when prices exceeded expected values by a significant amount. The bubble ultimately burst, and prices approached expected value by the end of the period. If this is feasible in a simple market, where every investor obtains the same information, it is clearly feasible in complex financial markets, where there is much more differential information and much greater uncertainty about expected value.

Types of Technical Indicators   Because technical indicators are built on the premise of investor irrationality, it makes sense to classify these indicators according to their particular type of irrationality. Here are some of the relevant observations.

1. *Investors overreact to information announcements.* Research in experimental psychology suggests that people tend to overreact to unexpected and dramatic events. In revising their beliefs, individuals tend to overweight recent

FIGURE 8-11   Experimental study of price behavior

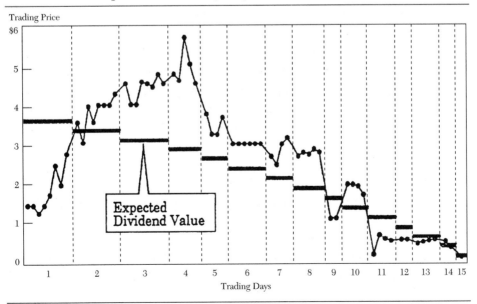

information and underweight prior data. Several technical indicators are built on these observations.

- *The odd-lot rule* looks at the proportion of odd-lot trades (i.e., trades of less than 100 shares) versus total trades. Because odd lots are usually traded by small investors, this rule indicates what small investors think about the stock. It then assumes that the small investors are wrong and pursues strategies opposite to their thinking.

- *The cash position of mutual funds,* a statistic that is widely reported, measures the cash held by mutual funds as a percentage of total funds. A low number here would indicate that fund managers are bullish about stocks, and a high number would indicate bearishness. Historically, the argument goes, mutual fund cash positions have been greatest at the bottom of a bear market and lowest at the peak of a bull market. Hence, investing against this statistic may be profitable.

- *Bullishness among investment advisers* is another widely used indicator. Again, it makes sense to buy when investment advisers are most bearish about a stock or a market, and to sell when they are most bullish.

2. *Investors' mood changes lead to shifts in demand and supply.* The notion that prices are determined by demand and supply is one that all investors would agree on, but some technical analysts argue that shifts in demand and supply can be detected by price and volume patterns. One indicator is the *breadth of the market,* which is a measure of the number of stocks in the market that have advanced, relative to those that have declined. Thus, a market that goes up with little breadth is considered to be a market on the verge of a downward shift in demand (and thus in price). For individual stocks, scores of price patterns are viewed as precursors of shifts in demand and hence in prices—for instance, when the price breaks through a *resistance line* (viewed as a bullish sign) or through a *support line* (viewed as a bearish sign), or when the price exceeds the *moving average* of prices over some prior period (viewed as a bullish sign) or drops below the moving average (viewed as a bearish sign).

3. *Markets learn slowly.* The argument here is that, because markets learn slowly, investors who are a little quicker than the market in assimilating and understanding information will earn excess returns. In addition, there will be price drifts (i.e., prices will move up or down over extended periods), and technical analysts can detect these drifts and take advantage of them.

There is evidence, albeit mild, that prices do drift after significant news announcements. A follow-up on price changes after announcements of large earnings surprises provided the evidence in Figure 8-12. Portfolio 10 includes

FIGURE 8-12   Price reactions to earnings announcements

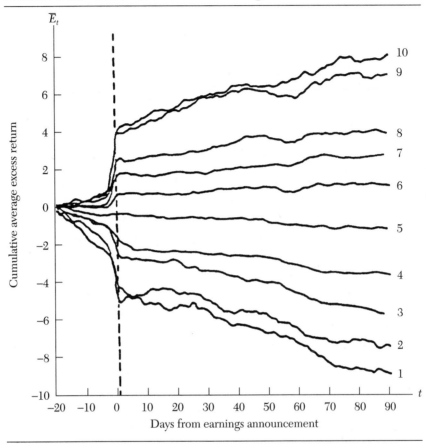

Days from earnings announcement

those stocks with the biggest positive earnings surprises, and portfolio 1 those stocks with the most negative earnings surprises. Figure 8-12 graphs out the price behavior of stocks in each portfolio in the 60 days following the announcement. Note the price drift, especially after the most extreme earnings announcements.

One of the indicators most widely used by momentum investors is the *relative strength* of a stock: the ratio of its current price to its average over a longer period (e.g., six months). The momentum rule suggests buying stocks that have the highest relative strength (which will also be the stocks that have gone up the most in that period), and selling stocks that have gone down the most.

4. *Markets are controlled by external forces.* Some technical indicators are based on the premise that markets are governed by "external" factors; without prejudice, one could call this the "Karma Approach"[19] to investing. For instance, the Elliot wave posits that the market moves in waves of various

sizes, from those encompassing only individual trades to those lasting centuries, perhaps longer. As one proponent put it, "[By] classifying these waves and counting the various classifications it is possible to determine the relative positions of the market at all times." There can be no bull or bear markets of one, seven, or nine waves, for example.

In the *Dow Theory*, the market is always considered as having three movements, all active at the same time: (1) the narrow movement (daily fluctuations), from day to day; (2) the short swing (secondary movements), from two weeks to a month; and (3) the main movement (primary trends), covering at least four years' duration.

5. *Follow the smart investors.* The final set of technical indicators is built on two assumptions: some investors are smarter than others, and indicators that can capture what the "smart" investors are doing will allow others to make excess returns. A good example of such an indicator would *the specialists' short sales ratio*, which measures short selling by specialists (who presumably know more about the stock than other investors) as a proportion of total trading volume. High short selling by specialists would be viewed as a bearish indicator.

Another indicator looks at *insider buying or selling;* high insider buying (selling) would be viewed as a bullish (bearish) indicator. There is some empirical evidence that buying stocks where insider buying is strong and selling stocks where insider selling is strong may yield excess returns, and that these returns increase with the "importance" of the insider. A CEO buying stock in his or her own company is a more positive indicator than a subordinate doing the same. This evidence has to be tempered by counterbalancing evidence that these excess returns are related to *when an investment is made.* A purchase made on the date of an insider report to the SEC may make excess returns, but these returns may dissipate if the investment is made when the actual SEC report is made public.

This approach is often in direct contradiction to the assumption that investors overreact. Thus, the same indicator that leads some investors (the contrarians) to sell may lead other investors (the followers of smart investors) to buy.

Usage and Empirical Evidence   There has long been a deep divide between what nontechnicians think about technical analysis and the viewpoint of its adherents. The former are convinced that charts and technical indicators are useless in finding undervalued assets, and technical analysts are equally adamant in claiming that the indicators are essential. Until recently, each side was able to cite studies that showed its view of the world was right. Given the strong biases within each group, these findings were not surprising. In recent years, however, many researchers have uncovered surprisingly strong evidence that there *are* predictable patterns in the prices of assets. These findings should come as small consolation for technical analysts, however; many of the patterns are long-term and are unlikely to be captured by most technical indicators. Two patterns—long-term price reversals, and price momentum—are reviewed here.

1. *Long-term price reversals.* There is substantial negative correlation in long-term return intervals, suggesting that markets reverse themselves over very long periods. Because such behavior, if true, would be a serious challenge to market efficiency, the phenomenon has been examined in extensive detail. Studies that break down stocks on the basis of market value have found that the serial correlation is more negative in five-year returns than in one-year returns, and is much more negative for smaller stocks than for larger stocks. Figure 8-13 summarizes one-year and five-year serial correlation by size class, for stocks on the New York Stock Exchange. The phenomenon has also been examined in

FIGURE 8-13   One-year and five-year serial correlations, by size class

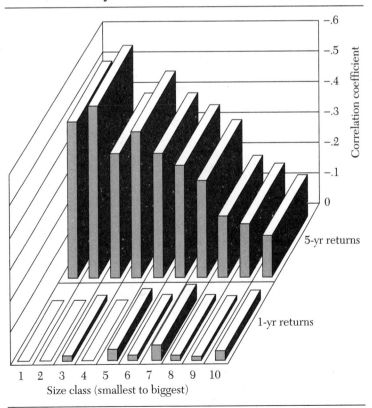

other markets, and the findings have been similar. There is evidence that returns reverse themselves over a long time period.

Since there is evidence that prices reverse themselves in the long term for entire markets, so it seems worthwhile to examine whether such price reversals occur on classes of stock within a market. For instance, are stocks that have gone up the most over the last period more likely to go down over the next period, and vice versa? To isolate the effect of such price reversals on extreme portfolios, DeBondt and Thaler[20] constructed a winner portfolio of the 35 stocks that had gone up the most over the prior year, and a loser portfolio of the 35 stocks that had gone down the most over the prior year, in each year from 1933 to 1978. They examined returns on these portfolios for the 60 months following the creation of the portfolio. Figure 8-14 summarizes the excess returns for the winner and loser portfolios.

The analysis suggests that the loser portfolio clearly outperformed the winner portfolio in the 60 months studied. This evidence is consistent with market overreaction and correction in long return intervals.

Many academics, as well as practitioners, suggest that these findings may be interesting but they overstate potential returns on "loser" portfolios. For instance, there is evidence that loser portfolios are more likely to contain low-priced stocks (selling for less than $5), which generate higher transactions

FIGURE 8-14   Cumulative average residuals for winner and loser portfolios of 35 stocks, one to 60 months after portfolio formation; length of formation period: 5 years

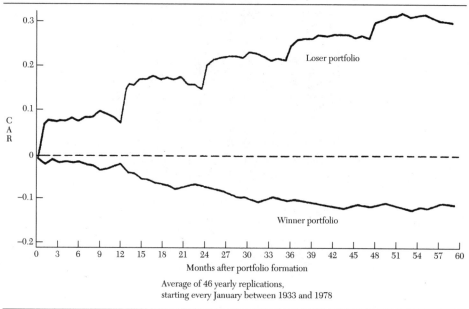

Average of 46 yearly replications,
starting every January between 1933 and 1978

costs and are also more likely to offer heavily skewed returns; that is, the excess returns come from a few stocks' making phenomenal returns rather than from consistent performance. One study of the winner and loser portfolios attributes the bulk of the excess returns of loser portfolios to low-priced stocks and also finds that the results are sensitive to when the portfolios are created. Loser portfolios created every December earned significantly higher returns than portfolios created every June.

2. *Price momentum.* In direct contradiction of the finding on winners and losers is a pattern that was uncovered by Jegadeesh and Titman (1993).[21] They tested a trading strategy of buying past winners and selling past losers, based on price performance over the previous six months, and holding for the next six months, and they realized an excess return of 12 percent. Furthermore, they found that these excess returns persisted even after correcting for other known anomalies such as market capitalization. This approach lost money in January, but made excess returns in every other month of the year. They attributed much of the excess returns to a delayed reaction to information, since the winner (loser) stocks made much of their positive (negative) excess returns around earnings announcements. This should offer solace to technical analysts who use relative strength (both price and earnings), since it is a measure of past price and earnings performance.

Limitations of Technical Analysis   The empirical evidence that has emerged in recent years on patterns that exist in stock and bond prices has made technical analysis more respectable. In addition, a combination of better data (intraday price movements), more sophisticated approaches to analyzing price and volume data (for instance, the emergence of chaos theory and neural networks), and more powerful computers has allowed technical analysis to move beyond charts and broad-volume indicators. Each of these advances, however, has come with costs. The proliferation of data has opened up the possibility of "data mining"—a researcher looking at a large enough data set, and using enough technical indicators and models, will always find a few that work over a specific period, but they are unlikely to provide excess returns in the future. This problem worsens as models become more complex and mathematical (and less intuitive). Some of the findings on stock price predictability emerging from the "new" technical methods (chaos theory, neural networks, etc.) have to be used with caution.

Private Information

The term *private information* refers to information about an asset that is available only to one or a few investors interested in it, and not to others. It remains the surest way of making excess returns in a market, but it may also have a fatal flaw. In some markets, its use is specifically prohibited. Insider trading laws forbid it in the stock markets in the United States.

What Is Private Information?   Private information is actually difficult to define. It is information about an investment that is available only to a subset of investors—not to all—and its value is diluted rapidly as the size of the subset increases. The information itself may take several forms. It may be about *a specific event* relating to a firm, such as an earnings announcement or a takeover bid that has not been made public yet but will be in the near future. It may be a more *general aggregation* of private information about the prospects for a firm, such as an increase in the availability of new projects, or improvements in profitability of key segments that might not be visible to other investors, that will lead to an increased value for the asset. Insider trading laws generally prevent investors from trading on the former but not on the latter.

Private information can also be categorized based on the precision of the information. It can be *perfect,* in which case there is no likelihood that the information is false or that the effects on the price of the asset are unambiguous (at least in terms of direction). Thus, a true insider (such as a manager in the firm, or a director) may be able to get precise information about a takeover bid that will be made tomorrow. It can be "noisy": there is a chance that the information is either false or misleading. This may be the case when an outsider learns of this information through second-hand sources or, as is often the case in markets, through rumors. An investor may also have private information about a firm but can be uncertain about its implications for value. Profits are certain in the first scenario (where the information is perfect), but they are uncertain in the latter situation, where it is noisy or its implications are uncertain. On average, however, there should be positive returns associated with getting even imprecise private information.

Using Private Information   The way in which investors use private information to pick assets is determined by the precision of the information and the legality of using the information. At one end of the continuum, an investor in possession of perfect inside information with no constraints on legality of trading can take full advantage of the information by trading in the asset or its derivatives directly, and buying and selling the maximum amount of that asset or derivative. There will be no need to hedge risk or hold a diversified position; a payoff is guaranteed, though its exact magnitude may be unclear. At the other end of the continuum, an investor who hears a rumor about an asset and is unclear about both the authenticity of the information and its effect on the asset's price may decide to: take a very limited position in the asset; take a larger position and hedge the risk partially; or take positions in more than one asset (i.e., diversify). When trading on the asset is illegal, investors cannot take positions in either the traded asset or its derivatives without running afoul of the law. This possibility has not deterred investors from doing so anyway, by using intermediaries and third parties to disguise their actions.

Usage and Empirical Evidence   Do investors use private information to pick under- and overvalued assets? Do they make excess returns when they do? We do not need extended studies to know that the answer to both questions is *Yes.* In fact, since it is illegal to do the former, no study that uses public databases of insider trading, such as the SEC official summary of insider trading, is going to be able to answer these questions. The indirect evidence is overwhelming, though, that insiders make significant profits in most markets. On the first question, the price run-up that we often observe before significant information announcements (e.g., earnings and merger announcements) suggests either an incredibly perceptive market or information leakage somewhere along the way. The surge in trading volume, often in the derivatives markets, before significant news announcements is additional evidence that investors do have access to private information and use it. On the second question, the evidence is partly anecdotal. It comes from looking at the profits of insiders who get caught using private information, and at the subset of insider trading that is legal and hence is summarized in the SEC databases.

The SEC defines an insider to be an officer or director of a firm, or a major stockholder (holding more than 5 percent of the firm's outstanding stock). Insiders are barred from trading in advance of specific information on the company being traded, and they are required to file with the SEC when they buy or sell stock in the company. If it is assumed, as seems reasonable, that insiders have better information about the company—and consequently, better estimates of value than other investors—the decisions by insiders to buy and sell stock should affect stock prices. Figure 8-15, derived from an early study of insider trading by Jaffe (1974),[22] examines excess returns on two groups of stock, classified on the basis of insider trades. In the "buy group," buys exceeded sells by the biggest margin, and in the "sell group," sells exceeded buys by the biggest margin. Note the positive returns associated with the first group.

Limitations of Private Information   There is a case to be made that the difference between a successful and an unsuccessful investor is the difference in the quality of information possessed by each. Three requirements have to be met to invest successfully with private information:

1. The investor has to have and maintain access to high-quality private information.

FIGURE 8-15   Cumulative returns following insider trading: Buy group versus sell group

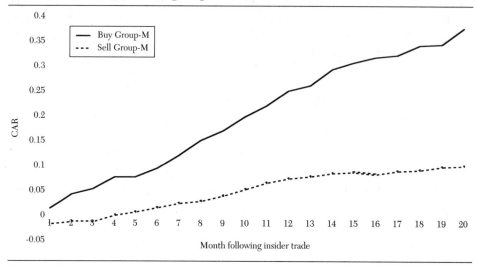

2. The investor has to be able to trade on that information without revealing it instantaneously.

3. The use of the information has to be legal.

There are problems with meeting each of these requirements. First, it is difficult to have access to good private information without being an insider, either as a top manager in the firm or firms affected by the information, or as an adviser (investment banker or accountant) to these firms. These are exactly the conditions under which trading is illegal, at least in the United States, so the third requirement of legality cannot be met. For an outsider, access to this information comes either second-hand or through rumors, which effectively reduces the quality of the information and makes acting on it more hazardous.

Second, even if an investor has access to good private information, the process of trading on that information may itself reveal the nature of the information (whether it is good or bad news) to the rest of the market and reduce or eliminate the excess returns that can be earned. This is of particular concern because strategies that try to take advantage of private information tend to be short-term and create substantial transactions costs.

Third, an investor who has acquired good private information and traded on it effectively may become the target of a probe by the SEC; the existence of large profits evokes suspicion that insider information may have been used. Ultimately, there may be no legal sanction, but the process is costly and risky, given the vagueness of the insider trading laws[23] regarding who exactly is an insider and what comprises insider trading.

In summary, the profits from using private information make it seem like an attractive option to many investors. However, strategies that use private information may actually be much highly risky in practice, from both an economic and a legal standpoint.

PASSIVE ASSET SELECTION

The strategies described so far are active strategies that attempt to find undervalued and overvalued securities, using valuation models, multiples, charts, or private information. These strategies vary immensely in their philosophical bases and their execution, but they share some common characteristics. They are all costly, in terms of the time and the resources that are needed to find the misvalued securities and the transactions costs, which may vary across strategies. They are also likely to result in portfolios that overweight some sectors, relative to their value, and underweight others, leading to a loss in diversification benefits. Investors are willing to live with these costs as long as the benefits that they provide exceed the costs. In this section, we examine whether active asset selection, at least on average, yields a benefit that exceeds the cost, and we consider the passive alternative (indexing), which allocates the portfolio across assets in each asset class, based on market value.

THE CASE AGAINST ACTIVE ASSET SELECTION

The best case against active asset allocation is made, ironically, by active portfolio managers. Professional money managers operate as the experts in the field of investments. They are supposed to be better informed and smarter, to have lower transactions costs, and to be better investors overall than smaller investors. The earliest study of mutual funds, by Jensen,[24] suggested that this supposition might not hold in practice. His findings, summarized in Figure 8-16 as excess returns on mutual funds, were that the average portfolio manager actually underperformed the market between 1955 and 1964. These results have been replicated with mild variations in the conclusions. In the studies that are most favorable for professional money managers, they break even against the market after adjusting for transactions costs; in those that are least favorable, they underperform the market even before adjusting for transactions costs. To those who would argue that these results occur because of "risk" adjustments that are unfair to money managers, the underperformance of active money managers can be illustrated by looking at their performance relative to the S&P 500. Figure 8-17 summarizes the percentage of active

FIGURE 8-16   Mutual fund performance, 1955–1964: The Jensen study

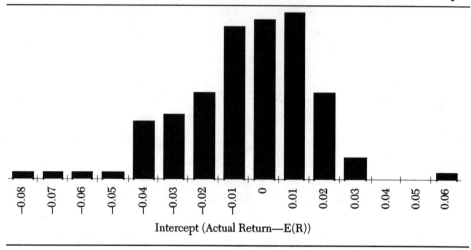

Intercept (Actual Return—E(R))

equity money managers who were beaten by the S&P 500 index between 1986 and 1995.

The evidence is no more promising when we look at Figure 8-18, which summarizes the performance of active bond fund managers relative to a bond index. The average bond fund underperformed the Lehman index by approximately 1.5 percent.

FIGURE 8-17   Percentage of general equity funds outperformed by the Standard & Poor's 500

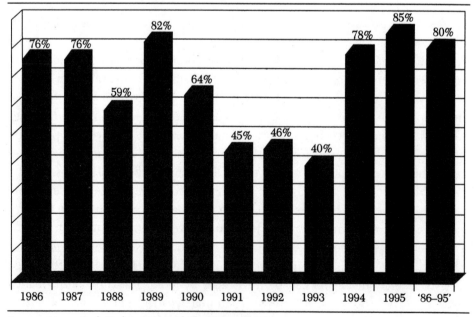

Source: Lipper Analytical Services and The Vanguard Group.
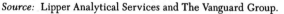

FIGURE 8-18   Bond funds versus Lehman Bond Index—cumulative returns (1983–1992)

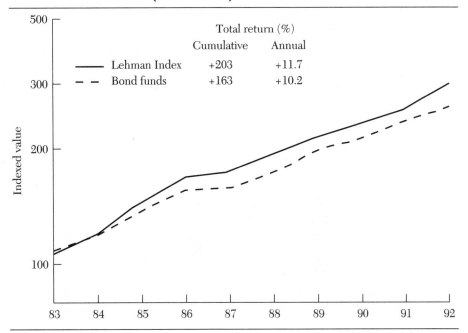

The results, when categorized on a number of different bases, do not offer much solace. For instance, Figure 8-19 shows the excess returns from 1983 to 1990, and the percentage of money managers who beat the market, categorized by investment style. Money managers in every investment style underperformed the market index.

Figure 8-20, from the same study, looks at the payoff to active portfolio management by examining the added value from trading actively during the course of the year, and finds that returns dropped from 0.5 percent to 1.5 percent a year as a consequence. The study, like others before it, found no evidence of continuity in performance. It classified money managers into quartiles and examined the probabilities of movement from one quartile to another, in each year from 1983 to 1990. The results, summarized in Table 8-5, indicate that a money manager who was ranked in the first quartile in a period had a 26 percent chance of being ranked in the first quartile in the next period and a 27 percent chance of being ranked in the bottom quartile. There is some evidence of reversal in the portfolio managers in the lowest quartile, though some of that evidence may be a reflection of the higher risk portfolios that they had put together.

The sole hopeful note in the studies is that there are a few areas where active money managers seem to have outperformed the indexes. One positive area is in international asset allocation, where active money managers have

FIGURE 8-19 Performance of equity funds, 1983–1990

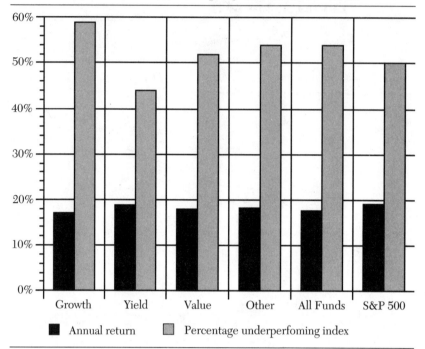

FIGURE 8-20 The payoff to active money management: Equity funds

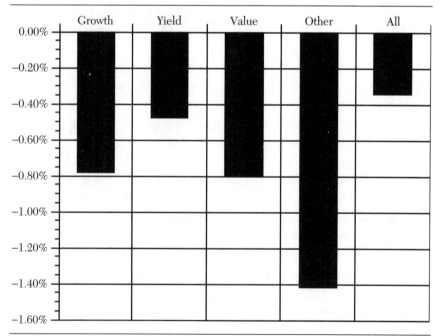

TABLE 8-5   Probabilities of transition from one quartile to another

Ranking This Period	Ranking Next Period			
	1	2	3	4
1	26%	24%	23%	27%
2	20	26	29	25
3	22	28	26	24
4	32	22	22	24

beaten the "passive" allocation model recently, though almost all of the outperformance in recent years can be attributed to managers' underweighting Japanese stocks in their portfolios. The other positive area is active funds in "emerging" and "information-poor" markets, which do better than passive funds in these markets. This may be attributable to the better information and superior execution skills that these funds seem to have, compared to other investors in these markets.

In summary, active portfolio managers, on average, underperform market indexes. The underperformance is broad-based and cannot be attributed to "risk" adjustments or to a few poor active money managers. Given that investors have to pay extra fees for active money management, it is not surprising that many of them turn to indexing.

INDEXING

The case against active investing is strong enough for some investors to consider an alternative, which is to allocate the portfolio across assets in the asset class, based on the market value of each asset. This approach is called *indexing,* and an index fund attempts to replicate a market index for the asset class. With stocks, index funds often try to replicate the S&P 500; with bonds, they look to the Lehman Bond Index, and with international stocks, to the Morgan Stanley Capital Index.

Mechanics of Indexing

The mechanics of creating an index fund are simple. The first step is to identify the index that the fund plans to replicate. Diversification would argue for replication of the widest possible index, but transactions costs and the dependability of the indexes in use may result in narrower indexes being chosen. Thus, in the United States, the most widely replicated index is the S&P 500, even though the NYSE composite or the Wilshire 5000 may be broader indexes. The second step is to estimate the market values of the assets in the index and to calculate the market value weights of the assets. The final step is to create a portfolio of the assets in the index, using the same market value weights. This process, which allows for perfect replication, becomes costly when the index contains thousands of assets. In such a case, the index fund may reduce its costs by using sampling to create a portfolio with the same characteristics (sector weights, market capitalization etc.) as the index. This sampling strategy does come with a cost: the index fund will no longer perfectly replicate the index, but will follow the index with noise.

Index funds are, for the most part, self-correcting, because assets in the fund and assets in the index essentially move together. Adjustments are needed as new assets enter the index and old assets leave the index.

Advantages of Indexing

Index funds have two of the advantages of traditional actively managed funds. First, no information costs or analyst expenses are associated with running these funds, and transactions costs associated with trading are low. Most index funds have turnover ratios of less than 5 percent, indicating that the total dollar volume of trading was less than 5 percent of the market values of the funds. Transactions costs for these funds are 0.20 percent to 0.50 percent, or less than one-third the costs at most actively managed funds. Second, the index funds' reticence to trade reduces the tax liabilities that they create for investors. In a typical actively managed fund, the high turnover ratios create capital gains and tax liabilities even for those investors who buy and hold these funds.

Limitations of Indexing

The primary limitation of index funds is that they cannot deliver more than their promise to keep up with the index. To the extent that an investor wants to beat the market, this may not be satisfactory. It can also be argued that the tendency of index funds to replicate just a few well known indexes (such as the S&P 500) can result in the stocks in these indexes becoming overvalued, especially as index funds become more popular. Furthermore, the most popular indexes may not be the most diversified. This is a problem, not with index funds per se, but with how most of them are constructed.

CONCLUSION

Investment strategies that claim to find misvalued assets abound. They can be categorized into four groups:

1. Strategies that use discounted cash flow models to value assets.
2. Relative valuation strategies that compare the pricing of individual assets to the pricing of assets that are "comparable" to them.
3. Technical analysis strategies that use price and volume indicators to predict shifts in market sentiment.
4. Strategies that attempt to use private information to find assets that are under- or overvalued.

Many investors subscribe to more than one of these groups of strategies, but very few investors seem to succeed in using them to earn returns in excess of what they would have earned by adopting a passive strategy of buying and holding a diversified portfolio of the assets. This gap between the performance that is promised by those who develop these strategies and the performance that is delivered by those who use these strategies suggests that there are significant costs and problems in execution: higher transactions costs, a price impact while trading, and imitation by other investors. The promise of "beating the market" is powerful enough, however, to induce investors to keep trying to come up with new and improved strategies. Far from bemoaning this fact, we should be celebrating it, since it is precisely this search for value that makes market price reflect information and value in the first place.

9 INVESTMENT STRATEGY

Robert D. Arnott

Portfolios do not manage themselves. Nor can they weather the ages unaltered. With each passing day, portfolios that we carefully crafted yesterday become ever less-than-optimal. Change is the investor's only constant. Investment strategy is the adaptation to change: We monitor client circumstance, investment return prospects, and market risks, managing portfolios to accommodate change.

Investment strategy hinges on an essential tension: the explicit cost of trading versus the opportunity cost of not trading. Errors more often occur in the natural human predisposition to act. Warren Buffett once marveled at the inability of investment managers to "sit quietly": Patience is a virtue that many investors lack. The essence of asset management lies in appropriate response to this tension between the cost of trading and the cost of inaction.

Trading imposes certain costs, including commissions, the price impact of trading, and the opportunity costs of trades that never occur. The cost of not trading is more subtle. It may mean that the portfolio has drifted into an asset allocation that is riskier, or less risky than suitable, for the client. It can mean retaining an investment that has become overpriced, offering inferior prospective returns. It can mean that the portfolio no longer fits the needs of the client.

The cost of transacting can also be nonfinancial. A client may grow concerned with turnover that he or she believes is excessive, and lose confidence in the investment manager. Critically, ours is a business of trust. Perhaps the greatest error an investment manager can make is to exceed the (often indiscernible) risk tolerance of the client. Finance theory suggests that investment managers should optimize client utility rather than maximize return. Even if a strategy triggers trading that is timely and profitable, that process is useless if the client abandons it.

Just as a transaction requires an investment decision, not trading is, itself, a decision that imposes costs. Suppose we have the wisdom to design a perfect portfolio for our client at any instant; after one day, even one hour, that portfolio is no longer completely optimal. On the other hand, the cost of transacting is real; it rarely makes sense to restructure a portfolio one day after it is altered: Trading rarely makes sense when there are only small differences between the current portfolio and the new optimum.

THE LOSER'S GAME

A useful approach to investment strategy begins with an examination of the errors that occur in investment management. Charles Ellis promotes the counterintuitive premise that investing is a "loser's game," in which the winners are often those who make the fewest egregious errors, rather than those who act on strokes of genius. There are many misconceptions about and many discrepancies between investment theory and its practice. Some investors churn portfolios in response to basic human emotion and crowd psychology. Others choose the latest fad, investing in markets or assets after they have earned good profits for their earlier investors, and bailing out only after damage has already been inflicted on their own wealth. Some of these errors are so obvious that they would be downright amusing if they were not so very costly.

The costliest errors in investment management are firmly rooted in human nature. They often stem from a quest for comfort, which the capital markets inherently intend not to reward. In the investment management business, when one has too much company, success is improbable. The capital markets price comfortable investments to reflect the fact that the investment management community *demands less reward from such assets*. Conversely, the markets price out-of-favor investments low, to reflect a demand for reward. Those who invest conventionally and comfortably perforce reap substandard rewards.

Many investors are fond of suggesting that, "if it ain't broke, don't fix it." This all-too-human model suggests that what goes up will forever rise and that strategies or investments that have floundered are en route to oblivion. History belies this notion. In business, this is sometimes true; in investments, it is rarely true. Indeed, common sense tells us that recently successful investments are priced to offer less reward today than yesterday. The optimal portfolio changes. This means that if it "ain't broke," we probably *should* fix it!

Conversely, consider investment managers who scramble to fix their strategy when their style falls out of fashion. They may merely change their approach as a period of poor performance ends, just before results rebound. Clients often suffer this same all-too-human temptation. How many times have we seen managers enjoy a burst of new accounts on the crest of a performance wave, and a rush to the exits as they approach their nadir? Ironically, if it *is* broke, the best course is often patience: Recently disappointing investments are typically priced to offer superior returns and are unlikely to attract the often-wrong crowd. Myra Drucker of Xerox once remarked, only partly in jest, that it makes sense to choose which managers and strategies to hire or fire, and then take action two years later!

It is not comfortable to employ a manager whose style has produced poor returns, and it is even less comfortable to take money from a manager who has been successful. In asset allocation, it is uncomfortable to move from a recently successful market into one that has been dismal. It is uncomfortable for an investment manager to maintain an investment style in the face of poor results.

The basis for this counterproductive pattern is something that is known in finance theory as "cognitive bias," which is based on statistical evidence that investors are not rational, that they favor comfort and shun uncertainty. This is the theoretical framework that suggests that comfortable investments *should* yield inferior rewards, and uncertainty *should* lead to pricing below fair value. Therefore, one might choose to observe the patterns of the investments community, look at the strategies from which investors are pulling back, notice which managers are getting their pink slips, and then buy into these out-of-step styles and likely earn a higher return than those chasing the latest investment fad.

CLASHING CULTURES

Some of the errors in investment management can be traced to something that we call "a clash of cultures." The successful business culture has long favored the survival of the fittest, depending on a pattern of aggressively rewarding success and ruthlessly punishing failure often called "economic Darwinism." In so doing, the successful grow and prosper by constantly weeding out any products, individuals, and business strategies that cannot compete. Management of most large investment portfolios is overseen by the investment committee of a board of directors. These committees are typically peopled by titans of industry, who have long since learned that the most successful *corporations* achieve their ends by favoring past successes over past failures.

Successful *investors* often trade in a counterintuitive fashion: increasing turnover when they are performing well, while enduring disappointment patiently. This behavior is at odds with human nature and with the corporate culture of most investment committees. When investments have performed poorly, instinct directs fixing of "the problem" by changing the portfolio. Yet, that portfolio is now priced to provide better returns than when it was first constructed. If the investments were attractive at higher prices, are they less attractive today? Conversely, if investments have performed well, human nature conditions us to coast in complacence with our winning strategy. Yet, recently successful investments are no longer priced to offer the rewards that first attracted us.

FIDUCIARIES AND THEIR CLIENTS

Successful investment strategies require that managers know their markets *and* know their clients. If they can effectively and profitably translate this knowledge into action, they earn their keep. This might mean selling stocks when, for example, in late-1972 or mid-1987, yields fell well below 3 percent, buying bonds during the peak yields of the early 1980s, or buying stocks in the wake of the 1987 Crash. Effective investment management requires courage, selling when few fear a major market decline, or buying when most investors find a multitude of reasons for fear.

The process of effective investment management involves a tension between comfort and profit, and a related tension between action and patience. Investors with the courage to shun comfort, and managers with the communication skills to encourage their clients to stay that course, are the winners in this game.

The committed contrarian rejoices when markets fall and tends to rue rising markets. This counterintuitive way of viewing markets is the correct view: A newly fallen market permits new investments and income reinvestment at improved prospective returns, thereby improving the long-term compounded rate of return. In effect, unless we are withdrawing money from our investment portfolios far faster than we are adding money, we should not be pleased when our stocks and bonds trade at all-time highs; we should dread the reduced prospective return.

A FIDUCIARY TIGHTROPE

Investment managers and fiduciaries face a tightrope walk. Seasoned investment managers know that performance will often be improved by pursuing an unconventional and often uncomfortable strategy. They also know that such strategies tend to attract scrutiny; most particularly they can expect second-guessing if the strategy goes awry.

In effect, not only do investment managers have customers, but often customers also have customers. An investment manager's client might be the investment officer of a pension fund, endowment, or foundation. Of equal or greater import, that investment officer clearly has a customer: the financial officers of the company, as well as the investment committee of the board of directors. Ironically, in the case of a pension fund, the investment officer's most relevant customer is typically not the pension beneficiary; the investment committee of the board of directors is the group responsible for the pension officer's livelihood, and therefore is the more influential "customer."

However prospectively rewarding a strategy might seem, the most profitable strategies can sometimes exceed the risk tolerance of a customer (or, at least as important, a customer's customer). No one will typically object to risk or surprise, when an investment strategy is more profitable than expected. But common sense tells us that any strategy that can generate favorable surprise can also generate unfavorable surprise. The unsophisticated or underinformed customer will generally be intolerant to adverse surprise.

One of the most important responses to this fiduciary tightrope is education. The educated client, chief financial officer, or investment committee of a board of directors is less likely to be taken by surprise. Each step in this process increases the likelihood that the client will have the patience to tolerate investment strategies that are uncomfortable (contrarian strategies). If clients are well-educated as to the importance of asset allocation, the importance of patience during periods when a strategy is unsuccessful, the costly nature of strategic "flip flops," and the impact that a few basis points can have on future corporate wealth, they are in a position to respond in an intelligent fashion to the choices that they face. Investment managers, investment officers, or CFOs who fail to educate their clients, *right up to the board level,* do so at their peril.

ARE MARKETS EFFICIENT?

The investment world can be broken into two principal camps: those who believe that markets are efficient, and those who believe they are inefficient. The capital markets of today function primarily on the basis of trading among those who believe that markets are inefficient. Advocates of inefficient markets believe that market pricing does not correctly reflect all available information. They seek mispricing in markets or in an individual asset that can lead to improved returns, with risk control as a secondary objective. Advocates of efficient markets believe that pricing already reflects all publicly available information; this leads to a very strong bias in favor of "passive management," with a focus on risk control first and investment performance as a secondary (or even nonexistent) objective. There are even theoretic foundations for both schools of thought: Equilibrium models provide a theoretic basis for observed market behavior in the context of "efficient pricing," while behavioral finance suggests that mispricing is inherent in human behavior.

Sound evidence is presented by both camps. Advocates of efficient markets point to the fact that many supposed demonstrations of market inefficiency are not statistically significant, and those that are statistically significant often vanish after receiving public scrutiny. Those who suggest that markets are *inefficient* like to point to the many times highly significant relationships are found between various independent variables and subsequent market or asset returns.

What is often lacking in this dialogue is an acknowledgment of the obvious: It is possible (even likely) that markets are inefficient, that active management can potentially add value, but that the inefficiencies are neither simple nor static nor inexpensive to exploit. In other words, part of the nature of market inefficiencies is that they tend to disappear. This means that once a market inefficiency is isolated and becomes widely known, it *should* begin to diminish or disappear as more money pursues the same inefficiency.

Indeed, essentially all categories of active management presume that markets are mispriced or inefficient. They presume to add value by investing in a market or an asset that is in some fashion mispriced. Yet any market inefficiency is inherently an arbitrage opportunity: If enough money pursues the same market inefficiency, it must disappear. It is reasonable to surmise that inefficiencies that are uncomfortable, that produce increased return at the cost of reduced comfort, should not attract enough investors to "arbitrage away" the opportunity. Accordingly, these inefficiencies might be expected to offer long-term gains for the patient investor.

Evidence from Asset Allocation

Evidence of inefficiencies can be found in a host of different articles and studies. Table 9-1 presents evidence of the link between risk premia and subsequent excess returns. For example, the difference between stock earnings yield and bond yield is sometimes called the equity risk premium. In the United States, if the earnings yield rises 100 basis points relative to bond yields, the

TABLE 9-1   Relative return coefficients

Country	Stock Earnings Yield minus Bond Yield	Stock Earnings Yield minus Cash Yield	Bond Yield minus Cash Yield
Australia	−0.25	−0.32	0.03
Austria	1.09	0.42	0.36[b]
Belgium	0.24	0.18[a]	0.12[b]
Canada	0.33	0.22	0.28[a]
Denmark	0.05	0.01	0.26[a]
France	0.16	0.95[b]	0.34[b]
Germany	0.46	0.35[a]	0.22[b]
Italy	0.04	0.32	0.24[b]
Japan	1.39[a]	1.64[a]	−0.09
Netherlands	1.64[b]	0.61[b]	0.27
Spain	2.90[b]	0.72	0.14
Sweden	0.79	0.24	0.01
Switzerland	0.86[a]	0.28	0.16[b]
United Kingdom	1.36[b]	0.14	0.06
United States	0.36	0.37[b]	0.30[a]
Average	**0.76[b]**	**0.41[b]**	**0.17[b]**

Source: R. Arnott, and Henriksson, "A Disciplined Approach to Global Asset Allocation," *Financial Analyst Journal,* March/April 1989.

[a] Significant at the 5 percent level.
[b] Significant at the 1 percent level.

stock market outperforms bonds by an average of 36 basis points *per month* until the stock versus bond risk premium returns to normal.

This research was first carried out in the United States. If markets are efficient, this relationship should not export particularly well: A seemingly powerful relationship in the U.S. that is only a statistical fluke should not be observed outside the U.S. Yet the world average for this relationship (which was a true out-of-sample test when the research was first performed in 1987) is twice as powerful as the U.S. relationship.

Similar results are found for other risk premium relationships. Stock earnings yield minus cash yield is a strong predictor for stock performance relative to cash in most of the major markets in the world. If we subtract cash yields from bond yields, we have a simple measure of the slope of the yield curve, often called a bond risk premium. When the yield curve is steep (hence, the bond risk premium is large), bonds subsequently offer a larger-than-normal excess return relative to cash equivalents in almost all markets in the world. In the United States, for example, a 100-basis point higher-than-normal slope of the yield curve is accompanied by a 30-basis point excess of return of bonds over cash until equilibrium is restored. As with the equity market relationships, this relationship is found worldwide.

TABLE 9-2   Relative return coefficients

Country	Bond Yield minus Cash Yield per 1% Increase in PPI
Australia	−0.06
Belgium	−0.12[a]
Canada	−0.91
Denmark	−0.47
France	−0.20[b]
Germany	−0.92[b]
Italy	−0.73[b]
Japan	−0.01
Netherlands	−0.25
Sweden	−0.46
Switzerland	−0.35[b]
United Kingdom	−0.78
United States	−0.90[b]
Average	**−0.47[b]**

Source: R. Arnott, and Henriksson, "A Disciplined Approach to Global Asset Allocation," *Financial Analyst Journal*, March/April 1989.

[a] Significant at the 5 percent level.
[b] Significant at the 1 percent level.

We also find that macroeconomic relationships are consistent around the world. In Table 9-2 you can see that the excess return of bonds over cash is strongly related to Producer Price Index (PPI) inflation, in every country that has a PPI measure. A rise in PPI inflation is generally followed by a rise in bond yields, hence underperformance of bonds.

You can see in Tables 9-3 and 9-4 that labor conditions also affect the capital markets. Rising unit labor costs hurt stocks and bonds worldwide, and, ironically, rising unemployment helps stocks and bonds worldwide. In effect, if less money is flowing to labor, more can flow to reward capital, while increased flows to labor decrease the available pool for rewarding capital investment. This relationship, like many of the others, was first identified in the United States, but the global evidence indicates that the inefficiencies identified in U.S. markets also exist overseas. This increases our confidence that these inefficiencies are legitimate.

Evidence from Stock Selection

Research into investment management styles also suggests that there are certain persistent inefficiencies in the capital markets. There is a risk model, designed by the investment consulting firm known as BARRA, that breaks stock

TABLE 9-3   Relative return coefficients: 1 percent increase in unit labor costs

Country	Stocks − Cash	Bond − Cash
Belgium	−0.51	−0.11
Canada	−0.06	0.02
Denmark	−0.30	−0.67
France	−2.03[b]	−0.84
Germany	−0.30	0.01
Italy	−0.40	−0.17[a]
Netherlands	−1.16[a]	−0.70
Sweden	−0.04	−0.13
United Kingdom	−0.02	−0.54
United States	−0.44	−0.50
Average	**−0.53[b]**	**−0.36[b]**

Source: R. Arnott and Henriksson, "A Disciplined Approach to Global Asset Allocation," *Financial Analyst Journal,* March/April 1989.

[a] Significant at the 5 percent level.
[b] Significant at the 1 percent level.

behavior into categories that reflect investment management styles, such as P/E ratios, growth rate, liquidity (trading volume), company size, dividend yield, reliance on foreign income, and so forth. Table 9-5 presents the mean return for each of the 13 BARRA factors. It also shows the standard deviation and t-statistic for these factor returns. Many of these mean returns for factors are statistically significant.

TABLE 9-4   Relative return coefficients: 1 percent increase in unemployment

Country	Stocks − Cash	Bond − Cash
Australia	0.40	0.80
Belgium	−0.16	−0.08[b]
Canada	0.23[b]	−0.13
Denmark	−0.24	0.36
France	−0.07	0.49[a]
Germany	0.96[a]	0.12[a]
Japan	0.39[b]	0.02
Netherlands	0.21	0.09
Switzerland	2.09	0.16
United Kingdom	0.23	0.22
United States	0.69[b]	0.35
Average	**0.40**	**0.23[b]**

Source: R. Arnott and Henriksson, "A Disciplined Approach to Global Asset Allocation," *Financial Analyst Journal,* March/April 1989.

[a] Significant at the 5 percent level.
[b] Significant at the 1 percent level.

TABLE 9-5   Monthly common factor returns (January 1973 through December 1990)

Factor	Mean (%)	Standard Deviation (%)	t-Statistic
BARRA Factor:			
Variability in markets	−1.0	1.43	−1.0
Success	0.24	1.16	3.0
Size	−0.13	0.82	−2.3
Trading activity	−0.08	0.76	−1.5
Growth exposure	−0.08	0.76	−1.5
Earnings/price	0.29	0.76	5.6
Book/price	0.25	0.73	5.0
Earnings variation	−0.01	0.67	−0.2
Financial leverage	−0.04	0.48	−1.2
Foreign income	−0.03	0.36	−1.2
Labor intensity	0.03	0.59	0.7
Dividend yield	0.06	0.82	1.1
Low capitalization	−0.19	1.91	−1.5
Other factors:			
Earnings revisions	0.50	0.60	9.9
Residual reversals	−0.52	0.90	−6.9

Source: Arnott, Dorian, and Macedo, "Style Management: The Missing Element in Equity Portfolios," *First Quadrant,* 1991, No. 1. Subsequently published in *Global Investing,* November/December 1991.

There is much debate in academic journals regarding the source of these "anomalies." Relatively few academicians (and even fewer practitioners), however, deny that these anomalies or inefficiencies *have existed in the past.* The problem is in extrapolating past market inefficiencies into the future.

It is in the nature of capital markets that any anomaly or inefficiency is an arbitrage opportunity: If enough money pursues the same anomaly or inefficiency, it ought to disappear. For many quantitative investment practitioners, it is a source of persistent frustration to note that, once a market inefficiency is amply documented in the academic journals, it has an odd habit of disappearing. In effect, it is dangerous to surmise that yesterday's inefficiency will persist tomorrow, if it is well-enough known to have attracted significant investment capital.

Table 9-6 provides compelling evidence of another class of market inefficiencies. This table examines cases in which publicly available information is predictive of the subsequent performance of an investment management "style." For example, the equity risk premium (which we define as the earnings yield on the S&P 500 index minus Treasury bill yields) is strongly correlated with the *subsequent* performance of several BARRA factors of return. When the equity risk premium is high, and investors are frightened, investors are evidently rewarded for investing in high "variability in markets" stocks (in effect, high-beta stocks), small stocks, and stocks with high earnings variation or with

TABLE 9-6   Sensitivity of factor returns to market variables

Factor	Equity Risk Premium		Stock Market Volatility		Cash − Yield Change	
	Correlation	t-Statistic	Correlation	t-Statistic	Correlation	t-Statistic
Variability in markets	0.29	4.5	0.19	2.8	−0.14	−2.0
Success	−0.15	−2.2	−0.20	−2.9		
Size	−0.14	−2.0	−0.14	−2.0	0.15	2.2
Trading activity	0.16	2.3	0.14	2.0		
Growth exposure	0.18	2.6	0.17	2.5	−0.16	−2.3
Earnings variation			0.16	2.3	−0.13	−1.9
Financial leverage	0.13	1.9	0.20	2.9	−0.15	−2.2
Foreign exposure					−0.18	−2.6
Dividend yield					−0.16	−2.3

Source: Arnott, Dorian, and Macedo, "Style Management: The Missing Element in Equity Portfolios," *First Quadrant,* 1991, No. 1. Subsequently published in *Global Investing,* November/December 1991.

a leverage balance sheet. Investors are also rewarded for investing in growth stocks at such times, because of the long-term nature of those investments. In effect, when the risk premium is high, suggesting that investors are pricing equities to reflect a demand for heightened reward relative to bonds or cash, one is rewarded for investing in "risky" stocks.

We find a similar linkage with stock market variability. Stock market turbulence rewards these same kinds of stocks with riskier attributes. High-beta stocks, leveraged stocks, stocks with high earnings variation, and growth stocks are all likely to do well when the markets have recently been turbulent. This link is consistent with behavioral finance: When markets are turbulent, investors are fearful; when investors are frightened, they tend to shy away from risky assets. It makes sense that the investor with the courage to invest where and when most investors are afraid should earn incremental reward, because fear makes an asset less expensive. Conversely, when markets are stable, and volatility is low, it makes sense that investors should become complacent; an investor should not be rewarded for bearing risk at such a time.

As in the asset allocation tables, we also find linkages between economic conditions and stock performance. These are detailed in Table 9-7. Here, you can see that the rate of change in PPI is a powerful predictor for the rewards on stocks that are dependent on foreign income. This is consistent with our knowledge of global capital flows: Accelerating PPI inflation should tend to push up bond yields, which will typically attract foreign investment capital, which boosts the value of the dollar, thereby damaging the prospects of companies that are dependent on foreign income. We also find that a rising PPI hurts the high-yielding stocks. Once again, this is sensible: Rising inflation should push up interest rates; rising bond and cash yields should have the effect of forcing up yields on high-yield stocks.

**TABLE 9-7   Sensitivity of factor returns to
economic variables**

Factor	Correlation	t-Statistic
1 Percent Change in PPI:		
Foreign income	−0.31	−4.6
Yield	−0.23	−3.4
Size	0.15	2.2
1 Percent Change in Leading Indicators:		
Earnings/Price	0.22	3.2
Financial leverage	0.16	2.3
Labor intensity	0.16	2.3

Source: Arnott, Dorian, and Macedo, "Style Management: The Missing Element in Equity Portfolios," *First Quadrant,* 1991, No. 1. Subsequently published in *Global Investing,* November/December 1991.

The Business Cycle and Stock Selection

Leading indicators also provide an interesting gauge. If leading indicators have risen in the past year, typical of a recovery from a recession, we find that heavily leveraged companies and labor-intensive companies are likely to do well. Typically, during the recession that precedes an upturn in leading indicators, most labor-intensive companies have already cut costs; they enter the new economic cycle lean and well-positioned for the ensuing economic recovery. Also, when leading indicators have risen in the past year, growth stocks have likely already made their move; accordingly, the value stocks (high earnings-to-price ratio stocks) would tend to do particularly well.

In each of these cases, we are not looking at coincident relationships, but predictive relationships. One might surmise that, in an efficient market, this kind of publicly available information is already fully factored into the price of stocks. Evidently, that is not the case.

So, Are the Capital Markets Efficient?

According to the empirical evidence, the capital markets do not appear to be efficient. There are enough statistically significant and economically defensible relationships between readily available *public* information and subsequent rewards to suggest that there is some predictability to capital markets returns. This holds true at the "macro level," for the asset allocation decision, and at the "micro level," in the selection of individual stocks (or bonds). We find linkages between risk premium measures and subsequent asset allocation returns or subsequent returns of certain categories of stocks. Similarly, we find linkages between economic conditions and capital market returns. Well-known value-oriented effects such as earnings-to-price and book-to-price ratios seem persistently useful for stock selection, albeit with the occasional poor year. While we do not study the evidence in this chapter, certain calendar effects also appear to be highly significant all over the world, presumably as a consequence of year-end tax planning and/or year-end portfolio "window dressing."

Theory suggests that rational investors should price the capital markets efficiently, accurately incorporating all publicly available information into the price of individual stocks and of markets. If the capital markets are not efficient, it must therefore be true that investors are not entirely rational, that investors' utility is not solely a function of wealth, that investors exhibit different risk or tax preferences, or that investors are not particularly prompt in incorporating new public information into asset pricing.

Behavioral finance forms an important theoretic basis for market inefficiencies: Investors tend to avoid perceived risk, but perceived risk need not be the same thing as the "diversifiable risk" contemplated in the capital asset pricing model. The root of risk perception can be found in human emotion; we are social creatures craving agreement and the shared consensus of others. Failing conventionally is often much less painful than unconventional failure. Accordingly, investors are more willing to risk a high likelihood of conventional failure than a low likelihood of unconventional failure; this gets factored into the pricing of assets.

The cynic might well ask, "If the market is inefficient, why is there only one Warren Buffett? Did he get rich through luck or skill?" There are three logical explanations for this.

- Market inefficiencies are (and should be) subject to change. It would be naive to presume that the inefficiencies in the capital markets never change. Indeed, the inefficiencies described in Tables 9-5, 9-6, and 9-7 may *all* fail in the years ahead, if too many investors seek to exploit them.

- Many market inefficiencies are predicated on the notion that capital markets return to some semblance of equilibrium; here again, equilibrium relationships change, and should be expected to change. This phenomenon can confound any investment process that is based on the tenet that markets return to long-term historical equilibrium relationships (often called "regression to the mean").

- Risk tolerance is usually lower than expected. Few investors have the tolerance for loss or shortfall that *even they* think they have. If they look at historical evidence for a particular investment strategy, and see a sound history of profit interspersed with brief periods of disappointment, most investors would likely say, "I could tolerate that disappointment." Living through disappointment is very different from looking at it on paper: Many investors do not have as much patience for risk tolerance *as they believe they have.*

The advocate of efficient markets would also point to a fourth "reason" for dismissing the empirical evidence: data mining. Statisticians calculate the likelihood that a relationship (such as the risk premium relationships described earlier) could be pure luck; anything smaller than a 5 percent likelihood of pure chance is often described as "statistically significant." What this means is that, even in an efficient market, 1 out of 20 randomly selected relationships will be statistically significant at the 5 percent level. Studying thousands of possible relationships should reveal dozens of "highly significant" relationships. The efficient markets advocates would say of Warren Buffett that 250 million individuals in the United States should yield one who tosses "heads" 28 times in a row. Suppose each of those "heads" leads to a doubling of wealth; then Warren Buffett need only have started with $40 to achieve his current wealth. This view is statistically defensible, but dubious on all other counts.

Inefficiencies can disappear. Indeed, they should be expected to disappear. The essence of the message here is a simple one: While good investment ideas are not eternal, we do observe that contrarian strategies often persist. This is because contrarian investing is inherently uncomfortable for the average investor. The use of price/earnings ratios or dividend yields to select stock have both shown good longevity, stretching back many decades. These disciplines, simple as they are, tend to favor the most unattractive and unloved companies on the stock market, and therefore the best opportunities for improved investment returns. Therein lies the fundamental appeal: Such companies might be expected to be priced to offer superior returns for those with the cast-iron stomach required to hold such out-of-favor assets.

Equilibrium models are not static. Figure 9-1 provides evidence of changing equilibriums drawn from research on asset allocation. The solid line represents the difference between the earnings yield on U.S. stocks and Treasury bill yields. Squares mark important market peaks, and circles show market bottoms. Following the disastrous 1973–1974 bear market, investors were so shaken that they priced equities to reflect the demand for heightened reward; this held true not just immediately following the bear market, but for years afterward. Important market tops have *always* occurred at a lower risk premium (less of a gap between earnings yields and Treasury bill yields) than this moving average, and important market bottoms have always occurred at higher risk premium levels. "Regression to the mean" is more than a theoretic principle; it is an evident reality. The problem here is a simple one: What mean are we regressing to?

FIGURE 9-1   Changing equilibriums

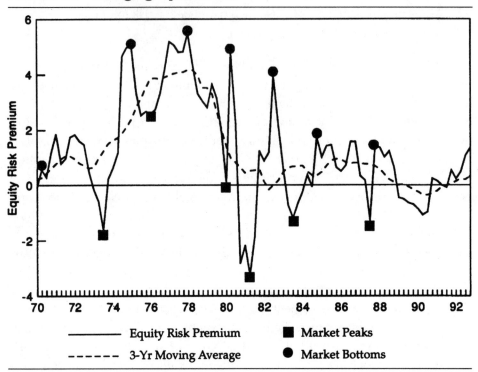

Source: First Quadrant Corp.

THE PROBLEM OF DATA MINING

With the enormous growth in computing power and data availability in recent years, data mining is one of the most serious risks in institutional asset management today. Fischer Black of Goldman Sachs has observed that there are two paths to expected returns: theory and data. He believes that both are flawed. Most finance theory (apart from behavioral finance) overlooks the possibility that there may be true anomalies or inefficiencies. Data are also a false guide: They can lead to a false sense of security.

If we look at historical relationships showing statistical significance at the 0.1 percent level, we may think we have found the path to assured wealth. Yet one out of a thousand *random* relationships will evidence this level of significance, and a true inefficiency can disappear quickly after being identified, as countless others in the investment world may start pursuing it at the same time. Identifying ways the market has been inefficient in the past does not necessarily help us in the future.

Professor Stephen Ross, at Yale, has also noted that, when empiricism seems to contradict theory, often a little digging or careful reasoning (a "thought experiment") can eliminate the conflicts. False inefficiencies abound.

- For example, Robert Shiller, also of Yale, has suggested that markets are too volatile to be efficient; market prices are far more volatile than the dividends that form the basis for wealth accumulation in stocks.[1] This simple comparison of volatilities overlooks an equally simple, but indisputably pertinent, fact: A modest 0.5 percent change in the discount rate that investors require for real returns can move the stock market as much as 15 percent. Since 15 percent is the normal annual volatility for the stock market, it is easy to surmise that, *absent any change in underlying fundamentals,* a standard deviation of 0.5 percent in the real rate of return that investors price into the stock market would account for *all* equity markets volatility.

- Some have cited the example of closed-end mutual funds that routinely trade at a discount, suggesting that this demonstrates a market inefficiency. Yet, the net present value of the expense ratio for a closed-end mutual fund should translate into a meaningful discount. For example, a fund with a 1 percent expense ratio (most are actually higher than this) ought to trade at a 10 percent or 20 percent discount to the net asset value of a fund. This is actually a fairly typical discount to NAV in the closed-end mutual fund world.

The problem of "disappearing inefficiencies" also plagues us. In the early 1980s, the small-stock effect was widely publicized; small stocks beat large in three years out of four by an average margin that is quite large. Similar research demonstrated that small stocks beat large stocks in almost every January, and that U.K. stocks also rallied almost every year in January. Subsequent to these well-publicized findings, small stocks began a seven-year bear market in which a dollar invested in small stocks was ultimately worth half as much as a dollar invested in large stocks. Similarly, the January effects in both the U.S. and the U.K. became much less reliable.

With data readily available and computer power cheaper than many might have imagined possible just a few years ago, data mining is inevitable. A cynical view of the historical data is in order. If we examine 1,000 relationships and find that 50 are statistically significant at the 5 percent level, we should not be ecstatic over identifying 50 "market inefficiencies." Even so, it is important not to reject examination of historical data merely because the activity can lead to data mining. Rather, we should become practical and intelligent historians.

We should question the theoretic underpinnings of these relationships, should question whether our use of data may have strayed too far into "data mining" territory, and pursue only those "inefficiencies" that are consistent with our understanding of capital markets behavior, that stand up to historical scrutiny, and that are not so widely known as to be arbitraged away.

Market inefficiencies likely exist and are relatively easy to identify in historical prospective. The question is a simple one: How many of these *historical* inefficiencies will prove profitable in the *future?* The implications for investment strategy, particularly in quantitative asset management, are significant.

QUANTITATIVE INVESTMENT MANAGEMENT

In the past 15 years, quantitative techniques have moved from radical fringe to mainstream. With that shift come a host of challenges and opportunities. An awareness of the strengths and limitations of quantitative investment techniques will be an increasingly important part of investment management in the years ahead. We need a clear understanding of what quantitative investment methods are, and what differentiates them from qualitative methods. The distinction is not as obvious as it seems.

We might begin by stating the obvious. Quantitative techniques are not magic; they are merely tools for effecting investment strategies with more discipline than traditional qualitative methods. Quantitative disciplines can be good, indifferent, or downright awful. But, unlike many qualitative investors, they are *disciplined*.

Quantitative methods are not inherently better than traditional subjective methods. After all, the human brain is an analytic instrument, capable of assessing the diverse impact and repercussions of a thousand or more variables, factors, and nuances. Quantitative tools, though, tend to break down when weighing more than a handful of variables. The brain is also a tool to deal with history, weighing and relating current market conditions to hundreds of comparison points drawn from history. Quantitative tools can help us draw comparisons only with the information that is in an often narrow database. The brain can assess why historical relationships might no longer apply; most quantitative tools can do no such thing. Of course, the words, "things are different this time," are uttered far more often than they are true!

Perhaps best of all, each brain can interact with other brains. We call this conversation, or teamwork. Computers can interact precisely only as and when we instruct them to do so. They are high-speed idiots, even when equipped with so-called artificial intelligence. Computer visionary Alan Kay, the inventor of the Macintosh/Windows user interface, challenged his colleagues at the

1985 International Artificial Intelligence Conference to back off on their attempts to mimic narrow aspects of human intellect and "build me a good cat." So far, the challenge is unmet.

But, for all of its strengths, the brain comes with excess baggage. We are social creatures with a yen for company. The capital markets inherently reward the unconventional view. We are creatures of emotion, seeking comfort. The markets inherently penalize the comfortable view. Asset prices change only partly because of news or objective changes in value; more powerful by far is the price change triggered by changes in the comfort that an asset provides investors in the aggregate, and therefore in the discount rate that the market applies to future expectations.

The human mind has a strong tendency to focus on recent history. In essence, we tend to fight yesterday's battle, forgetting the lessons—and the facts—learned in battles of years gone by. Our short-term memory is far better than our long-term memory. So our high-speed idiots (computers) can often, but not always, earn us higher returns than the finest minds in the business world.

Twenty years ago, quantitative methods were merely intriguing theoretical ideas. Few investors were so reckless as actually to commit assets on the basis of such abstract and quirky ideas as the capital asset pricing model, betas, and dividend discount models. Fifteen years ago, the earliest such applications were wildly and consistently successful, in large part because of their rare application. Today, quantitative investing attracts some of the finest minds in the scientific community, who now apply scientific methods in the investment world, and the margins of success are much smaller than they once were.[2]

As a result, it is no longer enough to be a "quant." We must be better-than-average quants if we are to earn profits for our clients. Today there is perhaps as much as a half-trillion dollars committed worldwide to strategies wholly or largely based on quantitative techniques. It is no longer as easy as it once was. As an aside, such opportunities still exist outside of the United States, where at most $20–40 billion is managed using quantitative disciplines.

Quantitative techniques are not magic. They can have good and bad months, quarters, and years. Yet we often hold them to a higher standard than we apply to those finest minds in the investment world. Why? Because if a brilliant individual delivers a bad year, we can empathize. We can often fully understand with hindsight the reasons for the flawed decisions. If a computer has a bad year, we surely do *not* empathize! More important, we often cannot fully comprehend the rationale for the failed investment.

What good are quantitative techniques? The answer is only partly better long-term performance. Well-reasoned and well-constructed quantitative techniques may well add value, although not so much in the United States as they perhaps once did. More important, they can serve as tools to avoid or to redress the greatest errors in investing, by stripping emotion out of an investment management strategy, and by eliminating the slippage that can erode long-term investment returns and reduce eventual wealth.

CONCLUSION

Is there a payoff to active money management? While the money managers who win at the game of professional money management tend to be the ones who make the fewest mistakes, many of these mistakes can be traced to human nature—the quest for comfort, the belief in trends, and the desire to switch styles and philosophies after failure. Some of the mistakes in portfolio management can be traced to the failure of money managers to understand their clients and to understand the markets that they invest in, and some mistakes can be attributed to the fiduciary tightrope that money managers have to walk between earning high returns and not exceeding the desired risk tolerance of their clients.

Empirical studies of financial markets have unearthed numerous inefficiencies that could potentially be exploited to time markets and pick misvalued securities, and these findings seem to make an argument for active money management. These results have to be considered with skepticism, especially since the inefficiencies that have been chronicled are noisy, subject to change, and may be a result of mining the data rather than reflections of real inefficiencies.

PART FOUR

PORTFOLIO EXECUTION

One of the most striking features of the empirical evidence accumulated on the efficiency of financial markets is the disconnection between studies on whether individual strategies beat the market and those on whether portfolio managers, who often adopt these same strategies, beat the market. There seem to be dozens of individual strategies that show promise in terms of beating the market, but very few portfolio managers actually accomplish the same objective consistency. One very important reason is that most studies fail to factor in both the difficulties and the costs associated with executing strategies.

There are three dimensions to portfolio execution: cost, trading speed, and management of risk. The cost of execution involves far more than the brokerage fees that are incurred when trades are made. The true cost actually has three components. The first component is the *bid ask spread*, which leads investors to buy at a high price and sell at a lower price. For low-priced stocks, this cost can dwarf the brokerage costs ranging as high as 20 percent of the price of the stock. The second component is the *price impact* of a trade; investors push the price up as they buy and push it down as they sell. In illiquid markets, this cost can be substantial, especially for large trades. The final component is the *tax impact* associated with trading. The ultimate objective in portfolio management is maximization of after-tax returns. When considered in aggregate, the trading costs will be high for both small investors (who often face a larger spread and higher brokerage costs than large investors) and large investors (who have a much greater price impact when they trade). The trading costs will vary widely across different investment strategies, depending on the trading frequency and the urgency associated with each strategy.

The second dimension to portfolio execution is trading speed. Generally speaking, the need to trade fast and the desire to keep transactions costs low will come into conflict. Investors who are willing to accept trades spread out over longer periods will generally incur much lower trading costs than investors who need to trade quickly. Recalling the investment strategies developed in Part Three, long-term-value investors should be less affected by trading costs than short-term investors who trade on information.

The final dimension to portfolio execution is the ongoing management of the risk in the portfolio. Portfolio risk characteristics do change over time, as do client objectives. The portfolio manager's job is to keep the portfolio in sync, at minimum cost. The expansion of the derivatives markets has provided portfolio managers with additional tools that can be used to hedge risk and add to returns over time.

The first chapter in this section, by Robert Arnott, looks at the tradeoff between cost and speed in trading. Aswath Damodaran then probes the hidden costs of trading—the bid ask spread, the price impact, and the opportunity cost of not trading. The final chapter, by Roger Clarke, looks at vehicles and strategies for hedging portfolio risk.

The Investment Process

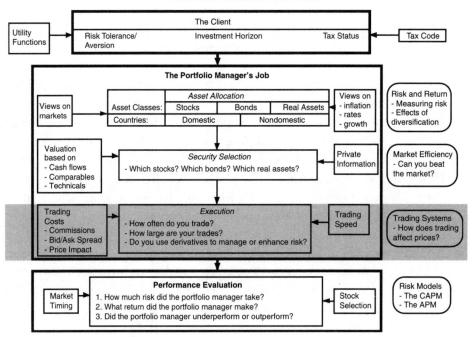

10 TRADING COSTS

Robert Arnott

Every portfolio manager is affected to some degree by the cost of transacting, but the costs vary widely across portfolio managers, depending upon their investment strategies. For active money managers with short term trading strategies, whose investment strategies require frequent trading, the drag on performance is much larger than for those with more long term strategies. For passive investors, who have stable asset allocation mixes and index assets in each class, the transactions costs can be negligible. All of this is based, however, on the premise that transactions costs can be measured accurately. In this chapter, the difficulties in measuring the cost of trading are exposed, and the trade offs that investors have to make between immediate trading (and the costs associated with it) and waiting (and the opportunity costs associated with it) are examined.

TRADING COSTS

Besides portfolio slippage from a drifting asset mix, from idle cash reserves, or from the natural human tendencies to bail out after disappointment and to stay with successful investments, slippage shows up in another way—trading costs. This is a topic that may offend many in the financial services industry. If we total up the revenues of the brokerage world, the arbitrage community, the mutual fund industry, investment managers, investment consultants, and all of the rest who earn a living in the capital markets, the sum is staggering. The revenues of these institutions comfortably exceed $150 billion per year. If we divide that sum by the total capitalization of the stock and bond markets in the United States, we come up with a rate between 1.5 percent and 2.0 percent per year. This proportion is removed from our capital market system by the intermediaries who serve to facilitate capital formation and capital flows in our economy.

While 1.5 percent removed from the capital market system per year seems a staggering sum, it is not wasted money. We have the most efficient capital formation structure and the most efficient structure for economic reallocation of capital in the world. This 1.5 percent figure actually compares favorably with every other major economy in the world. It *is* the cost of our economic structure, a cost soundly and sensibly paid to create an efficient economy.

In the 20 years from 1975 through 1994, we earned strong returns on assets, in part because investors priced stocks and bonds to reflect a gradual lessening in their demands for rewards. One could argue that intermediaries in the capital market systems earned their 1.5 percent by creating such a fluid system. This fluid system itself contributes to the comfort that has allowed investors to demand less reward, thereby creating the tremendous bull market of the past 20 years.

But, there is an irony: This is a sum that any single investor can choose not to pay. The investor who indexes to a 60 percent stock–40 percent bond mix, and rebalances solely through the direction of cash flows (thereby incurring only those trading costs that cannot be avoided) is a free rider. Over the years 1981 to 1989, suppose a fund chose to invest 60 percent in the S&P 500 and 40 percent in the Lehman Government/Corporate Bond index, with no idle cash reserves and with annual rebalancing. This fund would have outpaced fully 90 of the 100 largest pension funds in the United States during that nine-year span, outdistancing the average fund by 180 basis points per annum.[1]

Perhaps this passive free rider could not have earned the strong returns of the 1980s if others had been unwilling to pay the freight. Yet, even if we need our intermediaries, and even if the capital market system is paying a fair price for their facilitating effect on the economic structures upon which we depend, we are foolish to pay more of this cost than necessary.

Trading Costs: The Friction in Investment Strategy

In effect, the essence of investment strategy is the tension between the perceived reward for changing a portfolio and the cost of trading. How costly is trading? Various studies have suggested that equity trading costs are 10 basis points, 50 basis points, or 1,000 basis points. Yet, ironically, the truth is that a precise measurement of trading costs is fundamentally impossible.

A true measure of trading costs is not the commission paid to the broker, nor is it the difference between trade price and the average execution price of the day (a popular gauge of trading costs); nor can it be derived from stock price movements in the days before and after a trade is executed. The cost of trading is the difference between the execution price and the price that would have prevailed in the *absence of the trade*. Unfortunately, the trade execution itself prevents the pricing information that would allow us to measure trading costs accurately. This difference, which we can never observe, is the true trading cost.

Even this definition of trading costs can be applied only to trades that actually take place. For many investors, a much larger trading cost is associated with unexecuted trades. It is fair to say that if we want to buy two stocks trading at $50 a share, and one quickly soars up to $60 while the other plunges to $40, we will surely wind up owning the latter and quite likely not the former. The opportunity costs associated with these unexecuted trades represent an equally unmeasurable and often larger trading cost than the "price impact" trading cost described.

Given a simple definition of trading costs, it is important to recognize that trading costs can never be *negative*. For trades that are executed, the price would always be the same or lower in the absence of our trade; by the same token, absent our desire to sell, the price would always be the same or higher without our transaction. The same applies to the opportunity cost associated with unexecuted trades. The cost of unexecuted trades is always positive, at least on a short-term basis, because these unexecuted trades are the issues that move in the intended direction before we can trade.

Just as our own trade decisions affect trading cost, the actions of investors pursuing similar strategies will also have an effect. In essence, trading costs are embedded in the mechanics of our own investment strategy and the capital markets themselves. Because prices that would have prevailed, absent our trading, are unobservable, true trading costs are inherently unmeasurable.

Even so, it is useful for managers to look at their trading costs. Commercially available measurement techniques can still provide valuable insights into the investment process. Trading costs are probably not as inexpensive as the commission plus the bid-ask spread, nor are they as expensive as some market observers suggest. Even if modest, however, they are large enough to merit the focused attention of any serious investor. To some extent, we can control trading costs, and our efforts can have a profound impact on long-term investment success.

Studies demonstrate that the actions of like-minded investors can affect our trading costs.

- Prices tend to overact in response to important news, as an overabundance of buyers and sellers compete to be the first investors to effect their transactions, as is demonstrated in work by De Bondt and Thaler.[2]
- Market makers will absorb any temporary excesses in supplier demand, subject to an expectation that they can trade out of the position later at a profit.[3]

The net impact of both of these effects is that our own trading costs are inextricably entwined in the stock market mechanism and in the investment process of ourselves and our competitors (particularly like-minded traders who may be trading the same issues at the same time for the same reasons).

The decision every investor faces on every transaction is a choice between the "immediacy cost" of forcing a transaction quickly as against the "opportunity cost" associated with missing an opportunity that we correctly anticipated. Jack Treynor originated this paradigm for trading cost management, which is illustrated in Figure 10-1. He also notes that continuously available liquidity is not a free good; it must be manufactured by the intermediaries (dealers and specialists), who provide liquidity whenever the offsetting natural trade cannot be quickly identified. These intermediaries

FIGURE 10-1   Transaction cost

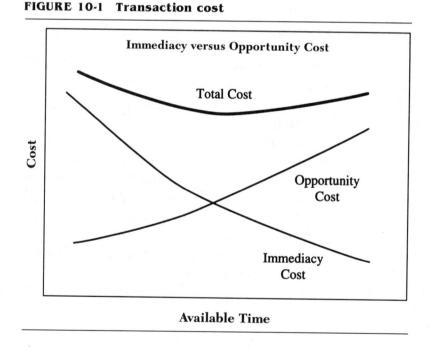

demand good compensation for the risk that they bear in providing this service. Some research suggests that the average transaction involves six intermediaries as an asset makes its way from a natural long-term seller to a natural long-term buyer.[4]

Immediacy cost will tend to decrease when the transaction can be worked patiently. Opportunity cost rises as the marketplace comes to recognize the information that forms the basis of the trade. In instances of fast-breaking news or with momentum-based strategies, we find this crossover point occurs very quickly, requiring rapid and aggressive execution, and typically incurring fairly large trading costs. Investors who react to fast-breaking news or who respond to momentum should be willing to pay the immediacy cost in order to avoid a fast-rising opportunity cost. Investors who rely on the purchase of out-of-favor investments, low P/E stocks, or long-depressed issues typically experience a much slower opportunity cost, where the half-life of the investment idea may be measured in months and not minutes. These investors should favor the use of crossing networks, limit orders, and other trading techniques that are designed to delay until the natural trade counterparty chooses to transact. Any trader who can wait for the natural trade counterparty actually operates much more like a dealer, providing liquidity rather than demanding liquidity. This approach does *not* work for investors who trade on the basis of fast-developing ideas.

This trade-off between immediacy cost and opportunity cost is one of the main reasons that it is imperative that investors know the nature of their own investment process. If we do not know ourselves, we may transact too soon or too late, at a large ultimate cost to our long-term investment success. A trading cost is the sum of the two curves: a downward-sloping immediacy cost and an upward-sloping opportunity cost. This combined cost has a minimum, reflecting the degree of patience that an investor should aim to find. Finding this minimum is not as easy as the diagram might suggest. The minimum is not observable; it changes not only from one investment strategy to another but also with the market liquidity of the day and the market liquidity of the specific individual trade. The art of trading is a balancing act between avoiding high immediacy cost by trading too quickly and avoiding high opportunity cost by trading too patiently.

Are Trading Costs High?

Some market observers suggest that trading costs are very large indeed. Given the cost of all of the market intermediaries who provide the service of liquidity, Jack Treynor concludes that the bid-ask spread is not a true measure of trading cost. He suggests that the true measure is the spread between what the long-term economic buyer pays and what the long-term economic seller receives, which may well be in the 10 percent range. In effect, Treynor suggests that an asset that is sold to an intermediary is not the same as an asset sold to a long-term investor: It is in the hands of someone looking for a positive trading return and is still for sale. It is not truly sold until it is out of the hands of the whole series of intermediaries and in the hands of an investor who seeks long-term investment.

A seminal analysis of the degree of the immediacy cost of trading includes dealer quotations on a selection of companies and trade sizes.[5] This work suggests that the round-trip cost of *immediate* trading can range from 1.1 percent to 43.8 percent. The extraordinarily high upper bound is, not surprisingly, associated with large block transactions in small companies. In effect, this is a test of the cost of demanding instant liquidity from brokers, a test that demonstrates that liquidity is not a free good, and that the rational investor will seek to avoid paying for unneeded immediacy on trades and strategies that have a reasonable "half life."

Are Trading Costs Low?

Some investors believe that trading is almost a zero-sum game. They dismiss even the bid-ask spread, pointing out that if the stock trades at the bid, the seller incurs a trading cost, while the buyer benefits; the converse holds true for a transaction at the ask. In effect, this view of the world suggests that there is a winner and a loser for every trade, so that only the commission is a true trading cost. This zero-sum game argument assumes that all investors who transact are long-term investors. It overlooks the fact that there is an intermediary (a dealer, a specialist, an arbitrageur) who will trade only in the expectation of offloading the position at a profit fairly quickly. In effect, these immediaries help to define the bid-ask spread. Natural long-term buyers who demand immediacy are unlikely to encounter a natural seller who, at that same instant, wishes to sell in the open market.

One might surmise that at least the intermediaries can enjoy negative trading costs, because they transact with an expectation of profiting very quickly as they unwind the position. They do not enjoy negative trading cost. Given the price they would like to trade at, even intermediaries must compromise in order to effect a transaction. They must accept a price that is both attractive enough to motivate the other side of the transaction, yet better than that of any other intermediary who is aware of the potential trade. They simply overcome their modest trading cost as a consequence of their expertise in short-term market behavior.

The truth is that all investors and traders incur positive trading costs, which reduce the ultimate success of their individual investment strategies.

The advocates of low trading costs disagree that trading costs are enormous. They suggest that every trading desk has developed a trading strategy that minimizes total trading cost, and, even if the trading strategy is unsuccessful, the trade counterparty is a winner with negative trading costs. The argument fails to explain the shortfall that we observed earlier in actively managed equity portfolios.

The danger in underestimating trading cost is that it can build a false sense of security. Suppose trading costs are perceived as small, or, worse yet, suppose that we surmise a skill that will allow us to benefit from negative trading costs. This would mean that investments can be made without regard to trading costs, and that one should pounce on the smallest opportunities. The consequence is trading that is too aggressive and *true* trading costs that mount prodigiously over time. The result is a large shortfall in the comparison between simulated results for a strategy and the observed results.

Andre Pérold suggests that a comparison between a real-time simulation to the concurrent live-asset returns is the most meaningful measure of trading costs.[6] This comparison would be more accurate than a comparison of historical simulations to subsequent live-asset returns. Few investors carry out such concurrent calculations. The fiduciary focus on best execution tends to focus much of the attention on controlling commissions. The control of commissions, though, can actually create a *disincentive* for the broker to work on an investment manager's behalf to gain best overall execution. Ironically, low commissions can actually work to the benefit of the dealer and the arbitrage community.

For all these reasons, it is possible for a trader to look good (low commission payouts) and an investment strategy to look good (results for paper buy and sell recommendations), but the overall investment result be well below the benchmark. In effect, successful execution of investment strategy involves the combined efforts of research and implementation teams. Research is the quest for the best possible investment strategies, which, on paper, provides superb results. Implementation is the effort to capture as much of that success as possible.

Measurement of trading effectiveness is an imprecise science. If it is used as a basis to seek better self-awareness and more effective execution, then it can be a good thing. If it is used as a basis for grading the trader and gauging the competence of the implementation team, it can actually serve to drive a wedge between effective investment strategy and effective implementation.

The solution is to treat the trading process as an "implementation department," which has the goal of capturing as much of the return associated with an investment strategy as possible. Excellence in trading is rewarding—most important, it is achievable. Without effective implementation, an investment idea is only an idea. Poorly effected implementation can undo the best ideas.

CONCLUSION

In the aggregate, transactions costs do absorb a significant proportion—up to 1.5 percent—of portfolio assets each year, though the exact magnitude of the cost is difficult to estimate because trading costs are difficult to measure for two reasons. The first is that on trades that do occur, the execution of the trade can affect the price, making it impossible to measure the true trading cost— the difference between the execution price and the price that would have prevailed in the absence of the trade. The second is that it does not capture the opportunity cost of trades not made because the price moved before the trade could be executed. No matter how trading costs are measured, investors have to trade off the cost of transacting quickly against the opportunity cost of waiting and missing the opportunity.

There are two schools of thought on trading costs. One school, using the broadest definition of trading costs, estimates trading costs at 10 percent or more, and argues that these costs are too high. The other school of thought is that trading is a zero-sum game and that while costs might be greater for some strategies than others, there the excessive costs incurred by some traders allows others to make gains.

Trading costs can explain why strategies that work well on paper and in simulations do not always earn investors excess returns in practice.

11 THE HIDDEN COSTS OF TRADING

Aswath Damodaran

The costs of trading clearly impose a drag on the performance of portfolio managers. As we debate the extent of these costs, we need to get a measure of what the costs are, how they vary across investment strategies, and how investors can minimize them. In the previous chapter, Robert Arnott discussed some of the difficulties associated with the measurement of trading costs, and noted the debate between those who think trading costs are too high, taking an expansive view of what comprises these costs, and those who argue that the costs are negligible from the perspective of the entire market.

This chapter takes a middle road. We will look at the ingredients that go into trading costs, and examine strategies where trading costs are likely to be high and strategies where they will generally be low.

THE TRADING COST DRAG

While we debate what constitutes trading costs and how to measure them, there is a fairly simple way in which we can at least estimate how much trading costs affect the return realized by the average portfolio manager. Active money managers trade because they believe that there is profit in trading, and the return, for any active money manager, has three ingredients:

$$\text{Return} = \text{Expected Return}_{Risk} + \text{Return from Active Trading} - \text{Trading Costs}$$

Among all active money managers, the average expected return has to be equal to the return on the market index. Thus, subtracting the average return made by active money managers from the return on the index should give us a measure of the payoff to active money managers:

$$\text{Average Return}_{\text{Active Money Managers}} - \text{Return on Index} = \frac{\text{Return from}}{\text{Active Trading}} - \text{Trading Costs}$$

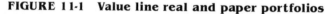

In Chapter 8, we noted that the average active money manager has underperformed the index in the past decade by about 1 percent. If we take the view that active trading, on average, adds no excess return, then the trading costs, at a minimum, should be 1 percent of the portfolio on an annual basis. If we take the view that active trading *does* add to the returns, the trading costs will be greater than 1 percent of the portfolio on an annual basis.

When real portfolios have been constructed to replicate hypothetical portfolios, the magnitude of the trading costs is illustrated starkly. Figure 11-1 shows the difference in returns, from 1979 to 1991, between the fund that Value Line has run and the paper portfolio that Value Line has used to compute the returns that its stock picks would have had. The paper portfolio had an annual return of 26.2 percent, whereas the Value Line fund had a return of 16.1 percent. Part of the difference can be attributed to Value Line's waiting until its subscribers had a chance to trade, but a significant portion of the difference can be explained by the costs of trading.

FIGURE 11-1   Value line real and paper portfolios

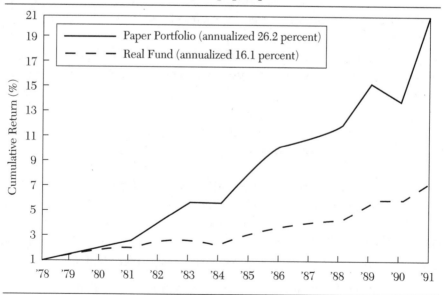

From the evidence, we would draw two conclusions. First, money managers either underestimate the trading costs or overestimate the returns to active trading—or both. Second, trading costs are a critical ingredient in any investment strategy; they can make the difference between a successful and an unsuccessful portfolio manager.

THE COMPONENTS OF TRADING COSTS

Some investors undoubtedly operate under the misconception that the only cost of trading is the brokerage commission that they pay when they buy or sell assets. This might be the only cost that they pay explicitly, but other costs that they incur in the course of trading generally dwarf the commission cost. When trading any asset, three ingredients go into the trading costs:

1. The *spread* between the price at which one can buy an asset (the dealer's ask price) and the price at which one can sell the same asset at the same point in time (the dealer's bid price).
2. The *price impact* that an investor can create by trading on an asset— pushing the price up when buying the asset, and pushing the price down when selling.
3. As first proposed by Jack Treynor,[1] an *opportunity cost* is associated with waiting to trade. Being a patient trader may reduce the first two components of trading cost, but the waiting can cost profits both on trades that are made and on trades that would have been profitable if made instantaneously but became unprofitable as a result of the waiting. The sum of these costs, in conjunction with the commission costs, makes up the trading cost for an investment strategy.

THE BID–ASK SPREAD

There is a difference between what a buyer will pay and what the seller will receive, at the same point in time and for the same asset, in almost every traded asset market. The *bid–ask spread* refers to this difference. In this section, we examine why this difference exists, how large a cost it is, the determinants of its magnitude, and its effects on returns in different investment strategies.

Why Is There a Bid–Ask Spread?

In most markets, a dealer or market maker sets the bid–ask spread to cover three types of costs that he or she faces: (1) the risk cost of holding inventory,

(2) the cost of processing orders, and (3) the cost of trading with more informed investors. The spread has to be large enough to cover these costs and yield a reasonable profit to the market maker.

The Inventory Rationale

Amihud and Mendelson[2] present a simple model of a market maker who has to quote the bid prices and ask prices at which he or she is obligated to execute buy and sell orders from investors. The investors could be trading because of information they have received (informed traders), for liquidity (liquidity traders), or because they believe that an asset is under- or overvalued (value traders). Setting too high a bid price will result in an accumulation of inventory to the market maker, and setting too low an ask price will result in an increase in the market maker's short position.

Amihud and Mendelson argue that market makers operate with inventory constraints, some of which are externally imposed (by the exchanges or regulatory agencies) and some of which are internally imposed (for financial and risk reasons). When the market maker's inventory position deviates from an optimal position, the prices will be different from the preferred prices. If the inventory is too high, the prices will be lower than the preferred prices; if the inventory is too low, the prices will be higher than the preferred prices.

The Processing Cost Argument

Because market makers incur a processing cost for the paperwork and fees associated with orders, the bid–ask spread, at the minimum, has to cover these costs. The costs are likely to be very small for large orders of stocks traded on the exchanges. They become larger for small orders of stocks, which might be traded only through a dealership market. Furthermore, because a large proportion of this cost is fixed, these costs, as a percentage of the price, will generally be higher for low-priced stocks than for high-priced stocks.

The Adverse Selection Problem

The adverse selection problem arises from the different motives investors have for trading an asset—liquidity, information, and views on valuation. Because investors do not announce their reasons for trading at the time of the trade, the market maker always runs the risk of trading against more informed investors. The expected profits from such trading will be negative, so the market maker has to charge an average spread that is large enough to compensate for these potential losses. This theory would suggest that spreads will increase with: the proportion of informed traders in an asset market; the "differential" information possessed, on average, by these traders; and uncertainty about future information on the asset.

The Magnitude of the Bid–Ask Spread

The New York Stock Exchange reported[3] that the average bid–ask spread across all NYSE stocks in 1996 was $0.23, which seems trivial when one considers that the average price of a NYSE stock is between $40 and $50 per share. This average, however, obscures the large differences in the cost as a percentage of the price across stocks, based on capitalization, stock price level, and trading volume. A study by Thomas Loeb,[4] in 1983, reported the spread as a percentage of the stock price for companies as a function of their market capitalization for small orders. The results are summarized in Table 11-1.

Note that the spread is as high as 6.55 percent of the price for small capitalization stocks, and drops to 0.52 percent of the price for large capitalization companies. Another study, by Huang and Stoll,[5] found that the stocks in the top 20 percent in terms of trading volume had an average spread of only 0.62 percent, and the stocks in the bottom 20 percent had a spread of 2.06 percent. There are also large differences in bid–ask spreads across different exchanges in the United States. Looking at only NASDAQ stocks, Kothare and Laux[6] found that the average was almost 6 percent of the price in 1992, and much higher for low-priced stocks on the exchange. Some of the difference can be attributed to the fact that NASDAQ stocks are generally much smaller and riskier than stocks listed on the NYSE or AMEX.

TABLE 11-1   Bid–ask spread as a function of market capitalization; common stock bid–ask spreads: Small orders

Sector	From (millions)	To (millions)	Number of Issues	Percent of U.S. Market	Average Price	Average Spread	Spread Price
1 (small)	$ 0	$ 10	1,009	.36%	$ 4.58	$.30	6.55%
2	10	25	754	.89	10.30	.42	4.07
3	25	50	613	1.59	15.16	.46	3.03
4	50	75	362	1.60	18.27	.34	1.86
5	75	100	202	1.27	21.85	.32	1.46
6	100	500	956	15.65	28.31	.32	1.13
7	500	1.000	238	12.29	35.43	.27	.76
8	1.000	1.500	102	8.87	44.34	.29	.65
9 (large)	1.500	99.999	180	57.48	52.40	.27	.52

These studies looked only at traded U.S. equities; there are bid–ask spreads in other markets as well. No single comprehensive study of all these spreads exists, but the following conclusions seem warranted:

1. The spreads in U.S. government securities are much lower than the spreads on traded stocks in the United States. For instance, the typical bid–ask spread on a Treasury bill is less than 0.1 percent of the price.
2. The spreads on corporate bonds tend to be larger than the spreads on government bonds. Safer (higher rated) and more liquid corporate bonds have lower spreads than riskier (lower rated) and less liquid corporate bonds.
3. The spreads in non-U.S. equity markets are generally much higher than the spreads on U.S. markets, reflecting the lower liquidity in those markets and the smaller market capitalization of the traded firms.
4. The spreads in the traded commodity markets are similar to those in the financial asset markets; the spreads in other real asset markets (real estate, art, and so on) tend to be much larger.

The Determinants of the Bid–Ask Spread

A number of studies have looked at the variables that determine (or, at the very least, correlate with) the bid–ask spread. Studies[7] by Tinic and West (1972), Stoll (1978), and Jegadeesh and Subrahmanyam (1993) found that spreads as a percentage of the price are correlated negatively with the price level, volume, and number of market makers, and positively with volatility. Each of these findings is consistent with the theory on the bid–ask spread. The negative correlation with price level can be explained by the higher processing cost as a percentage of the price. Higher volume reduces the need for market makers to maintain inventory, and allows them to turn over their inventory rapidly, resulting in lower inventory costs. The higher volatility leads to higher bid–ask spreads, partly because the adverse selection problem is greater for more volatile stocks; there will generally be more informed traders, a greater "information differential," and greater uncertainty about future information on these stocks. It is also worth noting that variables such as price level, volatility, and trading volume are not only correlated with each other, but are also correlated with other variables such as firm size.

The study by Kothare and Laux quoted in the previous section, looked at average spreads on the NASDAQ and also at differences in bid–ask spreads across stocks on the NASDAQ. In addition to noting similar correlations among the bid–ask spreads, price level, and trading volume, they uncovered an interesting new variable: Stocks where institutional activity increased significantly had the biggest increase in bid–ask spreads. Some of this can be attributed to the concurrent increase in volatility in these stocks; it might also reflect a perception on the part of market makers that institutional investors tend to be informed investors with more, or better, information.

Role in Investment Strategies

From the evidence, it is clear that bid–ask spreads will affect the returns from investment strategies, but the effect will vary, depending on the strategy. A strategy of buying undervalued companies and holding for the long term should not be affected very much by bid–ask spreads. A strategy of buying small over-the-counter stocks or emerging market stocks on information, and trading frequently, might lose a substantial portion of its allure when bid–ask spreads are factored into the returns.

To show the effect of the bid–ask spread on returns, consider the strategy of buying "losers." DeBondt and Thaler[8] (1985) presented evidence that a strategy of buying the stocks that have the most negative returns over the previous year, and holding them for a five-year period, earns significant excess returns. A follow-up study, however, noted that many of these "losers" were low-priced stocks, and that putting a constraint on this strategy (the prices had to be greater than $10) resulted in a significant drop in the excess returns. Because bid–ask spreads tend to be largest for low-priced stocks, it is an open question as to whether an investment strategy of buying losers will yield excess returns in practice. In fact, similar concerns should exist about any strategy that recommends investing in low-priced, inactive, and small-cap stocks, or in asset classes that have high volatility and low liquidity.

THE PRICE IMPACT

Most investors assume that trading costs become smaller as portfolios become larger. This is true for brokerage commissions, but it is not always the case for the other components of trading costs. For one component, the impact that trading has on prices, larger investors bear a more substantial cost than do smaller investors. If the basic idea behind successful investing is to buy low and sell high, pushing the price up as you buy, and then pushing it down as you sell, reduces the profits from investing.

Why Is There a Price Impact?

There are two reasons for the price impact, when investors trade. The first reason is that markets are not completely liquid. A large trade can create an imbalance between buy and sell orders, and the only way in which this imbalance can be resolved is with a price change. The price change that arises from lack of liquidity will generally be temporary and will be reversed as liquidity returns to the market.

The second reason for the price impact is informational. A large trade attracts the attention of other investors in that asset market because the trade might be motivated by new information that the trader possesses. Notwithstanding claims to the contrary, investors usually assume, with good reason, that an investor buying a large block is buying in advance of good news, and that an investor selling a large block has come into possession of some negative news about the company. This price effect will generally not be temporary, especially when we look across all stocks involved where such large trades are made. Investors are likely to be wrong about the informational value of large block trades a fair proportion of the time, but there is reason to believe that they will be right almost as often.

How Large Is the Price Impact?

There is conflicting evidence on how much of an impact large trades have on stock prices. On the one hand, studies of block trades on the exchange floor seem to suggest that markets are liquid and that the price impact is small and can be reversed quickly. These studies, however, have generally looked at heavily traded stocks at the New York Stock Exchange. On the other hand, others argue that the price impact is likely to be large, especially for smaller and less liquid stocks.

Studies of the price reaction to large block trades on the floor of the exchange conclude that prices adjust to such trades within a few minutes. Dann, Mayers, and Raab[9] examined the speed of the price reaction by looking at the returns an investor could make by buying stock right around the block trade and selling later. They estimated the returns as a function of how many minutes the acquisition took place after the block trade, and found that only trades made within a couple of minutes of the block trade had a chance of making excess returns. (See Figure 11-2.) Put another way, the prices adjusted to the liquidity effects of the block trade within five minutes of the block. This may be understated because of the fact that these were block trades on large stocks on the NYSE, but it is still fairly strong evidence of the capacity of markets to adjust quickly to imbalances between demand and supply.

These and similar studies suffer from a sampling bias—they tend to look at large block trades in liquid stocks on the exchange floor—and from a selection bias—they look only at actual executions. The true cost of market impact arises from trades that would have been done in the absence of a market impact but were not, because of the perception that they would be large. In one of the few studies of how large this cost could be, Thomas Loeb collected bid and

FIGURE 11-2 **Returns around block trades***

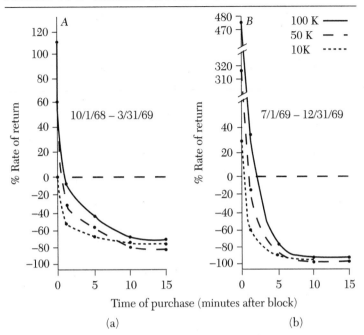

° Annualized rates of return on the −4.56 rule. (From Dann, L., D. Mayers, and R. Raab, "Trading Rules, Large Blocks, and the Speed of Adjustment," reprinted from *The Journal of Financial Economics,* January 1977, 18.)

ask prices from specialists and market makers, at a point in time, for a variety of block sizes. Thus, the differences in the spreads as the block size increases can be viewed as expected price impacts from these trades. Table 11-2 summarizes Loeb's findings across stocks, classified by market capitalization. The sectors refer to market capitalization, and they show the negative relationship between size and price impact. Note the effect of increasing block sizes on expected price impact within each sector: larger trades elicit much larger price impact than do smaller trades.

The Loeb findings were challenged by Leinweber,[10] who looked at 13,651 equity transactions, totaling about $2 billion, by a large corporate pension plan in 1991. In contrast to the positive relationship between block size and the trading costs presented in the Loeb study, he found a very weak relationship between trade size and trading cost. Figure 11-3 presents his findings on the percent of trading cost and the size of the trade as a percent of the three-day average trading volume. Note the bulge around the smallest trades, which seem to have both the lowest-cost and the highest-cost trades.

Figure 11-4 presents the net trading loss by order size. Smaller trades (< 25,000 shares), on average, had lower trading losses than larger trades, but they cumulatively accounted for almost 30 percent of the total trading costs for

TABLE 11-2 Round-trip transactions costs as a function of market capitalization and block size

Sector	\$5	25	250	500	1,000	2,500	5,000	10,000	20,000
				Dollar Value of Block (\$ Thousands)					
1 (small)	17.3%	27.3%	43.8%						
2	8.9	12.0	23.8	33.4%					
3	5.0	7.6	18.8	25.9	30.0%				
4	4.3	5.8	9.6	16.9	25.4	31.5%			
5	2.8	3.9	5.9	8.1	11.5	15.7	25.7%		
6	1.8	2.1	3.2	4.4	5.6	7.9	11.0	16.2%	
7	1.9	2.0	3.1	4.0	5.6	7.7	10.4	14.3	20.0%
8	1.9	1.9	2.7	3.3	4.6	6.2	8.9	13.6	18.1
9 (large)	1.1	1.2	1.3	1.7	2.1	2.8	4.1	5.9	8.0

Source: Thomas F. Loeb, "Trading Cost: The Critical Link Between Investment Information and Results," *Financial Analysts Journal, 39,* no. 3 (May/June 1983): 41–42.

FIGURE 11-3   Percent of trading costs and rade size

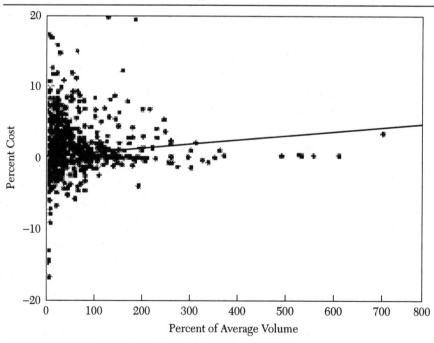

Source: David J. Leinweber.

FIGURE 11-4   Net trading loss by order size

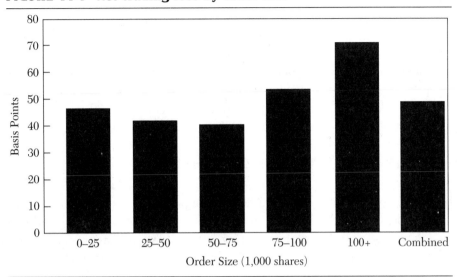

Source: David J. Leinweber.

the fund. Thus, it may be just as important to worry about trading costs on small trades as on large trades, especially given the sheer number of small trades made by many portfolio managers and investors.

Determinants of the Price Impact

Looking at the evidence, the variables that determine the price impact of trading seem to be the same variables that drive the bid–ask spread. That should not be surprising. The price impact and the bid–ask spread are both functions of the liquidity of the market. The inventory costs and adverse selection problems are likely to be largest for stocks where small trades can move the market significantly.

In many real asset markets, the difference between the price at which one can buy an asset and the price at which one can sell it, at the same point in time, is a reflection of both the bid–ask spread and the expected price impact of the trade on the asset. Not surprisingly, this difference can be very large in markets where trading is infrequent; for example, in the collectibles market, this cost can amount to more than 20 percent of the value of the asset.

Role in Investment Strategy

The fact that assets that have high bid–ask spreads also tend to be assets for which trading can have a significant price impact makes it even more critical to examine skeptically investment strategies that focus disproportionately on these assets. With the price impact, the effect of the size of the portfolio becomes much more critical because large portfolios beget large trading blocks, which, in turn, have the biggest price impact. Thus, a strategy of investing in low-priced stocks that are not followed by analysts may yield excess returns, even after the bid–ask spread is considered, for a portfolio of $25 million, but will cease to be profitable if that same portfolio becomes $500 million.

THE OPPORTUNITY COST OF WAITING

The final component of trading costs is the opportunity cost of waiting. An investor could reduce the bid–ask spread and price impact costs of trading by waiting. If there were no cost to waiting, even a large investor could break up trades into small lots and buy or sell large quantities without affecting the price or the spread significantly. There is, however, a cost to waiting. In particular, the price of an asset that an investor wants to buy because of a belief that it is undervalued may rise while the investor waits to trade, and this, in turn, can lead to one of two consequences: (1) the investor will eventually buy, but at a much higher price, reducing the expected profits from the investment, or (2) the price rises so much that the asset is no longer undervalued and the investor does not trade at all. A similar calculus applies when an investor wants to sell an asset that is believed to be overvalued.

The cost of waiting will depend in great part on the probability that the price will rise (fall) while the investor waits to buy (sell). We would argue that this probability will be a function of why the investor thinks the asset is under- or overvalued. In particular, the following factors should affect this probability:

1. *Is the valuation assessment based on private information or on public information?* Private information tends to have a short shelf life in financial markets, and the risks of sitting on private information are much greater than the risks of waiting when the valuation assessment is based on public information. Thus, the cost of waiting is much larger when the strategy is to buy because of rumors (or information) of a possible takeover than it would be when the strategy is to buy low PE ratio stocks.

2. *How active is the market for information?* Building on the first point, the risk of waiting, when one has valuable information, is much greater in markets where other investors are actively searching for the same information. Again, in practical terms, the costs of waiting might be greater when dozens of analysts are following the target stock than when few other investors are paying attention to it.

3. *How long term or short term is the strategy?* The generalization does not always hold, but short-term strategies are much more likely to be affected by the cost of waiting than long-term strategies. This can be partly attributed to the fact that short-term strategies are more likely to be motivated by private information, whereas long-term strategies are more likely to be motivated by views on value.

4. *Is the investment strategy a "contrarian" or "momentum" strategy?* In a contrarian strategy, where investors are investing against the prevailing tide (buying when others are selling, or selling when others are buying), the cost of waiting is likely to be smaller precisely because of this behavior. In contrast, the cost of waiting in a momentum strategy is likely to be higher because the investor is buying when others are buying and selling when others are selling.

In summary, the cost of waiting is likely to be greatest for short-term investment strategies based on private information or momentum, in markets with active information gathering. The cost will be less of an issue for long-term investment strategies based on public information, and for contrarian strategies.

THE MANAGEMENT OF TRADING COSTS

The preceding discussion makes clear not only how significant the trading cost problem is for active money managers, but also how difficult it is to develop a strategy to minimize the collective cost. Actions taken to reduce one type of trading cost (say, the brokerage commission or bid–ask spread) may increase another (for instance, the price impact). Strategies designed to minimize the collective impact of the bid–ask spread and the price impact (such as breaking up trades, or using alternative trading routes) may increase the opportunity cost of waiting. In this section, we examine five steps for managing trading costs within the broader construct of maximizing portfolio returns, given an investment philosophy.

Step 1. Develop and stay within a coherent investment philosophy and a consistent investment strategy. Portfolio managers who pride themselves on style switching or moving from one investment philosophy to another bear the biggest burden in terms of transactions costs, partly because style switching increases turnover and partly because it is difficult to develop a trading strategy without a consistent investment strategy.

Step 2. Estimate the cost of waiting, given the investment strategy that is being followed. As noted in the previous section, the cost of waiting is likely to be small for long-term, contrarian strategies, and greater for short-term, information-based, and momentum strategies. If the cost of waiting is very high, then the objective has to be to minimize this cost, which essentially translates into trading as quickly as one can, even if the other costs of trading increase as a consequence.

Step 3. Given the cost of waiting, look at the alternatives available to minimize the effect of the bid–ask spread and the price impact on portfolio returns. We have talked about trading primarily in terms of trading on the floor of the exchange, but an investor can use a number of other options to reduce the trading costs. Rose and Cushing[11] make the following suggestions to reduce trading costs on a portfolio:

1. Take advantage of the alternatives to trading on the floor of the exchange. Among these alternatives are: using the upstairs block market (where large buyers and sellers trade with each other), the dealer market (where trades are made with a dealer), and crossing networks (where trades are executed over a network). The tradeoff is straightforward; the approaches that yield the most liquidity (the exchange floor and the dealer market) also have the highest trading costs.

2. Trade portfolios rather than individual stocks, when multiple orders have to be placed. Portfolio trades generally result in lower trading costs and allow for better risk management and hedging capabilities.

3. Use technology to reduce the paperwork associated with trading and to keep track of trades that have already been made. By giving traders information on whether new trades have been executed, and on trades that have already been made, technology can help control costs.

4. Be prepared, prior to trading, with ways to control liquidity and splits between manual and electronic trading. "Pretrade" analysis allows traders to identify the least costly and most efficient way to make a trade.

5. After a trade has been executed, do a posttrade analysis of the details of the trade, in addition to a market impact analysis, which lists, among other information, the benchmarks that can be used to estimate the price impact, including the midpoint of the bid–ask spread before the trade, and the previous day's close. Posttrade analyses can then be aggregated across types of trades, securities, and markets, to give portfolio managers a measure of where their costs are greatest and how to control them.

Step 4. Stay within a portfolio size that is consistent with the investment philosophy and the trading strategy that has been chosen. Most portfolio managers are tempted to view portfolio growth as the fruit of past success, but a danger arises from allowing portfolios to become too big. How big is too big? It depends on both the portfolio strategy that has been chosen and the trading costs associated with that strategy. A long-term value investor who focuses on well-known, large-capitalization stocks might be able to allow a portfolio to increase to almost any size. An investor in small-cap, high-growth stocks or emerging market stocks may not have the same luxury, because of the trading costs enumerated in our earlier sections.

Step 5. Consider whether the investment strategy is yielding returns that exceed the costs. The ultimate test of an investment strategy lies in whether it earns excess returns after transactions costs. For an investor who has gone through the first four steps, the moment of truth always arrives when the performance of the portfolio is evaluated. If a strategy consistently delivers returns that are lower than the costs associated with implementing the strategy, the investor has one of two choices: (1) switch to a passive investing approach (such as an index fund) or (2) adopt a different active investing strategy—one that has higher expected returns or lower trading costs, or both.

CONCLUSION

Trading costs are an integral part of any investment portfolio. They can make the difference between a portfolio that beats the market and one that does not. The overall evidence suggests that trading costs impose a significant drag on portfolio returns, and may explain why active money managers underperform the market. One reason for high trading costs is that they include not just brokerage costs, but also the costs associated with the bid–ask spread, the price impact created by trading, and the cost of waiting. They are difficult to control because actions taken to reduce one component of trading costs tend to increase the other components.

Trading costs do not impose a uniform burden on all investment strategies. They punish short-term, information-based strategies far more than they do long-term value-based strategies, and they affect strategies that focus on small, less-liquid assets far more than strategies built around liquid assets. No matter what strategy is used, the portfolio manager's job is to manage trading costs, given the constraints of the strategy, and to earn an excess return that covers these costs.

12 MANAGING PORTFOLIO RISK

Roger Clarke

The risk characteristics of the investor should drive both the asset allocation and asset selection components of portfolio construction. Once portfolios are created, however, the risk in the portfolio still has to be monitored and managed. The client's risk characteristics might change, temporarily or permanently, creating a need for a concurrent change in the portfolio. Alternatively, the portfolio managers views of markets might necessitate risk hedging; for instance, a portfolio manager who believes that stocks are overvalued in the aggregate but does not want to sell of his or her stock holdings might look for a way to hedge stock market risk.

Effective risk management requires a decision as to how much of the risk should be hedged and at what cost. Analytical tools are required if one wants to be more precise about measuring risk. As a result, we frequently resort to mathematical expressions to capture the central concepts. Understanding these concepts is critical if the investor wants to apply risk management techniques in practice. In fact, the rigor of the mathematics makes the subject easier to understand and apply, not more difficult. Nonmathematical explanations follow each important mathematical expression.

HEDGING VEHICLES FOR MANAGING RISK

Two of the most frequently used generic vehicles for hedging risk involve either linear or nonlinear payoff patterns. Derivative securities are the most

274

common hedging vehicles. They are referred to as *derivatives* because they "derive" their value from the price of an underlying security or index. The most common linear derivatives are futures and forward contracts; the nonlinear derivatives involve options. Futures and forwards can deal most easily with risk that is symmetric, while options are usually required to deal with asymmetric or downside risk.

Futures and Forwards

A *forward contract* provides an opportunity to contract now for the purchase or sale of an asset or security at a specified price, but to delay payment for the transaction until a future settlement date. A forward contract can be either purchased or sold. An investor who purchases a forward contract commits to the purchase of the underlying asset or security at a specified price at a specified date in the future. An investor who sells a forward contract commits to the sale of the underlying asset or security at a specified price at a specified date in the future.

The date for future settlement of the contract is usually referred to as the *settlement* or *expiration date*. The fact that the price is negotiated now but payment is delayed until expiration creates an *opportunity cost* for the seller in receiving payment. The opportunity cost is the interest the investor might have earned by receiving the payment now and investing it until the maturity of the forward contract. As a result, the negotiated price for future delivery of the asset is usually different from the current cash price in order to reflect the cost of waiting to get paid.

For example, if an investor sells stock currently worth $250,000, but has to wait 30 days to be paid, the opportunity cost or interest lost over that 30-day period at a current interest rate of 6 percent would be:

$$\text{Opportunity Cost} = \$250,000 \ (0.06)(30/360) = \$1,250$$

The fair price for the stock if payment is deferred by 30 days is thus:

$$\$250,000 + \$1,200 = \$251,200$$

Strictly speaking, such a contract is referred to as a forward contract. A *futures contract* has many of the same elements as a forward contract, but any gains or losses that accrue as the current price of the asset fluctuates relative to the negotiated price in a futures contract are realized on a day-to-day basis. This daily realization is referred to as the *mark-to-market* convention. The total gain or loss is generally the same for a futures contract as for a forward contract with the same maturity date, except that the accumulated gain or loss is realized on a daily basis with the futures contract instead of in total at the forward contract's settlement date. Futures contracts also require the posting of a performance bond or deposit with the broker to initiate the trade. The purpose of this deposit is to reduce the chance that one of the parties to the trade might build up substantial losses and then default. This performance bond is referred to as *initial margin.* The amount of initial margin varies for different futures contracts, but it usually amounts to between 2 percent and 10 percent of the contract value, depending on the volatility of the specific market or underlying security. More volatile contracts usually require higher margins than less volatile contracts.

Another difference between forward and futures contracts is that futures contracts have standardized provisions specifying maturity date and contract size, so they can be traded interchangeably on organized exchanges such as the Chicago Board of Trade or the Chicago Mercantile Exchange. Most contracts that are traded actively are futures contracts, although an active forward market for foreign exchange exists through the banking system. Futures markets are regulated by the Commodity Futures Trading Commission, but forward markets are not. Table 12-1 provides a brief summary of the differences between futures and forward contracts.

Although forward and futures contracts are not exactly the same, the two terms are often used interchangeably. Research shows that, if interest rates are constant and the term structure is flat, the two will be priced the same.[1] [See Cox, Ingersoll, and Ross (1981).] These conditions are not met

TABLE 12-1   Comparison of futures and forward contracts

	Futures	Forward Contracts
Contract size	Standardized	Flexible
Maturity	Fixed maturities usually in three-month increments	Flexible
Pricing	Open outcry process at the futures exchange	Bid and offer quotes by each bank or broker
Collateral	Initial margin and daily mark to market	Standing lines of credit
Counterparty	Exchange serves as the guarantor of the trade	Individual bank or broker with whom the contract is negotiated
Commissions	Fixed rate per contract paid to the broker	Usually embedded in the bid and offer quotation
Settlement	Position is usually reversed by an offsetting transaction in the futures market	Often settled in cash at the expiration of the contract. Some contracts require physical delivery.

precisely in practice, but the difference in price between a futures and forward contract is usually small [see Cornell and Reinganum (1981), and Park and Chen (1985)].

The fair pricing of a futures or forward contract is usually maintained because market mechanisms provide the opportunity to create a riskless position for a gain if the contract is mispriced in excess of any transaction costs incurred to structure the arbitrage. The arbitrage relationship creates an equivalence between the return from either investing directly in the security itself or purchasing a futures contract while holding an equivalent amount of cash in an interest-bearing cash reserve. Creating an equivalent return pattern using a futures contract is sometimes referred to as creating a *synthetic security*. One behaves like the other in its risk and return characteristics; that is, the two sides of the relationship in Equation (1) have the same risk and return profile:

$$\text{Forward Contract} + \text{Cash Reserve} \leftrightarrow \text{Underlying Security} \qquad (1)$$

At times the investor may find it more advantageous to create the risk–return profile of the security by using the futures or forward contract instead. Futures and forwards provide a convenient and cost-effective way to create quick exposure to selected foreign exchange, fixed-income, equity, and commodities markets.

The fair price of a forward contract can be represented as:

$$F_0 = \text{Current Security Price} + \text{Interest Opportunity Cost}$$
$$- \text{Cash Distribution Paid by the Security} \qquad (2)$$
$$= S_0(1 + rt) - C_t$$

where: F_0 = current price of the forward contract
S_0 = current price of the underlying security
r = annualized riskless interest rate corresponding to maturity date t (reflecting the interest the seller loses by waiting to be paid)
t = maturity of the forward contract (fraction of a year)
C_t = cash distribution from the underlying security paid through date t (i.e., dividends or interest)

Equation (2) expresses the fair price of a forward contract as equal to the current security price plus the interest opportunity cost of delayed payment minus the interest or dividends received from the security over the period.

This pricing relationship shows how we can create a synthetic security by purchasing the forward contract and investing an equivalent amount of cash in an interest-bearing account earning at rate r until time t. The value of the cash reserve at the maturity of the forward contract will be $S_0(1 + rt)$. The gain or loss on the forward contract at maturity will be equal to $(F_t - F_0)$. At expiration the price of the forward contract will converge to the price of the security. Using this relationship allows us to write the value of the synthetic security at expiration as:

$$
\begin{aligned}
\text{Value of the Synthetic Security at } t &= S_0(1 + rt) + (F_t - F_0) \\
&= S_0(1 + rt) + [S_t - S_0(1 + rt) + C_t] \qquad (3) \\
&= S_t + C_t
\end{aligned}
$$

The term $(S_t + C_t)$ represents the value the investor would have at time t if the underlying security had been purchased initially and the interest or dividends subsequently received. The investor has created the same risk and return characteristics with a forward contract as with the underlying security.

Futures and forwards also provide a convenient and cost-effective way to hedge risk in their respective markets. Rearranging the synthetic security relationship in Equation (1) shows how derivatives can be used for hedging:

$$\text{Underlying Security} - \text{Forward Contract} \leftrightarrow \text{Synthetic Cash Reserve} \qquad (4)$$

The insight from Equation (4) comes by noting that holding the underlying security and selling a forward contract results in creating a *synthetic cash reserve*. That is, the risk in the underlying security is offset by a short position in the forward contract. The arbitrage relationship in the pricing of the forward contract is such that the return earned on the hedge is consistent with a riskless rate.

Using the fair price of the forward contract also allows us to see how hedging can eliminate the risk in the underlying security. The gain or loss on the short forward position cancels out the risk in the underlying security, giving the value of the hedged position at expiration as:

$$
\begin{aligned}
\text{Value of the Hedged Position at Expiration} &= S_t + C_t - (F_t - F_0) \\
&= S_t + C_1 - [S_t - S_0(1 + rt) + C_t] \qquad (5) \\
&= S_0(1 + rt)
\end{aligned}
$$

Notice that the value of the hedged position is not dependent on the value of the underlying security at expiration. All of the risk has been eliminated by creating a synthetic cash reserve earning a rate r so that the value of the position at expiration including interest is $S_0(1 + rt)$.

In essence, creating a hedged position is an attempt to eliminate the primary risk in the underlying security and to shift it to others in the futures market willing to bear the risk. The risk can always be shifted by doing away with the underlying security position, but this may interfere with the nature of the investor's business or disrupt a continuing investment program. The futures or forward market provides an alternate way to control temporarily or eliminate much of the risk in the underlying security position while continuing to hold the security.

The impact of hedging can be seen by examining the effect of hedging on a portfolio's return profile and probability distribution. Figure 12-1 illustrates the return on the hedged portfolio relative to the return on the underlying security. A partially hedged position reduces the slope of the return line, so that the hedged portfolio does not perform as well as the underlying security when returns are high, but it also does not perform as poorly when returns are low. The greater the portion of the portfolio that is hedged, the less slope the return line will have. A full hedge produces a flat line, indicating that the hedged portfolio will generate a fixed return no matter what the underlying asset does. This fixed return should be equal to the riskless rate if the future or forward is fairly priced.

Figure 12-2 shows how the forward hedge changes the probability distribution of returns. If the return distribution for the underlying security is symmetric with a wide dispersion, hedging the portfolio with forwards or futures gradually draws both tails of the distribution in toward the middle, and the mean return shrinks back somewhat toward the riskless rate. A full hedge draws both tails into one place and puts all of the probability mass at the riskless rate.

Hedging with futures or forwards will affect both tails equally. One of the main differences between options and futures is that options can affect one tail

FIGURE 12-1   Return profiles for hedged portfolios

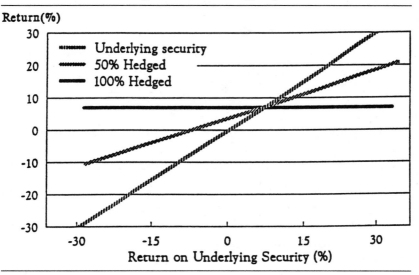

Return(%)

Underlying security
50% Hedged
100% Hedged

Return on Underlying Security (%)

FIGURE 12-2 Return distributions for hedged portfolios

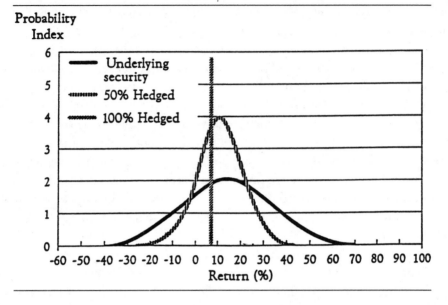

more dramatically than the other, so the distribution becomes quite skewed. Figure 12-3 illustrates the difference in the return distributions caused by a partial futures hedge versus a partial hedge created by using a put option. The put option hedge reduces the downside risk while leaving much of the upside potential. (The use of options for hedging is explained in more detail later.)

FIGURE 12-3 Return distributions for hedged portfolios

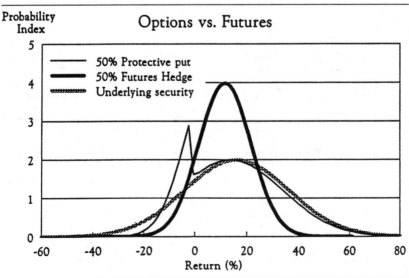

Pricing a Futures or Forward Contract

The price of a forward contract is related to (1) the price of the underlying security or asset, (2) the interest opportunity cost until the date of expiration, and (3) any expected cash distributions by the underlying asset before expiration. The fair pricing of a forward contract can be derived from the investment position called *cash-and-carry arbitrage*. The arbitrage argument is as follows: Suppose a security with a current price S_0 pays a cash distribution worth C_t at time t (fraction of a year) and ends with a value of S_t. Table 12-2 shows two different investment strategies that both result in holding the security at time t.

Because both strategies begin with the same dollar investment and result in the investor owning the security at time t, the ending values should also be equal to avoid one strategy from dominating the other. That is, the value of the security position at expiration should be equal to the principal and interest from the cash reserve plus the net gain or loss on the forward contract:

$$S_t + C_t = S_0(1 + rt) + (S_t - F_0) \qquad (6)$$

Solving for the forward price in Equation (21) gives:

$$F_0 = S_0(1 + rt) - C_t \qquad (7)$$

The fair price of a forward contract represents the current price of the security adjusted for the opportunity cost of delayed settlement. The seller of the security is compensated for waiting to receive the money by earning interest on the current value of the security. In addition, the forward price is reduced by any cash distributions the seller receives before settlement while still owning the security. This adjustment to the current security price to arrive at the fair forward price is sometimes referred to as the *net cost of carry* or *net*

TABLE 12-2   Cash-and-carry arbitrage

Strategy	Value Now	Value at Time t
Strategy I		
Purchase the security	S_0	$S_t + C_t$
Strategy II		
Invest equivalent \$ amount until time t at rate r	S_0	$S_0(1 + rt)$
Purchase a forward contract on the security for settlement at time t for price F	—	$S_t - F_0$
Total value for Strategy II	S_0	$S_0(1 + rt) + (S_t - F_0)$

carry. If the forward contract is not priced in this way, one of the alternatives for achieving the security returns will dominate the other.

For any given forward price, the investor can infer what interest rate the buyer has to pay to compensate the seller. This rate is usually referred to as the *implied repo rate* (repo stands for "repurchase"). The market tends to price the forward contract such that the implied rate equals a fair market interest rate. The rate usually varies between the short-term Treasury bill rate and the Eurodollar rate. If the implied rate is higher than the market rate, investors could create a riskless arbitrage to capture the increased return. A rate higher than the market rate could be earned by selling an overvalued forward contract and buying the security. Funds could be borrowed below market rates by buying an undervalued forward contract and selling the security.[2]

Equity Index Futures Pricing

The fair price of an equity index futures contract is established according to the cash-and-carry arbitrage relationship:

$$F_0 = \text{Index} + \text{Interest} - \text{Dividend Income} = S_0(1 + rt) - D_t \qquad (8)$$

where: F_0 = fair value futures price
S_0 = equity index
r = annualized financing rate (money market yield)
D_t = value of dividends paid before expiration
t = time to expiration (fraction of a year)

Because dividend yields are often less than short-term interest rates, the equity index futures price is often greater than the index price.

Consider, as an example, a contract on the S&P 500 index that is traded on the Chicago Mercantile Exchange with quarterly expiration in March, June, September, and December. The size of the contract is equal to $500 times the value of the S&P 500 index. The contract does not require the purchase or sale of actual shares of stock but is cash-settled in an amount equal to the change in value of the shares. Assume the index is at 900, and the expiration time for the contract is 34 days hence. The financing rate is 6.6 percent a year, and expected dividends through expiration in index points are 2.24. Thus, according to the general form for the price of an equity index futures contract,

$$F_0 = 900\left[1 + \frac{0.066(34)}{360}\right] - 2.24 = 903.37$$

If the actual futures price is quoted at 903.09, the future would appear to be underpriced by 0.28 index points relative to fair value. Whether this difference is material enough to be arbitraged away by market participants depends on the transaction costs of constructing the arbitrage.

Treasury Bond and Note Futures Pricing

The pricing of a note or bond futures contract is somewhat more complicated than for an equity index contract:

$$F_0 = \text{(Price + Interest Cost} - \text{Coupon Income)/Delivery Factor}$$
$$= \frac{P_0(1+rt)-Bc(t+a)}{f} \tag{9}$$

where: B = par value of the cheapest-to-deliver note or bond
P_0 = market price of note or bond B + accrued interest
r = annualized financing rate (money market yield)
c = annualized coupon rate
t = time to expiration (fraction of a year)
a = period of accrued interest (fraction of a year)
f = delivery factor of note or bond B

Equation (9) indicates that the fair price of a Treasury note or bond contract is equal to the current security price plus the interest opportunity cost less the coupon interest paid, all of which is adjusted by the *delivery factor.* Treasury bond futures contracts are traded on the Chicago Board of Trade with quarterly expiration dates ending in March, June, September, and December. The size of the contract is equal to \$100,000 face value of eligible Treasury bonds having at least 15 years to maturity and not callable for at least 15 years.[3] The contract requires the actual purchase or sale (called *delivery*) of Treasury bonds if it is held to expiration.

Because different notes and bonds have different coupon payments and different maturities, the actual Treasury note or bond that can be selected for delivery by the short seller is adjusted in price by a delivery factor to reflect a standardized 8 percent coupon rate. This adjustment normalizes the Treasury notes and bonds eligible for delivery so that the short-seller has some flexibility in choosing which note or bond to deliver to make good on the contract. The factor associated with any note or bond is calculated by dividing by 100 the dollar price that the note or bond would command if it were priced to yield 8 percent to maturity (or to first call date if the note or bond is callable). The pricing of the futures contract generally follows the price of the note or bond that is the cheapest to deliver at the time. The futures price itself is quoted in 32nds, with 100 being the price of an 8 percent coupon note or bond when its yield to maturity is also equal to 8 percent.

The fair price of the Treasury note and bond futures contract is also a function of the interest opportunity cost (P_0rt) and the size of the coupon payments up to the expiration date of the futures contract [$Bc(t + a)$]. Thus, the theoretical price of the Treasury bond future with 98 days to expiration is:

Current market price	(7.25% due in 2016)	78.16
+ Interest cost	78.16(0.066)(98/360)	= 1.40
− Coupon income	−100(0.0725)(98 + 9)/360	= −2.16
		77.40
÷ Delivery factor		0.9167
= Theoretical futures price		84.43 or $84\frac{14}{32}$

The actual price of this contract is $84^{12}/_{32}$, a mispricing that is equal to $-^2/_{32}$.

If the short-term interest rate is less than the coupon rate on the cheapest-to-deliver (CTD) note or bond, the futures price will be lower than the note or bond's price. If the short-term interest rate is higher than the coupon rate on the note or bond, the futures price will be more than the bond's price. Because short-term rates are generally lower than long-term rates, the futures price is often lower than the note or bond's market price.

Eurodollar Futures Pricing

Eurodollar futures are another popular futures contract. They are traded on several exchanges, but most of the trading volume occurs on the International Monetary Market at the Chicago Mercantile Exchange. Eurodollar futures have the same monthly expiration dates (March, June, September, and December) as do futures on Treasury notes and bonds. These contracts are settled in cash, and each contract corresponds to a $1 million deposit with a three-month maturity. Eurodollar futures are quoted as an index formed by subtracting from 100 the annualized percentage forward rate for the three-month London Interbank Offer Rate (LIBOR) at the date of expiration of the contract.

The pricing formula for a Eurodollar futures contract is:

$$F_0 = 100(1 - f_t), \tag{10}$$

where f_t is the annualized three-month LIBOR forward rate beginning at time t. For example, if the current forward interest rate 35 days forward is 6.31 percent, the futures price would be quoted as 93.96 (100 − 6.31).

A price quotation of this sort does not appear to have the same arbitrage conditions as the other contracts. The arbitrage process, however, is working to keep these forward interest rates consistent with the implied forward rates in the market term structure of interest rates. A short review of interest rate relationships and forward rates is given in Clarke (1993).[4]

Treasury Bill Futures Pricing

Futures on three-month Treasury bills are also traded on the International Monetary Market. The Treasury bill contracts have the same maturity months as Treasury notes and bonds and the Eurodollar contracts, and have a face value of $1 million. Settlement at expiration involves delivery of the current three-month Treasury bill. The Treasury bill futures contract is quoted the same way as the Eurodollar future. The forward interest rate used to calculate the index, however, is the three-month forward discount rate on Treasury bills at the expiration date of the futures contract.

The price for a Treasury bill contract is calculated as:

$$F_0 = 100(1 - d_t) \tag{11}$$

where d_t is the annualized three-month forward discount rate on a Treasury bill beginning at time t. For example, if $d_t = 7.32$ percent and $t = 45$ days, the futures price would be quoted as 92.68.

The volume of trading in Treasury bill futures has been declining in recent years, and the volume of Eurodollar futures has been increasing. The Eurodollar future is now more widely used and is the more liquid contract.

Foreign Currency Futures Pricing

Futures contracts in foreign currencies are traded on the International Monetary Market with the same expiration cycle of March, June, September, and December. Settlement at expiration involves a wire transfer of the appropriate currency two days after the last trading day. Each contract has specified size relative to the foreign currency:

Currency	Contract Size	
Australian dollar	100,000	AUD
British pound	62,500	BP
Canadian dollar	100,000	CAD
Deutsche mark	125,000	DM
French franc	250,000	FF
Japanese yen	12,500,000	JY
Swiss franc	125,000	SF

The fair pricing of a foreign exchange futures contract follows the same arbitrage process as that of the other futures contracts resulting in the relationship:

$$F_0 = \frac{S_0(1 + r_d t)}{(1 + r_f t)} \tag{12}$$

where S_0 is the spot exchange rate, r_d is the annualized domestic interest rate, and r_f is the annualized foreign interest rate of maturity t. This arbitrage relationship is often called *covered interest arbitrage*. Equation (12) indicates that the fair price of a foreign exchange futures contract is equal to the current spot exchange rate times the ratio of one plus the interest rate in the respective countries.

To understand this relationship, consider several investment alternatives. In the first case, one unit of the domestic currency is invested for t fraction of a year at an annualized rate of r_d. As an alternative, the investor could convert the domestic currency to the foreign currency at a spot exchange rate of S_0 ($\$$/foreign currency), receive interest at the foreign interest rate, and then contract to convert back to the domestic currency at the forward foreign exchange rate F_0. Each investment is invested in riskless securities, and the currency risk has been neutralized, so both strategies should generate a riskless return. To avoid one riskless return from dominating the other, both should result in the same value at time t. Equating the two values gives:

$$(1 + r_d t) = \frac{F_0(1 + r_f t)}{S_0} \tag{13}$$

The forward foreign exchange rate would have to be set at its fair value in order for both strategies to give the same rate of return. If the forward exchange rate deviated from this fair value, the difference could be arbitraged to give profits with no risk. Solving for the appropriate forward exchange rate from the equation above that eliminates arbitrage profits gives:

$$F_0 = \frac{S_0(1 + r_d t)}{(1 + r_f t)} \tag{14}$$

The calculation of a fair forward exchange rate, given interest rates in Japan and the United States, and using the covered interest rate arbitrage relationship is shown below. Assume the Japanese interest rate is 3.5 percent, the U.S. interest rate is 6.2 percent, and the time to expiration is 35 days. The exchange rate is 0.00960 dollars per yen or 104.16 yen per dollar. The fair forward foreign exchange rate is:

$$F_0 = \frac{0.00960 \left(1 + \dfrac{0.062(35)}{360}\right)}{\left(1 + \dfrac{0.035(35)}{360}\right)} = 0.00963 \ \$/\text{yen, or} \ \frac{1}{0.00963} = 103.89 \ \text{yen}/\$$$

The futures price reflects the relative difference in interest rates between countries over the time period. The higher interest rate in the United States results in a higher forward exchange rate of 0.00963 $/yen for future delivery as against the spot rate of 0.00960 $/yen.

Options

The two basic types of options are a *call option* and a *put option.* The call option gives the investor the right to buy a security at a specified price within a specified period of time. For example, a call option on the S&P 500 gives an investor the right to buy units of the S&P 500 index at a set price within a specified amount of time. The put option gives the investor the right to sell a security at a specified price within a particular period of time.

Options have several important characteristics. One is the *strike* or *exercise price.* This price gives the value at which the investor can buy or sell the underlying security. The *maturity* of the option defines the time period within which the investor can buy or sell the security at the exercise price.

Three terms—*at the money, in the money,* and *out of the money*—identify where the current security price is relative to the strike or exercise price. An option that is in the money means that the option would result in a positive value to the investor if exercised. For example, a call option that has a strike price of $100 when the security price is $120 is in the money, because the investor can buy the security for less than its market price. Similarly, a put option with a strike price of $100 while the security is priced at $90 would be in the money, because the investor can sell the security for more than its current market price.

Some options can be exercised early, but some can be exercised only on the specific maturity date. An option that can be exercised early is called an *American* option; an option that can be exercised only at the maturity date is a *European* option. Most of the options traded on organized U.S. exchanges are American options, although a few European option contracts are traded as well.

Analysts have come to think of the option price or premium as being composed of two parts—the *intrinsic value* and the *time value*—as illustrated in Figure 12-4. The intrinsic value depends on the relationship between the security price and the exercise price of the option. The intrinsic value of a call option is the maximum of either zero or the difference between the security price and the exercise price $(S - K)$. If $S - K$ is positive, the call option is in the money and has a positive intrinsic value. If $S - K$ is negative, the call option is out of the money and has zero intrinsic value. The intrinsic value of a put option is just the reverse: the maximum of zero or $K - S$. If $K - S$ is positive, the put option is in the money. If $K - S$ is negative, the put option is out of the money and has zero intrinsic value.

FIGURE 12-4 Option price

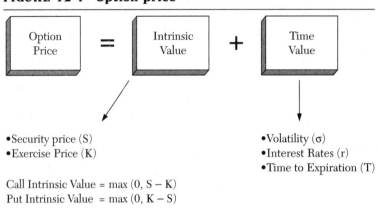

•Security price (S)
•Exercise Price (K)

•Volatility (σ)
•Interest Rates (r)
•Time to Expiration (T)

Call Intrinsic Value = max (0, S − K)
Put Intrinsic Value = max (0, K − S)

For example, suppose the current foreign exchange rate between the U.S. dollar and the Deutsche mark is 0.62 $/DM. A put option with a strike price of 0.64 $/DM would have an intrinsic value of:

$$\text{Put Intrinsic Value} = \max (0, K - S)$$
$$= \max (0, 0.64 - 0.62)$$
$$= 0.02 \ \$/DM$$

If the size of the option contract covers 62,500 DM, the dollar amount of the intrinsic value would be:

$$0.02 \ \$/DM \times 62{,}500 \ DM = \$1{,}250$$

At the same time, the intrinsic value of a call option with the same strike price would be zero:

$$\text{Call Intrinsic Value} = \max (0, S - K)$$
$$= \max (0, 0.62 - 0.64)$$
$$= 0$$

In this instance the put option would be in the money, and the call option would be out of the money.

The time value of an option is a function of the security's volatility, or risk (σ); the current level of interest rates (r); and the option's maturity, or time to expiration (T). The volatility of the underlying security and the time to expiration are particularly important to the price of an option. Volatility is important because the higher the volatility of the underlying security, the greater the potential payoff of the option if it expires in the money. Therefore, an option on a more risky security should be worth more than an option on a less risky security. Time to expiration is also important. An option with a short time to expiration has less time to reach a value where the option will pay off. Consequently, an option with more time to expiration will be worth more than an option with only a short time to expiration.

The difference between the option price and intrinsic value is the time value. The option's positive time value gradually approaches zero at expiration, with the option price at expiration equal to its intrinsic value. The option price's convergence to its intrinsic value at expiration is similar to the convergence of a futures contract to the underlying security price at expiration.

Insight into the characteristics of options can be obtained by looking at how options behave and what value they have at expiration. A matrix is a simple technique for showing the value of option positions at expiration:

Value at Expiration

	$S < K$	$S > K$
Call	0	$S - K$
Put	$K - S$	0
Security	S	S

At expiration of the put or call option, its intrinsic value depends on whether the security price is lower than the exercise price or more than the exercise price. The value of the underlying security is the same, S, whether it is below or above the option's exercise price. These values form the basic building blocks for option strategy analysis.

Figure 12-5 illustrates the payoff pattern at expiration for a call option. On the horizontal axis is plotted the security price. The vertical axis measures the payoff at expiration. The case representing the security's value is shown by the dashed line. For example, if the security ends with a value of K dollars, the security will have a payoff of K dollars. The call option has a value of zero until the security price reaches the exercise price K, after which the call option increases one for one in price as the security price increases. The investor, however, must first purchase the option. So the net payoff from buying a call option is negative until the security price reaches the exercise price, and then it starts to rise (the dotted line). This line represents the payoff the investor receives net of the cost of the option. The investor breaks even with zero net profit at the point where the security price equals the strike price plus the call option premium.

Note that the call option has a kinked or asymmetric payoff pattern. This feature distinguishes it from a futures contract. The future has a payoff pattern that is a straight line, as does the underlying security. This payoff asymmetry

FIGURE 12-5   Payoff profile of a call option

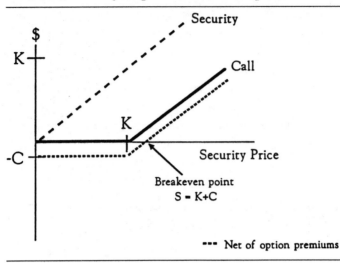

allows options to take specialized return patterns that are unavailable through futures contracts.

Figure 12-6 illustrates the behavior of a put option. The put option has an intrinsic value of zero above the exercise price. Below there, it increases one for one as the security price declines. If an investor buys a put option, the net payoff of the option is the dotted line. The investor breaks even, with zero net profit, at the point where the security price equals the strike price less the put option premium.

FIGURE 12-6   Payoff profile of a put option

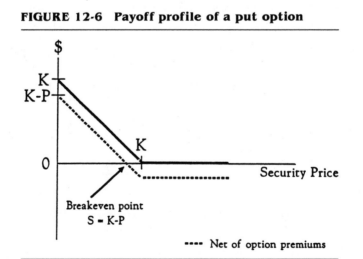

Pricing an Option: The Black–Scholes Model

Our understanding of options and how to price them has been one of the most important developments in finance in the last 25 years. The Black–Scholes model for pricing a call option was first published by Black and Scholes in 1973. It has since become the most common method for valuing options. The pricing formula is relatively difficult to calculate by hand, but many computer programs are available and are easy to use.

The Black–Scholes model for a call option can be written as:

$$C = S_0 N(d) - Ke^{-rT}N(d - \sigma\sqrt{T}) \tag{15}$$

where:

$$d = \frac{\ln(S_0 / K) + (r + \tfrac{1}{2}\sigma^2)T}{\sigma\sqrt{T}}$$

$$N(d) = \text{Cumulative Normal Distribution}$$

The Black–Scholes model indicates that the call option is equal to the security price (S_0) times a probability $N(d)$ minus the present value of the exercise price (Ke^{-rt}) times another probability $N(d - \sigma\sqrt{T})$. The probabilities are given by the cumulative normal distribution represented in Figure 12-7, and are similar to what we saw earlier.

Notice that the call price depends on the current security price (S_0) and the exercise price K; it also depends on the rate of interest (r), the time to expiration (T), and the risk of the underlying security (σ). As we noted in the discussion of the payoff of an option, the intrinsic value is dependent on both the security price and the strike price of the option. Furthermore, the potential size of the payoff, and the probability of being in the money are affected by the volatility of the underlying asset. Finally, it is not surprising that the time

FIGURE 12-7   Standard normal curve

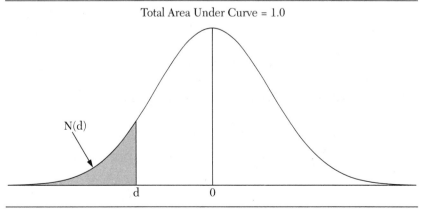

to achieve the threshold of the strike price is another factor that has a bearing on the price of the option.

The price of the put option can be found from the Black–Scholes model by using the *put/call parity relationship:*[5]

$$
\begin{aligned}
P &= C - S_0 + Ke^{-rT} \\
&= S_0[N(d) - 1] - Ke^{-rT}N(d - \sigma \sqrt{T})
\end{aligned}
\tag{16}
$$

where d and $N(d)$ are defined as in the Black–Scholes equation for a call option. By substituting in the price of the call option developed by Black–Scholes, we can derive the price of the put option. The formula is similar to the call option formula: the security price times a probability minus the present value of the strike price times another probability. The associated probabilities are again drawn from the cumulative normal distribution. A table of values for the cumulation normal distribution is given in Appendix A.

To illustrate the calculation of option prices using the Black–Scholes model, assume the security price (S_0) is \$100, the strike price (K) is also \$100, the riskless rate (r) is 5 percent, and the volatility of the security price (σ) is 22 percent. For an option with a maturity (T) of one year, d would equal 0.34; $N(d)$ 0.6331; and $N(d - \sigma \sqrt{T})$ 0.5478. The price for the call option is:

$$
C = 100(0.6331) - 100(0.9512)(0.5478) = \$11.20
$$

and the price for the put option is:

$$
P = 100(-0.3669) - 100(0.9512)(-0.4522) = \$6.32
$$

For a call option with one-quarter of a year to expiration, d equals 0.17; $N(d)$ 0.5675; $N(d - \sigma \sqrt{T})$ 0.5239. The prices for the call and put options are:

$$
C = 100(0.5675) - 100(0.9876)(0.5239) = \$5.01
$$
$$
P = 100(-0.4325) - 100(0.9876)(-0.4761) = \$3.77
$$

Use of the Black–Scholes model requires a knowledge of the current security price, the exercise price, the expiration date, the current interest rate, and the volatility of the underlying security (represented by the standard deviation of returns). The first three parameters are well-defined and readily observable. The interest rate generally used in the formula corresponds to a riskless rate with a horizon equal to the expiration date of the option. Strictly speaking, the interest rate should be a continuously compounded rate. To convert a simple annualized rate R to a continuously compounded rate r, we can use the relationship:

$$
\ln(1 + R) = r
$$

Although the continuously compounded rate will always be lower than the simple interest rate, any mispricing in an option with a short maturity caused by the use of the simple rate instead of the continuous rate will generally be small, because the option price is not overly sensitive to the interest rate assumption for short horizons.

The annualized volatility of returns for the underlying security is the last element in the model. It is represented by the standard deviation of the continuously compounded return on the security. Analysts pricing options typically use some measure of historical volatility, such as daily, weekly, or monthly returns. If daily returns are used to estimate annual volatility, the daily variance is typically multiplied by 250 (trading days in a year) to obtain an annualized number. If weekly returns are used, the variance is multiplied by 52, or if monthly returns are used, the variance is multiplied by 12. A review of the basic assumptions of the Black–Scholes model along with some of its modifications is contained in Appendix B.

The Black–Scholes model allows us to examine one other important relationship used in designing hedge relationships. It is important to know how the price of an option changes with respect to the price of the underlying security. This change in option price as the underlying security price changes is called the option's *delta*. For example, if a call option has a delta of 0.4, this implies that if the security price increases by \$1, the option price will increase by \$0.40 ($1 \times 0.40 = 0.40$). It can be shown that the delta of a call option using the Black–Scholes model is equal to the cumulative normal probability:

$$\Delta_{\text{Call}} = N(d) \tag{17}$$

It follows from the put/call parity relationship that the delta of a put option is equal to the delta of a call option minus 1 where the put and the call options have the same strike price and maturity:

$$\begin{aligned} \Delta_{\text{put}} &= \Delta_{\text{call}} - 1 \\ &= N(d) - 1 \end{aligned} \tag{18}$$

Since the cumulative normal probability can take on values from 0 to 1, the delta of the call option will range from 0 to 1, and the delta of a put option will range from 0 to -1. A deep out-of-the-money option will have a delta close to 0, indicating that the option price will not change in value much as the security price changes. This implies that a deep in-the-money call option will have a delta close to 1.0 and a deep in-the-money put option will have a delta close to -1.0 so that they will move nearly dollar for dollar with a change in the security price. At-the-money call options have a delta of approximately 0.5, while at-the-money put options would have a delta of approximately -0.5. The delta on such options indicates that for every \$1 increase in the underlying security price, the call option would increase in value by $0.50, and the put option would decrease in value by $0.50.

A GENERAL FRAMEWORK FOR HEDGING RISK

Figure 12-8 presents a simple framework for thinking about available alternatives for dealing with risk. There are three basic alternatives: (1) eliminate the risk by liquidating the underlying positions that generate the risk, (2) retain the risk and receive the resulting benefits or drawbacks, or (3) transfer the risk to someone else by hedging. Eliminating the source of the risk by liquidating the underlying positions is frequently awkward or expensive in dealing with short-run risk but may be a viable alternative to deal with undesirable risk in the long run. Retaining the risk is often acceptable if the risks are small, or

FIGURE 12-8 Alternatives for dealing with investment risk

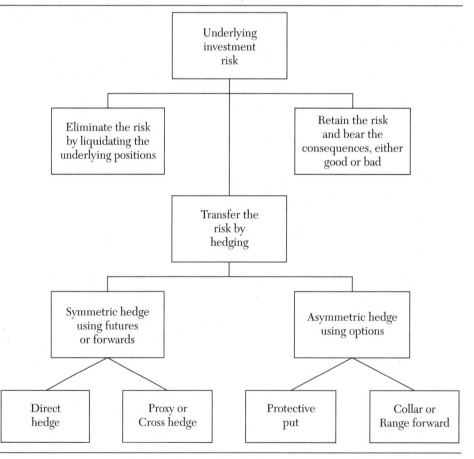

if there is sufficient compensation expected for bearing the risk. The final alternative is to transfer the risk to someone else by hedging. In many situations, investors may move among all three alternatives, depending on their expectations of market movements and their time horizons.

Two types of hedging alternatives are typically available, symmetric and asymmetric. Symmetric hedges can be constructed using forward or futures contracts, while asymmetric hedges require the use of some form of an option. A wide variety of complex hedging strategies might be designed to cover a specific situation, but we will deal with the most generic techniques in this chapter. Hedges have different advantages. Symmetric hedges deal best with risk described by variance or standard deviation, because these measures are symmetric in the way they treat deviations from a central point. Options deal better with measures of risk that address one side of the probability distribution or the other. Put options affect the downside of the probability distribution the most, which makes them ideal for dealing with the probability of shortfall, the expected shortfall, and the downside risk or relative semivariance. Conversely, call options affect the upside of the distribution, and can be used either to capture upside potential or truncate it.

Direct Hedge Ratios: Symmetric Hedges

A *hedge ratio* represents the amount of one security used to construct a hedge relative to the amount of the underlying security being hedged. In some cases, there is a direct way to calculate the appropriate hedge ratio between two securities. This technique can be used when the security used for hedging is tied directly to the underlying security being hedged. This is often the case when broad market risk is being hedged using futures, forwards, or option contracts to construct the hedge position. Hedge ratios can be calculated easily, because there is a direct link between the change in the value of the underlying security or portfolio and a change in the value of the associated derivative contract.

To develop this idea, suppose an investor holds one unit of a security S and wants to hedge it with another security F (this is often a futures or option contract). The change in the value of the combined position V as the security prices change is:

$$\Delta V = \Delta S + h \Delta F \qquad (19)$$

where h represents the number of units of security F used to hedge security S (the hedge ratio). Solving for the hedge ratio directly from Equation (19) gives:

$$h = \frac{\Delta V - \Delta S}{\Delta F} \qquad (20)$$

For a complete hedge, or market-neutral hedge ($\Delta V = 0$), the hedge ratio would be equal to the negative of the ratio of relative price changes between the security being hedged and the hedging security:

$$h = \frac{-\Delta S}{\Delta F} \qquad (21)$$

This simple way of calculating an appropriate hedge ratio can be illustrated by supposing S is a diversified equity portfolio, F is a futures contract on the S&P 500 index, and $\Delta S/\Delta F$ is assumed to equal 0.95. That is, when the S&P 500 futures contract moves by $1, the underlying equity portfolio moves by only $0.95, indicating that the portfolio is slightly less volatile than the broad market represented by the S&P 500 index. For a market-neutral hedge, the hedge ratio is:

$$h = -\frac{0.95}{1.00} = -0.95$$

An investor would sell futures contracts worth 95 percent of the value of the equity portfolio to create the hedge. Because the equity portfolio does not move one for one with the S&P 500 futures contract in the example, the investor does not want to use a hedge ratio of -1.0 to hedge the equity risk in the underlying securities. A market-neutral hedge requires fewer futures contracts to be used, because the underlying equity portfolio has only 95 percent of the movement of the futures contract.

If the investor wants only a partial hedge ($\Delta V = \frac{1}{3}\Delta S$, for example), the hedge ratio is:

$$h = \frac{\frac{1}{3}\,\Delta S - \Delta S}{\Delta F} = \frac{-2}{3}\left(\frac{\Delta S}{\Delta F}\right) = -0.63$$

This example also shows what the hedge ratio must be if only a partial hedge is created to protect against the price movement in the underlying securities. If the combined hedged position is targeted to have one-third of the movement of the underlying securities, a hedge ratio of -0.63 is needed. The investor then sells futures contracts worth only 63 percent of the value of the equity portfolio to create the partial hedge.

The arbitrage relationship between the forward or futures contract and the underlying security links the two prices together. This relationship can be used to calculate how the fair price of the forward or futures contract will change as the price of the underlying security changes. To see how this relationship can be used to estimate the hedge ratio directly, suppose that the price changes of both the security to be hedged and the forward or futures contract are proportional to the change in a common index I in the following way:

$$\Delta S = \beta_S \Delta I \text{ , and } \Delta F = \beta_F \Delta I$$

where β_s and β_F represent the sensitivity to the index of the security being hedged and of the futures contract, respectively.

Because both are tied to the same underlying index, the hedge ratio is proportional to the ratio of their respective sensitivities. That is:

$$h = \frac{-\Delta S}{\Delta F}$$

$$= -\frac{\beta_S}{\beta_F}$$

(22)

If the investor has a measure of how the prices of the futures contract and the hedged security change relative to the price of the common index, the investor can calculate the appropriate hedge ratio directly.

Equity Hedges

Suppose the price of an equity portfolio changes by a constant factor (represented by β_s) relative to the market index used by the futures contract. The change in the unit value of the portfolio is given by:

$$\Delta S = \beta_S \Delta I$$

(23)

and the short-term price change in the futures contract with t fraction of a year to maturity is given by:

$$\Delta F = (1 + rt)\Delta I$$

(24)

where ΔI is the change in the market index.[6]

The hedge ratio for an equity portfolio can then be calculated as the ratio of relative price changes:

$$h = \frac{-\Delta S}{\Delta F}$$

$$= \frac{-\beta_S}{(1 + rt)}$$

(25)

As an example, consider the calculation of the hedge ratio and the number of futures contracts required to hedge a $50 million equity portfolio with a beta of 1.05 relative to the S&P 500 index. If the futures contract has 35 days to expiration, the current interest rate is 8.6 percent, and the index stands at 930, the hedge ratio is:

$$h = \frac{-1.05}{\left[1 + \left(\dfrac{0.086 \times 35}{360}\right)\right]} = -1.04$$

The contract size for the S&P 500 is 500 times the value of the S&P 500 index, or $465,000 (500 × 930), so the number of futures contracts required to be sold is:

$$n = \frac{h(\text{Hedge Value})}{\text{Contract Size}} = \frac{-1.04(50,000,000)}{465,000}$$

$$= -111.8 \text{ Contracts}$$

Notice that the hedge ratio is slightly less than the relative risk or beta of the portfolio. The short-term hedge ratio allows for the slightly larger volatility in the index futures contract caused by its arbitrage pricing relationship. This additional volatility will shrink toward zero as the contract gets closer to maturity.

Foreign Exchange Hedges

For a foreign exchange contract, the change in the forward or futures contract's price relative to the change in the spot exchange rate is equal to:

$$\Delta F = \frac{\Delta S(1 + r_d t)}{(1 + r_f t)} \tag{26}$$

where r_d represents the domestic riskless interest rate, and r_f represents the foreign riskless interest rate with maturity t. Consequently, the hedge ratio is equal to the ratio of gross interest rates given by:

$$h = \frac{-\Delta S}{\Delta F} = \frac{-(1 + r_f t)}{(1 + r_d t)} \tag{27}$$

To calculate a hedge ratio for foreign exchange exposure, consider a hedge against a 100 million Deutsche mark position in which the futures contract expires in 42 days, the U.S. interest rate (r_d) is 5.5 percent, and the German interest rate (r_f) is 10.3 percent. The contract size is 125,000 marks.

The hedge ratio is:

$$h = \frac{-(1 + r_f t)}{(1 + r_d t)} = \frac{-\left(1 + \dfrac{[0.103(42)]}{360}\right)}{\left(1 + \dfrac{[0.055(42)]}{360}\right)}$$

$$= -1.006$$

and the number of futures contracts required is:

$$n = \frac{h(\text{Hedge Value})}{\text{Contract Size}} = \frac{[-1.006(100,000,000)]}{125,000}$$

$$= -805$$

FIGURE 12-9   Futures for interest rate hedging

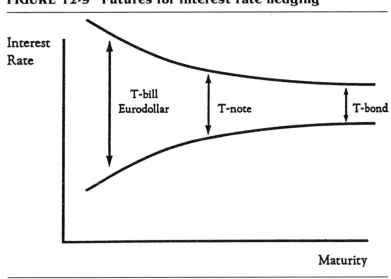

With the hedge ratio equal to -1.006, 805 contracts need to be sold to hedge the 100 million Deutsche mark position. In this case, the relative interest rates over the short time horizon are close enough that the short-term hedge ratio is only slightly different than an equal-dollar match of 800 contracts.

Interest Rate Hedges

Figure 12-9 shows the most popular futures contracts used in hedging interest rates of different maturities. Short-term rates tend to fluctuate more widely than longer-term rates, and Treasury bill futures and Eurodollar futures are useful in hedging short-term rate fluctuations. The Treasury note futures have a somewhat longer maturity, and the Treasury bond futures are positioned at the long end of the curve. The hedge ratios are calculated in exactly the same manner for the Treasury bonds and notes, but there are some differences for the Treasury bill and Eurodollar futures.

Treasury Bill Hedges.   The change in the price per dollar face value of a Treasury bill with t fraction of a year to maturity is equal to:

$$\Delta S = -t \Delta d \qquad (28)$$

where Δd is the change in the discount rate on the Treasury bill. Because of the way Treasury bills are quoted and priced, the change in the price of the futures contract per dollar face value is equal to:

$$\Delta F = 0.25 \Delta d_f \tag{29}$$

where Δd_f is the change in the discount rate on the futures contract. Consequently, the hedge ratio is:

$$h = \left(\frac{-t}{0.25} \right) \left(\frac{\Delta d}{\Delta d_f} \right) \tag{30}$$

where $(\Delta d / \Delta d_f)$ represents the movement in the discount rate for the underlying Treasury bill relative to the futures discount rate. This ratio would typically be equal to 1.0 for parallel moves in the yield curve when all rates move up or down together by the same absolute amount.

As an example of hedging the risk in a Treasury bill, consider a \$50 million exposure with 15 days to maturity. The ratio of Δd to Δd_f is assumed to be 1.0, and the contract size is \$1 million. The hedge ratio is:

$$h = \frac{-\left(\dfrac{15}{360} \right)}{0.25} (1.0) = -0.167$$

The number of contracts required is:

$$n = \frac{h(\text{Hedge Value})}{\text{Contract Size}} = \frac{-0.167(50,000,000)}{1,000,000}$$

$$= -8.35$$

With a hedge ratio of -0.167, about eight futures contracts have to be sold to hedge the exposure. Only a small number of contracts is needed, because each contract represents the interest exposure for 90 days on a \$1 million Treasury bill. The bill to be hedged has only 15 days of interest exposure left, so each contract can hedge the interest rate exposure of more than \$8 million of principal.

Eurodollar Hedges.   For a security such as a Eurodollar deposit paying a fixed interest rate, the change in the price of the security per dollar of principal from a change in the market yield of the security is equal to the change in interest earned discounted back to the present:

$$\Delta S = \frac{-t \Delta r}{1 + rt} \tag{31}$$

The change in the price of a Eurodollar future per dollar of face value is equal to:

$$\Delta F = 0.25 \Delta r_f \tag{32}$$

where Δr_f represents the change in the interest rate embodied in the futures contract. Thus, the hedge ratio is:

$$h = \frac{-t}{0.25(1 + rt)}\left(\frac{\Delta r}{\Delta r_f}\right) \qquad (33)$$

where $(\Delta r \, / \, \Delta r_f)$ is the relative movement in the interest rates between the security being hedged and the Eurodollar futures contract.

An example will illustrate calculation of the hedge ratio for a \$20 million position in securities that has 45 days left before maturity with a current yield of 7.83 percent. The relative movement in the interest rates on the security and the Eurodollar futures $(\Delta r \, / \, \Delta r_f)$ is assumed to be 1.0, and the contract size is \$1 million. The hedge ratio is equal to:

$$h = \frac{-\left(\dfrac{45}{360}\right)(1.0)}{0.25\left(1 + \dfrac{0.0783(45)}{360}\right)} = -0.495$$

and the number of contracts required is:

$$n = \frac{-0.495(20,000,000)}{1,000,000} = -9.9 \text{ Contracts}$$

The hedge position requires only half as many contracts as an equal-dollar matched position, because the securities have only 45 days of interest exposure left, but the futures contract embodies 90 days of interest exposure. Each contract can cover approximately twice the interest exposure per dollar face value of the security position.

Treasury Note and Bond Hedges.   In the fixed-income market, *duration* is used as a measure of interest rate sensitivity. It is expressed in years similar to the maturity of the note or bond, and represents the weighted average timing of the cash flows. The duration of a traditional fixed-income security with coupon payments and return of principal at maturity is less than or equal to the maturity of the security.

The change in the value of a note or bond from a change in its yield to maturity is proportional to the duration of the security:

$$\Delta B = -D^{\circ}B\Delta y_B \qquad (34)$$

where B is the security price, D° is the modified duration of the security (in years), and Δy_B is the change in the security's annualized yield to maturity. The change in the value of the Treasury note or bond futures contract is equal to:

$$\Delta F = D_F^{\circ}F\Delta y \qquad (35)$$

where F represents the futures price, D_F^* is the modified duration of the futures contract (in years), and Δy is the change in the annualized yield to maturity of the cheapest-to-deliver (CTD) note or bond. Duration is a convenient measure that serves to link the change in bond price to changes in interest rates.

A review of duration and its relationship to a change in the price of a fixed-income security is given in Clarke (1993). Using the concept of duration to measure interest rate risk allows us to write the hedge ratio as:

$$h = \frac{-D^* B}{D_F^* F} \left(\frac{\Delta y_B}{\Delta y} \right) \tag{36}$$

To illustrate calculation of the hedge ratio, consider a \$38 million bond position hedged with Treasury bond futures contracts. The security price is 96 2/32 (96.0625), the futures price is 95 16/32 (95.50), and the modified durations of the security and the futures contract are 10.3 years and 9.4 years, respectively. The ratio of the change in yield to maturity of the security to that of the CTD note or bond ($\Delta y_B / \Delta y$) is assumed to be 0.95, and the CTD contract size is \$94,500. The hedge ratio is:

$$h = \frac{-10.3(96.0625)}{9.4(95.50)} (0.95) = -1.05$$

which would require that approximately 422 futures contracts be sold to hedge the \$38 million position in underlying securities:

$$n = \frac{-1.05(38,000,000)}{94,500} = -422.2 \text{ Contracts}$$

Minimum-Variance Hedge Ratios: Symmetric Hedges

We developed in Equation (19) a simple framework for structuring a symmetric hedge between a security S and its hedge position F using a hedge ratio h. The change in the value of the combined position as the security prices change was given as:

$$\Delta V = \Delta S + h \Delta F \tag{37}$$

The variance of the change in position value can be written as the sum of the respective position variances plus the interaction between the two securities:

$$\sigma_V^2 = \sigma_S^2 + h^2 \sigma_F^2 + 2hC_{SF} \tag{38}$$

where: σ_V^2 = the variance of ΔV
σ_S^2 = the variance of ΔS
σ_F^2 = the variance of ΔF
C_{SF} = the covariance between ΔS and ΔF

The covariance term can also be written in terms of the correlation between the two securities as:

$$C_{SF} = \rho_{SF}\sigma_S\sigma_F \qquad (39)$$

where ρ_{SF} represents the correlation coefficient between ΔS and ΔF.

The hedge ratio that minimizes the variance of the change in position value can be represented as the ratio of covariance to the variance of the hedging security as:

$$h = \frac{-C_{SF}}{\sigma_F^2} = \frac{-\rho_{SF}\sigma_S}{\sigma_F} \qquad (40)$$

which when substituted into the variance Equation (38) gives the minimum position variance equal to:

$$\sigma_v^2 = \sigma_S^2\left(1 - \rho_{SF}^2\right) \qquad (41)$$

This hedge ratio is often referred to as the *minimum-variance hedge ratio*.[9]

Less-then-perfect correlation between the two securities will leave the hedged position with some variance at its minimum point. If ΔS and ΔF are perfectly positively correlated ($\rho_{SF} = 1.0$), the minimum-variance hedge ratio will be:

$$h = \frac{-\sigma_S}{\sigma_F} \qquad (42)$$

and the variance of the hedged position will be zero.

Figure 12-10 shows the general pattern of variance of the hedged position as a function of the hedge ratio. The minimum-variance ratio can occur on either side of -1.0, depending on the size of the correlation coefficient and the relative volatilities of the two assets. Since the correlation coefficient cannot be greater than 1.0, the hedge ratio will be less than 1.0 if the security to be hedged has a smaller variance than the security used for hedging. In this example, the asset used for hedging (F) has a higher variance than the asset being hedged (S), because $\sigma_F = 0.25$ and $\sigma_S = 0.20$. The correlation coefficient between the two is assumed to be 0.90.

Notice that the minimum variance occurs at a hedge ratio of:

$$h = \frac{-0.90(0.20)}{0.25} = -0.72$$

resulting in a minimum variance of:

$$\sigma_v^2 = \sigma_S^2(1 - \rho_{SF}^2)$$
$$= (0.20)^2(1 - 0.9^2)$$
$$= 0.0076$$
$$\sigma_v = 0.087$$

FIGURE 12-10   Position variance versus hedge ratio

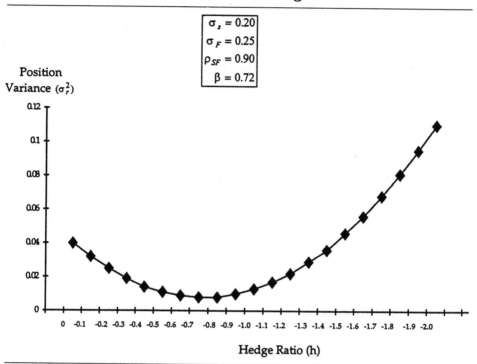

A common way to estimate the minimum-variance hedge ratio is to regress the change in ΔS on ΔF:

$$\Delta S = \alpha + \beta \Delta F + \epsilon \tag{43}$$

The slope coefficient from this linear regression is:

$$\beta = \frac{C_{SF}}{\sigma_F^2} = \frac{\rho_{SF}\sigma_S}{\sigma_F} \tag{44}$$

which can be used to estimate of the minimum-variance hedge ratio:

$$h = -\beta \tag{45}$$

For example, suppose that a regression of the change in unit price of an equity portfolio is regressed on the change in the value of the S&P 500 index, resulting in a regression coefficient of 0.83. The minimum-variance hedge ratio would be equal to:

$$h = -0.83$$

indicating that for every dollar in the equity portfolio, only $0.83 of S&P 500 futures contracts would need to be sold to create the hedge.

Direct hedge ratios are equivalent to minimum-variance hedge ratios when there is a perfect linkage between the underlying security and the futures or forward contract used for hedging. This can be seen by noting that the standard deviations of the securities are equal to the sensitivity coefficients times the standard deviation of the underlying index. Because the security and the futures contract are essentially perfectly correlated, the minimum-variance hedge ratio would be:

$$h = \frac{-\rho_{SF}\sigma_S}{\sigma_F} = \frac{-\beta_S\sigma_I}{\beta_F\sigma_I}$$

$$= \frac{-\beta_S}{\beta_F} = \frac{-\Delta S}{\Delta F} \tag{46}$$

As a result, the minimum-variance hedge ratio is equal to the direct hedge ratio when both securities are perfectly correlated to a common index.

A cross-hedge is one constructed with a hedging security that is somewhat dissimilar to the security being hedged. This usually results in a lower correlation and a less perfect hedge than if the hedging security were more tightly coupled together with the security to be hedged. For example, a portfolio of corporate bonds might be hedged with Treasury bond futures contracts or foreign exchange exposure in the Italian lira might be hedged with a position in Deutsche marks. The effectiveness of the hedge in reducing risk will be enhanced, the greater the correlation between the two positions.

Table 12-3 lists the alternatives usually discussed in formulating hedge ratios. The equal-dollar matched hedge ratio is a simple and quick alternative, but it is a special case of a more general framework, which tries to minimize the tracking error in the hedge. This hedge ratio, which minimizes the variance of the change in position value, is referred to as the minimum-variance hedge ratio. Regression analysis is often used to estimate the minimum-variance parameters. Finally, if the price movement in the underlying portfolio to be

TABLE 12-3   Hedge ratio alternatives

Ratio	Equation
Equal-dollar match	$h = -1$
Minimum-variance	$h = -\rho_{SF}\sigma_S / \sigma_F$
Statistical estimation	h = Negative of the slope coefficient of regression of ΔF on ΔS
Direct calculation	$h = \Delta S / \Delta F$

hedged is tied to the change in price of a hedging instrument like a futures contract, a direct hedge ratio can be calculated from the pricing of the futures or options contract. This hedge ratio if evaluated empirically should be quite close to the minimum-variance hedge ratio.

The framework for constructing a minimum-variance hedge ratio can be extended to accommodate the investor's willingness to trade off some risk in exchange for additional return. To illustrate this decision process we use the mean-variance framework. In this case, the investor chooses a hedge ratio to maximize a risk-adjusted return for the hedge position by using both Equations (37) and (38) for the expected incremental return and variance.

The risk-adjusted portfolio objective can be written as trying to maximize expected return minus a penalty for risk:

$$E(\Delta V) - \lambda \sigma_V^2 \qquad (47)$$

where λ represents the investor's willingness to trade off additional risk for some additional expected return. Solving for the optimal hedge ratio using the same optimization techniques as for the minimum variance hedge ratio gives:

$$h = \frac{E(\Delta F) - 2\lambda C_{SF}}{2\lambda \sigma_F^2} \qquad (48)$$

Notice that the optimal hedge ratio is a function of the expected change in value of the hedging security less a penalty for the interaction risk between the two securities. The greater the expected change in the price of the hedging security, the more the investor will want to hold a positive position (or less of a negative position). Notice also that the minimum-variance hedge ratio is a special case of the more general hedge ratio. The general hedge ratio reduces to the minimum-variance hedge ratio if the expected change in the price of the hedging security is equal to zero, or if the investor's penalty for the trade-off between expected return and risk is very large.

Using the values in the previous minimum-variance example, and assuming that the expected change in price for the hedging security is 0.05, the risk–return hedge ratio for an investor with a trade-off parameter of 2.0 is:

$$h = \frac{0.05 - 2(2.0)(0.90)(0.20)(0.25)}{2(2.0)(0.25)^2} = -0.52$$

Because the expected change in price for the hedging security is positive, it changes the hedge ratio from -0.72 to -0.52. Less of the hedging security would be sold to construct the hedge than previously, because the investor is willing to trade off some additional risk in order to get some expected return.

One of the difficult things about using the more general hedging framework is knowing what risk aversion parameter to use. This trade-off is specific to the individual investor and depends on the investor's tolerance for risk.

A slightly more complex situation would involve the use of two different securities to hedge the underlying security. In this case, the change in the value of the portfolio would be:

$$\Delta V = \Delta S + h_1 \Delta F_1 + h_2 \Delta F_2 \tag{49}$$

where h_1 and h_2 represent the hedge ratios for the hedging securities F_1 and F_2, respectively. The variance of the change in value would be:

$$\sigma_V^2 = \sigma_S^2 + h_1^2 \sigma_1^2 + h_2^2 \sigma_2^2 + 2h_1 C_{S1} + 2h_2 C_{S2} + 2h_1 h_2 C_{12} \tag{50}$$

where: σ_1^2, σ_2^2 = variance of ΔF_1 and ΔF_2, respectively
 C_{S1}, C_{S2} = covariance of ΔS with ΔF_1 and ΔF_2, respectively
 C_{12} = covariance of ΔF_1 with ΔF_2

Solving for the optimal hedge ratios using the same optimization techniques as for the single-security hedge ratio gives:

$$h_1 = \frac{[E(\Delta F_1)\sigma_2^2 - E(\Delta F_2)\sigma_1^2] - 2\lambda(\sigma_2^2 C_{S1} - C_{12}C_{S2})}{2\lambda(\sigma_1^2 \sigma_2^2 - C_{12}^2)} \tag{51}$$

$$h_2 = \frac{[E(\Delta F_2)\sigma_1^2 - E(\Delta F_1)\sigma_2^2] - 2\lambda(\sigma_1^2 C_{S2} - C_{12}C_{S1})}{2\lambda(\sigma_1^2 \sigma_2^2 - C_{12}^2)} \tag{52}$$

Notice that the expression for each hedge ratio has a form similar to that of the single-security hedge, except that the terms are somewhat more complex to reflect the interaction of the two hedging securities with the hedged security and with each other.

If the investor has a very high risk aversion parameter (λ), the expected returns on the hedging securities become irrelevant, and the hedge ratios that minimize the variance of the hedged position become:

$$h = \frac{-(\sigma_2^2 C_{S1} - C_{12}C_{S2})}{(\sigma_1^2\sigma_2^2 - C_{12}^2)} \tag{53}$$

$$h = \frac{-(\sigma_1^2 C_{S2} - C_{12}C_{S1})}{(\sigma_1^2\sigma_2^2 - C_{12}^2)} \tag{54}$$

To illustrate the use of multiple securities to hedge the risk in a security position, suppose we continue with the same values, as follows:

$$
\begin{array}{lll}
\sigma_S = 0.20 & E(\Delta F_1) = 0.5 & \\
\sigma_1 = 0.25 & E(\Delta F_2) = 0.4 & \\
\sigma_2 = 0.20 & \rho_{S1} = 0.9 & C_{S1} = 0.045 \\
\lambda = 2.0 & \rho_{S2} = 0.6 & C_{S2} = 0.024 \\
 & \rho_{12} = 0.2 & C_{12} = 0.010 \\
\end{array}
$$

Using these values in Equations (51) and (52) for the optimal hedge ratios gives:

$$h_1 = \frac{[0.5(0.20)^2 - (0.4)(0.25)^2] - 2(2.0)[(0.20)^2(0.045) - (0.010)(0.024)]}{2(2.0)[(0.25)^2(0.20)^2 - (0.010)^2]}$$

$$= -0.70$$

$$h_2 = \frac{[0.4(0.25)^2 - (0.5)(0.20)^2] - 2(2.0)[(0.25)^2(0.024) - (0.010)(0.45)]}{2(2.0)[(0.25)^2(0.20)^2 - (0.010)^2]}$$

$$= -0.39$$

The optimal hedge ratios that balance the trade-off between expected return and risk equal -0.70 for Security 1 and -0.39 for Security 2. This requires selling 0.70 units of Security 1 and 0.39 units of Security 2 for every unit held of the underlying security to be hedged.

The minimum-variance hedge ratios can be found by using Equations (53) and (54). Using the same data, we can calculate the minimum-variance hedge ratios as:

$$h_1 = -0.65$$
$$h_2 = -0.44$$

The use of multiple securities to construct hedges that are not perfectly correlated with the underlying security is another example of a cross-hedge relationship. Even though neither security is a perfect match with the underlying security being hedged, the combination is able to make the hedge more efficient than using either individually. This will be true as long as the hedging securities are not perfectly correlated with each other, so that the hedge can benefit from the diversification between the two.

Asymmetric Hedges

The construction of an asymmetric hedge that responds differentially to positive market returns and to negative market returns usually requires the use of an option or a strategy that replicates an option. The two most common strategies to hedge market exposure are the (1) protective put, and (2) the collar, range forward, or fence. There are other more complex strategies available and some of these are reviewed in Dengler and Becker (1984).

Protective Put

A protective put is constructed by holding the underlying security and buying a put option. The value matrix at expiration for this strategy is:

Protective Put Value at Expiration

	$S < K$	$S > K$
Security	S	S
Put	$K - S$	0
Total value	K	S

The value of the security is S whether it finishes above or below the exercise price. The value of the put option is $K - S$ below the option's exercise price and zero above the exercise price. The total value of the protective put is found by adding up the value in each column. Below the exercise price, the portfolio is worth K dollars at expiration. Above the exercise price, it is worth S.

This strategy is depicted graphically in Figure 12-11. The dashed line again represents the security value. The solid line represents the value of the security plus the put option. Below the exercise price, the put option compensates for the decline in the security price. Once the original cost of the put option is accounted for, the net payoff is represented by the dotted line. The break-even point occurs when the security price is equal to the strike price less the cost of the put option. Below this point, the protective put strategy gives a better payoff than holding just the security by itself.

The benefit of this strategy occurs below the break-even point. If the security price falls below this level, the portfolio is always worth more than the security itself. This protection is of great benefit if the market is going down.

FIGURE 12-11   Payoff profile of a protective put

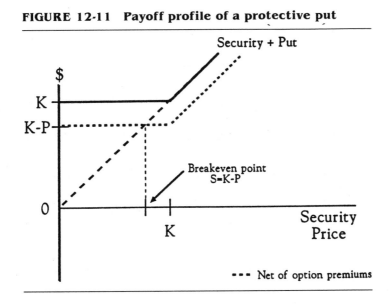

The market does not give this protection for free, however. Above the break-even point, the protected portfolio is always worth a little bit less than the security. The price paid for the option results in a slightly lower return on the upside. This strategy is sometimes called *portfolio insurance,* because the put option protects the value if the security price falls while maintaining some market exposure if the price rises.

To illustrate the impact of currency options to hedge currency exposure, suppose a U.S. investor holds a portfolio worth 10 million DM. Assume that the current exchange rate is 0.6000 $/DM. Below we illustrate the effect of a currency hedge using a put option if the Deutsche mark appreciates or depreciates by 5 percent over the next six months.

	Exchange Rate ($/DM)	Portfolio Value (DM)	Unhedged Portfolio Value ($)	Portfolio Percentage Change ($)
Current	0.60	10,000,000	6,000,000	
After six months	0.63	10,000,000	6,300,000	5.0
After six months	0.57	10,000,000	5,700,000	−5.0

Suppose the investor hedges the currency risk by purchasing a six-month put option with a strike price of 0.60 $/DM at a cost of $207,000. If the exchange rate declines to 0.57 $/DM, the value of the put option at expiration will be:

$$10,000,000 (0.60 - 0.57) = \$300,000$$

The net value of the portfolio in US dollars will be:

$$5,700,000 + (300,000 - 207,000) = \$5,793,000$$

representing a decline of 3.5 percent. The value of the portfolio in US dollars has declined by less than the 5 percent decline because of the initial cost of the option. The option will finish in the money and contribute some value to the portfolio. Without the option position, the unhedged value of the portfolio would have declined by the full 5.0 percent.

If the exchange rate increases to 0.63 $/DM, the value of the option at expiration will be zero, giving a net value of the portfolio in U.S. dollars of:

$$6,300,000 - 207,000 = \$6,093,000$$

representing an increase of 1.6 percent. With the cost of the options, the hedged portfolio will underperform the unhedged portfolio, which returns a full 5.0 percent.

Collar (Range Forward or Fence)

The *collar, range forward, or fence* is constructed by selling a call option in addition to the purchase of a put option. The sale of the call brings in cash, which reduces the cost of purchasing the put option. The maturity of the call option is typically the same as that of the put, but it is at a higher strike price. The sale of the call option eliminates the benefit of positive security returns above the level of the call's strike price. If the strike price of the call option is set close enough, the cost of the put option can be offset entirely by the sale of the call option. This is typically referred to as a zero-cost collar.

To accommodate the difference in strike prices between the put and the call options, the value matrix must be expanded. As a result, the value matrix for the collar is:

Collar Value at Expiration

	$S < K_P$	$K_P < S < K_C$	$S > K_C$
Security	S	S	S
Put	$K_P - S$	0	0
Call	0	0	$-(S - K_C)$
Total Value	K_P	S	K_C

K_P represents the put strike price and K_C represents the strike price for the call option. If the security price is below the strike price of the put at expiration, the payoff will be equal to the strike price of the put. If the security price is above the strike price of the call option, the payoff will be equal to the strike price of the call option. In between the two strike prices, the payoff will be equal to the underlying security price.

The payoff of the collar is shown graphically in Figure 12-12. The solid line represents the value of the security plus the payoff from the options. The dotted line represents the value of the strategy once the net cost of the options is considered. A zero-cost collar would have no net option cost, so the dotted line converges to the solid line. The dashed line represents the value of holding the security unhedged. The benefit of this strategy occurs below the exercise price of the option, similar to the protective put. The exact break-even point depends on the price of the call option sold to truncate some of the upside potential. This loss of upside potential beyond the break-even point of the short call position is the disadvantage of using the collar.

Suppose a call option is sold at a strike price of 0.62 $/DM for $135,000 and a put option purchased at a strike price of 0.60 $/DM. If the exchange rate drops to 0.57 $/DM, the put option will have value, but the call option will expire worthless. The net value of the portfolio will be:

$$5,700,000 + (300,000 - 207,000) + 135,000 = \$5,928,000$$

FIGURE 12-12   Payoff profile of a collar

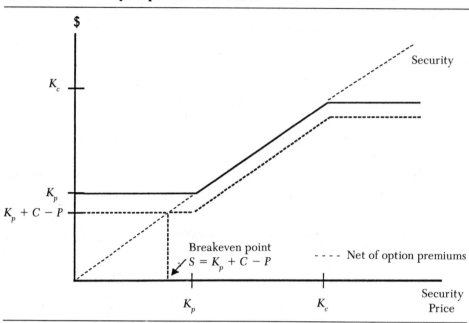

representing a decline of 1.2 percent compared to the currency decline of 5 percent. The sale of the call option has helped offset the cost of the put option hedge, which previously showed a decline of 3.5 percent.

If the exchange rate increases, on the other hand, the put option will expire worthless, and the value of the call option at expiration will be:

$$10,000,000 \ (0.62 - 0.63) = -\$100,000$$

The net value of the portfolio will be:

$$6,300,000 - 207,000 + (135,000 - 100,000) = \$6,128,000$$

representing a net increase of 2.1 percent. A comparison of the protective put strategy with the collar shows that the investor is better off using the collar if the exchange rate declines, but could be worse off if the exchange rate increases sufficiently beyond the strike price of the call option.

In the example here, the loss on the intrinsic value of the call option is not quite as great as the premium received when the option is sold, so the investor has done slightly better than the straight protective put strategy even though the exchange rate increased. If the exchange rate increases beyond 0.6335, the loss on the call option will be greater than its cost, causing the collar to perform worse than the protective put strategy. In general, the collar or range forward works well as long as the market does not increase beyond the strike price of the call option. If the market rallies much beyond that point, the investor will not participate in the upside market gains.

Probability Distribution of Returns

In addition to using payoff diagrams to describe the effect of options, an investor can look at the probability distribution of returns for various strategies. Consider first the protective put strategy. Figure 12-13 shows the probability distribution of returns for an underlying security with and without the use of put options. Note the way the shape changes as an increasing proportion of put options are purchased relative to the underlying security position. Purchasing put options draws the portfolio distribution back gradually on the left side and increases the chance that an investor will receive only moderate returns. Buying put options on 100 percent of the portfolio completely truncates the left-hand side of the probability distribution: The investor has a very high probability of receiving moderate returns and no probability of receiving low returns. Most of the probability of receiving high returns is preserved, however.

Figure 12-14 illustrates the effect of selling call options and buying put options simultaneously (a fence or collar). The combination causes quite a severe misshaping of the probability distribution in both tails. The distribution is

FIGURE 12-13   Probability distribution for a protective put

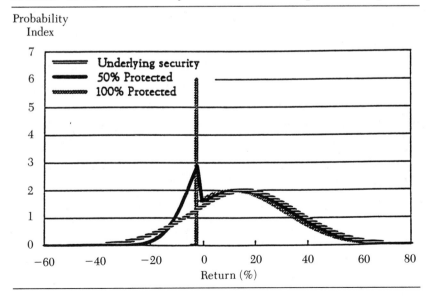

FIGURE 12-14 Probability distribution for a collar

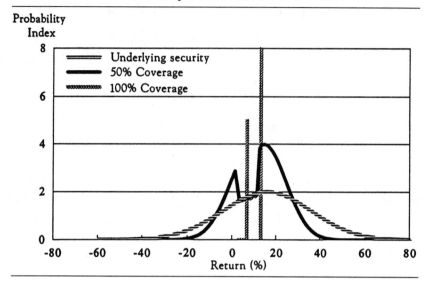

no longer smooth and symmetric. The asymmetry of options allows an investor to shape and mold the probability distribution of truncating some parts and adding to others. Call options affect the right-hand tail most dramatically, while put options affect the left-hand tail.

Notice that the collar provides similar downside protection but loses its potential for upside participation if the security return is positive beyond the level of the call's strike price. Selling a call option with the same strike price as the put option would protect against downside losses, but would also eliminate any upside participation. This would make the hedge symmetric, much as selling a futures or forward contract. Indeed, the short call and long put position with the same strike price creates a synthetic future or forward contract, which produces a symmetric hedge. This can be seen from the stylized put/call parity relationship in Equation (55), which indicates that a combination of a cash reserve with purchase of a call option and sale of a put option will behave the same as if the security were purchased:

$$\text{Synthetic Security} \leftrightarrow \text{Cash Reserve} + \text{Call Option} - \text{Put Option} \quad (55)$$

Rearranging the relationship to create a synthetic cash reserve instead of a synthetic security indicates that the combination of the underlying security plus a put option minus a call option creates a cash equivalent position:

$$\text{Underlying Security} + \text{Put Option} - \text{Call Option} \leftrightarrow \text{Synthetic Cash Reserve} \quad (56)$$

In this case, the short call option and the long put option work to create a synthetic future or forward that offsets the risk in the underlying security, resulting in a cash-equivalent position.

Synthetic Option Positions Using Dynamic Hedging

The return effects of an option can be mimicked using futures or forward contracts to adjust the hedge ratio in a systematic way as the price of the underlying security moves. Selling more futures contracts as the price falls creates the protection a put option provides. Buying futures as the price rises reduces the impact of the hedge, and allows some upside participation in market returns. On the other hand, selling futures contracts as the price rises will create the effect of having sold a call option—upside returns will be truncated. Investors may prefer to construct an option position using dynamic hedging instead of purchasing options directly because the available options may not have the exact parameters in maturity or strike price needed. The investor may also expect the market to have a different volatility going forward from the market consensus expressed in the current option prices.

The effectiveness of the dynamic hedge to mimic the price movement of an option depends on knowing how the price of the option will respond to a change in the underlying security price and on the ability to change the futures hedge smoothly. Both the actual option position and the synthetic option position protect the portfolio against adverse market returns while capturing the benefit of favorable returns. The synthetic option created through dynamic trading achieves its goal with some uncertainty, however, because it is only an approximation. If the ex post volatility of security prices is lower than the volatility implied in pricing the actual option, the synthetic option will generally be less expensive. Actual volatility higher than the implied volatility will increase the cost of the synthetic option. Sharp market moves or gaps do not allow the investor to change the hedge ratio smoothly, and the synthetic option will have more tracking error than the actual option, thus increasing the cost of the dynamic replication.

Problems associated with gapping markets and subsequent difficulties in adjusting the hedge ratio were particularly noticeable in the stock market break in October 1987. Dynamic hedging strategies were then used quite extensively by many investors who had difficulty in revising their hedge ratios smoothly. As a result, the option positions their hedges were designed to mimic were not replicated very accurately.

Dynamic option creation requires some calculations in order to provide protection with a specific floor return for the portfolio as a whole. This is because the return floor usually includes the original cost of the option positions as part of the portfolio protection. For example, suppose the total value of a portfolio is equal to n units of the underlying security valued at S_0 plus the net value of the put and call options valued at P_0 and C_0, respectively that are used to create the hedge:

$$V_0 = n(S_0 + P_0 - C_0) \tag{57}$$

The number of units of the security that can be held, given a fixed initial investment, is:

$$n = \frac{V_0}{S_0 + P_0 - C_0} \tag{58}$$

For the total value of the portfolio at the expiration of the options to be equal to the floor value V° if the market declines, we must have:

$$
\begin{aligned}
V^\circ &= n[S_t + (K_P - S_t)] \text{ for } S_t < K_P \le K_C = nK_P \\
&= \frac{K_P V_0}{S_0 + P_0 - C_0}
\end{aligned}
\tag{59}
$$

The problem in calculating the appropriate strike price for the put option lies in the fact that choosing V° does not automatically determine the strike price of the put option, because the number of units invested in the security is also a function of the put's strike price K_P through its dependence on P_0. The choice of the correct strike price for the put option requires an iterative calculation for a given V°, V_0, S_0, and C_0 until the appropriate strike price K_P can be found.[8]

Table 12-4 illustrates the procedure for a simple portfolio with a security valued at $100. The security is assumed to have an annualized volatility of 15 percent, the maturity of the option is 90 days, and the current annualized interest rate is 6.0 percent, with a yield on the security of 2.0 percent. The total value of the portfolio to be protected is currently $10,000,000 while the floor value is set at $9,500,000. Notice that the strike price on the put option needs to be set at 96.02 in order for the total portfolio value to be protected below $9,500,000.

Once the composition of the portfolio is established as if options are going to be purchased and sold to hedge the portfolio, the dynamic hedge can be created. To see how this can be done, suppose an investor wants to mimic the change in the portfolio value over time as the price of the underlying security changes. Taking the change in value at time t using Equation (57) gives:

$$\Delta V_t = n(\Delta S_t + \Delta P_t - \Delta C_t) \tag{60}$$

Dynamic hedging can be done by configuring a portfolio composed of the underlying security (or a synthetic security) and cash reserves. As the security

TABLE 12-4 Calculation of put option strike price for portfolio protection

Put Option Strike Price	Option Price	Put Option Delta	Protected Floor (000s)	Portfolio Shares (000s)	Initial Portfolio Value (000s)
$ 90	$0.19	−0.06	$8,983	99.82	$10,000
91	0.26	−0.08	9,076	99.74	10,000
92	0.36	−0.10	9,167	99.63	10,000
93	0.48	−0.13	9,255	99.52	10,000
94	0.64	−0.16	9,340	99.36	10,000
95	0.84	−0.20	9,421	99.17	10,000
96	1.07	−0.24	9,498	98.94	10,000
96.02*	1.08	−0.24	9,500	98.94	10,000
97	1.35	−0.28	9,571	98.67	10,000
98	1.68	−0.33	9,638	98.35	10,000
99	2.06	−0.38	9,700	97.98	10,000
100	2.49	−0.43	9,757	97.57	10,000

*The put option strike price must be set at this level to protect a $10 million portfolio at $9.5 million with a 90-day investment horizon. The put option is priced using a modified Black–Scholes model for a European option assuming that the current security price is $100, volatility is 15 percent, the annualized 90-day interest rate is 6 percent, and the annualized dividend yield is 2 percent.

price changes, the change in the value of the replicating portfolio that holds cash, units of the underlying security and H futures contracts would be:

$$\Delta R_t = m_t \Delta S_t + H_t \Delta F_t \tag{61}$$

where ΔR_t is the change in the aggregate value of the replicating portfolio, m_t is the number of units of the security held at time t, H_t is the number of futures contracts held at time t and ΔF_t is the change in the price of a futures contract.

The change in value at time t for the hedged portfolio and the replicating portfolio will be equal if the number of units of the security in the replicating portfolio and the number of futures contracts are set such that the change in value is the same for both positions. That is:

$$n(1 + \Delta_{put}^t - \Delta_{call}^t)\Delta S_t = m_t \Delta S_t + H_t \Delta F_t \tag{62}$$

where Δ_{put}^t and Δ_{call}^t represent the deltas of the associated put and call options respectively at time t that are to be replicated in creating the hedge.

If no futures contracts are used in adjusting market exposure ($H_t = 0$), the proportion of units of the security needing to be held in the replicating portfolio relative to the original units being replicated is:

$$\frac{m_t}{n} = 1 + \Delta_{put}^t - \Delta_{call}^t \tag{63}$$

Consequently, the proportion of the replicating portfolio held in the risky asset is:

$$\frac{m_t S_t}{V_t} = \frac{n(1 + \Delta_{put}^t - \Delta_{call}^t)S_t}{V^t}$$

$$= \left(\frac{V_0}{V_t}\right) \frac{S_t(1 + \Delta_{put}^t - \Delta_{call}^t)}{S_0 + P_0 - C_0} \tag{64}$$

The remainder of the replicating portfolio would be held in cash.

On the other hand, if no actual units of the security are held in the replicating portfolio, but futures are used to mimic the return on the security (thereby creating a synthetic security), the proportion of futures contracts in the replicating portfolio relative to the original units of the security being replicated is:

$$\frac{H_t}{n} = (1 + \Delta_{put}^t - \Delta_{call}^t)\left(\frac{\Delta S_t}{\Delta F_t}\right) \tag{65}$$

where $\Delta S_t / \Delta F_t$ can be thought of as the security's market sensitivity relative to the futures contract.

As the market price of the underlying security fluctuates over time, the deltas of the appropriate put and call options will also change, creating a need to rebalance the number of units of the security or futures contracts in the replicating portfolio. It is this rebalancing over time that produces the dynamic replication of the hedged portfolio. As the market falls, the delta of the put option will approach minus one, causing the dynamic hedge to reduce the number of units or futures contracts held in the replicating portfolio and increase the allocation to cash. The reverse happens as the market rises. More units or futures contracts are held and less is allocated to cash as the delta on the put option approaches zero, resulting in an increased allocation to the risky asset. If a collar is being replicated, the delta of the call option will approach one as the market rises, and gradually reduce the portfolio allocation to the risky asset.

Table 12-5 shows the results of implementing a dynamic hedge using the values in Table 12-4 in Equation (59). The table shows that 75,486 units are initially held in the replicating portfolio, leaving $24,514 in cash. The protective put strategy increases the proportion of the portfolio allocated to the risky asset as it increases in value and decreases the proportion as it falls in value. The portfolio value can actually fall below the floor before the expiration of the option, but because the portfolio is all in cash at that point, the interest earned up to expiration on the cash will bring the portfolio back up to the floor value.

**TABLE 12-5   Dynamic portfolio allocation to replicate a
protected portfolio**

				Beginning of Period		
Day	Security Price	Put Option Delta	Shares in Replicating Portfolio (000s)	Portfolio Value (000s)	Portfolio Cash (000s)	Percent of Portfolio in the Risky Security
0	100	−0.24	75.49	10,000	2,451	75.5
1	101	−0.20	79.44	10,076	2,053	79.6
2	102	−0.16	82.96	10,156	1,693	83.3
3	103	−0.13	86.05	10,239	1,376	86.6
4	102	−0.16	83.14	10,153	1,672	83.5
5	101	−0.19	79.76	10,070	2,014	80.0
6	100	−0.23	75.89	9,991	2,402	76.0
7	99	−0.28	71.51	9,915	2,835	71.4
8	98	−0.33	66.66	9,844	3,311	66.4
9	97	−0.38	61.38	9,778	3,825	60.9
10	96	−0.44	55.72	9,717	4,368	55.1
11	95	−0.50	49.81	9,662	4,931	49.0
12	94	−0.56	43.75	9,613	5,501	42.8
13	93	−0.62	37.70	9,571	6,065	36.6
14	92	−0.68	31.80	9,534	6,608	30.7
15	91	−0.74	26.21	9,503	7,118	25.1
16	90	−0.79	21.06	9,478	7,583	20.0
17	89	−0.83	16.46	9,458	7,993	15.5
18	88	−0.87	12.50	9,443	8,343	11.7
19	87	−0.91	9.21	9,432	8,631	8.5
20	86	−0.93	6.57	9,424	8,859	6.0
21	85	−0.95	4.54	9,419	9,033	4.1
22	84	−0.97	3.05	9,416	9,160	2.7
23	83	−0.98	2.01	9,414	9,248	1.8
24	82	−0.99	1.31	9,414	9,306	1.1
25	81	−0.99	0.87	9,414	9,343	0.8
26	80	−0.99	0.61	9,415	9,366	0.5
27	79	−1.00	0.46	9,416	9,379	0.4
28	78	−1.00	0.38	9,417	9,387	0.3
29	77	−1.00	0.34	9,418	9,392	0.3
30	76	−1.00	0.32	9,419	9,395	0.3

A Portfolio of Options versus an Option on a Portfolio

When a portfolio has exposure to multiple securities, the investor may be able
to use an option on the portfolio of assets instead of options on each individual
asset to create a hedge. There is an important characteristic of an option on a
portfolio of assets—an option on a portfolio is theoretically less expensive than
a portfolio of options on the individual pieces.

This result comes from the fact that the portfolio of options will deliver the same protection as the option on the portfolio when each asset falls below its floor, but the portfolio of options will perform better when some assets are above and some are below their strike prices. Because the portfolio of options has the potential of giving a greater payoff than the option on the portfolio, the portfolio of individual options should cost more in constructing the hedge. Less-than-perfect positive correlation allows the diversification to create a portfolio with a smaller variance than the average variance of the individual components. This reduction in the variance of the portfolio helps reduce the cost of the portfolio option compared to the cost of the sum of the individual options.

As an illustration of this phenomenon, consider a portfolio containing equal proportions of two securities, each with a volatility of 20 percent. Table 12-6 shows the volatility of the portfolio for various values of the correlation between the two securities. Notice that the volatility of the portfolio is always smaller than the volatility of the individual securities as long as they are not perfectly positively correlated.

Table 12-6 also shows the value of an at-the-money put option on the portfolio compared to a portfolio of two individual at-the-money put options. Notice that except for the case of perfect positive correlation, the portfolio of put options always costs more than the put option on the portfolio.

TABLE 12-6   Value of at-the-money put option

| | | Option Prices as a Percent of Portfolio Value | |
Correlation Between Securities	Portfolio Volatility	Put Option on the Portfolio	Portfolio of Individual Put Options
1.0	20.0	3.37	3.37
0.8	19.0	3.17	3.37
0.6	17.9	2.96	3.37
0.4	16.7	2.72	3.37
0.2	15.5	2.49	3.37
0.0	14.1	2.22	3.37
−0.2	12.6	1.93	3.37
−0.4	11.0	1.62	3.37
−0.6	8.9	1.22	3.37
−0.8	6.3	0.71	3.37
−1.0	0.0	NA	3.37

Note: At-the-money three-month European put options reflected in the table are priced using the Black–Scholes model. Individual options are priced assuming a volatility of 20 percent and an annualized continuously compounded riskless rate of 5.0 percent. The portfolio is equally weighted between the two separate securities.

An option on a portfolio of securities is not always easily available. As a result, an investor may purchase the more expensive individual options to create the hedge. The dispersion of individual security returns may present opportunities to restructure the positions periodically during the course of the hedge to lower the overall cost. These opportunities may exist if the dispersion between returns is large enough so that the gains from one option position more than offset the losses from another option position. This can occur because the changes in an option price for equal percentage up moves and down moves in the underlying security are not symmetric. Gains in the price of a put option from an equal percentage move down will be larger than the losses from the same percentage move up. This difference often allows the investor to restructure the portfolio of options to provide the same floor but at a lower cost even after taking into account transaction costs.

Hedging with a Portfolio of Options

As an illustration of this technique, consider a simple two-currency portfolio composed of half Deutsche mark exposure and half Japanese yen exposure. Suppose individual put options are initially purchased to protect the portfolio over a six-month time horizon. The annualized U.S. interest rate for that horizon is assumed to be 4.0 percent, while it is 8.0 percent in Germany and 3.0 percent in Japan. Suppose also that after one month the Deutsche mark has depreciated by 2 percent, while the yen has appreciated by 2 percent, leaving the total portfolio value the same.

	Initial Value			Value One Month Later		
	Exchange Rate	FX	USD	Exchange Rate	FX	USD
Deutschemark exposure	0.6000 $/DM	8,333,333	$ 5,000,000	0.588 $/DM	8,333,333	$ 4,900,000
Yen exposure	0.0100 $/YEN	500,000,000	5,000,000	0.0102 $/YEN	500,000,000	5,100,000
Total			$10,000,000			$10,000,000

Furthermore, assume that an at-the-money put option on 8,333,333 DM with 180 days to expiration costs $240,000, while an at-the-money put option on 500,000,000 yen costs $190,000. After 30 days, when the Deutsche mark has depreciated by 2 percent and the yen has depreciated by 2 percent, the respective options will be worth $280,833 and $101,000.

These options could be sold and replaced by new at-the-money options with 150 days to expiration for less cost as shown below. (Options prices are estimated using the Black–Scholes model modified for currency options and assuming a 12 percent volatility.)

	Initial At-the-Money Options with 180 Days to Expiration	Initial Options with 150 Days to Expiration	New At-the-Money Options with 150 Days to Expiration
Deutschemark option	$240,000	$280,833	$190,000
Yen option	190,000	101,000	145,000
Total	$430,000	$381,833	$335,000

Because the portfolio value of the currency positions has not changed, replacing the initial put options with new at-the-money options maintains the portfolio protection, but does so at a cost savings of $46,833 (381,833 − 335,000). The cash generated by replacing the original options serves to reduce the initial outlay of $430,000. If the currency returns diverge again, the process can be repeated to generate additional cost savings. Experience shows that this technique can be used effectively to create portfolio protection without using an option on the portfolio as a whole. The greatest cost savings are achieved as the component currencies diverge in their returns around each initial exchange rate level.

CONCLUSION

Investment risk arises out of a variety of sources. The most common sources stem from exposure to changes in interest rates, equity markets, inflation, foreign exchange rates, credit quality, and commodity prices. Effective management of risk requires the investor to identify the source of the risk, estimate its magnitude, and design a hedge to reduce the risk.

Appropriate hedge design depends to some extent on what measures of risk are used and whether the investor is particularly sensitive to downside risk. Two general hedge structures are available to the investor: symmetric and asymmetric hedges. Futures and forward contracts are symmetric in their impact on portfolio returns, as they offset returns equally on the upside and the downside. Hedges can also be constructed either to minimize variance or explicitly trade off variance against expected return.

Options create asymmetric hedge patterns. Put options affect the downside of the portfolio return distribution; call options affect the upside. Asymmetric hedges are more natural to use if the investor is particularly sensitive to downside risk, because option strategies can be designed specifically to focus on that part of the return distribution while leaving the upside potential relatively intact.

APPENDIX A: STANDARD NORMAL DISTRIBUTION

d	0.00	0.01	0.02	0.03	Prob $(r \leq d) = N(d)$ 0.04	0.05	0.06	0.07	0.08	0.09
0.0	0.5000	0.5040	0.5080	0.5120	0.5160	0.5199	0.5239	0.5279	0.5319	0.5359
0.1	0.5398	0.5438	0.5478	0.5517	0.5557	0.5596	0.5636	0.5675	0.5714	0.5753
0.2	0.5793	0.5832	0.5871	0.5910	0.5948	0.5987	0.6026	0.6064	0.6103	0.6141
0.3	0.6179	0.6217	0.6255	0.6293	0.6331	0.6368	0.6406	0.6443	0.6480	0.6517
0.4	0.6554	0.6591	0.6628	0.6664	0.6700	0.6736	0.6772	0.6808	0.6844	0.6879
0.5	0.6915	0.6950	0.6985	0.7019	0.7054	0.7088	0.7123	0.7157	0.7190	0.7224
0.6	0.7257	0.7291	0.7324	0.7357	0.7389	0.7422	0.7454	0.7486	0.7517	0.7549
0.7	0.7580	0.7611	0.7642	0.7673	0.7704	0.7734	0.7764	0.7794	0.7823	0.7852
0.8	0.7881	0.7910	0.7939	0.7967	0.7995	0.8023	0.8051	0.8078	0.8106	0.8133
0.9	0.8159	0.8186	0.8212	0.8238	0.8264	0.8289	0.8315	0.8340	0.8365	0.8389
1.0	0.8413	0.8438	0.8461	0.8485	0.8508	0.8531	0.8554	0.8577	0.8599	0.8621
1.1	0.8643	0.8665	0.8686	0.8708	0.8729	0.8749	0.8770	0.8790	0.8810	0.8830
1.2	0.8849	0.8860	0.8888	0.8907	0.8925	0.8943	0.8962	0.8980	0.8997	0.9015
1.3	0.9032	0.9049	0.9066	0.9082	0.9099	0.9115	0.9131	0.9147	0.9162	0.9177
1.4	0.9192	0.9207	0.9222	0.9236	0.9251	0.9265	0.9279	0.9292	0.9306	0.9319
1.5	0.9332	0.9345	0.9357	0.9370	0.9382	0.9394	0.9406	0.9418	0.9429	0.9441
1.6	0.9452	0.9463	0.9474	0.9484	0.9495	0.9505	0.9515	0.9525	0.9535	0.9545
1.7	0.9554	0.9564	0.9573	0.9582	0.9591	0.9599	0.9688	0.9616	0.9625	0.9633
1.8	0.9641	0.9649	0.9656	0.9664	0.9671	0.9678	0.9686	0.9693	0.9699	0.9706
1.9	0.9713	0.9719	0.9726	0.9732	0.9738	0.9744	0.9750	0.9756	0.9761	0.9767
2.0	0.9772	0.9778	0.9783	0.9788	0.9793	0.9798	0.9803	0.9808	0.9812	0.9817
2.1	0.9821	0.9826	0.9830	0.9834	0.9838	0.9842	0.9846	0.9850	0.9854	0.9857
2.2	0.9861	0.9864	0.9868	0.9871	0.9875	0.9878	0.9881	0.9884	0.9887	0.9890
2.3	0.9893	0.9896	0.9898	0.9901	0.9904	0.9906	0.9909	0.9911	0.9913	0.9916
2.4	0.9918	0.9920	0.9922	0.9925	0.9927	0.9929	0.9931	0.9932	0.9934	0.9936
2.5	0.9938	0.9940	0.9941	0.9943	0.9945	0.9946	0.9948	0.9949	0.9951	0.9952
2.6	0.9953	0.9955	0.9956	0.9957	0.9959	0.9960	0.9961	0.9962	0.9963	0.9964
2.7	0.9965	0.9966	0.9967	0.9968	0.9969	0.9970	0.9971	0.9972	0.9973	0.9974
2.8	0.9974	0.9975	0.9976	0.9977	0.9977	0.9978	0.9979	0.9979	0.9980	0.9981
2.9	0.9981	0.9982	0.9982	0.9983	0.9984	0.9984	0.9985	0.9985	0.9986	0.9986
3.0	0.9987	0.9987	0.9987	0.9988	0.9988	0.9989	0.9989	0.9989	0.9990	0.9990

APPENDIX B: ASSUMPTIONS AND MODIFICATIONS OF THE BLACK–SCHOLES MODEL

The Black–Scholes model depends upon several assumptions. It was originally developed assuming that returns for the security are lognormally distributed and independent over time. It also is assumed that the underlying security has constant risk, or variance, and that the interest rate is constant over time. The model also assumes no instantaneous price jumps in the security; that is, over a very short period of time, the security can move a little but not a large amount. The original model also assumed no dividends or cash payments from the security and no early exercise. The model was developed for pricing a European-style option. Researchers have tried to develop models to relax most of these assumptions, and many of today's models are variations of the original 1973 Black–Scholes model. A more detailed treatment of option pricing and applications is given in Clarke (1993), Chance (1993) or Hull (1993).

The easiest assumption to relax is probably that of no cash distributions. If known dividends are to be paid on a stock before expiration of the option, the price of the option will adjust for the dividend payments. For known discrete dividends, the current stock price needs to be adjusted by the present value of the dividends before being used in the Black–Scholes model. For example, suppose the current stock price is S_0 with an expected dividend of D_T at time T. The adjusted stock price to use at each place in the Black–Scholes formula to price the option is:

$$S_0^* = S_0 - D_T e^{-rT} \tag{B1}$$

Incorporation of the dividend payment in a pricing model reduces the price of the call option and increases the price of a put option.

Another approach to adjusting the stock price is to assume that the dividend is paid continuously at a known yield [see Merton (1973)]. This assumption might take the form of the dividends on a stock index; because of the many different stocks in an index, looking at each dividend separately is difficult. In this case, if y represents the aggregate annual dividend yield, the adjusted stock price used to price an option with expiration date T is:

$$S_0^* = S_0 e^{-yT} \tag{B2}$$

Options on foreign exchange can also be put into this framework. In the case of foreign exchange options, the assumption is that the foreign currency pays continuous interest at rate r_f. The pricing of a foreign currency option can be found by using the Black–Scholes model with the modification: If S_0 represents the current exchange rate, substitute:

$$S_0^* = S_0 e^{-r_f T} \tag{B3}$$

for each occurrence of S_0 in the standard Black–Scholes formula.

The dividend and foreign exchange adjustments presented here assume that the options cannot be exercised early, but variations of the Black–Scholes model for American options allow for early exercise. Such variations are explored in Roll (1977), Geske (1979) Cox, Ingersoll, and Ross (1979) and Whaley (1981). The techniques used to price American options are typically more

TABLE 12-7   Modifications to the Black–Scholes model

Discrete cash payout	$S_0^{\circ} = S_0 - D_T e^{-rT}$
	D_T = payout at time T from the security
Continuous cash payout	$S_0^{\circ} = S_0 e^{-yT}$
	y = rate of continuous payout or yield from the security
Currency option	$S_0^{\circ} = S_0 e^{-r_f T}$
	r_f = foreign interest rate
Futures option	$S_0^{\circ} = F_0 e^{-(r-y)T}$
	F_0 = futures price
	y = rate of continuous payout or yield from the security

Note: The standard Black–Scholes model can be used to price European options on securities with cash payouts, options on currencies, or options on futures contracts by substituting S_0° for S_0 in the standard formula.

complex than those for European options and often require substantial numerical analysis for a solution.

Relaxing some of the other assumptions of the Black–Scholes model is more difficult. Some attempts have been made to develop models in which the underlying security price is not lognormally distributed. For example, Bookstaber and McDonald (1985) develop models with more general probability distributions, of which the lognormal is a special case. Relaxing the assumptions of constant variance and interest rates is yet more difficult. Specialized models for fixed-income options have been developed, however, by relaxing the assumption of constant interest rates [see Dattatreya and Fabozzi (1989), and Black, Derman, and Toy (1990)].

Table 12-7 summarizes the modifications that can be made to the Black–Scholes model to price various types of European options.

REFERENCES

Black, F., E. Derman, and W. Toy. "A One-Factor Model of Interest Rates and Its Application to Treasury Bond Options." *Financial Analysts Journal* (January/ February 1990), pp. 33–39.

Black, F., and M. Scholes. "The Pricing of Options and Corporate Liabilities." *Journal of Political Economy* (May/June 1973), pp. 637–659.

Bookstaber, R., and J. McDonald. "A Generalized Option Valuation Model for the Pricing of Bond Options." *Review of Futures Markets* (1985) 4, pp. 60–73.

Chance, D. *An Introduction to Options and Futures.* Chicago: The Dryden Press, 1989.

Clarke, R. *Options and Futures: A Tutorial.* Charlottesville, VA: Association for Investment Management and Research, 1993.

Cornell, B., and M. Reinganum. "Forward and Futures Prices: Evidence from Foreign Exchange Markets." *Journal of Finance* (December 1981), pp. 1035–1045.

Cox, J.C., J.E. Ingersoll, and S.A. Ross. "A Note on an Analytic Formula for Unprotected American Call Options on Stocks with Known Dividends." *Journal of Financial Economics* (December 1981), pp. 321–346.

_____. "The Relation Between Forward Prices and Futures Prices." *Journal of Financial Economics* (December 1979), pp. 375–380.

Dattatreya, R., and F. Fabozzi. "A Simplified Model for Valuing Debt Options." *Journal of Portfolio Management* (Spring 1989), pp. 64–73.

Dengler, W.H., and H.P. Becker. "19 Option Strategies and When to Use Them." *Futures* (June 1984).

Geske, R. "A Note on an Analytic Formula for Unprotected American Call Options on Stocks with Known Dividends." *Journal of Financial Economics* (December 1979), pp. 375–380.

Hull, J. *Options, Futures, and Other Derivative Securities.* 2nd Edition. Englewood Cliffs, NJ: Prentice-Hall, 1993.

Merton, R. "The Theory of Rational Option Pricing." *Bell Journal of Economics and Management Science* (Spring 1973), pp. 141–183.

Park, H.Y., and A.H. Chen. "Differences Between Futures and Forward Prices: A Further Investigation of Marking to Market Effects." *Journal of Futures Markets* (February 1985), pp. 77–88.

Roll, R. "An Analytic Valuation Formula for Unprotected American Call Options on Stocks with Known Dividends." *Journal of Financial Economics* (November 1977), pp. 251–258.

Von Neumann, J., and O. Morgenstern. *Theory of Games and Economic Behavior.* Princeton: Princeton University Press, 1944.

Whaley, R. "On the Valuation of American Call Options on Stocks with Known Dividends." *Journal of Financial Economics* (June 1981), pp. 207–212.

PART FIVE

PERFORMANCE EVALUATION

Portfolio management can be the most brutal of professions. Its only objective is to make money, and markets are harsh performance evaluators because they provide feedback, often instantaneously, on decisions. A decision that has been well researched and is backed up by great reasons carries no guarantee, nor even great odds, of success. Conversely, the rashest and most unsupportable investment decisions may yield great returns for a lucky investor.

In evaluating the performance of a portfolio manager, three questions have to be answered.

1. How much risk did the portfolio manager take on in creating the portfolio for the investor? Implied here is an adherence to a model of risk and return that quantifies the risk; in finance, the models in use tend to emphasize statistical measures of risk, based on historical data. They measure the risk represented by each investment within a diversified portfolio.

2. What return did the portfolio manager earn over the period for the investor? The answer may seem straightforward, but it can be complicated by cash inflows and outflows that occur over the period.

3. What return should the portfolio manager have made over the period, given the risk taken on and given what markets earned over the same period? To use the proper term: What was the *conditional expected return?* Comparison of the actual returns to the conditional expected return provides a measure of the success of the portfolio manager. Actual returns that exceed expected returns indicate that the manager outperformed the market; actual returns that are lower indicate underperformance.

327

Given the importance of performance evaluation to the profession, it should not be surprising that none of these measurements is free of controversy. In measuring risk, the question of which risk and return model to use is contentious, especially because performance numbers and rankings can be affected significantly by changing the model used. In measuring expected returns, the choice of a benchmark becomes an issue because different benchmarks yield different results. Portfolio managers, in their zeal to outperform the markets, try to outguess the performance evaluators, and take actions that might make their performance look better—at the expense of after-tax returns.

Portfolio managers often complain that they find the frequency of performance evaluations distracting, and that performance evaluations penalize them for following strategies that provide long-term returns. This might be true, but investors are unlikely to be willing to leave their money with a portfolio manager and simply trust the manager to do a good job. Conversely, as portfolio managers earn investors' trust by delivering superior returns, they are much less likely to come under pressure to deliver immediate returns.

In this section, Nancy Jacob looks at the measurement of portfolio performance, the evaluation of investment performance, and some of the ways in which portfolio managers try to beat the system. Robert Jeffrey then explores the relationship between taxes and performance evaluation, when after-tax returns are considered.

The Investment Process

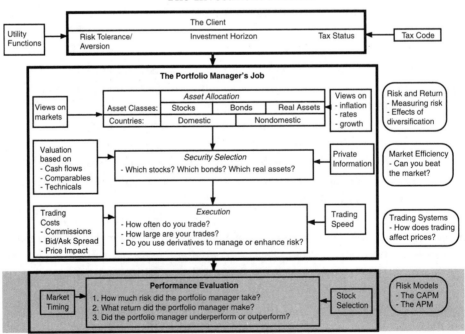

13 EVALUATING INVESTMENT PERFORMANCE

Nancy L. Jacob

In the investment business, you don't always get what you pay for, but you always pay for what you get.

Anonymous

It is hard for investors to resist using past performance to select investment managers. After all, choosing managers is both important and extremely hazardous. Making the wrong decision can be costly in time and money. Published performance histories, offered commercially by scores of financial periodicals and investment consultants and gratuitously by managers themselves, seem to be heaven-sent decision tools. They spring like welcome, objective oases out of a vast desert of ad hoc opinions, subjective evaluations, and questionable assertions that everyone hears about investment managers. After all, if managers *have* done well in the past, doesn't that augur well for their future results?

But, of what *real* predictive value are performance histories? How objective and accurate are they? Under what circumstances, if any, do they tell us what we want to know about managers' skills? And how useful are they to money managers themselves in assessing value added to clients and/or the effects of style on long-term performance?

The purpose of this chapter is to explain how performance numbers are constructed and presented, and to evaluate their strengths and weaknesses in the task of manager selection and performance attribution. We start with an overview of the computational underpinnings of performance measurement. We then turn to the practical uses, misuses, interpretations, and limitations of these measures for manager comparisons of skill.

RETURN CALCULATIONS—LOOKING "UNDERNEATH THE HOOD"

The most basic purpose of performance measurement is simply to account for changes in an investment's value over time. To answer the question, "How well did my portfolio do?", one must first specify a basic time interval for measurement purposes and then value the portfolio at the beginning and the end, taking into account any accrued income or cash additions and withdrawals during the period. *Total return* is the performance measure that results. Total return is defined as the percentage change in an asset's market value over a unit of time ("the compounding interval"), including all realized and unrealized capital gains and any accrued dividend and interest income, but excluding cash additions or withdrawals.

The formula for the total return of any marked-to-market asset or financial instrument (such as an individual security or managed portfolio of securities) is given by:[1]

$$R_t = [(MV_t) - (MV_{t-1}) + D_{t-1,t}]/(MV_{t-1})$$

where: R_t = total return between time $t - 1$ and t, stated as a decimal fraction
MV_t = market value of asset at end of period, or time t
MV_{t-1} = market value of asset at beginning of period, or time $t - 1$
$D_{t-1,t}$ = accrued income between time $t - 1$ and t

Example: *Calculation of a common stock's quarterly return (a three-month compounding interval)*

MV_{t-1} (end of December) equals $10 1/8 per share
MV_t (end of March) equals $11 1/2
The quarterly accrued dividend is $0.80

Therefore, R_1 = ($11.50 − $10.125 + $0.80)/($10.125) = 0.202, or 20.2%

Practical Issues in Total Return Calculations

Most investors accept at face value, and without question, the total returns that money managers present to them. Few ever ask how the results were derived, or whether the numbers have been verified. In fact, despite their appearance of precision, total returns are *always* approximations. They rest on frequently nonobvious assumptions. The most important of these relate to the treatment of management fees, and the choice of accounting methodologies for asset valuations, income, and cash flows.

Management Fees

Every investor should first ask, if it is not clear, whether the total returns presented are based on market values taken *before* the deduction of management fees and expenses or *after*. Management fees are almost always material items and can impact returns substantially.

Two general industry guidelines to be aware of: All published mutual fund returns are calculated net of fees. For individually managed accounts, returns are customarily reported either gross of fees, or both gross and net of fees.

Both gross and net numbers are useful. For instance, the Securities and Exchange Commission now requires the use of net-of-fee comparisons in public advertisements because these reflect actual investor results.[2] Gross-of-fee comparisons, however, reflect a manager's raw investment performance, and, because different fee schedules apply to different accounts, no single net-of-fee number can be accurate.

Accounting Methodologies

It is always preferable to use audited returns for which the calculation methodology is clearly described. This is not always possible, so investors need to ask for disclosure of all computational assumptions having a material impact on reported returns. Surprisingly, managers retain considerable flexibility in these matters.

The principal issues are: (1) the manager's asset valuation methodology, especially for any infrequently traded or nonmarketable assets that may be included in the portfolio (e.g., privately placed, nontraded debt or equity securities, real estate properties), (2) the manager's use of cash versus accrual accounting for income flows (the standard industry method is accrual), (3) the manager's use of trade date versus settlement date for portfolio returns (the industry standard is trade date), and/or (4) the manager's choice of adjustment methodologies for cash flows (portfolio contributions and withdrawals that occurred during the period). While for most portfolios of publicly traded stocks and bonds, these technical issues have little practical import, on occasion, and especially for hedge funds, venture capital portfolios, and distressed debt portfolios (where fixed-income securities may be nonperforming), they can be monumentally significant.[3]

Time-Weighted Returns

Since 1966, the time-weighted return (TWR) has been the industry standard method for computing an asset's total return over time periods encompassing multiple (or fractional) compounding intervals.[4] Prior to that time, rate of return calculations for portfolios of financial securities were made primarily for actuarial purposes and used internal rates of return (or IRRs) as the standard methodology. The IRR uses a discounting approach to measure the average rate of return earned by each dollar invested over the life of an investment. It is well-suited to answering questions related to the actuarial adequacy of earnings to meet anticipated liabilities in an insurance or pension portfolio. It is also well-suited to measuring returns on certain nonmarketable assets like venture capital partnerships, where it is still the predominant measure of asset multiperiod returns. It has one serious weakness, however. It is significantly affected by the timing and the magnitude of the portfolio owner's cash flows, over which most investment mangers have no control.[5]

The TWR eliminates the impact of portfolio cash flows and permits isolation of that portion of a portfolio's total return that is attributable solely to the manager's actions. Since the late 1960s, while the initial time-weighted return formula has been expanded and improved upon as computing technology has permitted increasingly more sophisticated, detailed, and accurate measurements, its basic formulation has remained unchanged. It is computed from asset total returns through *linked wealth relatives,* which are multiplicatively compounded over all intervals in the time horizon of interest.

The wealth relative for time t is just equal to the total return for time t plus 1.0. (Think of this sum as the ending dollar value of $1 invested in the portfolio at time $t - 1$.) Annualized time-weighted returns are derived from the resulting product of the linked wealth relatives, where the investment horizon is assumed to be made up of T compounding intervals, of which there are N compounding intervals per year:

$$TWR_{1, T+1} = [(1 + R_1)(1 + R_2) \cdots (1 + R_T)]^{(N/T)} - 1$$

where: $TWR_{1, T+1}$ = the annualized time-weighted return for a horizon of T compounding intervals starting on date 1 and ending on date $T + 1$

$1 + R_t$ = the wealth relative for compounding interval t; where $t = 1, 2, 3, \cdots, T$

T = the number of compounding intervals between date 1 and $T + 1$

N = the number of compounding intervals per year

Table 13-1 shows an example of TWR calculation using quarterly net returns for the Vanguard Windsor and Fidelity Magellan Funds over various time

**TABLE 13-1   Quarterly net-of-fee returns and performance statistics
Vanguard Windsor Fund versus Fidelity Magellan
(Ten Years: January 1985 through December 1994)**

Quarter Ended	Vanguard Windsor (%)	Fidelity Magellan (%)	Quarter Ended	Vanguard Windsor (%)	Fidelity Magellan (%)
Mar. 1985	7.52	11.87	Mar. 1990	−2.91	−2.09
Jun. 1985	8.46	9.13	Jun. 1990	1.37	6.61
Sep. 1985	−3.33	−3.50	Sep. 1990	−20.34	−16.48
Dec. 1985	13.57	21.47	Dec. 1990	7.78	9.53
Mar. 1986	14.55	22.41	Mar. 1991	18.25	20.23
Jun. 1986	3.21	6.23	Jun. 1991	0.74	−0.14
Sep. 1986	−0.89	−9.11	Sep. 1991	5.59	9.06
Dec. 1986	2.65	4.71	Dec. 1991	2.20	7.70
Mar. 1987	16.27	22.92	Mar. 1992	4.27	−0.70
Jun. 1987	6.17	2.57	Jun. 1992	5.55	0.65
Sep. 1987	0.77	6.42	Sep. 1992	−2.62	1.73
Dec. 1987	−18.63	−24.73	Dec. 1992	8.70	5.25
Mar. 1988	10.17	9.98	Mar. 1993	8.87	8.62
Jun. 1988	13.19	8.46	Jun. 1993	1.40	6.42
Sep. 1988	1.92	0.23	Sep. 1993	7.36	8.21
Dec. 1988	1.26	2.69	Dec. 1993	0.72	−0.34
Mar. 1989	6.89	9.52	Mar. 1994	−1.80	−1.59
Jun. 1989	6.95	9.61	Jun. 1994	3.79	−4.49
Sep. 1989	8.61	13.16	Sep. 1994	1.14	5.43
Dec. 1989	−7.36	−0.93	Dec. 1994	−3.15	−0.90

Annual Returns[a]

1985	28.03	43.11	1990	−15.50	−4.51
1986	20.27	23.74	1991	28.55	41.03
1987	1.23	1.00	1992	16.50	7.01
1988	28.70	22.76	1993	19.37	24.66
1989	15.02	34.58	1994	−0.15	−1.81

Five-Year Returns

1985–1989	18.20	24.20	1990–1994	8.57	12.02

Ten-Year Returns

1985–1994	13.28	17.95

Performance Summary

Statistical Performance Measures	Vanguard Windsor (%)	Fidelity Magellan (%)
Arithmetic Mean Return		
Quarterly	3.47	4.65
Annual	13.89	18.58
Time-Weighted (Geometric Mean) Return		
Quarterly	3.17	4.21
Annual	13.28	17.95
Standard Deviation		
Quarterly Returns	7.81	9.38
Annual Returns	15.62	18.75
Maximum Quarterly Return	18.25	22.92
Minimum Quarterly Return	−20.34	−24.73
Number Negative Quarters	9	12

Source: Ibbotson Associates and Morningstar, 1995.

[a] Computed by compounding quarterly returns.

periods during the ten years ended December 31, 1994. In the example, N equals 4, and T equals 40. Date 1 is December 31, 1984, and Date $T + 1$ is December 31, 1994. The annualized ten-year TWRs for the two funds are computed by taking the (N/T)th root (i.e., the 1/10 power) of the product of the 40 quarterly wealth relatives.

The TWR thus calculated assumes that all income and realized gains are reinvested at each compounding interval. If monthly total returns are linked to form an annualized TWR, then monthly compounding of dividends and interest is implicit. Similarly, the use of quarterly total returns implies quarterly compounding. Continuously compounded returns can be computed by assuming that interest and realized gains are reinvested instantaneously.

If the underlying compounding interval changes, the calculated TWR changes. Does this matter? In normal industry applications, the differences in compounding intervals are not significant, provided that the investor is aware of the frequency of compounding and always restricts across-manager comparisons to those having the same compounding interval.

More important is the treatment of external cash flows. There are three accepted methodologies for this purpose. One of them is exact and requires an asset valuation on the date of every cash flow; the two others assume that cash flows occurring *between* asset valuations are invested at a constant rate of return. The accuracy of the approximate methods depends on the length of the compounding interval (shorter is better) and the size of the cash flows in relation to portfolio value (less than 10 percent is best). For most nonmutual fund portfolios, monthly valuations are adequate. Mutual funds, which accept and distribute new monies daily, must have daily valuations.[6]

Arithmetic Average Returns

The TWR is also referred to as an asset's *geometric mean return*. As noted above, it is a fully compounded measure of investment performance; it therefore reflects the growth of earnings from reinvested realized capital gains and income.

The *arithmetic average return* is an alternative, noncompounded measure of multiperiod returns. It is computed by arithmetically averaging compounding interval returns. The formula for an asset's annualized arithmetic return over a time horizon starting with date 1 and ending with date $T + 1$ is:

$$AR_{1, T+1} = (N/T) \left[\Sigma_{t = 1, T} R_t \right]$$

As in the TWR formulation given earlier, N is the number of compounding intervals per year, and T is the total number of compounding intervals in the time horizon of interest.

In Table 13-1, the arithmetic average quarterly total returns on Windsor and Magellan are 3.47 percent and 4.65 percent, respectively. These are multiplied by four to obtain the corresponding annualized numbers of 13.89 percent and 18.58 percent.

In every case where an asset's returns fluctuate, the arithmetic average return will be higher than the geometric mean return over any time period. The arithmetic mean is used in performance measurement only to compute an asset's standard deviation (risk), and as part of risk-adjusted performance measures (discussed later in the chapter). On a stand-alone basis, arithmetic mean returns are properly interpreted only as an estimate of the asset's return in an "average" time period. They are *upward-biased* as a measure of true, multiperiod return.

INVESTMENT MANAGER PERFORMANCE PRESENTATIONS

Until the early 1990s, investment managers' performance presentations to the public were essentially unregulated, complicating across-manager comparisons because of lack of calculation uniformity. Misrepresentations were also commonplace. Some managers showed performance only for certain "representative portfolios"; others only for certain "representative" time periods.

In 1993, the Association for Investment Management and Research (AIMR) introduced the first industrywide performance presentation standards to promote greater comparability, accuracy, and fairness in performance presentations. The AIMR standards, founded on the mandatory use of the time-weighted total return, require full disclosure. They govern how a money manager's composite performance history must be presented, what it must include, how it should be described, and even aspects of calculation methodology. While compliance is voluntary, it happens that money managers who persistently violate them face professional ostracism. This gives the standards some force.

All investment activities, asset classes, and managed portfolios, including stocks, bonds, real estate, derivative securities, private investments, and international assets are covered by the AIMR standards. A summary of principal requirements is shown in Table 13-2.

Performance Composites

The AIMR standards concern themselves primarily with managers' *performance composites*. A composite is a collection of portfolios or accounts that are

TABLE 13-2   Highlights of AIMR performance presentation standards

To be considered in AIMR compliance a manager's presentations must incorporate

- Use of total return to calculate performance.
- Use of accrual, as opposed to cash, accounting.
- Use of time-weighted rates of return, with valuation on at least a quarterly basis and geometric (multiplicative) linking of wealth relatives.
- Inclusion of cash and cash equivalents in performance composites for equity and fixed-income portfolios.
- No linkage of simulated or model portfolios with actual portfolio performance.
- Market-value weighting of performance composites of individual accounts.
- Inclusion of terminated accounts (portfolios) for all periods prior to their termination, and exclusion thereafter.
- Presentation of annual returns for all years.
- Presentation of at least a ten-year performance record (or for the period since firm inception, if shorter).

Mandatory disclosures

- The number of portfolios (accounts) and amount of assets included in each composite, and the percentage of the firm's total assets each composite represents.
- Whether performance results are calculated gross or net of investment management fees, the manager's fee schedule, and for net results, the average weighted management fee.
- The use of settlement date rather than trade date valuations.
- If performance results are presented after taxes, the tax rate assumption.
- If the full performance record is not in compliance, the noncompliance periods and a description of how noncompliance periods are out of compliance.
- The existence of a minimum asset size below which portfolios are excluded from a composite.

Recommended guidelines and disclosures

- Revaluation of a portfolio whenever cash flows and market action combine to distort performance.
- Presentation of performance gross of investment management fees in one-on-one situations and before taxes.

Source: "Performance Presentation Standards: 1993," AIMR.

AIMR Definition of Composite: A composite is a collection of portfolios, accounts, or asset classes representing a similar strategy or investment objective. A composite may include only one portfolio if the portfolio is unique in its approach but fully discretionary. Mutual funds, commingled funds, or unit trusts may be treated as separate composites or be combined with other portfolios or assets of similar strategies. The construction of multiple composites is required if the use of a single composite would be misleading or otherwise inappropriate in the context of the presentation for which the composite results are being used. (For example, a presentation on the Magellan Fund should not include the performance of other equity mutual funds even if they have similar objectives.) All of a money manager's actual, fee-paying discretionary portfolios must be included in at least one composite, and composites must include only actual assets under management.

managed in a similar way or with a similar investment objective, such as all a manager's large-cap equity portfolios or intermediate-term bond portfolios. Any account that is fully discretionary—that is, in which the manager makes all purchase and sale decisions without being subject to significant client restrictions—and that meets prespecified minimum size must be included in the published composite.

What abusive practices do the standards prohibit? The standards are designed to eliminate misleading practices that lead to *selection bias,* making a manager's performance results appear to be better than investors' actual experience because not all portfolios are included for all time periods considered. Examples of non-AIMR complaint performance composites that lead to selection bias include:

- Performance composites that exclude some discretionary accounts.
- Performance composites covering arbitrary time periods.
- Performance composites that intermingle simulated, or backtested results with real portfolio performance.
- Performance composites that use unweighted simple averages of individual accounts, so that smaller accounts have disproportionate impact.
- Performance composites that eliminate all historical trace of terminated accounts.
- Performance composites that exclude uninvested cash balances in individual accounts.

An example of a well-constructed and clear performance presentation in compliance with AIMR standards is shown in Table 13-3. Notice the manager's detailed footnotes describing the methodology it used to construct the composites shown.

Time Periods and Performance Comparisons

Selection bias is especially troublesome to investors. Its most insidious forms involve the selection of apparently arbitrary time horizons after the fact. While AIMR standards have curbed the worst abuses, investors need constantly to remind themselves that performance results vary dramatically, depending on the starting date and time period chosen. An example will illustrate.

Nelson Publications annually publishes a quarterly periodical entitled the *World's Best Money Managers* that ranks time-weighted returns of the forty top-performing investment managers and mutual funds in different asset classes for the most recent quarter, year, three-year, five-year, and ten-year periods. Figure 13-1 shows Nelson's list of the top 20 top-performing

TABLE 13-3 Investment performance
XYZ Investment Management, Inc.
(performance periods ending March 31, 1995)

Fixed Income	YTD 3/31/95	Annualized as of 3/31/95			
		1 Year	3 Years	5 Years	10 Years
XYZ Full Range Duration	6.1%	5.2%	7.9%	9.8%	10.4%
Lehman Aggregate Index	5.0	5.0	6.8	8.9	10.3
Lehman Brothers Government/ Corporate Index	5.0	4.6	7.1	9.0	10.1
XYZ Intermediate Duration	4.9	5.0	7.3	9.3	10.0
Salomon Brothers Broad Investment Grade Medium Term Index	4.7	5.1	6.4	8.6	9.8
Lehman Government/Corporate Intermediate Bond Index	4.4	4.5	6.4	8.4	9.3
XYZ Short Duration	2.5	4.1	4.5	5.8	7.1
Salomon Brothers 1-Year Treasury Bill	2.5	4.9	4.4	6.0	N/A
XYZ Mortgage-Backed	5.0	5.6	7.4	9.5	N/A
Lehman Brothers Mortgage Index	5.1	5.0	6.9	9.0	10.3

Short and Full Range Duration performance is based on quarterly data and includes all fully discretionary, employee benefit, tax-exempt accounts over $10,000,000. Intermediate Duration performance is based on quarterly data and includes all fully discretionary, tax-exempt accounts over $10,000,000. Performance is calculated on a time weighted, trade-date basis, and is gross of all expenses and investment management fees which approximate 0.45% on the first $10 million invested and 35% thereafter. Mortgage-backed performance is based on a representative mortgege-backed account. Composites are calculated on a capitalization weighted basis. XYZ is in compliance with AIMR Performance Presentation Standards which were applicable for years 1993 and 1994. Prior years are presented according to industry standards applicable during those years. All XYZ composites are available upon request.

Past results are not indicative of future performance.

intermediate fixed-income managers in terms of three-year performance for the period ended December 31, 1994. It is a safe bet that most firms lucky enough to appear on this list ordered copies for their clients, their prospective clients, and maybe even members of the press. No matter that few remained in the top forty for very long, or that few of them simultaneously made the five-year, annual, or most recent quarter ended lists ending on the same date. How many of the firms that did drop off the list in subsequent quarters, or that did not again make a top-40 list, alerted their clients by sending the subsequent lists with their names missing? We guess probably none.

Sophisticated investors make no decisions based on arbitrary time horizons selected after the fact. They ask to see a firm's performance composites for each individual calendar year over at least a five- or ten-year time horizon, as well as shorter composites for rolling three- and five-year periods with different

FIGURE 13-1   Nelson's "Top 20" money managers—3-year returns

Product/Style Category:	**U.S. Intermediate Duration Fixed Income**
Performance Measurement Period:	**12 Quarters ending 12/31/94**
Ranking (Universe Size):	**Top 40 (out of 212 composites/funds)**

Lists the "Top 20" rates of return reported by the managers for this category and time period. All results are reported net of fees and inclusive of cash, as described in the introduction to this special report. For complete profiles of these managers, please refer to the indicated page in Nelson's Directory of Investment Managers—1995. Note: U.S. Equity products which are single-industry "Sector Funds" appear only in the "U.S. Concentrated Sector Equity" rankings and are not included in the "All Style" or other U.S. Equity rankings.

Rank	Firm Name (Profile Page Number) • Product Name	12 Qtr. Anlzd % Return	$ Assets in Composite
1	**Putnam Mutual Funds†** (Vol. I, Pg. 3837) • Putnam High Yield Advantage............................ *Composite represents 100.0% of assets under management in this style*	10.84%	710.2 mil
2	**Putnam Mutual Funds†** (Vol. I, Pg. 3837) • Putnam High Yield A... *Composite represents 10.0% of assets under management in this style*	10.44%	3268.2 mil
3	**Federated Investors** (Vol. I, Pg. 1558) • Fortress Bond Fund... *Composite represents 100.0% of assets under management in this style*	9.23%	142.3 mil
4	**Waddell & Reed†** (Vol. I, Pg. 4835) • United High Income II.. *Composite represents 100.0% of assets under management in this style*	9.18%	344.3 mil
5	**GW Capital** (Vol. I, Pg. 2133) • Sector Rotation Bond Management... *Composite represents 100.0% of assets under management in this style*	9.15%	52.7 mil
6	**Loomis Sayles & Company, L.P.** (Vol. I, Pg. 2793) • Medium Grade Fixed Income (MA)........... *Composite represents 100.0% of assets under management in this style*	8.46%	2811.0 mil
7	**Pension Management Company** (Vol. I, Pg. 3610) • Fixed Income..................................... *Composite represents 44.4% of assets under management in this style*	8.28%	10.0 mil
8	**Strong Capital Management†** (Vol. I, Pg. 4433) • Strong Income Fund................................. *Composite represents 100.0% of assets under management in this style*	8.02%	123.3 mil
9	**John Nuveen*** (Vol. I, Pg. 3415) • NY Performance Plus Municipal Fund............................... *Composite represents 100.0% of assets under management in this style*	7.77%	159.9 mil
10	**Caywood-Scholl Capital Mgmt.** (Vol. I, Pg. 882) • Fixed Income - Hybrid............................ *Composite represents 100.0% of assets under management in this style*	7.70%	273.0 mil
11	**GMG/Seneca Capital Management** (Vol. I, Pg. 2017) • Value Driven Fixed Income.................. *Composite represents 20.0% of assets under management in this style*	7.50%	158.6 mil
12	**FPA Fund Distributors†** (Vol. I, Pg. 1829) • FPA New Income... *Composite represents 99.9% of assets under management in this style*	7.50%	129.9 mil
13	**ARM Capital Advisors*** (Vol. I, Pg. 250) • Total Return Management.................................... *Composite represents 19.5% of assets under management in this style*	7.30%	583.6 mil
14	**John Nuveen*** (Vol. I, Pg. 3415) • NY Select Quality Municipal Fund................................... *Composite represents 100.0% of assets under management in this style*	7.08%	478.1 mil
15	**Morley Capital Mgmt†** (Vol. I, Pg. 3194) • Stable Value Assets....................................... *Composite represents 9.5% of assets under management in this style*	6.78%	601.1 mil
16	**Bradford & Marzec** (Vol. I, Pg. 635) • Full Quality Composite.. *Composite represents 98.7% of assets under management in this style*	6.78%	415.6 mil
17	**John Nuveen*** (Vol. I, Pg. 3415) • Premier Municipal Income Fund...................................... *Composite represents 100.0% of assets under management in this style*	6.73%	414.6 mil
18	**John Nuveen*** (Vol. I, Pg. 3415) • NY Investment Quality Municipal Fund............................. *Composite represents 100.0% of assets under management in this style*	6.56%	377.6 mil
19	**Morgan Grenfell Capital Mgmt** (Vol. I, Pg. 3155) • Fixed Income - Municipal Bonds............... *Composite represents 53.3% of assets under management in this style*	6.56%	346.4 mil
20	**Western Asset Management** (Vol. I, Pg. 4956) • WAM Intermediate Fixed Income................... *Composite represents 60.6% of assets under management in this style*	6.53%	432.0 mil

Reprinted with permission from Nelson's "World's Best Money Managers"—1995. © 1995 Nelson Publications.

* Reporting firm is not in compliance with AIMR Performance Presentation Standards
† Reporting firm did not indicate whether or not they are in compliance with AIMR PPS

starting dates. Observing a manager's year-by-year performance in both up- and downmarkets and over longer periods with different starting dates is necessary if one is to assess investment risk, manager investment style, and—ultimately—manager skill.

The Use of Portable and Backtested Returns

If every investor were sophisticated, no brand-new money management firms could get started. New firms are thus tempted to do one of two things: (1) present performance results a manager obtained while employed somewhere else (*portable returns*), or (2) present simulated results (*backtested returns*). AIMR standards allow both practices under certain circumstances, but only where fully and completely disclosed. Performance data from a prior firm can be used as supplemental information if the manager gives credit for the performance to the prior affiliation, and describes responsibilities while at the previous employer. Similarly, backtested results can only be used as supplementary information and identified as such.

Whether fully disclosed or not, both practices should invoke healthy skepticism. Portable returns don't allow the separate attribution of returns between the portfolio manager and the prior employer. Backtested results frequently ignore real world transaction costs and time delays, which can substantially impact real portfolio returns. Further, both practices probably entail healthy doses of selection bias. How was the starting date for a simulation chosen? What assumptions were made about which transactions were executed, when, and at what price? Did the manager time the departure from the prior employer in order to maximize the appeal of the portfolio performance history? When investors are in doubt, these questions need to be asked.

COMPARING RETURNS ACROSS MANAGERS

The time-weighted return describes a manager's *absolute* performance. It does not allow us to make judgments about the quality of that performance, however. Did the manager do well against his or her peers, or poorly? How did returns stack up against managed or unmanaged portfolios with similar objectives?

Two primary methodologies are used to compare manager performance: *performance benchmarks* and *performance universes*. Both are designed for performance attribution purposes (i.e., to separate the effects of various manager decisions for those of manager style or external, chance events).

Performance Universes

Performance universes are the most popular basis on which to compare portfolios. Let's look at how they are constructed.

Universe Construction

Performance universes are constructed electronically by aggregating market valuations and income accruals for a large number of individually managed portfolios. The data are supplied by independent investment advisors, brokerage firms, trust banks, and insurance companies that manage individual portfolios. They are used to compute quarterly TWRs for each portfolio in the universe, where a portfolio may be thought of as one account managed by one manager for one client.

This approach lets a variety of subuniverses by style and asset class exist within the larger universe. Subuniverses of individually managed portfolios can be constructed according to the type of portfolio owner (e.g., a pension plan sponsor versus an endowment), asset class (e.g., equities versus fixed-income), manager style (e.g., growth equities versus value equities), manager type (insurance companies versus banks), and so forth. TWR percentile rankings for the performance of managed portfolios within each definable subuniverse and for the universe of all managers and styles taken as a whole are then constructed. One portfolio may be included in more than one subuniverses and thus have multiple percentile ranks, depending on the context. The construction of subuniverses in this fashion helps us make relevant, "apples-to-apples" comparisons across portfolios and managers.

By industry convention, a first percentile performance ranking is the best; a 100th percentile ranking is the worst. Obviously, the larger the performance universe, the more significant a particular ranking is. Large universes permit finer subuniverse breakdowns with less sacrifice of statistical validity. The Wilshire Trust Universe Comparison Service (TUCS), the Frank Russell Company, SEI, and the Independent Consultant Co-op (I.C.C.) are the largest and most comprehensive proprietary databases. The largest purchased universes are offered by Lipper, CDA Investment Technologies, Morningstar, and Ibbotson Associates. Table 13-4 shows the relative size and composition of the proprietary universes as of the first quarter of 1995.[7]

Universe construction methodology differs across major vendors, but with some commonalities. For example, the Russell Universe includes portfolio returns submitted directly by investment managers, while Wilshire accepts data only from custodians and insurance companies. Both universes exclude

TABLE 13-4 Performance universes compared (all data as of the first quarter of 1995; dollars in billions)

Sponsor of Universe	Universe Size			Representative Subuniverses By:			
	Number of Portfolios	Collective Asset Base	Number of Managers	Portfolio Owner	Portfolio Type	Manager Type	Manager Style
Wilshire TUCS	4,904	$811.50	777	Endowments Foundations Defined benefit plans Life insurance Personal trust Profit sharing plans	Equity Fixed-income Cash Real estate properties Real estate securities Venture capital Convertible Optioned equity GIC Balanced	Bank Insurance Co. Investment advisor Internally managed	Large-company value Small-company value Large-company growth Small-company growth Mid-cap value Mid-cap growth High-yield fixed-income Core fixed-income Matched duration core fixed Domestic equity Foreign equity Global equity
Frank Russell Company	11,000	$138.60	715	Multi-employer Public Funds	U.S. equity U.S. fixed-income International equity Internat'l fixed-income Real estate Alternative investments Private partnerships Mutual funds		Value equity Market neutral equity Tactical asset allocators Emerging markets equity Global fixed-income (unhedged) Municipal bonds Small-cap equity Intermediate bonds Midcap equity
SEI	4,713	$541.40	1,575	Hospitals Local government State Taft-Hartley Corporate pension plans Canadian funds	Balanced Domestic equity Domestic fixed Real estate equity Real estate debt International equity		Small-cap equity Global bonds Pacific Basin equity Global equity Fixed-income—long duration Fixed-income—short duration
I.C.C.	7,336	$479.40	N/A		Balanced Company stock Cash Derivatives Real estate Venture capital GIC Convertibles Fixed-income Equity		Active equity Passive equity Active fixed-income Passive fixed-income Global fixed-income Immunized bonds

Note: This is a partial list. Some universe sponsors allow customization of subuniverses by portfolio size, asset mix, and so forth.

backtested portfolios and express all returns (except for mutual funds) gross of fees.

Style Considerations and the Assessment of Skill

A sample Wilshire TUCS performance universe comparison for one large-cap equity manager, which we shall call ABC Capital Management, Inc. (ABC), is summarized in Table 13-5. Note that ABC's percentile rank varies considerably depending on the time period and subuniverse selected as a comparison basis. How does the investor determine which of ABC's percentile ranks is the most valid?

The answer lies in understanding the impact of style on performance. Most managers, like ABC, tend to specialize in particular styles of investing. Their chosen styles require them to focus on particular sectors, or subsets, of the stock and/or bond markets. Value managers (of which ABC is an example) tend to purchase stocks whose P/E and price-to-book ratios are low and/or dividend yields high. Growth managers tend to shun such stocks unless their growth prospects are also excellent. Similarly, high-yield bond managers focus on noninvestment-grade bonds, while core bond managers typically focus on bonds rated Baa or higher.

Cycles in the performance of individual sectors in the stock and bond markets can differ dramatically from cycles in the performance of those markets taken as a whole. There are times when spreads widen between high-yield bonds and investment-grade bonds, and times when stocks in certain industries that have been driven down to low P/E multiples rebound relative to stocks in other sectors having higher P/E ratios. International equity managers have returns

TABLE 13-5 Total returns and Wilshire TUCS percentile ranks for ABC Capital Management (time periods ended 3/31/95)

Manager/Subuniverse Percentile Rank	First Quarter 1995	One Year	Two Year	Three Year
ABC Return	9.96%	11.86%	8.82%	10.99%
Managed Equities Rank	16	46	29	31
Managed Large-Cap Value Equities Rank	37	71	39	53
Managed Large-Cap Equities Rank	19	55	24	26
S&P 500 Return	9.96%	15.58%	8.27%	10.55%
S&P 500 Rank	19	55	24	26

Data courtesy of Wilshire TUCS. This table provides the gross-of-fees time-weighted quarterly returns and percentile rankings for a selected large-cap value equity account managed by ABC Capital Management over various time periods ending on 3/31/95 and for the S&P 500 over the same time periods.

that are differentiated both by geographic region of the world (e.g., Asia versus Europe), by capitalization (e.g., small stocks versus large-company stocks), and by style (value versus growth). Manager comparisons that do not take these differences into account are meaningless.

Figure 13-2 gives an example of these style effects. It illustrates historical performance cycles in small-capitalization stocks for the period from 1926 through the first quarter of 1995. Since 1926, small-cap stocks (generally defined as stocks with equity capitalization of $500 million or less) have experienced nine major performance cycles lasting an average of six (on the downside) to eight (on the upside) years. A client evaluating the five-year performance of a particular small-stock equity manager against a universe consisting of *all* managed equity portfolios might have been very impressed in 1982 with the manager's outstanding relative performance, and hired the manager on that basis. Later, in 1988, the client might fire the same manager for poor relative performance! Making decisions on the basis of "apples-to-oranges" comparisons such as this is a primary cause of a costly "hire high, fire low" investment decision cycle.

The guiding principle in subuniverse selection is to eliminate as completely as possible differences in manager style as a source of a manager's relative under- or overperformance. In this context, the more precise the definition of manager style, the better. Large-cap domestic equity growth managers should

FIGURE 13-2   Small stock performance relative to the S&P 500:
1926–1994

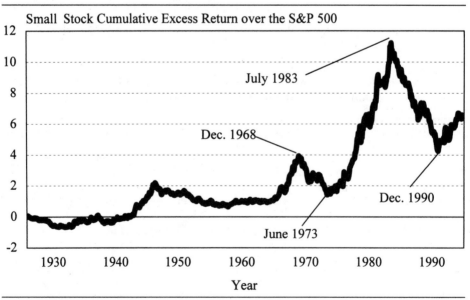

Source: Ibbotson Associates.

be compared only to other large-cap domestic equity growth managers. High-yield fixed-income, short-term, and convertible bond mangers, similarly, should not be compared to all fixed-income managers, but only to managers with the same fixed-income style.

In the case of ABC, a large-cap domestic value equity manager, the most valid style comparison is to other large-cap value equity managed accounts (portfolios). Over most time periods shown in Table 13-5, it can be inferred that value stocks outperformed growth stocks, and large-cap managers outperformed small. That is why ABC's percentile ranks against other large-cap value managers in that table are generally lower than its ranks against all managed equities and all large-cap equities. And, generally speaking, the longest time period affords the greatest indication of skill. Thus, the most meaningful number in the table is ABC's 53rd percentile rank against other large-cap value equity managers for the three years ended March 31, 1995.

Cognitive Errors

Cognitive errors in the use of universe comparisons are additional sources of the "hire high, fire low" decision cycle. Most unsophisticated investors, and many sophisticated ones who should know better, unwittingly fall into the dangerous traps these phenomena create.

The Illusion of Consistency. Cognitive errors arise when a decision-maker assumes, for example, that managers' relative performance is, or should be, relatively consistent over time. The assumption of consistency, for most of us, is an accepted fact of life. It is an unconscious carryover from our experience in arenas where consistency is the norm; i.e., games of skill, as opposed to games of chance. We routinely use baseball players' historical batting averages as informal guides to predicting future batting averages. If we see a basketball player try to make a particular shot of a type he has rarely missed in the past, we predict that he will make this one also.[8] Chess players are ranked on the basis of games won, lost, and drawn, and—although occasional upsets occur—chess rankings *are* reliable indicators of skill. There is scant evidence, however, that the same level of relative performance consistency is evident in investment management, a "game" that combines large elements of chance with elements of skill.

The Evidence for Consistency. A number of studies have examined the evidence for *performance consistency*.[9] One recent study, conducted by W. Scott Bauman and Robert E. Miller (1995), bases its evaluation on the quarterly performance of several hundred managed portfolios of diversified U.S. equities, as tracked by Callan Associates, a respected investment consulting firm, over five full market cycles between 1973 and 1992. The Bauman/Miller study shows weak evidence of correlation between managers' percentile universe rankings in one market cycle (peak-to-trough in the quarterly closing prices of the S&P 500) and their rankings in the subsequent market cycles, although the results are not unambiguously statistically significant in three of the four subsequent market cycles the study examined. In another study conducted by Edgar W. Barksdale and William L. Green (1990), and summarized in Table 13-6, a group of equity managers are ranked into performance quintiles for two different five-year periods and then reranked in the five-year period immediately following. It is discovered that managers who were in the top (first) quintile in the first five years of a decade are generally less likely to stay above the median in the second half of the decade than they are to fall below the median. While some other recent studies have found support for the proposition the winners do tend to repeat over very short periods of time, such as one to two years, the sum total of available evidence points to a surprising degree of inconsistency over long time periods. See Goetzmann and Ibbotson (1994) and Hendricks, Patel, and Zeckhauser (1993).

The Effects of Time on Skill Attribution.   A related cognitive error results from assuming that skill (or lack thereof) must be the cause of a manager's top (or bottom) quartile ranking. But suppose every manager in a universe is equally skilled. Given normal market randomness, some managers will perform better than others in the short run, even though their skills are equal. Universe rankings thus always produce short-run "winners" and "losers," whether or not differences in skill are present. This problem of confusing skill

TABLE 13-6   Percent of equity managers performing above the median during the second half of the 1980s[a]

Quintile Ranking of Managers During the First Half of the 1980s	1980–1984	1981–1985	1982–1986	1983–1987	1984–1988	1985–1989
First	31	52	48	45	48	45
Second	45	55	52	41	41	52
Third	37	50	57	61	61	43
Fourth	63	48	45	55	55	48
Fifth	57	45	48	48	45	57
Decade Analyzed	1975–1984	1976–1985	1977–1986	1978–1987	1979–1988	1980–1989

[a] The analysis examines a series of rolling 10-year intervals spanning the end of 1974 through 1989, using a database of more than 144 equity portfolios, all extending over the full 15-year period, managed by 135 firms. The portfolios' total market value exceeded $22 billion at the end of 1989.

with chance will not be solved by looking at a larger universe; it can be solved only by having more quarters of data on each manager.

All of this is reflective of a noisy statistical process in which the "signal" (i.e., the impact of the manager's skill on portfolio performance) is easily lost in a short-term jumble of miscellaneous chance elements beyond the manager's control (noise), as well as nonskill elements under manager control, of which portfolio risk is the most important. The noise, in the short run, at least, can effectively swamp the signal and contribute to the apparently random, inconsistent quarter-to-quarter universe performance rankings. Inconsistency is further amplified when the manager's portfolio is relatively undiversified and highly exposed to the impact of unique external chance events impacting individual stocks.

The alternative hypothesis, that the signal itself fluctuates dramatically over time, is far less intuitively appealing and implies that the whole exercise of performance comparisons is meaningless. It is more likely that the value added by *relatively constant skill levels* varies in the short run with *market cycles*. If this is true, and we believe it is, the solution to apparent short-run performance inconsistencies is to attempt to judge manager skill only over extremely long time periods in which the short-term noise cancels out and regresses to the mean. What is a long enough period reliably to separate the effects of skill from chance? The conventional statistical hurdle requires attainment of 95 percent confidence in the truth of a hypothesis before it can be accepted. Applying this standard to acceptance of the hypothesis that skill, rather than luck, is involved in a particular manager's performance history generally means we would need 20 or more years of quarterly returns to assess skill!

An example constructed by Peter Bernstein, editor of this book, illustrates the point.[10] He observed that over the period 1976–1994 the mutual funds included in Morningstar's growth category outperformed the S&P 500 by an average of 170 basis points (1.70 percent) a year, with a standard deviation (risk) of annual returns that was 120 basis points (1.20 percent) below the S&P. Does this excellent performance give us 95 percent confidence that skill is involved? No. We can be only 89 percent certain that the results in this case reflect skill. Another 16 years of similar results would be required to attain 95 percent confidence. And, if we were to take 50 basis points a year off the excess returns, an additional 50 years of data would be required for 95 percent certainty! Thus, a manager would have to beat the S&P 500 by 50 basis points a year for 69 years, or by 170 basis points a year for 35 years, before skill could be statistically confirmed.

The Effects of Risk on Skill Attribution.   Risk effects are often mistakenly attributed to skill in universe performance comparisons. Again, suppose every manager in a particular style subuniverse is equally skilled. Suppose that each differs materially from the other only in the degree of risk the portfolio assumes; i.e., some managers in the universe implement the chosen style with undiversified portfolios of stocks that are volatile and highly sensitive to market trends, while others select more diversified groupings of stocks insensitive to market trends.[11] Consider what will happen in a strongly trending market. In bull markets, when the market is rising, the "risky" managers will likely end up with the highest quarterly and annual universe percentile ranks. In these markets, their high risk pays off, giving them greater absolute returns than other managers. In bear markets, however, the "risky" managers end up in the bottom percentiles of the universe, as their stocks perform poorly in absolute terms. Observed performance inconsistencies of this nature cannot be eliminated by choosing a different style subuniverse, as noted.

The conclusion: The effects of risk must not be confused with evidence of manager skill. *Portfolio risk* profoundly affects portfolio performance—both in absolute terms and in terms of same-style universe rankings—yet it has little or nothing to do with skill.

Statistical Bias in Universe Comparisons

Statistical bias contributes very differently to the problem of performance attribution and skill assessment. Of the known sources of bias, *survivorship bias* is by far the most important. As Stephen Ross has commented, "Survivorship bias is endemic to everything researchers do when they use statistics in finance. It can do many things and never leave a clue as to what is happening."[12]

According to Ross, emerging markets performance studies provide a rich illustration of this problem. A number of academics and practitioners have looked at the performance of the so-called emerging stock markets over time and have variously concluded that their returns have been truly impressive, and that their diversification potential for traditionally balanced portfolios is enormous. It is on the basis of these studies that emerging markets equities products have proliferated, and billions of dollars of investor capital have flowed to them. What is wrong with this? Nothing, except that the historical studies on which capital flows were based do not look at yet-to-emerge markets like Bolivia, Haiti, Mongolia, Russia, or Iceland. They focus on emerg*ed* markets like Hong Kong, Brazil, Mexico, and Singapore, and backtest *their* performance. If yet-to-emerge markets were included in these studies, the results are unlikely to be as compelling, since some yet-to-emerge markets may never emerge. (As Ross comments, some investors have been waiting for the Mexican miracle for 30 years now.)

Thus, survivorship bias occurs when one evaluates the past performance of a *surviving* group of investment managers (or markets), as opposed to the past performance of a *starting* group of managers (markets) that were around at the beginning of the historical period. In the former approach, the managers who start out but fail, drop out, or otherwise do not "survive" to the end of the period are excluded.

Managers lose accounts for many reasons, including poor performance. When an account (client) is lost, the manager who lost it can no longer report on its performance to the universe sponsor. In other words, the account must be excluded from the universe rankings in subsequent quarters. What remains in the universe, then, is the group of survivors among this manager's client portfolios.

Survivorship bias is present in some form in all performance universes, no matter how carefully they are constructed. Table 13-7 shows one indication of its practical impact using the Wilshire TUCS data. The table compares the performance of a hypothetical "median" equity manager over the five-year period ended December 31, 1994, against the year-by-year universe median of all equity managers. Survivorship bias among the managers in this particular universe accounts for the fact that the manager ranks in only the 58th percentile against each of the five-year medians, as opposed to 50th against the year-by-year medians. The manager appears unskilled relative to the universe of other survivors, yet performance is precisely in the middle of the pack in each and every year.

The longer the historical time period involved in a comparison, the worse the impact of survivorship bias. Ten-year survivors are surprisingly few compared to five-year survivors or one-year survivors, as Table 13-8 illustrates.

Small-portfolio bias has a similar effect. Usually in any universe, there are a great many more small portfolios than large ones. Percentile or quartile ranks taken relative to the entire universe are unweighted by size, so that each

TABLE 13-7 **Wilshire Trust Universe performance ranks and rates of return for managed equity portfolios (over time periods ending on December 31)**

Percentile Rank	1994 (One Year)	1993 (One Year)	1992 (One Year)	1991 (One Year)	1990 (One Year)	1994 (Five Years)
5th percentile	6.19%	27.55%	22.48%	64.83%	8.02%	15.46%
25th percentile	2.21	17.20	12.93	40.38	0.57	11.33
Median	0.27	12.55	9.02	31.92	−3.95	9.73
75th percentile	−2.16	8.82	5.97	26.23	−8.66	8.59
95th percentile	−7.52	0.50	−0.57	15.96	−20.12	6.62
S&P 500	1.29	9.99	7.67	30.57	−3.18	8.69
	(37th)	(67th)	(81st)	(56th)	(44th)	(72nd)
"Median Manager"	0.27	12.55	9.02	31.92	−3.95	9.73
	(50th)	(50th)	(50th)	(50th)	(50th)	(58th)

TABLE 13-8 Wilshire Trust Universe Comparison Service (number of observations as a function of time horizon ending December 31, 1994)

Subuniverse	Current Quarter	One Year	Five Years	Ten Years
Total portfolios	5,170	4,511	2,168	669
Balanced portfolios	621	521	254	114
Managed equity portfolios	2,181	1,874	881	298
Managed fixed-income portfolios	1,163	1,047	555	144

Source: Wilshire TUCS. Ten-year horizon is actually nine years, three quarters.

portfolio has equal importance, whether it represents $2 million or $200 million in assets. Percentile ranks are thus influenced considerably more by the performance of the smaller portfolios than by the larger ones, even though the total assets under management in the universe may be dominated by large portfolios. Small accounts are frequently managed very differently from very large accounts; they may not be comparable, so bias can result.[13] Comparing an equity mutual fund with $10 billion in assets to a universe of portfolios in which 90 percent are under $1 billion in size gives a highly distorted picture of manager skill.

Other Problems

Universe comparisons suffer from other nettlesome structural defects. First, the comparisons are academic because they involve comparing *infeasible*, or *noninvestable*, alternatives. For example, Tables 13-1 and 13-7 reveal that the Windsor Fund underperformed the Wilshire Universe median for managed equity portfolios over the period 1990–1994. An investor who wants to switch out of Windsor on this basis will receive no help from the universe data in identifying anyone with greater skill. Think about it: How can the 25th percentile manager for the *next* five years be identified beforehand?[14]

Benchmarks and Performance Attribution

These shortcomings and others lead sophisticated investors to use performance *benchmarks* instead of universes as a basis for *performance attribution* studies. Benchmarks, unlike universes, permit one to control the effects of risk and style, while affording comparisons to similar style, identifiable-in-advance, investable alternatives.

Performance attribution using benchmark portfolios dates back to the late 1960s and early 1970s, when academicians began to apply the concepts of modern portfolio theory (MPT) and the capital asset pricing model (CAPM) to summarize the overall performance of investment managers relative to portfolio risk. The first attempts, by Sharpe (1966), Jensen (1968, 1969), and Treynor (1965), were directed at the development of risk-adjusted returns for use in performance comparisons. Then in 1972, Eugene Fama suggested decomposing the sources of a manager's returns in excess of a market index into the effects of his "selectivity," "risk," and "timing" decisions. Since that time, numerous formal performance attribution studies that assign components of observed returns to various prespecified factors have been conducted, using variants of Fama's conceptual framework. These studies have become quite sophisticated, with recent advancements in statistical methodology and in computing power.

Most begin by defining appropriate passive benchmarks for the managed portfolios being evaluated. The managed portfolios' returns in excess of their benchmarks are calculated for each historical compounding interval. The objective of this approach is to correlate these differences, or *excess returns,* with (or attribute them to) active decisions (called *factors* in the attribution model) that the manager has made. These decisions (factors) might include stock selection, market timing (such as whether to be fully invested and, if not, how much cash to hold), currency and country selection (in the case of international managers), asset allocation (in the case of balanced managers), sector and industry allocations, and so forth.

For in-depth discussion of performance attribution and manager style analysis using benchmarks, see Ankrin (1992), Rennie and Cowhey (1989), and Tierney and Winston (1991). Famous attribution studies include Brinson, Hood, and Beebower (1986) and Brinson, Hood, and Singer (1991).

Benchmarks Defined

To understand how formal performance attribution systems are set up and used to evaluate the effects of skill (or lack thereof), it is necessary first to understand the role and use of performance benchmarks.

Benchmark portfolios (alternatively called "bogeys" or "normal" portfolios) are unmanaged, investable, passive, or semipassive paper portfolios that reflect a manager's particular investment style. The primary purpose of a benchmark is to set a realistic, attainable performance standard, so that, by closely replicating a manager's style and chosen risk level, any short- or long-run differences in performance that arise between the manager and the benchmark can be attributed to the manager's active decisions, and thus—eventually—to manager skill. An appropriate benchmark should include the type of securities that are also representative of the manager's portfolio. In this respect, a benchmark could be a published market index, such as the S&P 500 or the Russell 1000, the S&P/Barra MidCap Growth Index, or a customized, proprietary portfolio unique to a particular manager. The source of the benchmark doesn't matter. What *does* matter are certain criteria.

A good performance benchmark is:

- Investable.
- Objectively constructed.
- Specifiable in advance.[15]

A good performance benchmark has:

- Unambiguous composition.
- Easily observed performance.
- Same style and risk as manager.

Using these criteria, we can see that the *world market portfolio,* a portfolio that includes all financial securities, real estate, commodities, and currencies, would not be a good benchmark. It is not investable (at least from a practical standpoint), and while it can be specified in advance, its performance is not easily measurable. Further, it is unlikely to reflect most managers' styles. Similarly, the "median high-yield fixed-income manager in the SEI universe" is a poor benchmark for a high-yield bond manager because the benchmark cannot be specified in advance and thus is not investable. But, the First Boston High Yield Bond Index, the S&P 500, the Russell 1000, the Russell 2000, the Lehman Aggregate Bond Index, the S&P MidCap 400, the MSCI EAFE Index, the CRSP 9-10 and so on, are examples of published market benchmarks that do generally meet the criteria (for certain managers, of course).

While the characteristics we specify are not "cast in stone," they are the most important ones. To be appropriate and meaningful in separating the effects of style and risk from skill, a benchmark should be investable, specified in advance, and roughly match the most important style and risk characteristics of a portfolio. These include such items as average market capitalization of the securities held (i.e., large-cap stocks versus small-), dividend yield, variability of returns, price-to-book ratio, concentration by sector and industry, market-related risk (i.e., correlations to relevant market indexes), and earnings growth.

Defining the Security Universe and Selection Process

One way to construct an appropriate benchmark is to define the stock universe from which a particular manager selects portfolio holdings and to mimic the manager's stock screening criteria within this universe. A large-cap value manager might, for example, start with all 987 stocks that make up the Russell 1000 Index and exclude those that have less than $3 billion in equity market capitalization, have been publicly traded for less than five years, have negative current earnings, and have higher-than-average P/E and price-to-book ratios. From there, the manager might next eliminate any nondividend-paying stocks and, perhaps, stocks in certain sectors, such as utilities. This reduced stock universe might then be analyzed, and those stocks that appear underpriced relative to forecasted future earnings purchased in equal dollar amounts. The relationship between the initial stock universe and the reduced stock universe used to construct a performance benchmark for this manager is graphically shown in Figure 13-3.

A growth-stock manager, on the other hand, might start with the same initial universe, apply identical screens on market capitalization, trading longevity, and current earnings, but then eliminate those stocks with lower-than-average forecasted earnings growth and P/E ratios.

What are appropriate benchmarks for managers who invest this way? One popular selection approach involves choosing a published market style index that mimics as closely as possible the style characteristics of the manager's portfolio. Tables 13-9 and 13-10 provide examples of several published large-cap value and growth indexes. From these lists, the managers in question might choose the index that most closely matches (1) their reduced universes after mechanical screening criteria have been applied, and (2) the style-related risk factors and characteristics of their respective portfolios, described above. Important statistical evaluation tools widely used for comparing and summarizing the risk and style characteristics of two portfolios— as opposed to merely comparing their holdings stock-by-stock—include the BARRA Model and the VESTEK On-Line System. These are PC-based software tools that can be used to dissect and compare portfolios in terms of their industry, sector, and risk factor exposures.

FIGURE 13-3   Available asset class securities

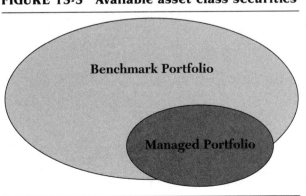

Benchmark Portfolio

Managed Portfolio

TABLE 13-9   Large-cap value indexes (data as of 12/31/94)

Name of Market Index	Number of Companies Represented	Weighting Method	Unweighted Average Capitalization ($billions)	Weighted Average P/E Ratio	Dividend Yield
Prudential Securities Large-Cap Value Index	470	Market cap	$4.2	11.7	2.4%
Rogers/Casey Value Index	149	Shares	$10.5	13.2	3.9%
Russell Large-Cap Value Index	499	Floating	$3.5	12.4	4.0%
S&P/BARRA Value Index	318	Market cap	$5.2	13.1	3.8%
Wilshire Large-Value Index	150	Market cap	$4.7	10.4	4.9%
S&P 500	500	Market cap	$6.7	14.9	2.9%

Source: Prudential Securities, *Benchmark Report V.V,* February 1995.

Let's look at an example. Table 13-11 shows the BARRA output for a structured mid- to small-cap growth portfolio that U.S. Trust Company of New York created for a client, as compared to its benchmark, an 80 percent/20 percent mixture of the S&P 400 MidCap and S&P 600 SmallCap Indexes. The upper portion of the table compares the two portfolios' exposure to the BARRA model's 13 attribution factors. These factors are *size* (a factor that distinguishes

TABLE 13-10   Large-cap growth indexes (data as of 12/31/94)

Name of Market Index	Number of Companies Represented	Weighting Method	Unweighted Average Capitalization ($billions)	Weighted Average P/E Ratio	Dividend Yield
Prudential Securities Securities Large-Cap Growth Index	348	Market cap	$3.1	18.8	0.7%
Rogers/Casey Growth Index	150	Shares	$11.0	16.0	1.7%
Russell Large-Cap Growth Index-	488	Floating	$3.9	17.6	1.8%
S&P/BARRA Growth Index	182	Market cap	$9.3	17.6	2.0%
Wilshire Large-Value Index	192	Market cap	$7.2	17.2	1.9%
S&P 500	500	Market cap	$6.7	14.9	2.9%

Source: Prudential Securities, *Benchmark Report V.V,* February 1995.

TABLE 13-11   BARRA benchmark comparisons for a mid- to small-cap managed equity portfolio (as of May 15, 1995)

BARRA Risk Factor	Managed Portfolio	Benchmark	Difference
Variability in markets	0.74	0.77	−0.02
Success	0.34	0.32	0.02
Size	−2.09	−2.09	−0.01
Trading activity	0.44	0.43	0.01
Growth	0.65	0.66	−0.01
Earnings/price	−0.016	−0.18	0.02
Book/price	−0.01	0.03	−0.03
Earnings variation	0.30	0.33	−0.03
Financial leverage	−0.22	−0.23	0.00
Foreign income	−0.64	−0.65	0.01
Labor intensity	0.24	0.22	0.02
Yield	−0.54	−0.56	0.02
Locap	−0.52	0.49	0.04

BARRA Risk Prediction

Annualized Standard Deviation of Return	17.07%	17.11%	
Systematic risk (beta) of portfolio relative to benchmark	1.0		
R-Squared (coefficient of determination)	0.995		

Comparison of sector allocations

Economic Sector Allocation	Percent of Portfolio Value	Percent of Benchmark Value	Difference
Raw materials production	7.29	7.11	0.18
Durable goods production	10.21	9.77	0.45
Integrated oils	0.26	0.45	−0.19
Other energy producers	3.96	4.03	−0.07
Consumer staples	1.78	2.12	−0.34
Healthcare	10.29	10.01	0.28
Consumer discretionary purchases	23.23	23.26	−0.03
Utilities	6.82	6.94	−0.11
Financial services	17.47	17.38	0.08
Autos and transportation	2.95	3.49	−0.54
Technology	15.73	15.44	0.29

Source: U.S. Trust Company of New York. The benchmark shown is an 80 percent/20 percent blend of the S&P 400 Midcap/S&P 600 Smallcap Indexes.

large stocks from small stocks), *trading activity* (which distinguishes stocks by their trading volume), *growth* (which distinguishes stocks by past and antici-pated earnings growth), *variability* (which distinguishes stocks by their volatil-ity), *yield, financial leverage* (which distinguishes firms by their debt to equity ratio and exposure to interest rate risk), and so forth. Each entry in the table is scaled so that on average across the entire universe of stocks the mean is zero, with a standard deviation of 1.0.

Thus, Table 13-11 reveals that both the portfolio and its benchmark are over two standard deviations below the universe mean in size (i.e., they are both significantly more small-cap than the universe as a whole); they are both above the universe mean in variability and growth, and below the mean in yield. The two portfolios are highly similar and have approximately the same risk level, as measured by standard deviation. Ninety-nine percent of the variability over time in the managed portfolio is associated with variability in the benchmark (this is the R-squared value in the table). Finally, the bottom portion of Table 13-11 compares the two portfolios' economic sector allocations. These are quite similar, as well.

Once a benchmark is selected, its total return is tracked in real time and compared, quarter-by-quarter, to the manager's total return. Any *excess return,* sometimes called *"active reward,"* earned by the manager over (under) the benchmark should reflect differences in stock selection, sector/industry allocations, and market timing relative to the benchmark. The manager whose portfolio is displayed in Table 13-11, for example, has overweighted healthcare stocks and durable goods manufacturers relative to the benchmark. The portfolio might also hold different individual stocks (stock selection) or have raised cash in market downturns (market timing), which affected returns relative to the benchmark. Over long periods of time, if the manager is skilled at these activities, the cumulative excess return should be positive, reflecting an active reward emanating from skill. One advantage of this approach to evaluating skill is its objectivity: It is impossible to manipulate the composition of a published, investable benchmark.

Problems with Published Benchmarks

When same-style benchmarks were first used for performance attribution in the early 1980s, benchmark quality received scant attention. The original proponents of customized or same-style benchmarks (mostly plan sponsors) faced numerous obstacles, including investment managers who actively resisted being pigeonholed, limited computer databases, and inadequate computer software. Any concerns over benchmark quality were temporarily set aside in the interests of implementing this innovative decision tool as quickly as possible.[16] As industry acceptance has improved and computing capabilities and databases expanded, more attention has been focused on these quality issues and on the associated problems that arise in benchmark construction.

The critical part of the benchmark construction process is the weighting of individual stocks in the benchmark portfolio. Weights can dramatically alter the benchmark's characteristics and performance, as well as influence the results of manager performance attribution relative to it. A large-cap equal-weighted benchmark will have a much lower average equity capitalization than one that is market cap-weighted. In the example of the large-cap value manager, the manager has an equally weighted portfolio of value stocks drawn from the Russell 1000, so its capitalization will likely be lower than any of the cap-weighted indexes shown. This introduces a large-cap bias in the benchmark. Often, too, equal-weighted benchmark will have lower yield and higher risk than a market cap benchmark of the same stock universe. It may not be possible to find a published style benchmark with the desired weighting characteristics.

Another problem is periodic rebalancing to keep the index's style characteristics intact. The Russell large-cap value and growth indexes, for example, are obtained by dividing the Russell 1000 into value stocks and growth stocks. Over time, if these portfolios are not rebalanced and the universe redivided along value and growth lines, some of the original value stocks will become "growthy" as their prices change, and some of the original growth stocks will take on value characteristics. The rebalancing process, which is conducted monthly in the Russell indexes, can introduce some aspects of active stock selection and even limit the "practical" investability of the benchmark. The alternative is equally unpalatable, however: comparison to a drifting style index over time, because that reduces the benchmark's effectiveness.

Gaming the Benchmark.   Mechanical rebalancing issues aside, a far more serious flaw in the use of published benchmarks relates to human behavior. This flaw is a manager's natural tendency to try to "game" the benchmark in one of two ways, either by: (1) trying to outperform it by investing in excluded assets, or (2) "mimicking" the benchmark and deviating from it in only minor ways, so as to avoid underperforming it. These activities are truly widespread. They often have the client's tacit acceptance, if not approval.

Consider Peter Lynch. By all accounts, he gained a reputation as a master stock-picker while managing the excellently performing Magellan Fund during the 1980s. The S&P 500 was the performance benchmark used by Fidelity and by virtually everyone who had occasion to assess Lynch's investing prowess. Yet, it was well-know at the time that Lynch had invested a significant portion (25 percent or so) or Magellan's assets in foreign stocks, which are not included in the S&P. During the last half of the 1980s, as the U.S. dollar weakened and Japan's market soared, foreign stocks as a group dramatically outperformed domestic stocks as a group. Was Lynch really a master stock-picker, or did he just shrewdly anticipate that foreign stocks would do better than U.S. stocks and thus (innocently) "game" his benchmark?[17]

Similarly, international equity managers who, in about 1989 or 1990, began including emerging markets investments in Hong Kong, Brazil, Singapore, Malaysia, and Mexico as part of broader international portfolios by 1994 appeared to be more skilled than the international managers who continued to confine themselves to investments in the mature, industrialized nations included in the MSCI EAFE Index, against which they were all being compared.[18] The former managers' outperformance, of course, was not attributable to superior skill in stock selection, but only to their taking "benchmark risk," and perceiving the potential that emerging markets would outperform EAFE markets. In the fourth quarter of 1994, when this benchmark risk turned against them, these managers suddenly appeared to be considerably less skilled than their more conservative brethren. As we mention earlier, the short-term "noise" from straying from one's benchmark can easily obscure the skill "signal."

The second type of benchmark gaming is even more subtle. Some managers clearly are reluctant to construct portfolios that stray significantly from the composition of their benchmark, for fear of underperforming it and being fired by the client. These managers typically dissect the benchmark and determine its percentage allocations (weights) by industry, economic sector, and individual stock. In the usual manifestation of this behavior, the manager forms acceptable ranges around those benchmark weights that equal, say, plus or minus half of the benchmark's percentage allocations. Thus, if utility stocks represent 13 percent of the benchmark, the manager may allow investment in utilities in a range of from 6.5 percent of the portfolio's market value to a maximum of 19.5 percent. Such managers may sense that, given a long enough period of benchmark underperformance, they will likely be fired. At the same time, they know they will not be fired for simply matching benchmark performance (presumably net of fees). This state of affairs produces and *asymmetric payoff function,* which means that the manager's self-interest is served by minimizing the risk of underperformance (rather than maximizing the chance of outperformance).

Herein lies the difference between "owner's risk" and "manager's risk."[19] The former reflects the chance that a portfolio's absolute returns will fall short of the portfolio owner's long-term investment objectives. The "manager's risk," however, is that of getting fired for relative underperformance. If both parties are rational, they will try to minimize their respective risks. At the same time, the manager's behavior is suboptimal from the owner's point of view. This situation results in what is commonly referred to as a "closet index fund," in which the client ends up paying the high fees associated with active management of a portfolio but receives only benchmark performance (which could have been directly for a presumably lower fee).[20]

Benchmark gaming in these various manifestations cannot be completely avoided, although its effects can be controlled through periodic reviews of the manager's portfolio composition relative to the benchmark.

The Role of Cash. Published market benchmarks, by definition, hold no cash balances. Managers, by contrast, virtually always maintain some uninvested "frictional" cash balances, even when they try to stay fully invested. These differences mean that the market index will tend to outperform managed portfolios in strongly rising markets and underperform them in downtrending markets, regardless of skill. Customized benchmarks, which include small "normal" cash balances, represent one solution.

Transaction Costs. Should a benchmark's returns be adjusted for real-world transaction costs? Because a benchmark portfolio is intended to represent a passive investment alternative to the investment manager's style, if there are costs associated with replicating this passive portfolio, those should be reflected in the benchmark's returns, or the comparison is not fair. Reasonable transaction costs that reflect the costs of initial investment and ongoing rebalancing, depending on the level of benchmark turnover, should be estimated and deducted from returns.

All in all, published benchmarks are analogous to unaltered, off-the-rack men's suits. A few accidentally fit well, but most suffer from flaws; the jacket gapes, or the sleeves are too short. The better fitting a benchmark, like a suit, the more powerful the performance attribution we can conduct with it.[21] It is best, where resources permit, to construct customized semipassive benchmarks using statistical optimization methodology. This affords more control over both benchmark risk and style.

Risk and Performance Attribution

As we note earlier in this chapter, risk has a particularly profound effect on a portfolio's absolute and relative performance over time. It must always be accounted for in benchmark construction. To understand how properly to account for it in the construction of customized benchmarks, we first explore its measurement.

Performance attribution studies rely on three main measures of risk. These are: *standard deviation* (often called "sigma"), *beta,* and *R-squared* (coefficient of determination). Two of these (beta and R-squared) measure a portfolio's risk *relative* to a market index. The third (standard deviation) measures portfolio risk in *absolute* terms.[22]

Standard Deviation. The standard deviation is a statistical measure of the dispersion of a portfolio's periodic time-weighted total returns around its *arithmetic mean return.* The true standard deviation (risk) of a risky asset can never be known; it is estimated from a sample of historical time-weighted returns using the formula:

$$\sigma_p = [\{1/(T-1)\} \{\Sigma_{t=1,\,T}(R_{p,\,t} - (1/T)\,(\Sigma_{I=1,\,T}R_t))^2\}]^{(1/2)}$$

where: σ_p = the portfolio's estimated standard deviation (sigma) per compounding interval

$R_{p,\,t}$ = the portfolio's TWR in compounding interval t, for $t = 1, 2, \ldots T$

This formula estimates a portfolio's standard deviation *per compounding interval;* the result can be annualized by multiplying it by the square root of N, the number of compounding intervals per year.

The standard deviation measures a portfolio's time-weighted return volatility (both up and down) from month to month, quarter to quarter, or year to year. Magellan's 9.38 percent quarterly standard deviation over the ten-year period from 1985 through 1994 tells us the dispersion of its actual quarterly returns around its average 4.65 percent quarterly return. An informal rule of thumb, according to certain standard statistical assumptions regarding normally distributed returns, allows us the infer the range of future quarterly returns. This rule of thumb states that in roughly two quarters out of three Magellan's actual return should lie within a 66 percent *confidence interval* of 4.65 percent plus or minus one standard deviation, or from −4.73 percent to +14.03 percent. The larger the standard deviation in relation to the arithmetic mean, the wider the resulting confidence interval, and the riskier Magellan is assumed to be.

Under the same assumptions, 95 percent of a portfolio's returns should fall within plus or minus two standard deviations of the arithmetic mean. In Magellan's case, the 95 percent confidence interval is −14.11 percent to +23.41 percent.

Beta.   Beta, in contrast, measures risk *relative* to a market index or benchmark. In this sense, it is a partial measure of risk, which focuses only on market-related variability. It quantifies the extent to which the movement of a portfolio's time-weighted return is affected by, or merely statistically associated with, contemporaneous movements of the market index or a particular benchmark.

Beta is a "dimensionless" number (similar in that sense, say, to Richter scale measurements for earthquakes). For conventional equity and bond portfolios, it varies over a range of from about −0.5 to +2.0. The average beta in the stock market is 1.0. A beta of 1.2 suggest that a 1 percent movement up or down in the benchmark's TWR over a particular compounding interval (whether a month, a quarter, or a year) is statistically associated with an average 1.2 percent movement *in the same direction* in the portfolio's TWR. Such a portfolio would be said to be *aggressive.* It behaves like a levered index fund, amplifying market trends. In contrast, a portfolio beta of 0.5 would mean that a 1 percent change in the benchmark's TWR on average historically has yielded a 0.5 percent change in the portfolio. In this case, the portfolio would be said to be *defensive*. It behaves like an index fund with half its money invested in cash, moderating market trends. Negative betas have similar interpretations, but signify portfolio moves in the *opposite* direction from the benchmark.

Statistically speaking, the formula for calculating the beta of a portfolio is the same as the equation for the slope of the line that results from regressing a managed portfolio's historical returns on those of a market index or benchmark:

$$\beta_p = r_{pm}(\sigma_p/\sigma_m)$$

where: β_p = portfolio beta (i.e., slope of the regression line)

r_{pm} = the correlation coefficient between the portfolio and the market index (or benchmark). (The correlation coefficient is the signed square root of R-squared.)

σ_p = the observed standard deviation of the portfolio's TWRs over a particular time horizon and compounding interval

σ_m = the standard deviation of the market index over the same time horizon and compounding interval

Note that beta is specific to a particular time horizon (e.g., five years) and compounding interval (e.g., monthly). Betas calculated for the same portfolio over *different* time horizons or compounding intervals vary from one another, sometimes significantly. As a general rule, at least 20 observations are needed for statistical reliability; if quarterly returns are used, one needs a minimum of five years of data. If monthly returns are employed, two to three years of data usually suffice. Five-year monthly betas seem to be an industry norm.

How does one decide which index or benchmark to use in the regression of historical returns? When different managed portfolios are being compared to one another, a common market index, such as the S&P 500 or the Lehman Aggregate (for bond managers), should be used for all. In this instance, one wishes to assess relative market-related risks across managers, which obviously requires a common standard for what constitutes the market. In other cases, however, such as where one is seeking to evaluate a managed portfolio's responsiveness to movements in its benchmark (as is the case in Table 13-11), the particular benchmark should be employed.

R-squared.   R-squared, or the coefficient of determination, is the square of the correlation coefficient given in the beta equation. It tells us what percent of the portfolio's total risk (its standard deviation) is market-related (i.e., associated with beta) and what percent is uniquely determined by the particular securities held. Market-related risk is often termed *systematic risk,* because it affects all securities in the market place to a greater or lesser degree, and thus is endemic to investments in that market. It cannot be avoided. Unique risk is termed *unsystematic risk,* because it reflects the business and financial risks associated with investing in individual securities in the portfolio. Unsystematic risk can be diversified away by holding a large number of different securities, but systematic risk cannot be diversified away within the particular market of interest. R-squared essentially measures how much of a portfolio's unsystematic risk has been diversified away and how much still remains.

Formally, R-squared is interpreted as the percentage of the portfolio's total risk explained by, or statistically associated with, movements in the market index. It can range from zero to 1.0. A value of zero signifies that the portfolio and the benchmark are highly dissimilar and typically move in totally unrelated ways over time; i.e., there is no statistical correlation (positive or negative) between them.[23] A value of 1.0, on the other hand, means the two portfolios have perfect correlation; i.e., they move in precise tandem (either in the same or the opposite direction). In practice, this would mean that they are literally the same portfolio (or one is merely the other sold short). Most of the time, R-squared falls *between* these two extremes. For managed equity portfolios whose benchmark is the S&P 500, for instance, typical R-squared values lie between about 0.70 and 0.98.

The higher a portfolio's R-squared value relative to the index or benchmark it is compared against, the more diversified a portfolio it is relative to the index, and the more similar the two portfolios can be assumed to be. The lower a portfolio's R-squared, on the other hand, the less diversified it is, and the more dissimilar it is to the index.

Choosing a Risk Measure.   The three risk measures are related. As can be seen, for example, beta equals the correlation between a portfolio and its benchmark (i.e., the signed ($+/-$) square root of its R-squared value) multiplied by the ratio of its standard deviation to the standard deviation of the market index.

Which risk measure should be used in performance attribution? That depends on the context. As Sharpe and Alexander (1990) observe in their widely quoted text, *Investments,* standard deviation is a good measure of risk for a well-diversified portfolio. But it is not a good measure of risk for a single asset held as part of a much larger portfolio that includes other types of assets. In that case, beta is the preferred measure of portfolio risk, because nonmarket-related risk, or unsystematic risk, is diversified away in the context of the broader portfolio.

Suppose a corporation seeks a small-cap equity manager to add to its multimanager, multiasset class pension portfolio. Suppose the vice president in charge of the pension plan interviews two small-cap managers—A and B—who, coincidentally, have had highly comparable historical average returns over the last one, three, and five years. Manager B, however, has achieved its returns with a significantly lower standard deviation than Manager A. The vice president, knowing that risk is "bad," might proceed to select Manager B. In this context, however, when the manager's portfolio will be added to the larger multimanager portfolio, the appropriate risk measure is *not* each manager's absolute or total variability, but rather the *market-related risk* that the manager adds to the existing overall portfolio including all other assets and managers. The two managers should be compared on the basis of their betas with respect to a common market index or, equivalently, the respective change in the overall portfolio's standard deviation that results after hiring each.

Risk-Adjusted Performance Measures

Risk-adjusted performance measures provide an easy means of making comparisons. If properly used, they provide a single comparative measure, for an effective ranking of a manager's value added relative to other managers (or, alternatively, to a benchmark).[24]

The Sharpe Ratio.   The *Sharpe ratio*, or *Sharpe reward-to-variability ratio*, was first suggested by Nobel Laureate William F. Sharpe. It is equal to a portfolio's arithmetic mean return, in excess of the risk-free interest rate, all divided by its standard deviation.[25] The risk-free interest rate is normally assumed to equal the annual income return on a U.S. Treasury instrument, such as 91-day Treasury bills or a Treasury bond of an appropriate maturity:

S_p = (Average Return in Excess of Risk-Free Rate)/(Portfolio Standard Deviation), or

$$S_p = \{(AR_{p, 1, T+1}) - RF_{1, T+1}\}/\sigma_p$$

where: S_p = Sharpe ratio
$AR_{p, 1, T+1}$ = portfolio's annualized arithmetic mean return between dates 1 and $T + 1$
$RF_{1, T+1}$ = average annualized risk-free interest rate between the same dates

> *Example: A manager has an annual arithmetic average return of 12 percent. The risk-free interest rate is 5 percent, and the manager's annualized standard deviation is 15 percent per year. The Sharpe ratio equals $(12\% - 5\%)/(15\%) = 0.466$.*

The Treynor Ratio.   The *Treynor ratio* differs only from the Sharpe ratio in its choice of risk measures.[26] Treynor uses beta to divide the portfolio's excess return over the risk-free interest rate:

$$T_p = \text{(Average Return in Excess of Risk-Free Rate)/(Portfolio Beta), or}$$

$$T_p = \{(AR_{p, 1, T+1}) - RF_{1, T+1}\}/\beta_p$$

where: T_p = Treynor ratio

> *Example: Assume the manager has a beta of 1.2. The manager's Treynor ratio is $(12\% - 5\%)/1.2 = 0.0583$.*

This measure is sometimes alternatively referred to as the *Treynor reward-to-volatility ratio.*

The Jensen Alpha. The *Jensen alpha,* sometimes alternatively called the *Jensen differential return,* is named after Michael Jensen, its developer.[27] Like the Treynor ratio, it quantifies the extent to which a manager has added value relative to the market, given the beta. For example, if a manager's beta is 1.5, and the market delivers an average annual excess TWR of 10 percent over the risk-free interest rate, the portfolio is expected to produce a TWR equal to 1.5 × 10 percent, or 15 percent over the risk-free interest rate. Suppose the manager instead earns 18 percent. The Jensen alpha in this case is +3 percent, indicating positive value added. If the manager delivers only 9 percent, the alpha is a −6 percent, for negative value added.

The Jensen alpha is computed as:

J_p = Average Return in Excess of Risk-Free Rate Minus Beta times the Market's Average Return in Excess of Risk-Free Rate, or

$$J_p = (AR_{p, 1, T+1} - RF_{1, T+1}) - \beta_p \times (AR_{m, 1, T+1} - RF_{1, T+1})$$

where: J_p = Jensen alpha

> *Example: The manager in the Sharpe and Treynor ratio examples has a Jensen alpha of $+1\% = (12\% - 5\%) - (1.2)(10\% - 5\%)$, if the market index's average return is 10%.*

The Jensen alpha is normally calculated by running a linear regression of the time series of portfolio returns in excess of the risk-free interest rate against the benchmark's returns in excess of the risk-free interest rate. The slope of the resulting line equals beta; the intercept is alpha. Alpha tells us whether a manager is adding value relative to the expected return, given the manager's beta.

Selecting the Right Risk-Adjusted Measure. In the pension plan example, suppose Manager A has a portfolio beta of 0.8, while Manager B, whose standard deviation is smaller, has a higher beta, equal to 1.2. If both managers have the same arithmetic average returns over the historical time horizon, Manager A's Jensen alpha and Treynor ratios will be higher than B's, but B's Sharpe ratio will be higher than A's. What conclusions should be drawn?

When you are in doubt, the Treynor ratio probably gives a more realistic picture. Why? Their Treynor ratios show that the manager with the lower beta is superior. An investor might conclude from looking at the Jensen measure that Manager A is more skilled in stock picking. Yet the Treynor ratio tells us that, when added to the existing portfolio, Manager A (who has the lowest beta) will add more return per unit of market-related risk than Manager B, and this is the more important conclusion. Thus, not all equally skilled managers are equally desirable in the context of a multi-manager portfolio. The Treynor ratio appropriately adjusts for the marginal risk–return contribution of a new manager added to an existing portfolio, while the Jensen alpha and the Sharpe ratios do not.

The Sharpe ratio should be used only for comparison of the performance of an entire multimanager balanced portfolio or an asset class within such a portfolio to appropriate broad market indexes. It is adversely affected by unsystematic risk in a portfolio relative to the market as a whole. Again, in the above example, Manager B has a higher Sharpe ratio, reflecting lower unsystematic risk than A, but B will add more market-related risk (beta) to the plan's combined portfolio than A will, while contributing no more return.

As with simple universe comparisons, it often requires many years of data to show evidence of skill at a high level of statistical confidence with risk-adjusted performance measures.

Customized Benchmarks

Formal performance attribution systems, as we have noted, compare the returns on managed portfolios to same-style, same-risk investable benchmarks. The insights gleaned from this approach depend heavily upon benchmark quality as a proxy for the managed portfolio. As manager acceptance for performance attribution has grown, and as statistical software to analyze portfolios has become commercially available, benchmark quality has become the focus of attention. The available software lets us construct customized, even proprietary benchmarks to meet desired quality standards and to overcome the problems with published, or generic, style benchmarks. The customized portfolios fit the manager more closely than any single generic benchmark can, as many managers have eclectic styles that cannot readily be pigeonholed into value or growth, large- or small-cap. Others' styles, and even asset allocations to specific markets, change with economic conditions. Thus, global equity managers, tactical asset allocators, and sector rotators cannot readily be de-scribed by a single generic benchmark.

William F. Sharpe has remarked that managers' returns are like "tracks in the sand."[28] If so, we can compare these to the "tracks" left by a *combination of generic style indexes* constructed to maximize their explanatory power over the manager's returns. Sector rotational managers, for example, who shift from autos to consumer nondurables at different points in the economic cycle might be compared to a blend of generic value and growth indexes. Using this idea, Sharpe developed a highly sophisticated approach to perfor-mance attribution that builds optimized, dynamic benchmarks form blends of published style benchmarks in order to maximize the percentage of "ex-plained" variation in the manager's returns over time.[29] In contrast to the benchmark construction procedure we describe earlier, no direct attempt is made to match the P/E, industry and economic sector allocations, or equity capitalization levels of the two portfolios. One needs only find a blended benchmark that does the best job of explaining the managers' historical re-turns. Such a benchmark should have significantly higher correlation with the manager's actual returns than will a single generic style benchmark, for two important reasons.

First, the use of a blend of several generic benchmarks should increase the portfolio's R-squared with the benchmark. Second, the use of a changing blend as the manager's portfolio changes should also increase the R-squared. Suffice it to say, however, that the quality of the "Sharpe benchmark" con-structed using this procedure depends on the relevance of the generic bench-marks selected as blending candidates.

The Sharpe approach divides the historical time horizon of interest into two segments. Returns in the first segment, the in-sample period, are used as a basis for constructing the optimized benchmark. The manager's returns in the second segment—which is usually a single compounding interval such as a month or a quarter—are then predicted using this specified-in-advance benchmark. The process is rolled forward quarter by quarter, each time allow-ing the benchmark weights to vary, and each time predicting a single month or quarter of the manager's returns.

Figure 13-4 (on pp. 368–369) illustrates the results of this approach. We show a small-cap equity account managed by Investment Advisers Inc (IAI). The four generic benchmarks used are the four Wilshire large- and small-cap value and growth indexes. IAI's monthly returns over the 36 months ended Au-gust 31, 1992, form the in-sample period. The initial benchmark selected by the optimizer was 30 percent invested in the Wilshire large-cap growth index and 70 percent in the Wilshire small-cap growth index. The in-sample period was then rolled forward a month at a time, until the end of March 1995. At that point, there are 31 months of predictions, using a blended benchmark whose weights vary five times during the period.

The conclusions that can be drawn are that IAI's portfolio is a classic small- to mid-cap growth portfolio, although its style has drifted more into small-cap stocks over time. By September 1994, the benchmark was 100 percent invested in the Wilshire small-cap growth index. How correlated is the benchmark with the manager? The portfolio's R-squared with the benchmark is 0.886, meaning that the benchmark explains 88.6 percent of the manager's returns, compared with only 79 percent explainable by the Russell 2000 small-cap index, the standard index against which virtually all small-cap managers like IAI are compared. Did IAI add value relative to this benchmark? Yes. IAI's cumulative annualized excess return over the return predicted by its benchmark is 2.52 percent.

Customized indexes of this type improve on our ability to distinguish style and risk effects from skill in performance attribution. They also help managers determine how their styles may have changed over time and how much value they are adding to client portfolios compared to feasible alternatives, in a way that static generic benchmarks simply cannot. When they are used as adjuncts to risk-adjusted return comparisons across managers, such tools mitigate the noise associated with skill assessment, reducing the years of data required for the attainment of the 95 percent confidence level.

A CLOSING OBSERVATION

Although we have not named it explicitly, luck is the pervasive chance element, or noise factor, that is endemic to all performance evaluations. Luck is what makes some managers attain higher short-run returns, and attract more new clients, than their equally competent peers. It is better to focus on finding "lucky" managers than finding skilled ones? We think not. Luck, like chance, is unsustainable and nonrepeatable over long time periods. It eventually cancels out across managers. For any given manager, luck regresses to the mean, while skill persists. Skill eventually is compensated in a competitive marketplace by those investors who seek it out and give it assets to manage.

Published performance numbers, as we have demonstrated, are ambiguous measures of manager skill. If this were not the case, eventually all unskilled managers would lose their clients, and the managers remaining would tend to have equal skills. This would negate the role of performance numbers as useful screening devices. As with most worthwhile endeavors, therefore, this one can never be easy, no matter how powerful statistical tools and computers become. The use of care and good judgment will always be in short supply.

FIGURE 13-4 JMC investment management style analysis

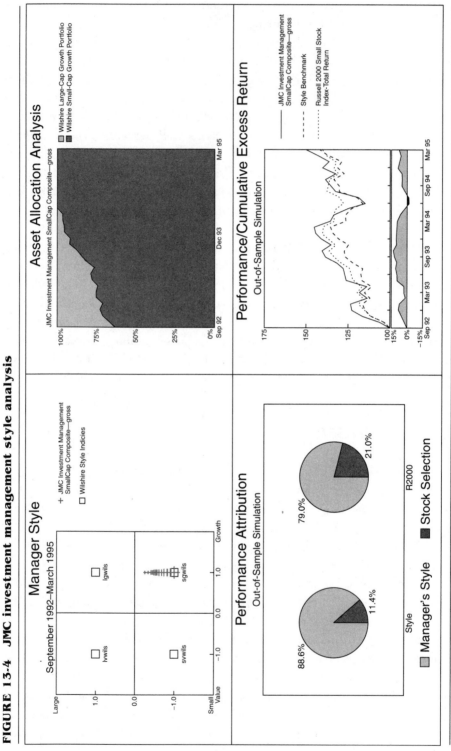

Source: Zephyr Style Advisor: Capital Trust Company

Optimization Results
JMC Investment Management SmallCap Composite—gross

	r2000			Asset Allocation						Style	
	Alpha	Beta	R2, %	Alpha	Igwils	Ivwils	sgwils	svwils	R2, %	Value-Growth	Small-Large
September 92–February 93	0.0074	1.0000	82.16	0.0054	0.2995	0.0000	0.7005	0.0000	91.07	1.0000	−0.4010
March 93–August 93	0.0047	1.0000	78.35	0.0046	0.2288	0.0000	0.7712	0.0000	88.61	1.0000	−0.5425
September 93–February 94	0.0034	1.0000	70.35	0.0029	0.0894	0.0000	0.9106	0.0000	84.46	1.0000	−0.8213
March 94–August 94	0.0009	1.0000	71.42	0.0013	0.0115	0.0000	0.9885	0.0000	85.27	1.0000	−0.9769
September 94–February 95	−0.0001	1.0000	73.14	−0.0003	0.0000	0.0000	1.0000	0.0000	86.67	1.0000	−1.0000
March 95	0.0030	1.0000	78.23	0.0012	0.0000	0.0000	1.0000	0.0000	88.20	1.0000	−1.0000

Out-of-Sample Simulation: 9209–9503
36-month moving windows (reoptimized monthly)

	Portfolio Performance, %			vs Style Benchmark					vs r2000			
	Annualized Return	Cumulative Return	Standard Deviation	Annualized Excess Return, %	Cumulative Excess Return, %	Annualized Turnover, %	Stddev of Excess Return, %	Explained Variance, % (Corr2)	Annualized Excess Return, %	Cumulative Excess Return, %	Stddev of Excess Return, %	Explained Variance, % (Corr2)
JMC Investment Management SmallCap Com	17.63	50.06	18.31	2.52	7.92	19.36	7.25	88.57	3.11	9.72	10.03	78.97

REFERENCES

Ankrin, Ernest M. "Risk-Adjusted Performance Attribution," *Financial Analysts Journal*, March/April 1992.

Bailey, Jeffery V. "Evaluating Benchmark Quality," *Financial Analysts Journal*, May-June 1992.

Barksdale, Edgar W., and William L. Green. "Performance is Useless in Selecting Managers," *Pensions and Investments*, September 17, 1990, p. 16.

Bauman, W. Scott, and Robert E. Miller. "Can Managed Portfolio Performance Be Predicted?" *The Journal of Portfolio Management*, Summer 1994.

Bauman, W. Scott, and Robert E. Miller. "Portfolio Performance Rankings in Stock Market Cycles," *Financial Analysts Journal*, March-April 1995.

Bernstein, Peter. Luncheon address to the AIMR Conference on "Performance Evaluation, Benchmarks, and Attribution Analysis," Toronto, November 16, 1994.

Bleiberg, Steven D. "The Nature of the Universe," *Financial Analysts Journal*, March/April 1986.

Bogle, John C. "Selecting Equity Mutual Funds," *The Journal of Portfolio Management*, Winter 1992.

Brinson, Gary, Larry Hood, and Gil Beebower. "Determinants of Portfolio Performance," *Financial Analysts Journal*, July/August 1986.

Brinson, Gary, Larry Hood, and Ron Singer. "Determinants of Portfolio Performance II: An Update," *Financial Analysts Journal*, May-June 1991.

Dietz, Peter O. in the article, "Pension Fund Investment Performance-What Method to Use When," *Financial Analysts Journal*, January/February 1966.

Dunn, P., and R. Theisen. "How Consistently Do Active Managers Win?" *Journal of Portfolio Management*, 1983.

Fama, Eugene F. "Components of Investment Performance," *Journal of Business*, June 1972.

Ferguson, Robert. "Performance Measurement Doesn't Make Sense," *Financial Analysts Journal*, May/June 1980.

Goetzmann, W. N., and R. Ibbotson. "Do Winners Repeat?" *Journal of Portfolio Management*, Winter 1994.

Hardy, Steve. "Style Analysis, Style Benchmarks, and Custom Core Portfolios," *Advances in Asset Allocation*, New York: John Wiley & Sons, 1994.

Hendricks, D., J. Patel, and R. Zeckhauser. "Hot Hands in Mutual Funds: Short-Run Persistence of Performance in Relative Performance," *Journal of Finance*, March 1993.

Jensen, Michael C. "The Performance of Mutual Funds in the Period 1945–1964," *Journal of Finance*, May 1968.

Jensen, Michael C. "Risk, the Pricing of Capital Assets, and the Evaluation of Investment Portfolios," *Journal of Business*, April 1969.

Prudential Securities, *Benchmark Report V.V*, February 1995.

Rennie, Edward P., and Thomas J. Cowhey. "The Successful Use of Benchmark Portfolios," in *Improving Portfolio Performance with Quantitative Models*, The Institute of Chartered Financial Analysts, 1989.

Roll, Richard. "Performance Evaluation and Benchmark Errors (I)," *Journal of Portfolio Management*, Summer 1980.

Roll, Richard. "Performance Evaluation and Benchmark Errors (II)," *Journal of Portfolio Management*, Winter 1981.

Ross, Stephen A. "Survivorship Bias in Performance Studies," in *Blending Quantitative and Traditional Equity Analysis*, AIMR, 1994.

Sharpe, William F. "Capital Asset Prices: A Theory of Market Equilibrium Under Conditions of Risk," *Journal of Finance*, September 1964.

Sharpe, William F. "Determining a Fund's Effective Asset Mix," *Investment Management Review*, November/December 1988, pp. 59–69.

Sharpe, William F. "Mutual Fund Performance," *Journal of Business*, January 1966.

Sharpe, William F. "The Sharpe Ratio," *Journal of Portfolio Management*, Fall 1994.

Sharpe, William F., and Gordon Alexander. *Investments*, 4th ed., Englewood Cliffs: Prentice-Hall, 1990.

Tierney, David E., and Kenneth Winston. "Using Generic Benchmarks to Present Manager Styles," *Journal of Portfolio Management*, Summer 1991.

Treynor, Jack. "How to Rate Management of Investment Funds," *Harvard Business Review*, January/February 1965.

Treynor, Jack, and Kay K. Mazuy. "Can Mutual Funds Outguess the Market?" *Harvard Business Review*, July/August 1966.

Troutman, Michael L. "The Steinbrenner Syndrome and the Challenge of Manager Selection," *Financial Analysts Journal*, March-April 1991.

14 TAXES AND PERFORMANCE EVALUATION

Robert Jeffrey

We emphasized tax considerations in Chapter 5. While doing performance evaluation, it is all too common to measure performance based on the returns earned prior to taxes. It, therefore, becomes just as important that we examine whether there were excess returns on the portfolio being evaluated after taxes. While few active portfolio managers earn excess returns, relative to the benchmark indices and after adjusting for risk, on a pretax basis, their numbers are thinned even further when we look at after-tax returns. In this chapter, we will begin with an examination of the differences between pretax and after-tax returns at large mutual funds, and note the effects of turnover on after-tax returns. We will then consider a number of strategies that portfolio managers can use to reduce the tax bite on their returns, including derivatives.

"IS YOUR ALPHA BIG ENOUGH TO COVER ITS TAXES?"

Given the tremendous negative leverage that turnover-generated taxes exert on returns, the overriding question for taxable investors is whether the trading activity will improve the portfolio's performance sufficiently to compensate for the attendant costs, which are not only the capital gains taxes, but also the other transaction costs plus the costs of the trader (i.e., the fees of the active manager if there be one). In an efficient market, frictional losses from transaction costs must always be considered, but for taxable investors the problem can be enormous. For small self-managed portfolios incurring significant trading costs, and for larger professionally managed portfolios, nontax-related costs can easily run to 200 basis points or more, and we have demonstrated here that capital gains taxes can add at least another 100. At some point, a convincing case for low-cost, low-turnover portfolio strategies—such as indexing—can obviously be made.

Robert Arnott and I made such a case in 1993 in our article "Is Your Alpha Big Enough to Cover Its Taxes?" using pretax and after-tax performance of 72 large equity mutual funds from 1982 through 1991.[1] Figure 14-1 (which comes from that article) compares these funds' pretax, after-tax, and after-deferred-tax results with the Vanguard Index 500 and with a hypothetical "Closed-End Index 500" fund. The latter was added because open-end index funds incur additional capital gains taxes that are unrelated to changes in the makeup of the index. (As noted earlier, The Vanguard Group subsequently recognized this shortcoming, and introduced in 1994 a series of low-fee index funds designed explicitly to minimize realized capital gains.)[2,3]

Figure 14-1 demonstrates that few actively managed funds outperform index funds on a pretax basis, and that the comparison is even worse when taxes—which are mostly capital gains taxes—are taken into consideration. While just 15 funds outperformed the "Closed-End Index 500" pretax over this period, only five did so after taxes, and of these only in two cases (CGM Capital and Magellan) are the outperformances significant.[4] And even after subtracting the deferred taxes on unrealized gains, the "Closed-End Index 500" is superior to all but ten actively managed funds.

FIGURE 14-1 **Ten-year pretax and after-tax growth of $1.00 invested in various mutual funds (1982–1991)**

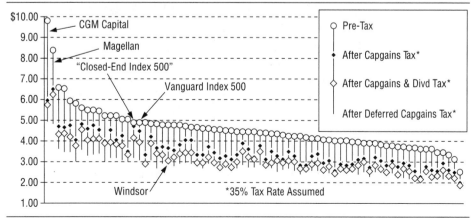

Joel Dickson and John Shoven (1993) undertook a similar but more detailed study, using a larger number of mutual funds over different and longer periods of time, and in 1994 they reported on the results of an index fund designed to minimize capital gains realizations. They conclude that "on average, there are large differences between the [performance] rankings which take taxes into account and those which do not, particularly for high tax individuals and [those with] long holding periods." Dickson and Shoven were surprised that their study does not show stronger negative correlation between fund turnover rates and after-tax performance. The explanation could well lie in the hockey stick phenomenon I describe earlier; nearly all the tax damage is done before turnover reaches 25 percent. Because there is little difference between the capital gains taxes incurred at 25 percent turnover and 200 percent, and because the turnover of most actively managed funds falls within this range, it is not surprising that Dickson and Shoven find so little correlation between turnover and performance. These writers would presumably concur with Jeffrey and Arnott's advice to taxable investors:

> Taxable investors should bear two simple points in mind. First, passive indexing is a very difficult strategy to beat on an after-tax basis, and therefore active taxable strategies should always be benchmarked against the after-tax performance of an indexed alternative. Second, while active management can conceivably add value on an after-tax basis, this will occur only with careful planning that results in maximizing the buildup of unrealized [and thus untaxed] capital gains [Jeffrey and Arnott (1993, p. 16)].

ARE THERE VIABLE ALTERNATIVES TO INDEXING FOR THE TAXABLE INVESTOR?

Given the compelling empirical evidence in favor of low-cost, low-turnover indexing, can a realistic case be made in taxable situations for active management? Robert Kirby, in his oft-quoted "Coffee Can Portfolio" (1984), provides anecdotal evidence supporting a combination of active management and very low turnover. It seems that after the death of a longtime client, Kirby was asked by the widow to review her deceased husband's portfolio. Kirby discovered that his late client had followed all his buy recommendations, but had done nothing about the sells, and, notwithstanding this one-sided approach, the portfolio had performed exceptionally well.

What happened, of course, was that Kirby's client was "riding his winners," a practice that, *up to a point,* is good advice for a taxable investor, but it is often not the advice that clients receive from their outside advisors.

> Too often, big winners are trimmed back or sold off at tremendous tax expense, not because the appreciated holding no longer fits the *owner's* circumstances, but rather because it "outgrows" the portfolio in which it originated, either in terms of its own market capitalization or, more often, because its increased weight . . . exceeds the *manager's* comfort level [Jeffrey (1991, p. 15) emphasis added].

Taxable clients, in particular, who employ outside advisors must always remember to ask, "Whose risk is being diversified?" And client-owners should understand that their risk is often quite different from that of their retained advisor, whose primary concern is not losing the account by having a large holding "torpedoed" in a sharp market decline.

The weakness in the coffee can portfolio's buy-and-hold strategy is that ultimately a diversification problem is likely to develop. Indeed, we eventually learn that this problem had already developed for Kirby's client—where one of the winners he had been riding was Xerox. This holding had grown so that it constituted over 50 percent of the portfolio, and, in retrospect, we know that at that time Xerox was already beginning to show signs of maturity.

Dealing with maturation is, or should be, the principal purpose of turnover, but, as Jeffrey and Arnott (1994) comment, the turnover activity required need not—and should not—be as great as it usually is:

> In a dynamic world, portfolios must be pruned to deal with the maturation process that is ever present; but because of transaction costs, and especially taxes, this pruning—this turnover—should be used as thoughtfully and as sparingly and with as much pre-planning as possible.
>
>   There is ample opportunity for active managers who understand that *there is a big difference—especially in taxable portfolios—between activity and accomplishment* [Jeffrey and Arnott (1994, p. 96), emphasis added].

If taxable investors should strive to reduce their turnover to, say, 10 percent or less, which is an average holding period of no more than ten years, how do they know when to commence selling a holding that seems to have matured? The traditional approaches of the money management community are often not very helpful, because they are typically based on information or opinions that have either a short useful life (e.g., weeks or months) or an alpha value that is insufficient to cover the taxes that a sale would trigger. Very low turnover, therefore, requires a nontraditional approach, in which the owner-client must play a leading role.

One such approach is to monitor the dividend growth of the portfolio holdings as distinct from their current market values (see Jeffrey, 1977). Steering the taxable portfolio ship by the slow-turning dividend compass rather than the more volatile earnings and market value dials can be a useful way to minimize turnover. This strategy relies implicitly on the assumption that dividend announcements have a high insider information content, i.e., that given the embarrassment of cutting a dividend, boards are assumed to know what they are doing when they raise their dividends and when they do not.

Most active managers would view this approach as naive and simplistic, but the fact is that both clients and managers typically spend too much time worrying about next quarter's earnings and which holdings are over or undervalued, and not enough time devising ways to minimize turnover. If the portfolio is taxable, the cost of implementing these value judgments will too often overwhelm the analyst's insights. But the problem has a silver lining. As I wrote in 1991, "The only advantage taxable investors have over their nontaxable counterparts is that the transaction cost nemesis is so tangibly apparent [because of the taxes] that turnover is more apt to be minimized" [Jeffrey (1991, n. 5, p. 18)].

REALIZING LOSSES, TAX SWAPPING, AND THE LIKE

The easiest way to minimize capital gains taxes is to realize losses in the portfolio whenever they become sufficiently large that the tax saving is not offset by the transaction costs of the sale. Jeffrey and Arnott say that "realized losses are almost like cash in the bank, because they can be essentially exchanged at the Treasury window for tax dollars that would be paid, or have been paid, or will be paid in the future" (1993, p. 21). (The IRS carry forward and carry back regulations pertain here, but the current rules afford considerable flexibility.)

Besides transaction costs, the only other limitation on realizing losses is the IRS's so-called wash sale rule, which prohibits holdings sold at a loss from being purchased within 30 days before or after the day of the sale, including purchases of "substantially identical" securities. Because the intent of the wash sale rule is to insure that the purpose of the transaction is not solely to avoid taxes, the taxpayer must always be at some risk when a loss sale is realized. It is not permissible, for instance, to hedge against the risk of a price rise during the wash sale period by buying a derivative of the holding being sold. But unless one assumes great skill in predicting short-term market prices, the known cash value of realizing a loss would seem to outweigh the unknown risk of being out of a stock for a month, especially if the proceeds of the sale were reinvested in a similar holding.

Perhaps the most common error of taxable investors is to wait until year end to realize losses. This is a poor practice for three reasons. First, a dollar saved in taxes in January is at least as valuable as a dollar saved in the following

December. Second, the January opportunity to save the dollar may well be gone by December (or by February or even the next day). For a taxpayer, who has realized (or expects to realize) gains that a loss would offset, to miss this opportunity is like seeing a dollar in the street and leaving it there.

The third problem with waiting until year end is simply that so many other taxable investors are doing the same thing. As a consequence, stocks whose prices have recently declined tend to be trading more cheaply at year end than replacement stocks whose prices have not declined, which results in a "sell cheap, buy dear" transaction. (Some believe that the tendency of the market to rebound in January, which has come to be known as the "January effect," is a natural response to the heavy tax loss selling in December.)

While applicable in principal to realizing a loss in one stock and reinvesting the proceeds in another, "tax swapping" is a practice more commonly applied to bond portfolios. In periods of rising interest rates, bond prices decline, thereby creating opportunities to realize capital losses. The wash sale rules that tend to inhibit "tax swapping" in equities are much less of a problem with bonds, because the replacement bond need only be different in some material feature such as maturity or coupon, and the issuer can be the same.

Taxable investors who are not relying on their bond portfolios for liquidity (as distinct from income) should bear in mind that the increased price volatility from a longer-duration portfolio may actually be advantageous, because the realizable losses when interest rates go up are larger, thereby providing more cash (by virtue of the tax recovery) with which to buy more replacement bonds, whose prices had declined at the same rate as the bonds that were sold. Kipling's advice that "if you can keep your head when all about you are losing theirs" is especially relevant in tax swapping. Astute taxable bond investors see rising interest rates as an opportunity to get a psychological advantage over their counterparties in swap transactions, who look only at the current market value of their portfolio, and thus see their fortunes slipping away.

The apparent free lunch from tax swapping turns out to be not quite so free when it is understood that eventually the replacement bond will mature and a taxable gain will be realized.[5] On the other hand, because of the time value of money, tax swapping is almost always a productive strategy, especially if the losses in the bond portfolio create opportunities to realize offsetting gains in the equity portfolio by disposing of matured stocks.

While realizing losses is usually found money, it should be understood that this tactic will not, except in unusual circumstances, resolve the taxable equity investor's chronic capital gains tax problem. Because stock prices go up more often than down over most long time periods, the realizable losses will rarely be sufficient to offset the unrealized gains. When a major bank in its "Tax Aware Equity Management" program for so-called high-net worth individuals offers to "scour client portfolios for an unrealized capital loss, and harvest the loss to off-set a gain," the client-owner should remember that once the accumulated losses of the past have been harvested, the tax costs of active management once again become a material consideration.[6] And the client-owner so approached might well also contemplate why it is necessary to retain an advisor to "scour" for losses that should already be apparent.

LONG-TERM AND SHORT-TERM CAPITAL GAINS

Short-term gains are taxed as ordinary income, while long-term gains are eligible for the usually lower rate on capital gains. Since 1986, the holding-period requirement for long-term treatment has been "more than one year." At other times, it has been as short as six months. In addition to, or in lieu of, allowing inflationary cost basis adjustments, one of the possibly more politically feasible ways to reduce the capital gains tax problem would be to create a descending rate schedule inversely related to holding period, in which after some fairly long period—say, five or ten years—the rate would be relatively low, and conceivably zero.

    If something like this occurs, taxable investors will obviously have a very important new consideration to bear in mind. It's normally been a "no brainer," even for money managers with tax-exempt mentalities, to remember to hold out for long-term treatment. But the time period involved was a maximum of only six months or a year, and the rate differential was relatively small. Were the law changed to incorporate a much larger rate differential tied in steps to a much longer holding period, the money management community, including those managing their own affairs, would almost certainly have to develop strategies to take advantage of these new opportunities.

    I bring this point up, one, because such changes are now being seriously discussed in Washington, and, two, because these new opportunities would be merely extensions—albeit more obvious to see—of the same opportunities to minimize taxes by deferring gains that we have been discussing here.

DIVERSIFICATION AND THE TAXABLE INVESTOR

Taxable investors with very large holdings to be sold relative to their total portfolio are faced with a Hobson's choice. The classic example occurs when a privately owned business sells part of its stock to the public or is merged into a large public company in a tax-free exchange of stock, but the problem can also arise from the excess appreciation of an extraordinarily successful investment decision. On the one hand, diversification is the first and foremost precept of prudent portfolio management; on the other hand, with an outsized holding leaving a very low basis, the cost of achieving diversification can consume as much as a third of the holding's value.

Having opted to effect the sale of the family business in a tax-free exchange of stock, owners are often loath to begin selling the stock they took in trade. The problem is compounded when an emotional attachment develops for the company to which they sold. The emotional problem is apt to be even worse when the stock being sold is that of "the engine that made the family what it is." When the public company holding is very large and/or where a member of the selling group is on the public company's board, the diversification problem becomes further complicated by insider trading considerations that limit the owners' ability to take advantage of short-lived selling opportunities. Owners contemplating the disposition of a private business would be advised to remember that, while they have most of their eggs in one basket, *they own the basket;* if they accept the public company's stock in trade, they still have most of their eggs in one basket, but *someone else owns the basket!* Needless to say, there is a big difference.

There are no easy answers to the diversification dilemma, but its importance should never be disregarded. Periodically, the undiversified owner should assess the consequences of a major decline in the large holding's stock price and/or its dividend. If the economic (or psychological) consequence of this worst case scenario is tolerable, and the large holding continues to appear healthy, it can presumably still be held and the taxes deferred. But if the worst case scenario is not tolerable, plans should be laid for reducing the holding to the point where the lack of diversification is no longer a serious potential problem. In cases of doubt, owners are strongly advised to err on the side of adequate diversification, notwithstanding the enormous loss in taxes. The costs of being wrong are simply too great.

As Fred Young advises, "The inconvenience of going from rich to poor is greater than most people can tolerate. . . . Staying rich requires an entirely different approach from getting rich" (1983, pp. 113–114). It might be said that one *gets* rich by working hard and taking big risks, and that one *stays* rich by limiting risk and not spending too much. Passive portfolio investors who are dependent on their portfolios to maintain their standard of living are incurring huge risks when they are not diversified.

USING DERIVATIVES TO MANAGE CAPITAL GAINS

The advent of liquid markets for derivative securities and their relatively low transaction costs gives the taxable investor considerably more flexibility in managing the timing of when taxes are incurred. For instance, an owner of a highly appreciated diversified equity portfolio who believes the stock market is overpriced can sell an equivalent amount of futures contracts (or options) on the S&P 500. This is sometimes referred to as an overlay strategy. If the stock market declines during the life of the contracts (which is relatively short), a gain results. The gain is taxable, but the after-tax balance is additional return to the owner. If the stock market goes up, a loss results, but this can be used to realize gains at no additional cost in taxes in the underlying equity portfolio, which the owner presumably now believes is even more overpriced than it was before.

If these offsetting gains in the underlying portfolio are the result of turnover that would have occurred in any case to maintain the portfolio's vitality, the derivatives overlay would be a win–win strategy. But overlays have their own costs, including commissions, fees, and collateral requirements. The killer cost, according to Jeffrey and Arnott, is "if the . . . overlay hedging bets were large, frequent, and often wrong, thereby necessitating *extra turnover* in the underlying portfolio to generate the offsetting capital gains" (1993, p. 22).

More exotic derivative strategies are now appearing, often with arcane names like "zero-cost collars" (also known as "synthetic shorts against the box") and equity swaps. In some cases, third parties are involved, which introduces another important and too often overlooked element of risk. Such strategies are sometimes appealing to owners of large concentrated holdings with low cost bases, but, as Nancy Jacob (1994) advises, they are not without their own trade-offs.

> These products exchange a large one-time cost—in this case, taxes—for smaller recurring expenses while, at the same time, shift[ing] the underlying portfolio's expected risk and return parameters in a pre-specified way to conform to the investor's performance and diversification objectives. Their desirability depends on the investor's time horizon, the degree to which risk and return can be significantly enhanced, the magnitude of the gains avoided relative to the recurring expenses of the swap, the likelihood of a premature, forced unwinding, and the potential for IRS challenges to the expected tax treatment of the exchange [Jacob (1994, p. 20)].

Derivatives can be an effective means of controlling the incidence of capital gains taxes, but owners must understand both the assumptions that are being made and the downside risks involved. The biggest risks are that the assumptions, which typically deal with relationships among different kinds of securities, will prove invalid in an unanticipated market condition.

PERSONAL RETIREMENT VEHICLES THAT SHELTER INCOME AND GAINS

IRAs, Keoghs, 401(k) plans, and so-called variable annuities all permit investments to compound tax-free. This is an important benefit to taxable investors, but, for that very reason, the investors must realize that, as in any other tax shelter, they must look behind the tax features to insure that the tax deferral advantages are not being wiped out by other costs, including, in particular, the promotors' fees. Investors should also pay special attention to their own future spending requirements, because early withdrawals from these various vehicles can trigger severe tax penalties.

An important but less obvious problem with tax-deferred retirement plans is the possibility that tax rates may be higher when the funds are ultimately withdrawn and become subject to tax. While investors usually assume that they will be in lower tax brackets on ordinary income at retirement, a substantial part of the funds that will be withdrawn will have been capital gains, which, outside of the retirement plan, would presumably have been subject to a lower tax. It is fairly hard to imagine a scenario in which using these tax deferral plans would be disadvantageous for a younger person, but the answer is less clear with an older person.

RECORD-KEEPING CONSIDERATIONS

Taxable investors should always maintain their portfolio records using the "specific lot" method whereby the cost bases of every purchase are recorded. In the absence of such records, the IRS will assume first-in, first-out, which, over a period of rising prices, will almost always work to the taxpayer's disadvantage. Using the specific lot method, sales should normally be made using the highest-cost lots, while the lowest-cost lots should be used for charitable contributions. Using low-basis stock for contributions is also a good way to reduce outsized holdings. (Under current law, however, the realized capital gain that is avoided in a gift of appreciated property is a so-called preference item in determining the alternative minimum tax (AMT).) The only record-keeping problem in using the specific lot method arises from stock splits, where the cost of the lot remains unchanged, while the number of shares increases and the cost per share decreases.

Mutual funds, unfortunately, present a special record-keeping problem, which is presumably why the IRS allows the average cost method for mutual funds but not for other investments. The record-keeping problem arises because every mutual fund income and capital gains dividend that is directly reinvested and not taken in cash constitutes another specific lot that must be recorded. Despite the additional record-keeping, mutual fund investors who are taxable should use the specific lot method for the same reasons noted above.

AFTER-TAX PERFORMANCE BENCHMARKS

The Association for Investment Management and Research (AIMR) formed a subcommittee in 1993 to develop standards for measuring the performance of taxable portfolios. The subcommittee's report issued in 1994 is directed primarily at the investment management community rather than client-owners. While more after-tax performance data on separate account managers (as distinct from mutual funds) will presumably be forthcoming in the future, its usefulness is yet to be determined. A major problem in presenting after-tax results on separate accounts is how to adjust the data for the taxes that are triggered not by the manager's trading decisions with the intent of improving the portfolio, but rather for liquidations to meet the client-owner's spending or liquidity needs. In taxable situations, the owner's spending requirements have a very real bearing on the portfolio's performance.

As noted earlier, in 1993 *Morningstar Mutual Funds* began reporting tax-adjusted historical returns on mutual funds. Morningstar reduces the historical pretax returns by the taxes on the fund's income and capital gains dividends (using assumed rates), and then reports the percentage of the after-tax to the pretax return. In addition, the "potential capital gains tax exposure" is calculated, which is basically the deferred capital gains taxes on the unrealized gains expressed as a percentage of the total assets. For after-tax benchmarking purposes at the present time, taxable investors might best select a fund or funds from Morningstar whose style is compatible with the investor's own situation, and use the after-tax returns.

Because of its exceptionally low fees, the after-tax results of the Vanguard Index 500 would be a good real-world proxy for the after-tax performance of the S&P 500. Vanguard's new (in 1994) Tax Managed Fund and the Schwab 1000 Fund (new in 1993) may eventually be even better after-tax index fund proxies, because both are explicitly dedicated to minimizing realized capital gains.[7] Given the increasing interest in after-tax performance, one might assume that Standard & Poor will eventually start reporting the after-tax performance of its index. The principal problem here is in determining which changes in the S&P 500 components are taxable events and which are not. For instance, the tax-free exchange of stock between two S&P 500 companies would not generate a tax.

CONCLUSION

While few portfolio managers beat the benchmark indices on a pretax return basis, even fewer succeed when we look at after-tax returns. In fact, on an after-tax return basis, index funds provide a much better return to the average investor than most actively managed mutual funds, a finding that can be attributed to their very low turnover ratios. For investors who want to follow active strategies, there are strategies available that can reduce the tax bite. One strategy is to reduce the trading involved by adopting value strategies, where investments are made for the long-term. A second strategy is to actively manage the tax liabilities on a portfolio by realizing investment losses and using them to offset capital gains on investments that have to be liquidated. A third is to use derivatives to manage the tax liability, though the very complexity of some of the strategies that use derivatives creates its own trade-offs. The success or failure of an investment portfolio will be based on whether it makes the investor wealthier on an after-tax basis and not a pretax basis.

APPENDIX A: DATA SPREADSHEET

z	Total return	9%
y	Yield	3%
x	Appreciation	6%
w	Dividend tax rate	45%
v	Capital gains tax rate	34%
u	1st year spending rate	3%
t	Spending growth rate	4%
s	Turnover rate	25%
r	Beginning cost/market	100%

"Spending" is the amount withdrawn each year from the fund. The spending growth rate is assumed to be the rate of inflation.

a	Year		1	2	3	4
b	Beginning cost	r^*c	100.00	99.64	100.01	100.95
c	Beginning market		100.00	104.14	108.07	111.86
d	Dividend income	y^*c	3.00	3.12	3.24	3.36
e	Dividend tax	w^*d	1.35	1.41	1.46	1.51
f	Appreciation	x^*c	6.00	6.25	6.48	6.71
g	Spending	u^*c; $g^*(1+t)$	3.00	3.12	3.24	3.37
h	Sales	$s^*(c+f)$	26.50	27.60	28.64	29.64
i	Cost of sales	$b^*(h/(c+f))$	25.00	24.91	25.00	25.24
j	Realized capital gain	$h-i$	1.50	2.69	3.64	4.41
k	Capital gain tax	v^*j	0.51	0.91	1.24	1.50
l	Purchases	$d-e-g+h-k$	24.64	25.28	25.94	26.62
m	Ending market	$c+f-h+l$	104.14	108.07	111.86	115.54
n	Ending cost	$b-i+l$	99.64	100.01	100.95	102.33
o	Cost/market %	n/m	96%	93%	90%	89%
p	Total return	$((m+g)/c)-1$	7.1%	6.8%	6.5%	6.3%
	Total return (cum/yr)		7.1%	7.0%	6.8%	6.7%

If the sales generated by the turnover assumption are insufficient to cover any shortfall between after-tax dividend income and the withdrawal for spending, the sales are increased accordingly, including a "gross-up" to cover the taxes on the additional sales. The turnover rate, however, is not adjusted.

Assumes liquidation of portfolio at end of 25th year.

5	6	7	8	9	10	....	25	25'
102.33	104.05	106.04	108.24	110.60	113.09	....	153.36	155.62
115.54	119.16	122.74	126.28	129.82	133.35	....	184.19	187.03
3.47	3.57	3.68	3.79	3.89	4.00	....	5.53	
1.56	1.61	1.66	1.70	1.75	1.80	....	2.49	
6.93	7.15	7.36	7.58	7.79	8.00	....	11.05	
3.51	3.65	3.80	3.95	4.11	4.27	....	7.69	
30.62	31.58	32.52	33.47	34.40	35.34	....	48.81	187.03
25.58	26.01	26.51	27.06	27.65	28.27	....	38.34	155.62
5.04	5.57	6.01	6.41	6.75	7.06	....	10.47	31.41
1.71	1.89	2.05	2.18	2.30	2.40	....	3.56	10.68
27.30	28.00	28.71	29.42	30.14	30.87	....	40.60	176.35
119.16	122.74	126.28	129.82	133.35	136.88	....	187.03	176.35
104.05	106.04	108.24	110.60	113.09	115.69	....	155.62	176.35
87%	86%	86%	85%	85%	85%	....	83%	100%
6.2%	6.1%	6.0%	5.9%	5.9%	5.8%	....	5.7%	-5.7%
6.6%	6.5%	6.4%	6.4%	6.3%	6.3%	....	6.0%	5.7%

REFERENCES

"AIMR Performance Presentation Standards: Report of the Subcommittee on Taxable Portfolios." Charlottesville, VA: Association for Investment Management and Research, 1994.

Bogle, John C. "Taxes and Mutual Funds," Chapter 11, in *Bogle on Mutual Funds*, Burr Ridge, IL: Irwin, 1994.

Dickson, Joel M., and John B. Shoven. "Ranking Mutual Funds on an After-Tax Basis." Center for Economic Policy Research, Publication No. 344. Stanford, CA: Stanford University, 1993.

Dickson, Joel M., and John B. Shoven. "A Stock Index Mutual Fund Without Net Capital Gains Realizations." National Bureau of Economic Research, Inc., Working Paper No. 4717, Cambridge, MA, 1994.

Ellis, Charles D. *Investment Policy: How To Win the Loser's Game.* Second Edition. Homewood, IL: Business One Irwin, 1993.

Flaherty, Francis. "Wall Street's New Ways to Blunt the Tax Blow," *The New York Times,* September 17, 1994.

Garland, James P. "Taxable Portfolios: Value and Performance." *Journal of Portfolio Management,* Winter, 1987.

Hertog, Roger, and Mark R. Gordon. "Equity Strategies for Taxable Investors." *Journal of Investing,* Fall 1994.

Jacob, Nancy L. "Taxes, Investment Policy, and the Diversification of Low Basis Assets." Portland, OR: CTC Consulting, Inc., 1994.

Jeffrey, Robert H. "Do Clients Need So Many Portfolio Managers?" *Journal of Portfolio Management,* Fall 1991, pp. 13–19.

Jeffrey, Robert H. "Internal Portfolio Growth: The Better Measure." *Journal of Portfolio Management,* Summer 1977, pp. 10–25.

Jeffrey, Robert H., and Robert D. Arnott. "Is Your Alpha Big Enough To Cover Its Taxes?" *Journal of Portfolio Management,* Spring 1993, pp. 15–25.

Jeffrey, Robert H., and Robert D. Arnott. " 'Is Your Alpha Big Enough To Cover Its Taxes?': Reply to Comment." *Journal of Portfolio Management,* Summer 1994, pp. 96–97.

Kirby, Robert G. "The Coffee Can Portfolio." *Journal of Portfolio Management,* Fall 1984, pp. 76–80.

Young, Fred J. *How To Get Rich and Stay Rich.* Hollywood, FL: Frederick Fell Publishers, Inc., 1983.

PART SIX

CORPORATE GOVERNANCE AND INVESTMENT MANAGEMENT

Investors all too often make investment decisions based on the status quo. They expect well-managed companies to continue being well managed and selling at high multiples, and they write off poorly managed companies as continuing to be poorly managed and to command low valuations. Investors who adopt this view of the business world are missing a critical ingredient that could earn them extraordinary returns. Just as there are markets for assets, there is a market for managers and for the control of corporations. When good managers get hired away by other firms, well-managed companies are put at risk. Conversely, poor managers may lose their jobs or retire, providing the catalyst for turning around poorly managed companies.

The market for corporate control is not restricted to the hiring and firing of managers. When a firm is poorly managed and incumbent management cannot be displaced by stockholders, there is an alternative process through which control can be wrested from their hands. Another company or individual might succeed in an attempt to take over the company in a hostile acquisition, and might then proceed to change the way the company is run. The changes can be far reaching: assets may be acquired and sold, and financial leverage may be altered. The restructuring of corporate America in the 1980s has been attributed, in great part, to the threat of hostile takeovers. Some of the hostile acquirers did overreach in their zeal to acquire firms, but, collectively, they had a salutary effect. They put the managers of the largest corporations in the United States on notice that poor performance might elicit a hostile bid.

Investors who become aware of such trends in corporate governance can profit handsomely. An active investor with substantial funds might invest in poorly managed firms and then push for internal change, thus gaining directly from the restructuring that follows. Smaller investors might adopt a less ambitious strategy of waiting for an activist to take a position, or a hostile takeover to create high returns. Generally, companies in which stockholders have more power over managers should sell for higher prices than similar companies that have entrenched managers.

In this section, Michael Jensen and Donald Chew review the trends in corporate governance in the 1980s and the lessons that can be drawn from them for the future. Much of these authors' discussion is directed toward the overall economic benefits of having an effective system of control over incumbent managers. There are also some useful insights for investors who want to consider these trends in designing their investment portfolios. Stockholders in other countries are beginning to realize that they *own* the firms that they have invested in, and that the managers of these firms work for them. This trend clearly has implications for portfolio managers looking to foreign markets for their investments.

15
U.S. CORPORATE GOVERNANCE: LESSONS FROM THE 1980s

Michael C. Jensen
with Donald H. Chew

Corporate governance is a concern of great importance to owners of common stocks, because stockholder wealth depends in large part upon the goals of the people who set the strategy of the corporation. Who is the boss, and whose interests come first?

The objectives of corporate managers often conflict with those of the shareholders who own their companies. Laws and regulations enacted since the 1930s have effectively put most of the power in the hands of management, frequently at the expense of the interests of the owners of the corporation. At the same time, boards of directors have tended to go along with management and to ignore the interests of the very party they were created to protect.

The takeover boom of the 1980s brought the subject of corporate governance to the front pages of the newspapers, as a revolution was mounted against the power complexes at corporate headquarters. The mergers, acquisitions, LBOs, and other leveraged restructurings of the 1980s constituted an assault on entrenched authority that was long overdue. Control of the corporation was transformed from a means of perpetuating established arrangements

This chapter draws heavily on Michael C. Jensen: "Corporate Control and the Politics of Finance," *Journal of Applied Corporate Finance*, Vol. 4, No. 2 (Summer 1991); and "The Modern Industrial Revolution, Exit, and the Failure of Internal Control Systems," *Journal of Finance*, Vol. 48 (July 1993). A shorter, less technical version of the latter is in *Journal of Applied Corporate Finance*, Vol. 6, No. 4 (Winter 1994).

into a marketplace where the highest bidder made certain that the owners' interests would prevail. In many cases, the result was a convergence of interest between management and owners. New methods of finance meant that even large companies were vulnerable to attack; the steady increase in the size of the deals culminated in the $25 billion buyout of RJR-Nabisco in 1989 by KKR, a partnership with fewer than 60 employees.

The effect of such transactions was to transfer control over vast corporate resources—often trapped in mature industries or uneconomic conglomerates—to those prepared to pay large premiums to use those resources more efficiently. In some cases, the acquirers functioned as agents rather than principals, selling part or all of the assets they acquired to others. In many cases, the acquirers were unaffiliated individual investors (labeled "raiders" by those opposed to the transfer of control) rather than other large public corporations. The increased asset sales, enlarged payouts, and heavy use of debt to finance such takeovers led to a large-scale return of equity capital to shareholders.

The consequence of this control activity has been a pronounced trend toward smaller, more focused, more efficient—and in many cases private—corporations. While capital and resources were being forced out of our largest companies throughout the 1980s, the small- to medium-sized U.S. corporate sector experienced vigorous growth in employment and capital spending. And, at the same time our capital markets were bringing about this massive transfer of corporate resources, the U.S. economy experienced a 92-month expansion and record-high percentages of people employed.

The resulting transfer of control from corporate managers to increasingly active investors aroused enormous controversy. The strongest opposition came from groups whose power and influence were being challenged by corporate restructuring: notably, the Business Roundtable (the voice of managers of large corporations), organized labor, and politicians whose ties to wealth and power were being weakened. The media, always responsive to popular opinion even as they help shape it, succeeded in reinvigorating the American populist tradition of hostility to Wall Street "financiers." The controversy pitting Main Street against Wall Street was wrought to a pitch that recalled the intensity of the 1930s. Newspapers, books, and magazines obliged the public's desire for villains by furnishing unflattering detailed accounts of the private doings of those branded "corporate raiders."

Barbarians at the Gate, for example, the best-selling account of the RJR-Nabisco transaction, is perhaps best described as an attempt to expose the greed and chicanery that went into the making of some Wall Street deals. And, on that score, the book is effective (although it's worth noting that, amid the general destruction of reputations, the principals of KKR and most of the Drexel team come across as professional and principled). But what also emerges from the 500-plus pages—although the authors seem to have failed to grasp its import—is clear evidence of corporatewide inefficiencies at RJR-Nabisco, including massive waste of corporate "free cash flow," that allowed KKR to pay existing stockholders $12 billion over the previous market value for the right to bring about change.

Since this control change, KKR defied skeptics by managing the company's huge debt load without losses, extracted some $6 billion in capital through asset sales, and brought the company public again in two separate offerings in March and April of 1991. KKR ended its investment in the RJR-Nabisco leveraged buyout in March 1995, by exchanging much of its stake in RJR for 100 percent ownership of Borden in a leveraged buyout of Borden. Its remaining shares of RJR were subsequently transferred to Borden to help improve the firm's balance sheet. As of April 1995, the consequences of the RJR buyout for pre-buyout shareholders, the banks, and junk bond investors were a remarkable $15 billion in added value over what an investment in the S&P 500 would have earned.[1] The deal was much less successful, however, for KKR's original equity investors in the RJR buyout. The return on their investment amounted to only 0.5 percent annually compounded,[2] substantially less than the S&P 500 earned during the same period, and dramatically below the 30 percent annual returns earned by its other investments.[3]

For economists and management scientists concerned about corporate efficiency, the RJR story is deeply disturbing. What troubles us is not so much the millions of dollars spent on sports celebrities and airplanes—or the greed and unprofessional behavior of several leading investment bankers—but rather the waste prior to the KKR buyout of billions in unproductive capital expenditures and organizational inefficiencies.[4] Viewed in this light—although, here again, the authors do not seem aware of what they have discovered—*Barbarians* is testimony to the massive failure of the internal control system under the lead of RJR's board of directors. As former SEC Commissioner Joseph Grundfest has put it, the real "barbarians" in this book were *inside* the gates.[5]

Moreover, the fact that Ross Johnson, RJR's CEO, was held up by *Fortune* as a model corporate leader only months before the buyout attests to the difficulty of detecting even such gross inefficiencies and thus suggests that organizational problems of this magnitude may extend well beyond RJR.[6] Although parts of corporate America may be guilty of underinvesting—as the media continually assert—there is little doubt that many of our largest U.S. companies have grossly *over*invested, whether in desperate attempts to maintain sales and earnings in mature or declining businesses or by diversifying outside of their core businesses.

This is what I mean by waste of corporate "free cash flow." Many of our best-known companies—GM, IBM, and Kodak come to mind most readily—

have wasted vast amounts of resources over the last decade or so. The chronic overinvestment and overstaffing of such companies reflects the widespread failure of our corporate internal control systems. And this fundamental control problem over free cash flow that gave rise to a large part of the corporate restructuring movement of the 1980s.

THE MEDIA AND THE ACADEMY

The role of takeovers and LBOs in curbing corporate inefficiency was not the story being told by our mass media. The journalistic method of inquiry is the investigation of selected cases, a process highly prone to "selection bias." The typical journalistic product is a series of anecdotes—stories that almost invariably carry with them a strong emotive appeal for the "victims" of control changes, but with little or no attention paid to long-run efficiency effects. So when media accounts do manage to raise their focus above the "morality play" craved by the public to consider broader issues of economic efficiency and competitiveness, the message is invariably the same: Leveraged restructurings are eroding the competitive strength of U.S. corporations by forcing cutbacks in employment, R&D, and capital investment.

Using very different methods and language, academic economists have subjected corporate control activity to intensive study. And the research contradicts the popular rhetoric. Indeed, I know of no area in economics today where the divergence between popular belief and the evidence from scholarly research is so great.

The most careful academic research strongly suggests that takeovers—along with leveraged restructurings prompted by the threat of takeover—have generated large gains for shareholders and for the economy as a whole. Our estimates indicate that during the period 1976–1994 over 45,000 control transactions occurred—including mergers, tender offers, divestitures, and leveraged buyouts, totaling $3.3 trillion (in 1994 dollars). The premiums paid to selling firms and their shareholders in these transactions totaled $959 billion (1994 dollars).[7] And this estimate includes neither the gains to the buyers in such transactions nor the value of efficiency improvements by companies pressured by control market activity into reforming *without* a visible control transaction.

To be sure, some part of the shareholder gains in highly leveraged transactions (HLTs) came at the expense of bondholders, banks, and other creditors who financed the deals. But total creditor losses probably did not exceed $25 billion through 1990, and accrued through 1994 were probably less than $50 billion in 1994 dollars.[8] (To put this number into perspective, IBM alone saw its equity value fall by $25 billion in a six-month period during 1991.) And thus far, there is no reliable evidence that any appreciable part of the remaining $900 billion or so of net gains to stockholders came at the expense of other corporate "stakeholders" such as employees, suppliers, and the IRS.[9]

These well-documented increases in shareholder value were largely dismissed by journalists and other critics of restructuring as "paper gains" having little bearing on the long-term vitality and competitiveness of American business. For such observers, these gains were interpreted as evidence of the "short-term" investor mentality that was said to be destroying American business.

For financial economists, however, theory and evidence suggest that as long as such value increases do not arise from transfers from other parties to the corporate "contract," they should be viewed as reliable predictors of increases in corporate operating efficiency. And, as I discuss later in the chapter, research on LBOs has indeed produced direct evidence of such efficiencies. Moreover, macroeconomic data suggest a dramatic improvement in the health and productivity of American industry during the 1980s.

THE REACTION

Toward the end of 1989 and in the first two years of the 1990s, restructuring transactions came to a virtual standstill. For example, total merger and acquisition transactions fell from a peak of $247 billion in 1988 to $108 billion in 1990 and to $71 billion in 1992. Although there have been a handful of hostile takeover attempts in recent years (principally by large companies for smaller ones), these acquisitions tended to be the value-destroying "strategic" type acquisition that we saw in the mid to late 1960s. They tended to be stock-for-stock deals (where overpayment caused no financial distress) or cash acquisitions funded by free cash flow.

Widespread savings and loan failures and a number of highly publicized cases of troubled HLTs have combined with the criminalization of securities law disclosure violations and the high-profile RICO and insider trading prosecutions to create a highly charged political climate.[10] Such political forces produced a major reregulation of our financial markets. The political origin of such regulatory initiatives was made clear by the fact that bad real estate loans dwarfed junk bond losses and troubled HLT loans as contributors to the weakness of S&Ls and other financial institutions at the time.

With the eclipse of the new-issue market for junk bonds, the application of HLT rules to commercial bank lending, and new restrictions on insurance companies, funding for large highly leveraged transactions all but disappeared. And, even in financing had been available, court decisions (including those authorizing the use of poison pills and defensive employee stock ownership plans) and state antitakeover and control shareholder amendments greatly increased the difficulty of making a successful hostile offer.

CONTRACTING PROBLEMS COMPOUNDED BY POLITICS

So what went wrong with the leveraged deals of the 1980s? The story in brief is as follows. As prices were bid up to more competitive levels in the second half of the 1980s, the markets "overshot." Contracting problems between the promoters of HLTs and the suppliers of capital—most important, too little equity capital put up by dealmakers and participating managements and front loaded fees for promoters that paid them for doing deals—led to too many overpriced deals. In this sense, the financial press was right in attributing *part* of the current constraints on our debt and takeover markets to unsound transactions. Such transactions, especially those completed after 1985, were overpriced by their promoters and, also overleveraged. The transactions, however, would have resulted in significant losses to the new owners, regardless of how they were financed; high debt converted the losses into financial distress in some cases.

But it is also clear that intense political pressures to curb the corporate control market greatly compounded the problems caused by this "contracting failure." However genuine and justified the concern about our deposit insurance funds, the reactions of Congress, the courts, and regulators to losses (which, again, were predominantly the result of real estate, not HLT loans) had several unfortunate side effects. They sharply restricted the availability of capital to noninvestment-grade companies, thereby increasing the rate of corporate defaults. They also limited the ability of financially troubled companies to reorganize outside of court, thus ensuring that most defaulted companies wound up in bankruptcy. And all of this, in my view, contributed greatly to the weakness of the U.S. economy in the early 1990s.

I begin by reviewing macroeconomic evidence on changes in productivity in American manufacturing that is sharply inconsistent with popular claims that corporate control transactions were crippling the U.S. industrial economy in the 1980s. Then I go on to show how the restructuring movement of the 1980s addressed a fundamental problem that still faces many large, mature public companies both in the U.S. and abroad: namely, excess capacity, and, more generally, the conflict between management and shareholders over control of corporate "free cash flow." Technological and other developments that began in the mid-20th century have led over the past two decades to rapid improvements in productivity, the creation of massive overcapacity, and, consequently, the requirement for exit. In the pages that follow, I discuss in some detail worldwide changes driving the demand for exit in today's economy. I also describe the barriers to efficient exit in the U.S. economy, and the role of the market for corporate control—takeovers, LBOs, and other leveraged restructurings—in surmounting those barriers during the 1980s.

With the shutdown of the capital markets in the 1990s, the challenge of accomplishing efficient exit has been transferred from the market for corporate control to corporate internal control systems. With few exceptions, however, U.S. managements and boards have failed to bring about timely exit and downsizing without external pressure. Although product market competition will eventually eliminate overcapacity, this solution generates huge unnecessary costs. (As I argue later, the costs of this solution have become apparent in Japan, where a virtual breakdown of corporate internal control systems, coupled with a complete absence of capital market influence, has resulted in enormous overcapacity—a problem that Japanese companies have only begun to address.)

I close with suggestions for reforming U.S. internal corporate control mechanisms. In particular, I see several features of venture capital and LBO firms such as Kleiner Perkins and KKR as worthy of emulation by large, public companies—notably (1) effective decentralization, (2) higher pay-for-performance, (3) smaller, more active, and better informed boards, and (4) significant equity ownership by board members as well as managers. I also urge boards and managers to encourage larger holdings and greater participation by people I call "active" investors.

NEW INSIGHTS FROM MACROECONOMIC DATA

While scholarly work has documented efficiency gains by LBO companies, we can also see productivity gains in the aggregate data on the 1980s. As summarized in the top two panels of Figure 15-1, the pattern of productivity and unit labor costs in the U.S. manufacturing sector over the period 1950–1989 is inconsistent with popular characterizations of the 1980s as the decade of the dismantling of American industry. Beginning in 1982, there was a dramatic increase in the productivity of the manufacturing sector (see Panel A)—a turnaround unmatched in the last 40 years. In Panel B, we see a sharp acceleration of the steady decline in real unit labor costs after 1982—a decline that had been going on since 1960 but had become stalled in the 1970s.

Such cost reductions and efficiency gains did not come at the expense of labor generally (although *organized* labor has certainly seen its influence wane). During the 1980s, as shown in Panels C, D, and E, there was a rise in total employment and hours worked after the end of the 1981–1982 recession; real

FIGURE 15-1   Trends in manufacturing, 1950–1989: Productivity, unit labor costs, employment, compensation, and capital

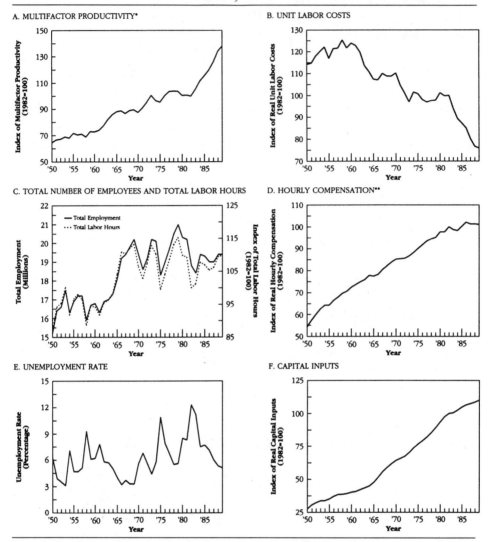

Sources: **Panels A and F**—Bureau of Labor Statistics, "Multifactor Productivity, 1988 and 1989," Table 3. **Panels B and D**—Bureau of Labor Statistics, "International Comparisons of Manufacturing Productivity and Labor Cost Trends, 1989," (July 1990) USDL #90-383, Table 2. **Panel C**—Bureau of Labor Statistics, "Employment and Earnings," supplement obtained from Office of Employment and Unemployment; Bureau of Labor Statistics, "International Comparisons of Manufacturing Productivity and Labor Cost Trends, 1989" (July 1990) USDL #90-383, Table 2. **Panel E**—Bureau of Labor Statistics, "Labor Force Statistics Derived from the Population Survey, 1948–1987," (August 1988) Bulletin 2307, Table A-35; Bureau of Labor Statistics, "Employment and Earnings, January 1990," Table 11.

° Multifactor Productivity is real output per unit of combined capital and labor.

°° Hourly Compensation includes wages and salaries, supplements, employer payments for social security, and other employer-financed benefit plans.

hourly compensation continued to rise after 1982 (although at a somewhat slower rate than before); and the percentage unemployed fell dramatically after 1982.

The Effect on Capital Investment

Critics of leveraged restructuring also claimed that corporate capital investment was a casualty of the M&A activity of the 1980s. But, as shown in Panel F, after a pause in 1982, real capital growth in the manufacturing sector continued to rise through the rest of the decade—although, again, at a slower rate than previously. This pattern is consistent with the "free cash flow" argument that corporate restructuring was a response to excessive capital in many sectors of American industry.

The pattern also suggests that, although capital was being squeezed out of the low-growth manufacturing sector by the payouts of cash and substitution of debt for equity, it was being recycled back into the economy. Some of that capital was transferred to smaller companies, including large inflows to the venture capital market. At the same time, the resulting organizational changes and efficiency gains at larger companies were providing the basis for renewed capital spending.[11]

The Effect on R&D

Another persistent objection to the control market is that it reduces valuable R&D expenditures. But, as shown in Figure 15-2, while M&A activity rose sharply after the 1982 recession (until plummeting in 1990), real R&D expenditures reached new highs in each year of the period from 1975 to 1990. R&D also rose from 1.8 percent to 3.4 percent of sales during this period.[12]

In short, although the macroeconomic data do not establish control market activity as a *cause* of the dramatic productivity improvements, they provide no support for the popular outcry against the workings of the corporate control market.

LEVERAGED RESTRUCTURING AND EXCESS CAPACITY

There is no doubt that the corporate restructuring movement resulted in changes painful to many individuals. With the shrinkage of some companies, there was loss of jobs among top management and corporate staff, although not among blue collar workers as a group.[13] Much of the contraction resulting from takeovers was fundamentally a reflection of larger economic forces, such

FIGURE 15-2 M&A activity vs. industry R&D expenditures (1975–1990)

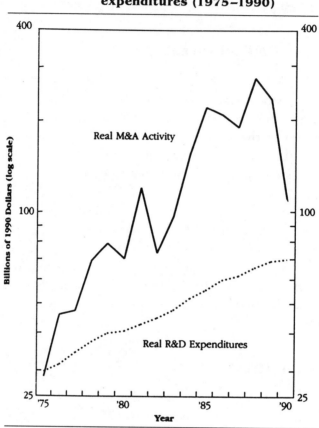

Source: Business Week, "R&D Scoreboard," annual; and Merrill Lynch, Mergerstat Review, 1990, Figure 5.

as intensified global competition, that dictated which changes had to be made if resources were to be used efficiently and industrial decline to be halted. Hostile takeovers typically achieve quickly—and thus, I would argue, with considerably lower social costs—the same end brought about in more protracted fashion by intense competition in product markets.

Consider the plight of the U.S. auto industry in 1991. Few industries had then experienced as drastic a retrenchment as the auto industry went through in the 1977–1982 period—and yet the restructuring forced upon American auto companies in the last few years was comparable in severity. In our view, it is precisely the auto industry's past immunity to takeover and major restructuring, along with government protection from foreign competitors, that is responsible for the extent of the recent downsizing required in the industry.[14]

At the end of the 1970s, when the Dow Jones average was around 900, Lester Thurow complained that one of the principal shortcomings of a "mixed" economy like ours is its inability to "disinvest"—that is, to move capital out of declining industries and into vital ones.[15] But this forced "disinvestment" is one of the primary accomplishments of the wave of restructurings in the 1980s. Such restructuring, I argue, reflects the efforts of a new breed of "active" investors to prevent management from wasting resources by reinvesting cash flow in mature, low-return businesses with excess capacity. This is why restructuring activity was concentrated in industries such as oil, tobacco, tires, food processing, retailing, publishing, broadcasting, forest products, commodity chemicals, and financial services.

Causes of Excess Capacity

Excess capacity can arise in at least four ways. The most obvious occurs when market demand falls below the level required to yield returns that will support the currently installed production capacity. This *demand-reduction* scenario is most familiarly associated with recession episodes in the business cycle.

Excess capacity can also arise from two types of technological change. The first type, *capacity-expanding* technological change, increases the output of a given capital stock and organization. An example of a capacity-expanding type of change is the Reduced Instruction Set CPU (RISC) processor innovation in the computer workstation market. RISC processors have brought about a ten-fold increase in power, but can be produced by adapting the current production technology. With no increase in the quantity demanded, this change implies that production capacity must fall by 90 percent to avoid overcapacity and declining prices. Of course, such price decreases increase the quantity demanded in these situations, thereby reducing the extent of the capacity adjustment that would otherwise be required. Nevertheless, the new workstation technology has dramatically increased the effective output of existing production facilities, thereby generating excess capacity.

The second type is *obsolescence-creating* change—change that makes the current capital stock and organization obsolete. For example, Wal-Mart and the wholesale clubs that are revolutionizing retailing are dominating old-line department stores, thereby eliminating the need for much current retail capacity. When Wal-Mart enters a new market, total retail capacity expands, and some of the existing high-cost retail operations must go out of business. More intensive use of information and other technologies, direct dealing with manufacturers, and the replacement of high-cost, restrictive work rule union labor are several sources of the competitive advantage of these new organizations.

Finally, excess capacity also results when many competitors simultaneously rush to implement new, highly productive technologies without considering whether the aggregate effects of all such investment will be greater capacity than can be supported by demand in the final product market. The winchester disk drive industry provides an example. Between 1977 and 1984, venture capitalists invested over $400 million in 43 different manufacturers of winchester disk drives; initial public offerings of common stock infused additional capital in excess of $800 million. In mid-1983, the capital markets assigned a value of $5.4 billion to 12 publicly traded, venture capital-backed hard disk drive manufacturers. Yet, by the end of 1984, overcapacity had caused the value assigned to those companies to plummet to $1.4 billion. William Sahlman and Howard Stevenson attribute this overcapacity to an "investment mania" based on implicit assumptions about long-run growth and profitability *for each individual company* [that,] . . . had they been stated explicitly, would not have been acceptable to the rational investor."[16]

Such "overshooting" has by no means been confined to the winchester disk drive industry. Indeed, the 1980s saw boom-and-bust cycles in the venture capital market generally, and also in commercial real estate and LBO markets. And, as Sahlman and Stevenson also suggest, something more than "investment mania" and excessive "animal spirits" was at work here. Stated as simply as possible, my own analysis traces such overshooting to a gross misalignment of incentives between the "dealmakers" who promoted the transactions and the lenders, limited partners, and other investors who funded them.[17]

During the mid to late 1980s, venture capitalists, LBO promoters, and real estate developers were all effectively being rewarded simply for doing deals rather than for putting together successful deals. Reforming the "contracts" between dealmaker and investor—most directly, by reducing front-end-loaded fees and requiring the dealmakers to put up significant equity—would go far toward solving the problem of too many deals. (As I argue later, public corporations in mature industries face an analogous, although potentially far more costly in terms of shareholder value destroyed and social resources wasted, distortion of investment priorities and incentives when their managers and directors do not have significant stock ownership.)

Current Forces Leading to Excess Capacity and Exit

The ten-fold increase in crude oil prices between 1973 and 1979 had far-reaching effects, forcing contraction in oil, chemicals, steel, aluminum, and international shipping, among other industries. In addition, the sharp crude oil price increases that motivated major changes to economize on energy had other, longer-lasting consequences. The general corporate reevaluation of organizational processes stimulated by the oil shock led to dramatic increases in efficiency above and beyond the original energy-saving projects. (In fact, I view the oil shock as the initial impetus for the corporate "process reengineering" movement that continues to accelerate throughout the world.)

Since the oil price increases of the 1970s, I have again seen systematic overcapacity problems in many industries similar to those of the 19th century. While the reasons for this overcapacity appear to differ somewhat among industries, there are a few common underlying causes.

Macro Policies

Major deregulation of the American economy (including trucking, rail, airlines, telecommunications, banking, and financial services industries) under President Carter contributed to the requirement for exit in these industries, as did important changes in the U.S. tax laws that reduced tax advantages to real estate development, construction, and other activities. The end of the Cold War has had obvious consequences for the defense industry and its suppliers. In addition, I suspect that two generations of managerial focus on growth as a recipe for success has caused many firms to overshoot their optimal capacity, thus setting the stage for cutbacks. In the decade from 1979 to 1989, Fortune 100 firms lost 1.5 million employees, or 14 percent of their workforce.

Technology

Massive changes in technology are clearly part of the cause of the current industrial revolution and its associated excess capacity. Both within and across industries, technological developments have had far-reaching impact. To give some examples, the widespread acceptance of radial tires (which last three to five times longer than the older bias-ply technology and provide better gas mileage) caused excess capacity in the tire industry; the personal computer revolution forced contraction of the market for mainframes; the advent of aluminum and plastic alternatives reduced demand for steel and glass containers; and fiber optic, satellite, digital (ISDN), and new compression technologies dramatically increased capacity in telecommunication. Wireless personal communication such as cellular telephones and their replacements promise to extend this dramatic change further.

The changes in computer technology, including miniaturization, have not only revamped the computer industry, but also redefined the capabilities of countless other industries. Some estimates indicate that the price of computing capacity fell by a factor of 1,000 over the last decade. This means that computer production lines now produce boxes with 1,000 times the capacity for a given price. Consequently, computers are becoming commonplace—in cars, toasters, cameras, stereos, ovens, and so on. Nevertheless, the increase in quantity demanded has not been sufficient to avoid overcapacity, and we are therefore witnessing a dramatic shutdown of production lines in the industry—a force that has wracked IBM as a high-cost producer. A change of similar magnitude in auto production technology would have reduced the price of a $20,000 auto in 1980 to under $20 today. Such increases in capacity and productivity in a basic technology have unavoidably massive implications for the organization of work and society.

Fiber optic and other telecommunications technologies such as compression algorithms are bringing about similarly vast increases in worldwide capacity and functionality. A 1991 Bell Laboratories study of excess capacity indicates, for example, that, given three years and an additional expenditure of $3.1 billion, three of AT&T's new competitors (MCI, Sprint, and National Telecommunications Network) would be able to absorb the entire long-distance switched service that was supplied by AT&T in 1990.

Organizational Innovation

Overcapacity can be caused not only by changes in physical technology, but also by changes in organizational practices and management technology. The vast improvements in telecommunications, including computer networks, electronic mail, teleconferencing, and facsimile transmission, are changing the workplace in major ways that affect how people work and interact. It is far less valuable for people to be in the same geographic or physical location to work together effectively, which is encouraging smaller, more efficient, entrepreneurial organizing units that cooperate through technology. This in turn leads to even more fundamental changes.

Through competition, "virtual organizations"—networked or transitory organizations in which people come together temporarily to complete a task, then separate to pursue their individual specialties—are changing the structure of the standard large bureaucratic organization and contributing to its shrinkage. Virtual organizations tap talented specialists, avoid many of the regulatory costs imposed on permanent structures, and bypass the inefficient work rules and high wages imposed by unions. In so doing, they increase efficiency and thereby further contribute to excess capacity.

In addition, Japanese management techniques such as total quality management, just-in-time production, and flexible manufacturing have significantly enhanced the efficiency of the organizations in which they have been successfully implemented throughout the world. Some experts argue that such new management techniques can reduce defects and spoilage by an order of magnitude. These changes in managing and organizing principles have contributed significantly to the productivity of the world's capital stock and labor force and economized on the use of raw materials, thus also contributing to excess capacity.

Globalization of Trade

Over the last several decades, the entry of Japan and other Pacific Rim countries such as Hong Kong, Taiwan, Singapore, Thailand, Korea, Malaysia, and China into worldwide product markets has contributed to the required adjustments in Western economies. Competition from new entrants to the world product markets promises to intensify.

With the globalization of markets, excess capacity tends to occur worldwide. The Japanese economy, for example, is currently suffering from enormous overcapacity, caused in large part by what I view as the breakdown of its corporate control system.[18] As a consequence, Japan now faces a massive and long-overdue restructuring—one that includes the prospect of unprecedented (for Japanese companies) layoffs, a pronounced shift of corporate focus from market share to profitability, and even the adoption of pay-for-performance executive compensation contracts (something heretofore believed to be profoundly "unJapanese").

Yet even if the requirement for exit were isolated in just Japan and the United States, the interdependence of today's world economy ensures that such overcapacity would have global implications. For example, the rise of efficient high-quality producers of steel and autos in Japan and Korea has contributed to excess capacity in those industries worldwide. Between 1973 and 1990, total capacity in the U.S. steel industry fell by 38 percent from 157 to 97 million tons, and total employment fell over 50 percent from 509,000 to 252,000 (and fell further to 160,000 by 1993). From 1985 to 1989 multifactor productivity in the industry increased at an annual rate of 5.3 percent, as compared to 1.3 percent for the period 1958–1989.[19]

Revolution in Political Economy

The rapid pace of development of capitalism, the opening of closed economies, and the dismantling of central control in communist and socialist states is occurring in various degrees in Eastern Europe, China, India, Indonesia, other Asian economies, and Africa. In Asia and Africa alone, this development will place a potential labor force of almost a billion people—whose current average income is less than $2 per day—on world markets. The opening of Mexico and other Latin American countries and the transition of some socialist Eastern European economies to open capitalist systems could add almost 200 million more laborers with average incomes of less than $10 per day to the world market.

To put these numbers into perspective, the average daily U.S. income per worker is slightly over $90, and the total labor force numbers about 117 million, and the European Economic Community average wage is about $80 per day with a total labor force of about 130 million. The labor forces that have affected world trade extensively in the last several decades (those in Hong Kong, Japan, Korea, Malaysia, Singapore, and Taiwan) total about 90 million.

While the changes associated with bringing a potential 1.2 billion low-cost laborers onto world markets will significantly increase average living standards throughout the world, they will also bring massive obsolescence of capital (manifested in the form of excess capacity) in Western economies as the adjustments sweep through the system. Such adjustments will include a major redirection of Western labor and capital away from low-skilled, labor-intensive industries and toward activities where they have a comparative advantage. While the opposition to such adjustments will be strong, the forces driving them will prove irresistible in this day of rapid and inexpensive communication, transportation, miniaturization, and migration.

One can also confidently forecast that the transition to open capitalist economies will generate great conflict over international trade as special interests in individual countries try to insulate themselves from competition and the required exit. And the United States., despite its long-professed commitment to "free trade," will prove no exception. Just as U.S. managers and employees demanded protection from the capital markets in the 1980s, some are now demanding protection from international competition in the product markets, generally under the guise of protecting jobs. The debate over the North American Free Trade Agreement is but one general example of conflicts that are also occurring in the steel, automobile, computer chip, computer screen, and textile industries. It would not even surprise me to see a return to demands for protection from *domestic* competition. This is currently happening in the deregulated airline industry, an industry faced with significant excess capacity.

The bottom line, then, is that with worldwide excess capacity and thus greater requirement for exit, the strains put on the internal control mechanisms of Western corporations are likely to worsen for decades to come. The experience of the United States in the 1980s demonstrated that the capital markets can play an important role in forcing managers to address this problem. In the absence of capital market pressures, competition in product markets will eventually bring about exit. But when left to the product markets, the adjustment process is greatly protracted and ends up generating enormous additional costs. This is the clear lesson held out by the most recent restructuring of the U.S. auto industry—and it's one that many sectors of the Japanese economy are now experiencing firsthand.

THE ROLE OF THE MARKET FOR CORPORATE CONTROL

There are four basic control forces bearing on the corporation that act to bring about a convergence of managers' decisions with those that are optimal from shareholders' (and society's) standpoint. They are (1) the capital markets, (2) the legal, political, and regulatory system, (3) the product and factor markets, and (4) the internal control system headed by the board of directors.

The capital markets were relatively constrained by law and regulatory practice from about 1940 until their resurrection through hostile tender offers in the 1970s. Prior to the 1970s, capital market discipline took place primarily through the proxy process.

The legal/political/regulatory system is far too blunt an instrument to handle the problems of wasteful managerial behavior effectively. (Nevertheless, the breakup and deregulation of AT&T is one of the court system's outstanding successes; I estimate that it has helped create over $125 billion of increased value between AT&T and the Baby Bells.[20])

While the product and factor markets are slow to act as a control force, their discipline is inevitable; firms that do not supply the product that customers desire at a competitive price will not survive. Unfortunately, by the time product and factor market disciplines take effect, large amounts of investor capital and other social resources have been wasted, and it can often be too late to save much of the enterprise.

Which brings us to the role of corporate internal control systems and the need to reform them. A large and growing body of studies document shareholder gains from corporate restructurings of the 1980s.[21] The size and consistency of such gains provide strong support for the proposition that the internal control systems of publicly held corporations have generally failed to cause managers to maximize efficiency and value in slow-growth or declining industries.

Perhaps more persuasive than the formal statistical evidence, however, is the scarcity of large, public firms that have voluntarily restructured or engaged in a major strategic redirection without a challenge from the capital markets or a crisis in product markets. By contrast, partnerships and private or closely held firms such as investment banking, law, and consulting firms have generally responded far more quickly to changing market conditions.

Capital Markets and the Market for Corporate Control

Until control transactions were largely shut down in 1989, the capital markets provided one mechanism for accomplishing change before losses in the product markets generated a crisis. While the corporate control activity of the 1980s has been widely criticized as counterproductive to American industry, few have recognized that many of these transactions were necessary to accomplish exit over the objections of current managers and other corporate constituencies such as employees and communities.

The solution to excess capacity in the tire industry, for example, came about through the market for corporate control. Every major U.S. tire firm was either taken over or restructured in the 1980s.[22] In total, 37 tire plants were shut down in the period 1977–1987, and total employment in the industry fell by over 40 percent.

Capital market and corporate control transactions such as the repurchase of stock (or the purchase of another company) for cash or debt accomplished exit of resources in a very direct way. When Chevron acquired Gulf for $13.2 billion in cash and debt in 1984, the net assets devoted to the oil industry fell by $13.2 billion as soon as the checks were mailed out. In the 1980s, the oil industry had to shrink to accommodate the reduction in the quantity of oil demanded and the reduced rate of growth of demand. This meant paying out to shareholders its huge cash inflows, reducing exploration and development expenditures to bring reserves in line with reduced demands, and closing refining and distribution facilities. Leveraged acquisitions and equity repurchases helped accomplish this end for virtually all major U.S. oil firms.

Exit also resulted when KKR acquired RJR-Nabisco for $25 billion in cash and debt in its 1986 leveraged buyout. The tobacco industry must shrink, given the change in smoking habits in response to consumer awareness of cancer threats, and the payout of RJR's cash accomplished this to some extent. RJR's LBO debt also prevented the company from continuing to squander its cash flows on wasteful projects it had planned to undertake prior to the buyout. Thus, the buyout laid the groundwork for the efficient reduction of capacity and resources by one of the major firms in the industry. And the recent sharp declines in the stock prices of RJR and Philip Morris are signs that there is much more downsizing to come.

The era of the control market came to an end, however, in late 1989 and 1990. Intense controversy and opposition from corporate managers—assisted by charges of fraud, the increase in default and bankruptcy rates, and insider trading prosecutions—led to the shutdown of the control market through court decisions, state anti-takeover amendments, and regulatory restrictions on the availability of financing. In 1992, the total value of transactions fell to $71 billion from $340 billion in 1988. Leveraged buyouts and management buyouts fell to slightly over $1 billion in 1991 from $80 billion in 1988.

The demise of the control market as an effective influence on American corporations has not ended the restructuring. But it has allowed many organizations to postpone addressing major problems until forced to do by financial difficulties generated by the product markets. Unfortunately, the delay means that some of these organizations will not survive—or will survive as mere shadows of their former selves.

The Failure of Corporate Internal Control Systems

With the shutdown of the capital markets as an effective mechanism for motivating change, exit, and renewal, we are left to depend on the internal control system to act to preserve organizational assets, both human and otherwise. Throughout corporate America, the problems that motivated much of the control activity of the 1980s are now reflected in lackluster performance, financial distress, and pressures for restructuring. General Motors, Kodak, IBM, Westinghouse, ITT, and many others have faced or are now facing severe challenges in the product markets. We therefore must understand why these internal control systems have failed and learn how to make them work.

By nature, organizations abhor control systems. Ineffective governance is a major part of the problem with internal control mechanisms; they seldom respond in the absence of a crisis. The General Motors board "revolt," which resulted in the firing of CEO Robert Stempel, exemplifies the failure, not the success, of GM's governance system. Although clearly one of the world's high-cost producers in a market with substantial excess capacity, GM resisted making major changes in its strategy for over a decade. The revolt came too late; the board acted to remove the CEO only in 1992, after the company had reported losses of $6.5 billion in 1990 and 1991.

GM is no isolated example. IBM is another testimony to the failure of internal control systems. The company failed to adjust to the substitution away from its mainframe business following the revolution in the workstation and personal computer market—ironically enough, a revolution that it helped launch with the invention of the RISC technology in 1974. Like GM, IBM is a high-cost producer in a market with substantial excess capacity. It too began to change its strategy significantly and removed its CEO only after reporting losses of $2.8 billion in 1991 and further losses in 1992 while losing almost 65 percent of its equity value.

General Electric is a notable exception to my proposition about the failure of corporate internal control systems. Under CEO Jack Welch since 1981, GE has accomplished a major strategic redirection, eliminating 104,000 of its 402,000-person work force (through layoffs or sales of divisions) in the period 1980–1990 without a threat from capital or product markets. These changes appear attributable almost entirely to the vision and leadership of Jack Welch, however, rather than the influence of GE's governance system.

General Dynamics provides another exceptional case. The appointment of William Anders as CEO in September 1991 resulted in a rapid adjustment to excess capacity in the defense industry—again, with no apparent threat from an outside force. The company generated $3.4 billion of increased value on a $1 billion company in just over two years. One of the key elements in this success story, however, was a major change in the company's management compensation system that tied bonuses directly to increases in stock value.[23]

Gordon Donaldson's account of General Mills' strategic redirection is yet another case of a largely voluntary restructuring.[24] The fact that it took more than ten years to accomplish exemplifies the social costs of continuing the waste caused by ineffective control. Internal control systems appear to have two faults: They react too late, and they take too long to effect major change. Changes motivated by the capital market are generally accomplished quickly—typically, within one to three years. No one has yet demonstrated social benefits of relying on internally motivated change that would offset the costs of the decade-long delay in the restructuring of General Mills.

In summary, it appears that the infrequency with which large corporate organizations restructure or redirect themselves solely on the basis of the internal control mechanisms—that is, in the absence of intervention by capital markets or a crisis in the product markets—is strong testimony to the inadequacy of these control mechanisms.

REVIVING INTERNAL CORPORATE CONTROL SYSTEMS

There are lessons to learn from board of directors problems, current active investors, and the history of CEOs and the venture capital industry.

Remaking the Board as an Effective Control Mechanism

The problems with corporate internal control systems start with the board of directors. The board, at the apex of the internal control system, has the final responsibility for the functioning of the firm. Most important, it sets the rules of the game for the CEO. The job of the board is to hire, fire, and compensate the CEO, and to provide high-level counsel. Few boards in the past decades have done this job well in the absence of external crises. This is particularly unfortunate, given that the very purpose of the internal control mechanism is to provide an early warning system to an organization before difficulties reach a crisis stage.

Reasons for the failure of boards are not completely understood, but we are making progress toward understanding these complex issues. The available evidence does suggest the CEOs are removed after poor performance, but this effect seems too late and too small to meet the obligations of the board.[25] I believe bad systems or rules, not bad people, are at the root of the general failings of boards of directors.

Board Culture

Board culture is an important component of board failure. The emphasis on politeness and courtesy at the expense of truth and frankness in boardrooms is both a symptom and a cause of failure in the control system. CEOs have the same insecurities and defense mechanisms as other human beings; few will accept, much less seek, the monitoring and criticism of an active and attentive board.

An example will illustrate the general problem. John Hanley, retired Monsanto CEO, accepted an invitation from a CEO to join his board—subject, Hanley wrote, to meeting with the company's general counsel and outside accountants as a kind of directorial due diligence. Says Hanley:

> At the first board dinner the CEO got up and said, "I think Jack was a little bit confused whether I wanted him to be a director or the chief executive officer." I should have known right there that he wasn't going to pay a goddamn bit of attention to anything I said.

So it turned out, and after a year Hanley quit the board in disgust.[26] The result is a continuing cycle of ineffectiveness. By rewarding consent and discouraging conflicts, CEOs have the power to control the board, which ultimately can damage the CEO's and the company's performance. This downward spiral makes corporate difficulties likely to culminate in a crisis requiring drastic steps, as opposed to a series of small problems met by a continuously self-correcting mechanism.

Information Problems

Serious information problems limit the effectiveness of board members in the typical large corporation. For example, the CEO almost always determines the agenda and the information given to the board. This limitation on information severely restricts the ability of even highly talented board members to contribute effectively to the monitoring and evaluation of the CEO and the company's strategy.

Board members should also have the financial expertise necessary to provide useful input into the corporate planning process, especially in forming the corporate objective and determining the factors that affect corporate value. Yet such financial expertise is generally lacking on today's boards. And it is not only the inability of most board members to evaluate a company's current business and financial strategy that is troubling. In many cases, boards (and managements) fail even to understand that their basic mission is to maximize the market value of the enterprise.

Legal Liability

The incentives motivating modern boards are generally not consistent with shareholder interests. Boards are moved to serve shareholders primarily by substantial legal liabilities through class action suits initiated by shareholders, the plaintiff's bar, and others—lawsuits that are often triggered by unexpected declines in stock price. These legal incentives are more often consistent with minimizing downside risk than with maximizing value. Boards are also concerned about threats of adverse publicity from the media or from the political or regulatory authorities. Again, while these incentives often provide motivation for board members to reduce potential liabilities, they do not provide strong incentives to take actions that create efficiency and value for the company.

Lack of Management and Board Member Equity Holdings

Much of corporate America's governance problem arises from the fact that neither managers nor board members typically own substantial fractions of their firm's equity. While the average CEO of the 1,000 largest firms owned 2.7 percent of his or her firm's equity in 1991, the median holding was only 0.2 percent—and 75 percent of CEOs owned less than 1.2 percent.[27] In addition, if outside board members held substantial equity interests, they would have better incentives.

Achieving significant direct stock ownership in large firms would require huge dollar outlays by managers or board members. To get around this problem, Bennett Stewart has proposed an approach called the "leveraged equity purchase plan" (LEPP), which amounts to the sale of slightly (say, 10 percent) in-the-money stock options. By requiring significant out-of-pocket contributions by managers and directors, Stewart's plan helps overcome the "free option" aspect (or lack of downside risk) that limits the effectiveness of standard corporate option plans.[28] By having the exercise price of the options rise every year at the firm's cost of capital, it also removes the problem with standard options that allows management to reap gains on their options while shareholders are losing.[29]

Boards should have an implicit understanding or explicit requirement that new members must invest in the stock of the company. While the initial investment could vary, it should seldom be less than $100,000 from the new board member's personal funds; this investment would force new board members to recognize from the outset that their decisions affect their own wealth as well as that of remote shareholders. Over the long term, the investment can be made much larger by options or other stock-based compensation. The recent trend to pay some board member fees in stock or options is a move in the right direction. Discouraging board members from selling this equity is also important so that holdings will accumulate to a significant size over time.

Oversized Boards

Keeping boards small can help improve their performance. When boards exceed seven or eight people, they are less likely to function effectively and are easier for the CEO to control.[30] Because the possibility for internal animosity and retribution from the CEO is too great, it is almost impossible for direct reports to the CEO to participate openly and critically in effective evaluation and monitoring of the CEO. Therefore, the only inside board member should be the CEO; insiders other than the CEO can be regularly invited to attend board meetings in an unofficial capacity. Indeed, board members should be given regular opportunities to meet with and observe executives below the CEO—both to expand their knowledge of the company and CEO succession candidates, and to increase other top-level executives' exposure to the thinking of the board and the board process.

The CEO as Chair of the Board

It is common in U.S. corporations for the CEO to hold the position of chair of the board. The function of a chair is to run board meetings and oversee the process of hiring, firing, evaluating, and compensating the CEO. Clearly, the CEO cannot perform this function apart from his or her personal interest. Without the direction of an independent leader, it is much more difficult for a board to perform its critical function. Therefore, for the board to be effective, it is important to separate the CEO and chair positions. The independent chair should, at a minimum, be given the rights to initiate board appointments, and board committee assignments, and (jointly with the CEO) to set the board's agenda. All these initiatives, of course, should be conditional on the ratification of the board.

An effective board will often experience tension among its members as well as with the CEO. But I hasten to add that I am not advocating continuous war in the boardroom. In fact, in well-functioning organizations the board will generally be relatively inactive and will exhibit little conflict. It becomes important primarily when the rest of the internal control system is failing, and this should be a relatively rare event. The challenge is to create a system that will not succumb to complacency during periods of prosperity and good management, and therefore be unable to rise early to the challenge of correcting a failing management system. This is a difficult task, because there are strong tendencies for boards to develop a culture and social norms that reflect optimal behavior under prosperity, and these norms make it extremely difficult for the board to respond early to failure in its top management team.

Attempts to Model the Process on Political Democracy

There have been a number of proposals to model the board process after a democratic political model in which various constituencies are represented. Such a process, however, is likely to make the internal control system even less accountable to shareholders than it is now. To see why, we need look no farther than the inefficiency of representative political democracies (whether at the local, state, or federal level) and their attempts to manage quasi-business organizations such as the Postal Service, schools, or power-generation entities such as the TVA.

Nevertheless, there would likely be significant benefits to opening up the corporate governance process to the firm's largest shareholders. Proxy regulations by the SEC severely restrict communications between management and shareholders and among shareholders themselves. Until recently, for example, it was illegal for any shareholder to discuss company matters with more than ten other shareholders without previously filing with and receiving the approval of the SEC. The November 1992 relaxation of this restriction now allows an investor to communicate with an unlimited number of other stockholders provided the investor owns less than 5 percent of the shares, has no special interest in the issue being discussed, and is not seeking proxy authority. But these remaining restrictions still have the obvious drawback of limiting effective institutional action by those investors most likely to pursue it.

As I discuss below, when equity holdings become concentrated in institutional hands, it is easier to resolve some of the free rider problems that limit the ability of thousands of individual shareholders to engage in effective collective action. In principle, institutional investors can exercise corporate control rights more effectively. Legal and regulatory restrictions, however, have prevented financial institutions from playing a major corporate monitoring role. Therefore, if institutions are to aid in effective governance, we must continue to dismantle the rules and regulations that have prevented them and other large investors from accomplishing this coordination.

Resurrecting Active Investors

A major set of problems with internal control systems are associated with the curbing of what I call "active investors."[31] Active investors are individuals or institutions that hold large debt and/or equity positions in a company and actively participate in its strategic direction. Active investors are important to a well-functioning governance system, because they have the financial interest and the independence to view firm management and policies in an unbiased way. They have the incentives to buck the system to correct problems early rather than late when the problems are obvious but difficult to correct. Financial institutions such as banks, pensions funds, insurance companies, mutual funds, and money managers are natural active investors, but they have been shut out of boardrooms and firm strategy by the legal structure, by custom, and by their own practices.

Active investors are important to a well-functioning governance system, and there is much we can do to dismantle the web of legal, tax, and regulatory apparatus that severely limits the scope of active investors in this country.[32] But even without such regulatory changes, CEOs and boards can take actions to encourage investors to hold large positions in their debt and equity and to play an active role in the strategic direction of the firm and in monitoring the CEO.

Wise CEOs can recruit large block investors to serve on the board, even selling new equity or debt to them to encourage their commitment to the firm. Lazard Frères Corporate Partners Fund is an example of an institution set up specifically to perform this function, making new funds available to the firm and taking a board seat to advise and monitor management performance. Warren Buffett's activity through Berkshire Hathaway provides another example. He played an important role in helping Salomon Brothers through its recent legal and organizational difficulties following the government bond bidding scandal.

Learning from LBOs and Venture Capital Firms

Finally, there are valuable lessons that come out of corporate takeover experience.

Organizational Experimentation in the 1980s

The evidence from LBOs, leveraged restructurings, takeovers, and venture capital firms has demonstrated dramatically that leverage, payout policy, and ownership structure affect organizational efficiency, cash flow, and hence value. Such organizational changes show that these effects are especially important in low-growth or declining firms where the agency costs of free cash flow are large.

Evidence from LBOs

LBOs provide a good source of estimates of the value increases resulting from changing leverage, payout policies, and the control and governance system. After an LBO transaction, the company has a different financial policy and control system, but essentially the same managers and the same assets. Leverage increases from about 18 percent of value to 90 percent, there are large payouts to prior shareholders, and equity becomes concentrated in the hands of managers and the board (who own about 20 percent and 60 percent, on average, respectively). At the same time, boards shrink to about seven or eight people, the sensitivity of managerial pay to performance rises dramatically, and the companies' equity usually becomes private (although debt is often publicly traded).

Studies of LBOs indicate that premiums to selling-firm shareholders are roughly 40 percent to 50 percent of the prebuyout market value, cash flows increase by 96 percent from the year before the buyout to three years after the buyout, and value increases by 235 percent (96 percent adjusted for general market movements) from two months prior to the buyout offer to the time of going public, sale, or recapitalization (about three years later, on average).[33] Large value increases have also been documented in voluntary recapitalizations—those in which the company stays public but buys back a significant fraction of its equity or pays out a significant dividend.[34]

A Proven Model of Governance Structure

LBO associations and venture capital funds provide a blueprint for managers and boards who wish to revamp their top-level control systems to make them more efficient. LBO firms like KKR and venture capital funds such as Kleiner Perkins are among the preeminent examples of active investors in recent U.S. history; they thus serve as models that can be emulated in part or in total by most public corporations. The two have similar governance structures, and have been successful in resolving the governance problems of both slow-growth or declining firms (LBO associations) and high-growth entrepreneurial firms (venture capital funds).

Both LBO associations and venture capital funds tend to be organized as limited partnership. In effect, the institutions that contribute the funds to these organizations delegate the role of the active investor to the general partners of the organizations. Both governance systems are characterized by:

- Limited partnership agreements at the top level that prohibit headquarters from cross-subsidizing one division with the cash from another.
- High equity ownership by managers and board members.
- Board members (mostly the LBO association partners or the venture capitalists) who through their funds directly represent a large fraction of the equity owners of each subsidiary company.
- Small board of directors (of the operating companies) typically consisting of no more than eight people.
- CEOs who are typically the only insider on the board.
- CEOs who are seldom the chair of the board.

LBO associations and venture funds also solve many of the information problems facing typical boards of directors. First, as a result of the due diligence process at the time the deal is undertaken, both the managers and the LBO and venture partners have extensive and detailed knowledge of virtually all aspects of the business. In addition, these boards have frequent contact with management, often weekly or even daily during times of difficult challenges. This contact and information flow is facilitated by the fact that LBO associations and venture funds both have their own staffs. They also often perform the corporate finance function for the operating companies, providing the major interface with the capital markets and investment banking communities. Finally, the close relationship between the LBO partners or venture fund partners and the operating companies encourages the board to contribute its expertise during times of crisis. It is not unusual for a partner to join the management team, even as CEO, to help an organization through such emergencies.

CONCLUSION

Beginning with the oil price shock of the 1970s, technological, political, regulatory, and economic forces have been transforming the worldwide economy on a scale not seen since the nineteenth century Industrial Revolution. As in the nineteenth century, technological advances in many industries have led to sharply declining costs, increased average (but declining marginal) productivity of labor, reduced growth rates of labor income, excess capacity, and the requirement for downsizing and exit.

Events of the last two decades indicate that corporate internal control systems have failed to deal effectively with these changes, especially excess capacity and the requirement for exit. The corporate control transactions of the 1980s—mergers and acquisitions, LBOs, and other leveraged recapitalizations—represent a capital market solution to this problem of widespread overcapacity. With the regulatory shutdown of the corporate control markets beginning in 1989, finding a solution to the problem now rests once more with the internal control systems, with corporate boards, and, to a lesser degree, with the large institutional shareholders who bear the consequences of corporate losses in value. Making the internal control systems of corporations work is the major challenge facing us in the 1990s.

STUDIES DOCUMENTING THE EFFECTS OF CAPITAL MARKET TRANSACTIONS ON SHAREHOLDER WEALTH

Baker, George, and Karen Wruck. "Organizational Changes and Value Creation in Leveraged Buyouts: The Case of O. M. Scott and Sons Company." *Journal of Financial Economics* 25, No. 2, (1989), pp. 163–190. For a less technical version of the same article, see Vol. 4, No. 1 (Spring 1991) of the *Journal of Applied Corporate Finance.*

Bhagat, Sanjai, Andre Shleifer, and Robert W. Vishny. "Hostile Takeovers in the 1980s: The Return to Corporate Specialization." Brookings Papers: Microeconomics 1990, pp. 1–84.

Brickley, James A., Gregg A. Jarrell, and Jeffrey M. Netter. "The Market for Corporate Control: The Empirical Evidence Since 1980," *Journal of Economic Perspectives* 2, No. 1, (1988), pp. 49–68.

Comment, Robert, and Gregg Jarrell. "Corporate Focus and Stock Returns." Bradley Policy Research Center, Working Paper MR 91-01, May 1991.

Dann, Larry Y., and Harry DeAngelo. "Corporate Financial Policy and Corporate Control: A Study of Defensive Adjustments in Asset and Ownership Structure." *Journal of Financial Economics* 20, (1988), pp. 87–127.

DeAngelo, Harry, Linda DeAngelo, and Edward Rice. "Going Private: Minority Freezeouts and Stockholder Wealth." *Journal of Law and Economics* 27, (1984), pp. 367–401. For a less technical version of the same article, see Vol. 4, No. 1 (Spring 1991) of the *Journal of Applied Corporate Finance.*

Denis, David J. "Organizational Form and the Consequences of Highly Leveraged Transactions: Kroger's Recapitalization and Safeway's LBO." *Journal of Financial Economics,* pp. 193–224. Oct 1994, Vol. 3b, No. 2.

Denis, David, and Diane Denis. "Managerial Discretion, Organizational Structure, and Corporate Performance: A Study of Leveraged Recapitalizations." *Journal of Accounting and Economics* (January 1993).

Donaldson, Gordon. "Voluntary Restructuring: The Case of General Mills." *Journal of Financial Economics* 27, No. 1, (1990), pp. 117–141. For a less technical version of the same article, see Vol. 4., No. 3 (Fall 1991) of the *Journal of Applied Corporate Finance.*

Healy, Paul M., Krishna G. Palepu, and Richard S. Ruback. "Does Corporate Performance Improve After Mergers?" *Journal of Financial Economics* 31, Vol. 2, 1992, pp. 135–175.

Holderness, Clifford G., and Dennis P. Sheehan. "Monitoring An Owner: The Case of Turner Broadcasting." *Journal of Financial Economics* 30, No. 2, (1991), pp. 325–346.

Jensen, Michael C. "The Agency Costs of Free Cash Flow: Corporate Finance and Takeovers." *American Economic Review* 76, No. 2, (1986), pp. 323–329.

Jensen, Michael C. "The Takeover Controversy: Analysis and Evidence." *The Midland Corporate Finance Journal* 4, No. 2, (1986), pp. 6–32.

Jensen, Michael C., and Brian Barry. "Gordon Cain and the Sterling Group (A) and (B)." Harvard Business School, #9-942-021 and #9-942-022, (1992).

Jensen, Michael C., Willy Burkhardt, and Brian K. Barry. "Wisconsin Central Ltd. Railroad and Berkshire Partners (A): Leverage Buyouts and Financial Distress." Harvard Business School #9-190-062, (1992).

Jensen, Michael C., Jay Dial, and Brian K. Barry. "Wisconsin Central Ltd. Railroad and Berkshire Partners (B): LBO Associations and Corporate Governance." Harvard Business School #9-190-070, (1992).

Kaplan, Steven N. "Campeau's Acquisition of Federated: Post-Bankruptcy Results." *Journal of Financial Economics* 35, (1992), pp. 123–136.

Kaplan, Steven N. "Campeau's Acquisition of Federated: Value Added or Destroyed." *Journal of Financial Economics* 25, (1989), pp. 191–212.

Kaplan, Steven N. "The Effects of Management Buyouts on Operating Performance and Value." *Journal of Financial Economics* 24, (1989), pp. 581–618.

Kaplan, Steven. "Management Buyouts: Evidence on Taxes as a Source of Value." *Journal of Finance* 44, (1989), pp. 611–632.

Kaplan, Steven N., and Jeremy Stein. "The Evolution of Buyout Pricing and Financial Structure in the 1980s." *Quarterly Journal of Economics* 108, No. 2, (1993), pp. 313–358. For a less technical version of the same article, see Vol. 6, No. 1 (Spring 1993) of the *Journal of Applied Corporate Finance.*

Kaplan, Steven N., and Jeremy Stein. "How Risky is the Debt in Highly Leveraged Transactions?" *Journal of Financial Economics* 27, No. 1, (1990), pp. 215–245.

Lang, Larry H. P., Annette Poulsen, and Rene M. Stulz. "Asset Sales, Leverage, and the Agency Costs of Managerial Discretion." *Journal of Financial Economics,* (Jan. 1995), pp. 3–37. Vol. 37, No. 1.

Lichtenberg, Frank R. *Corporate Takeovers and Productivity,* (Cambridge MIT Press, 1992). For a less technical summary of the findings, see Vol. 2, No. 2 (Summer 1989) of the *Journal of Applied Corporate Finance.*

Lichtenberg, Frank R., and Donald Siegel. "The Effects of Leveraged Buyouts on Productivity and Related Aspects of Firm Behavior." *Journal of Financial Economics* 27, No. 1, (1990), pp. 165–194.

Mann, Steven V., and Neil W. Sicherman. "The Agency Costs of Free Cash Flow: Acquisition Activity, and Equity Issues." *Journal of Business* 64, No. 2, (1991), pp. 213–227.

Murphy, Kevin J., and Jay Dial. "Incentives, downsizing, and value creation at General Dynamics," *Journal of Financial Economics* 37, (1995), pp. 261–314.

Palepu, Krishna G. "Consequences of Leveraged Buyouts." *Journal of Financial Economics* 27, No. 1, (1990), pp. 247–262.

Rosett, Joshua G. "Do Union Wealth Concessions Explain Takeover Premiums? The Evidence on Contract Wages." *Journal of Financial Economics* 27, No. 1, (1990), pp. 263–282.

Smith, Abbie J. "Corporate Ownership Structure and Performance: The Case of Management Buyouts." *Journal of Financial Economics* 27, (1990), pp. 143–164.

Tedlow, Richard. "Hitting the Skids: Tires and Time Horizons." Harvard Business School, (1991).

Tiemann, Jonathan. "The Economics of Exit and Restructuring: The Pabst Brewing Company." Harvard Business School, (1990).

Wruck, Karen H. "Financial Distress, Reorganization, and Organizational Efficiency." *Journal of Financial Economics* 27, (1990), pp. 420–444.

Wruck, Karen H. (1992), "Financial Policy, Internal Control, and Performance: Sealed Air Corporation's Leveraged Special Dividend." *Journal of Financial Economics,* forthcoming.

Wruck, Karen H. "What Really Went Wrong at Revco?" *Journal of Applied Corporate Finance* 4, (1991), pp. 79–92.

Wruck, Karen H., and Krishna Palepu. "Consequences of Leveraged Shareholder Payouts: Defensive versus Voluntary Recapitalizations." Working paper, Harvard Business School, (1992).

Wruck, Karen H., and Steve-Anna Stephens. "Leveraged Buyouts and Restructuring: The Case of Safeway, Inc." Harvard Business School Case #192-095, (1992).

Wruck, Karen H., and Steve-Anna Stephens. "Leveraged Buyouts and Restructuring: The Case of Safeway, Inc.: Media Response." Harvard Business School Case #192-094, (1992).

CHAPTER NOTES

Chapter 1: The Investment Setting

1. Like all generalizations, this one has exceptions. The reader will find a detailed discussion of investment results over time in Chapter 2.

2. The Rule of 72 is a quick and easy way to calculate either the rate of interest *or* the time required for doubling through compounding. Given a compound rate of interest, the number of years required to double the original investment is calculated by dividing the rate into the number 72. Or, given a number of years, the rate of interest required to double the starting sum is calculated by dividing the given number of years into 72.

3. Saulé Omarova, a student from Kazakhstan, "invested" several years studying scientific Communism at the University of Moscow, only to witness in her senior year the elimination—along with the Soviet Union and the Communist Party's power in the early 1990s—of all hope for the entire career for which she had prepared so conscientiously. The academic discipline she had mastered and the field in which she planned to teach were obliterated. She is now "investing" boldly in another career, studying Western political theory at the University of Wisconsin.

4. Such a blind trust is sometimes used by high-ranking elected officials to avoid any question about the independence of their decisions.

Chapter 2: Risk and Utility: Basics

1. D. Bernoulli, "Exposition of a New Theory on the Measurement of Risk," *Econometrica,* January 1954 (translation from 1738 version), pp. 23–36.

2. *Ibid.,* p. 29.

3. This approach was introduced by William Sharpe in an article entitled, "An Algorithm for Portfolio Improvement," *Advances in Mathematical Programming and Financial Planning*, Vol. 1, (Greenwich, CT: JAI Press, Inc., 1987).

4. This innovation was introduced by George Chow. For a more elaborate description, see G. Chow, "Portfolio Selection Based on Return, Risk and Relative Performance," *Financial Analysts Journal,* March/April 1995, pp. 54–60.

5. For example, see P. Samuelson, "Risk and Uncertainty: A Fallacy of Large Numbers," *Scientia,* April/May 1963, pp. 1–6; P. Samuelson, "Lifetime Portfolio Selection by Dynamic Stochastic Programming," *Review of Economics and Statistics,* August 1969, pp. 239–246; and Z. Bodie, A. Kane, and A. Marcus, *Investments* (Homewood, IL: Irwin, 1989), pp. 222–226.

6. For example, see J. Poterba and L. Summers, "Mean Reversion in Stock Returns: Evidence and Implications," *Journal of Financial Economics,* 22 (1988), pp. 27–59.

7. Samuelson addresses this result in P. Samuelson, "Longrun Risk Tolerance When Equity Returns are Mean Regressing: Pseudoparadoxes and Vindication of Businessman's Risk," in W. Brainard, W. Nordhaus and H. Watts, Eds., *Macroeconomics, Finance and Economic Policy: Essays in Honor of James Tobin* (Cambridge, MA: MIT Press, 1991) pp. 181–200.

8. Z. Bodie, R. C. Merton, and W. Samuelson, "Labor Supply Flexibility and Portfolio Choice in a Life-Cycle Model," *Journal of Economic Dynamics and Control,* Vol. 16, 1992, pp. 427–449.

Chapter 3:   Models of Risk

1. A utility function summarizes investors' preferences generically on the basis of some choice variables. In this case, investors' utility or satisfaction is stated as a function of wealth and allows us to answer questions such as: Will an investor be twice as happy if returns yield twice as much wealth? Does each marginal increase in wealth lead to less additional utility than the prior marginal increase? In one specific form of this function, the quadratic utility function, the entire utility of an investor can be compressed into the expected wealth measure and the standard deviation in that wealth, which provides a justification for the use of the capital asset pricing model (CAPM).

2. This procedure for annualization assumes that returns are uncorrelated across months, i.e., there is no relationship between the returns in one month and the returns in the following month.

3. Firms could conceivably diversify away competitive risk by acquiring their existing competitors. Doing so would expose them to attacks under the antitrust laws, however, and would not eliminate the risk from as-yet-unannounced competitors.

4. If investments are not held in proportion to their market value, investors are still losing some diversification benefits. There is no gain from overweighting some sectors and underweighting others in a marketplace with only random odds of finding undervalued and overvalued assets, and investors will not do so.

5. Stephen A. Ross, "The Arbitrage Theory of Capital Asset Pricing," *Journal of Economic Theory,* Vol. 13(3), 1976, pp. 341–360.

6. N. Chen, R. Roll, and S. A. Ross, 1986, "Economic Forces and the Stock market," *Journal of Business,* Vol. 59, 1986, pp. 383–404.

7. E. F. Fama and K. R. French, 1992, "The Cross-Section of Expected Returns," *Journal of Finance,* Vol. 47, pp. 427–466.

8. R. Roll, 1977, "A Critique of the Asset Pricing Theory's Tests: Part I: On Past and Potential Testability of Theory," *Journal of Financial Economics,* Vol. 4, pp. 129–176.

9. E. F. Fama and K. R. French, 1992, "The Cross-Section of Expected Returns," *Journal of Finance,* Vol. 47, pp. 427–466.

10. Y. Amihud, B. Christensen, and H. Mendelson, 1992, "Further Evidence on the Risk-Return Relationship," Working Paper, New York University.

11. L. K. Chan and J. Lakonsihok, 1992, "Are the Reports of Beta's Death Premature?", Working Paper, University of Illinois.

12. J. F. Weston and T. E. Copeland, 1992, *Managerial Finance,* Dryden Press, Orlando. Weston and Copeland used both approaches to estimate the cost of equity for oil companies in 1989 and came up with 14.4 percent with the CAPM and 19.1 percent using with the APM.

13. Barra, a leading beta estimation service, adjusts betas to reflect differences in fundamentals across firms (such as size and dividend yields). It is drawing on the regression studies that have found these to be good proxies for market risk.

14. Financial obligation refers to any payment a firm is legally obligated to make, e.g., interest and principal payments. It does not include discretionary cash flows, such as dividend payments or new capital expenditures, which can be deferred or delayed without legal consequences. (There may be economic consequences, however.)

Chapter 4: Alternative Measures of Risk

1. The symbol $\sum_i$ is a shorthand notation called a summation, which represents the sum of the terms following it.

2. The use of mean and variance can also be motivated by the use of a quadratic utility function. If quadratic utility describes how the investor evaluates the utility of wealth, the only measures that make a difference are the mean and variance of the distribution of wealth. Quadratic utility functions have some severe limitations, however, and don't describe the way people behave very well for extreme wealth values.

Chapter 5: Tax Considerations in Investing

1. "Magellan and Taxes," *Morningstar Mutual Funds,* December 23, 1994.

2. In theory, if very wealthy individuals were the only buyers, the yield of a tax-exempt bond should be virtually equal to the after-tax yield of a taxable bond that is comparable in all other respects. In practice, because many buyers, including corporations, have lower effective tax rates, municipal yields are usually higher than this calculation would indicate. That the municipal bond market is less efficient than the market for most taxable bonds, and certainly Treasury issues, is also a contributing factor.

3. Because of the 70 percent intercorporate dividend-received deduction, the effective corporate tax rate on dividends from domestic companies is 10.5 percent (35 percent of 30 percent), while the corporate capital gains tax rate is now 35 percent.

4. Because capital gains realizations are typically much more controllable than the flow of ordinary income, the 1986 Tax Reform Act was a great boon to intelligent investors. By effectively trading away the traditional capital gains rate differential for a much lower rate on ordinary income, many investors were far better off. And if one

concurs with Ellis that most tax shelters end up being poor investments, it can also be argued that the shelter-ending provisions of the 1986 TRA were beneficial to prospective investors.

5. Capital gains taxes increase over time as the portfolio's appreciation compounds, and thus the relationship between the taxes on capital gains and dividends is also changing. Figure 8-1 plots, for illustrative purposes, the tax costs in the tenth year of the portfolio's existence. If the cumulative tax costs over the entire ten years were plotted instead, the hockey stick curve would be somewhat less sharp, but the message that most of the tax damage occurs in the low turnover range remains essentially the same. Of the maximum capital gains tax at 100 percent turnover, 23 percent would have been incurred at 5 percent turnover, 42 percent at 10 percent turnover, and 73 percent at 25 percent turnover. (The anomaly in Figure 8-1 of a small capital gains tax at zero turnover relates to the assumed spending requirement.)

6. The spreadsheet in the Appendix is constructed so that, when the sales generated by the turnover assumption are insufficient to cover any deficit between after-tax dividend income and the withdrawal for spending, the sales from the portfolio are increased accordingly, including a gross-up for the capital gains taxes on the additional sales. These additional sales to meet spending needs are not reflected in the turnover rate. The $0.32 capital gains tax cost at zero turnover is the capital gains tax on the additional sales required to meet the spending requirement.

7. Because investing is mostly about growth rates, and because growth rates can only be depicted accurately using logarithmic scales, students of investing should become comfortable with their use. As a case in point, if I were to use an arithmetic scale in Figure 8-4, the curves would all turn upward, as if the growth rates progressively increased with time, when in fact just the opposite is true.

8. GAAP accounting requires corporations to set up a liability provision for the capital gains taxes that would be due in the unlikely event the entire portfolio were liquidated on the balance sheet date. This is actually a useful practice for all taxable investors to follow, because the deferred tax provision serves to remind owners that the assets generating the cash flow to meet their current spending requirements are greater, and often substantially greater, than the assets that would remain were the gains suddenly realized.

9. Roger Hertog and Mark Gordon are president and director of product development, respectively, at Sanford C. Bernstein & Co., Inc., a well-regarded active management firm in New York.

10. Using somewhat different assumptions, and making no provision for current spending, Hertog and Gordon calculate that at 25 percent turnover and liquidation after the 20th year, 58 basis points of added annual return would be necessary to offset the taxes.

Chapter 6:   Global Management and Asset Allocation

1. For example, see "Determinants of Portfolio Performance II: An Update," by Gary P. Brinson, Brian D. Singer, and Gilbert L. Beebower, *Financial Analysts Journal* (May/June 1991), pp. 40–48.

2. Some extensions of the CAPM allow investors to hold different market portfolios. These modifications include borrowing and lending rates that differ, the

availability of multiple portfolios with high correlation to the market portfolio, investors who have different time horizons, and assets that have different liquidities.

3. Many times investors assume that the market portfolio includes only the market in which they are interested. For example, investors examining Exxon may take the market to be the S&P 500 or some other U.S. equity index, often assuming that the market proxy should be limited to only their relevant investment arena. Problems with this method of analysis are addressed later.

4. A fuller presentation of the results in this section appears in Denis S. Karnosky and Brian D. Singer, "Global Asset Management and Performance Attribution," Association for Investment Management and Research (1994). Charlottesville, VA.

5. All variables in this derivation are in natural log terms (continuously compounded rates) for simplicity. The interest rates and rates of return are additive when expressed as logs, and cross-product concerns vanish.

6. Because of the equivalence of risk premiums for all investors, the asset mix of the optimal portfolio will also be identical across all countries and for all unrestricted investors.

7. Richard Roll and Stephen Ross have shown that a benchmark portfolio can be less than 25 basis points below the efficient frontier and produce measured betas of zero, even though the true betas may be quite large and significant. Although disturbing, this result points out an enormous source of potential error for researchers attempting to disprove beta's significance. "On the Cross-sectional Relation between Expected Returns and Betas" *Journal of Finance* (March 1994), pp. 101–121.

8. In other instances, one could argue that the U.S. market is a less significant proportion of the global portfolio than 15 years earlier, and therefore would have less impact. Equity markets around the globe, however, reacted in concert with the crash in the U.S.

9. Standard deviations and correlations can be more stable over shorter, more frequently sampled time periods, such as monthly periods calculated using daily data. Asset allocation is usually concerned with longer horizons, so we present longer horizon measures here.

10. The jumps in volatility in the global market do not appear quite as pronounced simply because there are other assets that act to diversify or dampen the influence of U.S. equities.

11. An examination of the risk premium for U.S. equities over the same long period reveals that the pattern in the shorter time frame in Figure 3-10 is not unusual. A period that is as anomalous occurred during the 1929 Crash and the subsequent Great Depression.

12. Alternatively, the investor could estimate covariances, but it is difficult to develop any intuition about these numbers. Instead, most optimizers work with correlations, as the covariances can be easily computed from the correlations and standard deviations.

13. The magnitude of the Sharpe ratio is determined by investors' utility functions. If investors are collectively highly risk-averse, they demand large amounts of compensation for bearing risk, and the Sharpe ratio would be relatively large. See William F. Sharpe, "The Sharpe Ratio," *Journal of Portfolio Management* (Fall 1994), pp. 49–58.

14. Recall that in a segmented/segmented world, investors will set the risk premium for an asset class solely on the basis of that asset's total risk. Given the risk assumptions here, the risk premiums would be:

Equities	4.13%
High-Yield Bonds	2.50%
Fixed-Income	1.50%

15. The investor should develop an assumption about the risk-free rate, dependent on expectations for inflation and the real rate of return.

16. A more complete discussion and a review of the historical evidence on this phenomenon is found in Denis S. Karnosky, "Global Investing in a CAPM Framework," *The CAPM Controversy: Policy and Strategy Implications for Investment Management*, Association for Investment Management and Research, Charlottesville, VA. (October 15, 1993), pp. 56–61.

17. We are not arguing here that a manager hired to manage a specific asset class should not be given a benchmark relevant to that class. We refer instead to the risk the investor assumes for the portfolio as a whole, and the success of the asset allocation in achieving the objective.

Chapter 7:   Active Asset Allocation

1. See R. D. Arnott and R. M. Lovell, "Rebalancing: Why? When? How Often?" *Journal of Investing*, Spring 1993, pp. 5–10; and W. A. R. Goodsall, "Rebalancing to Benchmark: An Asset Allocation Discipline for UK Pension Funds," First Quadrant Corp., 1994, No. 4.

2. Returns between 1926 and 1993, from *Stocks, Bonds, Bills and Inflation*, Chicago, IL: Ibbotson Associates, 1993.

Chapter 8:   Asset Selection: Strategies and Evidence

1. Even the notion that governments are default-free can be challenged in markets where governments have defaulted on debt in prior periods.

2. By discrete, we mean that the rating agencies assign a rating to broad group of companies, say AA, and do not discriminate within this group. Only when the risk changes sufficiently will the rating change to AA+ or AA−.

3. When book value weights are used, the costs of capital tend to be much lower for many U.S. firms, because book equity is lower than market equity. This pushes up the value of these firms. This method may be attractive to the sellers of these firms, but very few buyers would be willing to pay the asked price because it would require the debt used in their financing to be based on the book value debt ratio, often tripling or quadrupling the dollar debt in the firm.

4. Richard B. Carter and Howard E. Van Auken, 1990, "Security Analysis and Portfolio Management: A Survey and Analysis," *Journal of Portfolio Management*, Spring, pp. 81–85.

5. E. H. Sorensen and D. A. Williamson, 1985, "Some Evidence on the Value of the Dividend Discount Model," *Financial Analysts Journal*, Vol. 41, pp. 60–69.

6. Suzanne McGee, "The Small Cap Effect Is a Myth," *Wall Street Journal,* February 10, 1997.

7. E. Dimson and P. R. Marsh, "Risk, Return and Company Size Effects on the London Stock Exchange: The Thirty Year Record," Working Paper, London Business School.

8. G. L. Bergstrom, R. D. Frashure, and John R. Chisholm, "Stock Return Anomalies in Non-U.S. Markets," in Robert Z. Aliber and Brian R. Bruce, Eds., *Global Portfolios,* Richard D. Irwin, Inc., Homewood, IL, 1991.

9. Y. Hamao, "Japanese Stocks, Bonds, and Inflation, 1973–1987." *The Journal of Portfolio Management,* Winter 1989; updated in Yasushi Hamao and R. G. Ibbotson, "Stocks, Bonds, and Inflation, Japan 1989 Yearbook," Ibbotson Associates, Chicago, 1989.

10. B. Graham, D. Dodd, and S. Cottle, "Security Analysis," McGraw-Hill, New York, 1962.

11. B. Rosenberg, K. Reid, and R. Lanstein, 1985, "Persuasive Evidence of Market Inefficiency," *Journal of Portfolio Management,* Vol. 11, pp. 9–17.

12. E. F. Fama and K. R. French, 1992, "The Cross-Section of Expected Returns," *Journal of Finance,* Vol. 47, pp. 427–466.

13. L. K. Chan, Y. Hamao, and J. Lakonishok, 1991, "Fundamentals and Stock Returns in Japan," *Journal of Finance,* Vol. 46, pp. 1739–1789.

14. C. Capaul, I. Rowley, and W. F. Sharpe, 1993, "International Value and Growth Stock Returns," *Financial Analysts Journal,* pp. 27–36.

15. E. F. Fama and K. R. French, 1992, "The Cross-Section of Expected Returns," *Journal of Finance,* Vol. 47, pp. 427–466.

16. A. J. Senchack, Jr. and J. D. Martin, 1987, "The Relative Performance of the PSR and PER Investment Strategies," *Financial Analysts Journal,* Vol. 43, pp. 46–56.

17. B. I. Jacobs and K. N. Levy, 1988a, "Disentangling Equity Return Irregularities: New Insights and Investment Opportunities," *Financial Analysts Journal,* Vol. 44, pp. 18–44.

18. R. Levy, 1967, "Relative Strength as a Criterion for Investment Selection," *Journal of Finance,* 22, pp. 595–610.

19. In Indian mythology, the sequence of worldly events is assumed to follow a preordained path, set by the gods, and no amount of human intervention or analysis will change this sequence.

20. W. F. M. DeBondt and R. Thaler, 1985, "Does the Stock Market Overreact?", *Journal of Finance,* Vol. 40, pp. 793–805.

21. N. Jegadeesh and S. Titman, 1993, "Returns to Buying Winners and Selling Losers: Implications for Stock Market Efficiency," *Journal of Finance,* March 1993, pp. 65–92.

22. J. Jaffe, 1974, "Special Information and Insider Trading," *Journal of Business,* Vol. 47, pp. 410–428.

23. The vagueness of the insider trading laws is intentional, since it leaves investors uncertain about what exactly comprises insider information and makes them less likely to trade on information that they might obtain. Recent rulings in the U.S. courts have expanded the definition of "insiders" to include those with fiduciary relationships with a firm.

24. M. C. Jensen, 1969, "Risk, the Pricing of Capital Assets, and the Evaluation of Investment Portfolios," *Journal of Business*, Vol. 42, pp. 167–247.

Chapter 9:   Investment Strategy

1. See, for example, Robert J. Shiller, "Do Stock Prices Move Too Much To Be Justified By Subsequent Changes In Dividends?," *American Economic Review*, Volume 71(3), 1981, pp. 421–436; and "Market Volatility and Investor Behavior," *American Economic Review*, Volume 80(2), 1990, pp. 58–62.

2. See Peter L. Bernstein, *Capital Ideas*, New York: John Wiley & Sons, 1992.

Chapter 10:   Trading Costs

1. See Robert D. Knott and Robert M. Lovell, "Winning in the Eighties: What it Took," *Journal of Investing*, Spring 1994, pp. 5–11.

2. Werner F. De Bondt and Richard H. Thaler, "Does the Stock Market Overreact?" *Journal of Finance*, July 1985, pp. 793–805.

3. Jack Treynor, "The Economics of the Dealer Function," *Financial Analysts Journal*, November/December 1988, pp. 27–34.

4. Kent A. Logan, "The Institutional Equity Business: A House Divided," Paine Webber, November 30, 1988.

5. Thomas F. Loeb, "Trading Costs: The Critical Link Between Investment Information and Results," *Financial Analysts Journal*, May/June 1983, pp. 39–43.

6. Andre F. Pérold, "Implementation Shortfall: Paper vs. Reality," *Journal of Portfolio Management*, Spring 1988, pp. 4–9.

Chapter 11:   The Hidden Costs of Trading

1. This was proposed in his article titled "What Does It Take to Win the Trading Game?", *Financial Analysts Journal* (January–February 1981).

2. This model is presented in Y. Amihud and N. Mendelson, titled "Liquidity, Asset Prices and Financial Policy," *Financial Analysts Journal* (November/December 1991).

3. See *1996 NYSE Fact Book* for a listing of the average spread across all NYSE stocks, by month.

4. See T. Loeb, "Trading Cost: The Critical Link Between Investment Information and Results," *Financial Analysts Journal* (May/June 1983).

5. R. D. Huang and H. R. Stoll, "Major World Equity Markets: Current Structure and Prospects for Change," *Monograph Series in Finance and Economics*, 1991–1993, NYU Salomon Center, 1991.

6. See M. Kothare and P.A. Laux, "Trading Costs and the Trading Systems for NASDAQ Stocks," *Financial Analysts Journal* (March/April 1995).

7. See S. Tinic and R. West, "Competition and the Pricing of Dealer Service in the Over-the-Counter Market," *Journal of Financial and Quantitative Analysis* (June 1972); H. Stoll, "The Pricing of Security Dealer Services: An Empirical Analysis of NASDAQ Stocks," *Journal of Finance* (November 1978); and N. Jegadeesh and A.

Subrahmanyam, "Liquidity Effects of the Introduction of the S&P 500 Futures Contract on the Underlying Stocks," *Journal of Business* (April 1993).

8. See F. M. DeBondt and R. Thaler, "Does the Stock Market Overreact?" *Journal of Finance* (July 1985).

9. L. Dann, D. Mayers, and R. Raab, "Trading Rules, Large Blocks and the Speed of Adjustment," *Journal of Financial Economics,* 1977, pp. 3–22.

10. D. J. Leinweber, "Using Information from Trading in Trading and Portfolio Management," *Execution Techniques, True Trading Costs and Microstructure of Markets,* Association for Investment Management and Research, Charlottesville, 1993.

11. See J. D. Rose and D. C. Cushing, "Making the Best Use of Trading Alternatives," *Execution Techniques, True Trading Costs and the Microstructure of Markets,* Association for Investment Management and Research, Charlottesville, 1993.

Chapter 12: Managing Portfolio Risk

1. The term structure of interest rates refers to the pattern of interest rates according to the maturity of the obligation. The term structure is flat if you can borrow funds for one year at the same annualized interest rate as borrowing for ten years, for example.

2. For some securities or commodities, selling the futures or forward contract is easier than shorting the underlying security. This can create an asymmetry in the arbitrage conditions. The forward price rarely goes to excess on the upside, but it sometimes goes to excess on the downside, because creating the downside arbitrage by buying the forward contract and selling the security may be more difficult. Thus, futures or forward prices can be more easily underpriced than overpriced, as indicated by implied repo rates that are sometimes less than riskless market interest rates.

3. Treasury note futures contracts are priced in the same way as Treasury bond futures contracts except that the eligible notes for delivery must have at least six and a half years to maturity at the time of delivery.

4. A full discussion of forward rate relationships is beyond the scope of this chapter, but the basic relationship serves to link two different rates in the term structure. For example, if the rate for a one-year investment is 6.0 percent, and the rate for a two-year investment is 7.0 percent, the implied forward rate for a one-year investment one year forward is found by equating the value of a two-year investment to a sequence of two one-year investments. That is,

$$(1 + i_2)^2 = (1 + i_1)(1 + f_1)$$

The one-year forward rate implied by the two market rates is

$$f_1 = \frac{(1 + i_2)^2}{(1 + i_1)} - 1 = 8.0\%$$

where i_2 = the two-year annualized interest rate
  i_1 = the one-year annualized interest rate
  f_1 = the implied one-year forward interest rate, one year from now

A sequence of investments earning 6.0 percent the first year and 8.0 percent the second year gives the same value as earning 7.0 percent compounded for two years.

The rate of 8.0 percent that equilibrates the two is referred to as the implied forward rate. Implied forward rates can be arbitraged using futures contracts if implied rates deviate very much from directly quoted forward rates in the futures market.

5. The put/call parity relationship is the arbitrage relationship that keeps the prices of the put and call options tied to the price of the underlying security. It is constructed in a similar way to the cash-and-carry arbitrage relationship for a forward contract.

6. We assume that expected dollar dividends to be paid will not change in the short run as the price of the security changes.

7. The hedge ratio that creates the minimum variance for the combined position can be found by taking the derivative of the position variance in Equation (53), setting it equal to zero, and solving for the hedge ratio.

8. The choice of the correct strike price of the call option again requires an iterative calculation since C_0 depends on the choice of K_C. For example, for $S_t > K_C$, we would have

$$V^{\circ\circ} = n[S_t - (S_t - K_C)] = nK_C = \frac{K_C V_0}{S_0 - C_0}$$

Chapter 13: Evaluating Investment Performance

1. "Marked to market" means revaluing an asset periodically on the basis of recent market quotations or actual trading prices for identical or highly comparable assets.

2. To be more precise, the SEC requires that all published performance information for periods beginning May 27, 1990, reflect the deduction of actual management fees and expenses, except where a manager is making a one-on-one presentation to an individual investor or to groups of individuals (such as consultants) who represent individual investors, where before-fee numbers may be used.

3. Investors in David Askin's Granite Partners a hedged fixed-income limited partnership investing in marketable collateralized mortgage obligations (CMOs) in 1994 lost virtually all of their investment because they accepted at face value the manager's asset valuations and reported returns based on those valuations. As it turned out, Askin valued assets at what *he* thought his securities were worth, rather than on the basis of dealers' offering prices, which Askin thought were "overly conservative."

4. Time-weighted returns were first introduced by Peter O. Dietz in "Pension Fund Investment Performance—What Method to Use When," *Financial Analysts Journal,* January/February 1966.

5. If an investor were to contribute a large amount of money to a portfolio just before a market downturn, and then withdraw it again at the bottom just before the market rebounded (an example of perverse market timing), the IRR would show a substantially more negative return than it would if the investor had left the amount invested constant. Managers should not be held accountable for an investor's poor market timing, nor should they be rewarded for an astute investor's excellent timing.

6. The most widely used method for handling cash flows is called the modified Dietz method. It asserts that the total return on an asset for each subperiod is equal to the change in market value plus income accrued plus any capital additions and withdrawals, all divided by the asset's beginning market value adjusted by a

weighted sum of the net capital additions and withdrawals occurring during the subperiod. The weights applied to each cash flow in the denominator reflect the percentage of the subperiod's days remaining at the time the cash flow occurs.

7. Proprietary universes are ones that the universe sponsor does not sell publicly, but may use in its own business license for use by certain subscribers for an annual fee. Purchased universes are widely available commercial databases and some require the user to construct his own rankings for any subuniverse.

8. Consider the theory of the "hot hand" in basketball. Ask a basketball fan whether a player is more likely to make his next shot if he has successfully made his last shot, and you will get a resounding "yes." Yet an exhaustive statistical analysis of the Philadelphia 76ers over a full season demonstrates that success on one shot or a series of shots has no predictive value for the next shot. In this case, the cognitive error is termed the "illusion of validity." It is different from the "illusion of consistency," in which the impact of chance events is attributed improperly to the effects of skill, but both these illusions directly contribute to predictive errors from extrapolations of past experience. See Michael L. Troutman, "The Steinbrenner Syndrome and the Challenge of Manager Selection," *Financial Analysts Journal,* March-April 1991.

9. See, for example: Edgar W. Barksdale and William L. Green, "Performance is Useless in Selecting Managers," *Pensions and Investments,* September 17, 1990, p. 16.; John C. Bogle, "Selecting Equity Mutual Funds," *Journal of Portfolio Management,* Winter 1992; W. Scott Bauman and Robert E. Miller, "Portfolio Performance Rankings in Stock Market Cycles," *Financial Analysts Journal,* March-April 1995, W. Scott Bauman and Robert E. Miller, "Can Managed Portfolio Performance Be Predicted?", *Journal of Portfolio Management,* Summer 1994; P. Dunn and R. Theisen, "How Consistently Do Active Managers Win?" *Journal of Portfolio Management,* 1983; W. N. Goetzmann and R. Ibbotson, "Do Winners Repeat?" *Journal of Portfolio Management,* Winter 1994; D. Hendricks, J. Patel, and R. Zeckhauser, "Hot Hands in Mutual Funds: Short-Run Persistence in Relative Performance," *Journal of Finance,* March 1993.

10. Address to the AIMR Conference on "Performance Evaluation, Benchmarks, and Attribution Analysis," Toronto, November 16, 1994.

11. In CAPM (capital asset pricing model) parlance, we are saying that the former group of managers have undiversified, high-beta portfolios, while the latter have diversified, low-beta portfolios.

12. Stephen A. Ross, "Survivorship Bias in Performance Studies," in *Blending Quantitative and Traditional Equity Analysis,* Charlottesville, VA: AIMR, 1994.

13. Some think that small accounts are easier to generate high returns with than large accounts, because equity position sizes can be smaller, and thus small account trades have less market impact. This view is debatable. But, still, one would hesitate to draw conclusions based on a comparison of College Retirement Equity Fund's $50 billion equity portfolio with that of a universe consisting of $1 million to $100 million 401(k) plan portfolios.

14. Strictly speaking, we should adjust Windsor's return to add back its average expense ratio before making this comparison, because the universe computes managers' ranks on the basis of gross-of-fee returns, and Windsor, being a mutual fund, reports its returns net of fees.

15. A benchmark that can be specified in advance is not necessarily investable, although the reverse is not true. An investable benchmark must be specifiable in advance.

16. See Jeffery V. Bailey, "Evaluating Benchmark Quality," *Financial Analysts Journal,* May-June 1992, for discussion of the characteristics of good benchmarks.

17. The point of this story is not to minimize Lynch's accomplishments. We merely suggest that it pays to ask: "Why was this particular benchmark selected? Is it broadly reflective of the type of securities the manager *really holds,* or is it biased in a material way?" Bond managers, for example, typically use the Lehman Government/Corporate Index as a benchmark because of its wide availability, yet many of these same managers invest extensively in mortgage-backed instruments that are excluded from that index. And large-cap domestic equity managers often stray into smaller-company stocks to boost performance against the S&P 500.

18. EAFE stands for "Europe, Australia, and the Far East." The index is a market capitalization-weighted index composed of individual industrialized nations' domestic equity market indexes.

19. We owe this terminology to Robert H. Jeffrey.

20. Hence: "In the investment business, you don't always get what you pay for, but you always pay for what you get."

21. Strictly speaking, this statement is true only up to a point: The ultimately best-fitting benchmark is one's own portfolio. By definition, however, it cannot be underperformed, so it is useless in performance attribution.

22. A fourth risk measure used in certain asset allocation applications is downside risk, or semi-variance. It has not yet received widespread acceptance in performance measurement applications, and space considerations prevent its discussion here.

23. To be precise, from a statistical point of view, lack of correlation means only that the two portfolios are linearly independent of one another. They may, however, be related in a more complex, nonlinear fashion that is undetectable using conventional statistical methodology.

24. For purposes of this discussion, we assume these ratios are annualized and reflect a one-year compounding interval.

25. For a more complete discussion, see William F. Sharpe, "The Sharpe Ratio," *Journal of Portfolio Management,* Fall 1994.

26. This measure was first proposed by Jack Treynor in "How to Rate Management of Investment Funds," *Harvard Business Review,* January/February 1965.

27. See Michael C. Jensen, "Risk, the Pricing of Capital Assets, and the Evaluation of Investment Portfolios," *Journal of Business,* April 1969.

28. William F. Sharpe, "Determining a Fund's Effective Asset Mix," *Investment Management Review,* November/December 1988, pp. 59–69.

29. For a description of Sharpe's returns-based "style analysis" methodology, see David E. Tierney and Kenneth Winston, "Using Generic Benchmarks to Present Manager Styles," *Journal of Portfolio Management,* Summer 1991, and Steve Hardy, "Style Analysis, Style Benchmarks, and Custom Core Portfolios," *Advances in Asset Allocation,* New York: John Wiley & Sons, 1994.

Chapter 14:   Taxes and Performance Evaluation

1. Using data from *Morningstar Mutual Funds,* the income and the capital gains dividends were "taxed" each year at 35 percent, and the "taxes" were deducted from the ending net asset value to arrive at after-tax returns.

2. In addition to realizing gains (or losses) when constituent companies are removed from the index (typically as a result of takeovers), index funds may also realize capital gains when liquidations are made to meet net shareholder redemptions. These realized gains, although incurred on behalf of the liquidating shareholders, who will pay their own capital gains taxes, are distributed at year end to the fund's remaining shareholders and are taxable to them. The little-known result is that *the Treasury temporarily collects two taxes on essentially the same gain*. (The second tax is temporary—assuming a stepped-up cost basis at death does not arise in the interim—because the continuing shareholders' cost bases are increased by the amount of the capital gains dividend.) Because of this double tax on redemption gains, the use of an open-end vehicle such as the Vanguard Index 500 as an after-tax performance benchmark *overstates* the tax impact of owning an S&P 500 index fund outright. See Bogle (1994).

3. Vanguard's Tax Managed Fund series seeks to minimize realized capital gains primarily by the imposition of fees (payable to the fund) on redemptions in less than five years, and by adopting the specific lot method of accounting for capital gains. In 1993, Charles Schwab introduced a somewhat similar product, the Schwab 1000.

4. While I do not intend to demean the spectacular long-term record of Fidelity Magellan, it should be noted that, over the period in question as well as since, the fund has enjoyed, because of its success, tremendous inflows of cash. This contributes to a "success breeds success" phenomenon to the extent that the fresh ideas purchased with the new cash dominate yesterday's mistakes.

5. Under the current law, the gain at maturity from a so-called market discount at the time of purchase is taxed as ordinary income. As the rate differential between capital gains and ordinary income increases, the benefits from tax swapping diminish. On the other hand, the tax-swapping benefit increases with the maturity of the replacement bond purchased, because the taxpayer has the use of the money longer.

6. See Flaherty (1994).

7. Using data developed by the Dickson and Shoven study, the Schwab 1000 expects to minimize and even eliminate capital gains realizations by realizing losses, but this strategy is dependent on having strong cash inflows into the fund with which to make new purchases. In a long-term rising market, without these new purchases at higher costs, the fund would have relatively few losses to realize during market downturns.

Chapter 15:   U.S. Corporate Governance: Lessons from the 1980s

1. "Taking Stock of the RJR Nabisco Buyout," by Steven Kaplan, *Wall Street Journal*, March 30, 1995.

2. The equity gains are based on the value of KKR's Borden holdings, $2.25 billion, at market close on 3/14/95 (the last day of trading before Borden shares were delisted), and the value of RJR shares transferred to Borden to strengthen its balance sheet on two separate occasions, during February 1995 and again during March 1995, $0.392 billion and $.640 billion, respectively. The original RJR LBO investors contributed about $3.2 billion in equity ($1.5 billion initially on 2/9/89 and $1.7 billion in the restructuring on 7/16/90).

3. Kaplan concludes that the poor return earned by KKR's equity investors was due to KKR's overpaying for RJR-Nabisco. Incidentally, he computes the return to

the equity investors to be "less than 3 percent." His return is slightly higher than the one we report because it is based on the average cost of KKR's investment rather than the actual cost, and apparently does not take account of the exact timing of the cash flows.

4. As revealed in the book, John Greeniaus, head of RJR's baking unit, told KKR that if "the earnings of this group go up 15 or 20% . . . I'd be in trouble." His charter was to spend the excess cash in his Nabisco division to limit earnings in order to produce moderate, but smoothly rising profits—a strategy that would mask the potential profitability of the business (Bryan Burrough and John Helyar, *Barbarians at the Gate* (New York: Harper & Row, 1990), pp. 370–371). Moreover, the *Wall Street Journal* reported that Greeniaus told it that the company was "looking frantically for ways to spend its tobacco cash," including a $2.8 billion plant modernization program that was expected to produce pretax returns of only 5 percent (Peter Waldman, "New RJR Chief Faces a Daunting Challenge at Debt-Heavy Firm, *Wall Street Journal,* March 14, 1989, p. A1).

5. Joseph Grundfest, "Just Vote No or Just Don't Vote," Stanford Law School, 1990.

6. Bill Saporito, "The Tough Cookie at RJR Nabisco," *Fortune* (July 18, 1988).

7. *Mergerstat Review* 1990, 1994, Merrill Lynch Business Brokerage and Valuation, Schaumburg, Illinois.

8. As reported by the Salomon Brothers High Yield Research Group ("Original Issue High-Yield Default Study—1990 Summary," January 28, 1991), as of the end of 1990, the face value of defaulted publicly placed or registered privately placed high-yield bonds in the period 1978–1990 was roughly $35 billion (about $20 billion of which entered bankruptcy). Given that recovery rates historically average about 40 percent, actual losses may well be below $20 billion. Not all of these bonds were used to finance control transactions, but I use the total to obtain an upper-bound estimate of losses. Although the authorities have not released the totals of HLT loans and losses, bankers have told me privately that such losses are likely to be well below $10 billion.

9. A 1989 study demonstrates that, contrary to popular assertions, LBO transactions result in increased tax revenues to the U.S. Treasury—increases that average about 60 percent per year on a permanent basis under the 1986 IRS code (Michael C. Jensen, Steven Kaplan, and Laura Stiglin, "Effects of LBOs on Tax Revenues of the U.S. Treasury," *Tax Notes,* Vol. 42, No. 6 (February 6, 1989), pp. 727–733).

Joshua Rosett (1990), analyzing over 5,000 union contracts in over 1,000 listed companies in the period 1973 to 1987, shows that less than 2 percent of the takeover premiums can be explained by reductions in union wages in the first six years after the change in control. Pushing the estimation period out to 18 years after the change in control increases the percentage to only 5.4 percent of the premium. For hostile takeovers only, union wages increase by 3 percent and 6 percent for the two time intervals, respectively.

10. Many of the most visible of these prosecutions by U.S. Attorney Giuliani were either dropped for lack of a case or reversed. The only RICO conviction, Princeton/Newport, was reversed (although other securities law violations have been upheld), and so too the GAF, Mulheren, and Chestman cases. For a brief discussion of pressures from Congress on the SEC to bring down investment bankers,

arbitrageurs, and junk bonds, see Glenn Yago, "The Credit Crunch: A Regulatory Squeeze on Growth Capital," *Journal of Applied Corporate Finance,* Spring 1991, pp. 99–100.

11. Safeway, for example, went through an LBO in 1986 and sold half its stores. It has since come back public and has also launched a record five-year $3.2 billion capital program focused on store remodeling and new store construction.

12. The discrepancy between the data and the impression left by critics turns on a confusion between the level and the rate of increase of R&D spending. While achieving record levels, R&D spending grew more slowly in the late 1980s.

In a study of 600 acquisitions of U.S. manufacturing firms during 1976–1985, Bronwyn Hall found that acquired firms did not have higher R&D expenditures (as a fraction of sales) than firms in the same industry that were not acquired. Also, she found that "firms involved in mergers showed no difference in their pre- and post-merger R&D performance over those not so involved." See "The Effect of Takeover Activity on Corporate Research and Development," Chapter 3 in *Corporate Takeovers: Cause and Consequences,* Alan Auerbach, Ed., Chicago: University of Chicago Press, 1988.

Moreover, a study by the Office of the Chief Economist at the SEC ("Institutional Ownership, Tender Offers, and Long-Term Investments," 4/19/85) concludes: (1) increased institutional stock holdings are not associated with increased takeovers of firms; (2) increased institutional holdings are not associated with decreases in R&D expenditures; (3) firms with high research and development expenditures are not more vulnerable to takeovers; and (4) stock prices respond positively to announcements of increases in R&D expenditures.

13. In their study of 20,000 plants involving control changes, Frank Lichtenberg and Donald Siegel find that changes in control reduce white collar employment in non-production facilities, but do not reduce blue collar or R&D employees. They also find significant increases in total factor productivity after both acquisitions and LBOs. See Frank Lichtenberg and Donald Siegel, "The Effect of Control Changes on the Productivity of U.S. Manufacturing Plants," *Journal of Applied Corporate Finance* (Summer 1989), pp. 60–67.

14. From 1977–1982, total employment fell by 336,000 from its high of over 1,000,000 in 1977. From 1982 to 1989, when the industry succeeded in gaining protection by means of import quotas, industry profits increased and employment in the industry rose to almost 840,000 even as U.S. automakers were losing significant market share.

15. Lester Thurow, *The Zero-Sum Society* (New York: Basic Books, 1980), p. 81.

16. See William A. Sahlman and Howard H. Stevenson, "Capital Market Myopia," *Journal of Business Venturing* 1, (1985), p. 7.

17. Stated more precisely, my argument attributes overshooting to "incentive, information, and contracting" problems. For more on this, see Jensen (1991), pp. 26–27. For some supporting evidence, see Steven N. Kaplan and Jeremy Stein (1993).

18. In 1991, I wrote, "As our system has begun to look more like the Japanese, the Japanese economy is undergoing changes that are reducing the role of large active investors and thus making their system resemble ours. With the progressive development of U.S.-like capital markets, Japanese managers have been able to loosen the controls once exercised by the banks. So successful have they been in bypassing banks that the top third of Japanese companies are no longer net bank borrowers. As

a result of their past success in product market competition, Japanese companies are now 'flooded' with free cash flow. Their competitive position today reminds me of the position of American companies in the late 1960s. And, like their U.S. counterparts in the 60s, Japanese companies today appear to be in the process of creating conglomerates."

My prediction is that, unless unmonitored Japanese managers prove to be much more capable than American executives of managing large, sprawling organizations, the Japanese economy is likely to produce large numbers of those conglomerates that U.S. capital markets have spent the last 10 years trying to pull apart. And if I am right, then Japan is likely to experience its own leveraged restructuring movement. ("Corporate Control and the Politics of Finance," *Journal of Applied Corporate Finance,* Vol. 4, No. 2, Summer 1991, p. 24, fn. 47.)

For some interesting observations attesting to the severity of the Japanese overinvestment or "free cash flow" problem, see Carl Kester, "The Hidden Costs of Japanese Success," *Journal of Applied Corporate Finance*, Volume 3, Number 4, Winter 1990.

19. See James D. Burnham, *Changes and Challenges: The Transformation of the U.S. Steel Industry,* Policy Study No. 115 (St. Louis: Center for the Study of American Business, Washington University), 1993, Table 1 and p. 15.

20. For this calculation, see Jensen (1993).

21. For a partial list of such studies, see the References.

22. In May 1985, Uniroyal approved an LBO proposal to block hostile advances by Carl Icahn. About the same time, BF Goodrich began diversifying out of the tire business. In January 1986, Goodrich and Uniroyal independently spun off their tire divisions and together, in a 50-50 joint venture, formed the Uniroyal-Goodrich Tire Company. By December 1987, Goodrich had sold its interest in the venture to Clayton and Dubilier; Uniroyal followed soon after. Similarly, General Tire moved away from tires; the company, renamed GenCorp in 1984, sold its tire division to Continental in 1987. Other takeovers in the industry during this period include the sale of Firestone to Bridgestone and Pirelli's purchase of the Armstrong Tire Company. By 1991, Goodyear was the only remaining major American tire manufacturer. Yet it too faced challenges in the control market: In 1986, following three years of unprofitable diversifying investments, Goodyear initiated a major leveraged stock repurchase and restructuring to defend itself from a hostile takeover from Sir James Goldsmith. Uniroyal/Goodrich was purchased by Michelin in 1990. See Tedlow (1991).

23. See Murphy and Dial (1992).

24. See Donaldson (1990). For a less technical version, see Donaldson (1991).

25. CEO turnover approximately doubles from 3 percent to 6 percent after two years of poor performance (stock returns less than 50 percent below equivalent-risk market returns [Weisbach (1988)], or increases from 8.3 percent to 13.9 percent from the highest- to the lowest-performing decile of firms [Warner, Watts, and Wruck (1988)]. See Michael Weisbach.

26. Myron Magnet, "Directors, Wake Up!" *Fortune* (June 15, 1992), p. 86.

27. See Kevin Murphy, *Executive Compensation in Corporate America*, 1992, United Shareholders Association, Washington, DC, 1992. For similar estimates based on earlier data, see Michael Jensen and Kevin Murphy, "Performance Pay and Top-Management Incentives," *Journal of Political Economy* 98, No. 2 (1990), pp. 225–264;

and Michael Jensen and Kevin Murphy, "CEO Incentives—It's Not How Much You Pay, But How," *Harvard Business Review* 68, No. 3 (May-June, 1990).

28. See G. Bennett Stewart III, "Remaking the Public Corporation From Within," *Harvard Business Review* 68, No. 4 (July-August, 1990), pp. 126–137.

29. This happens when the stock price rises but shareholder returns (including both dividends and capital gains) are lower than the opportunity cost of capital.

30. In their excellent analysis of boards, Martin Lipton and Jay Lorsch also criticize the functioning of traditionally configured boards, recommend limiting membership to seven or eight people, and encourage equity ownership by board members. (See Lipton and Lorsch, "A Modest Proposal for Improved Corporate Governance," *The Business Lawyer* 48, No. 1 (November 1992), pp. 59–77. Research supports the proposition that, as groups increase in size, they become less effective because the coordination and process problems overwhelm the advantages gained from having more people to draw on. See, for example, I. D. Steiner, *Group Process and Productivity* (New York: Academic Press, 1972) and Richard Hackman, Ed., *Groups That Work* (San Francisco: Jossey-Bass, 1990).

31. See Jensen, "LBOs, Active Investors, and the Privatization of Bankruptcy," *Journal of Applied Corporate Finance* (Spring 1989).

32. For discussions of such legal, tax, and regulatory barriers to active investors (and proposals for reducing them), see Mark Roe, "A Political Theory of American Corporate Finance," *Columbia Law Review* 91 (1991), pp. 10–67; Mark Roe, "Political and Legal Restraints on Ownership and Control of Public Companies," *Journal of Financial Economics* 27, No. 1 (September 1990); Bernard Black, "Shareholder Passivity Reexamined," *Michigan Law Review* 89 (December 1990), pp. 520–608; and John Pound, "Proxy Voting and the SEC: Investor Protection versus Market Efficiency," *Journal of Financial Economics* 29, No. 2, pp. 241–285.

33. For a review of research on LBOs, their governance changes, and their productivity effects, see Palepu (1990).

34. See Denis and Denis (1993); and Wruck and Palepu (1992).

GLOSSARY

Active management: Attempts to achieve portfolio returns more than commensurate with risk, either by forecasting broad market trends or by identifying particular mispriced assets within a market.

Actuarial liabilities: The estimated future payouts to beneficiaries of pension or medical funds predicted by the use of actuarial tables to estimate life expectancy, number of actual retirees, inflation and cost-of-living increases. These future payouts are then discounted by current interest rates and held as liabilities on a company's balance sheet.

Alpha: An investor's forecast of the rate of return on an asset in excess of the market's consensus. The latter is generally given by an estimated asset pricing model.

Alpha derivatives expense ratio: The annual operating expenses of a fund divided by the average assets under management. In taxable situations, expenses should properly also include capital gains taxes.

American option: An option that can be exercised at any time·

Annualized return: A return which, when compounded over the total number of years, produces the cumulative return from which it was derived.

Arbitrage: The simultaneous purchase and sale of essentially identical assets to profit from the price difference.

Arbitrage-free: No arbitrage opportunities exist.

Arbitrage-free valuation: Valuation of an asset that precludes arbitrage opportunities.

Arithmetic average: The probability weighted sum of a set of values. For example, the arithmetic average of a 10 percent rate of return that has a 60 percent chance of occurring and a 20 percent rate of return that has a 40 percent chance of occurring equals 14 percent.

Arrow-Debreu security: A security that pays $1 if a given state occurs and $0 otherwise. Also called state-contingent claim.

Ask price: The price at which an asset is offered for sale.

Asset: Something that is a store of future benefits.

Asset allocation: The allocation of investment funds to different assets or groups of assets.

At the money: An option for which the price of the underlying stock or bond equals the exercise price.

Balance sheet: The financial statement of a firm that lists the assets and liabilities.

Basis: Price difference between the underlying physical commodity and the futures contract. Cash price minus the futures price equals the basis of some futures, such as stock index futures that are usually priced above the cash price, the basis is often calculated as the futures price minus cash price so that the basis is a positive number.

Basis point: One hundredth of one percent, i.e., 0.01%.

Bearish: Pessimistic about a particular stock or the stock market as a whole.

Benchmark: An index or reference portfolio against which the investor's portfolio is compared.

Beta: A measure of the sensitivity of the rate of return of an asset to movements in the overall market.

Bid and ask spread: The difference between the bid price and ask price.

Bid price: The price that a potential buyer is willing to pay for an asset.

Black-Scholes model: A pricing model developed by Black and Scholes for a European option in an asset or security.

Bond yield: The yield-to-maturity on a debt instrument based on time to maturity, interest (or coupon) payments, and price of the bond.

Book-to-market ratio: The ratio of the book value of equity to the market value.

Book value: The value at which an asset is carried on the balance sheet, usually historic cost less depreciation.

Bullish: Optimistic about a particular stock or the stock market as a whole.

Call option: An option that gives the holder the right to buy the security at a specific price within a certain, fixed period of time.

Cap: An agreement that specifies an upper limit (a "cap") on the interest rate to be paid on a floating rate note. When interest rates exceed the cap level, the cap holder receives the difference between the interest rate and the cap rate.

Capital asset pricing model: A model of asset pricing that assumes that the expected risk premium of an asset (expected return minus the return on a risk-free asset) is proportional to its systematic risk, or beta.

Capital budgeting: The investment decision as to which projects a firm should undertake.

Capitalization: Total market value. A firm's equity capitalization is equal to its share price multiplied by the number of shares outstanding. An index is capitalization-weighted if the component securities are weighted by their relative market values.

Carry (cost of carry): A term associated with financing a commodity or a security until it is sold or delivered. This can include storage, insurance, and assay expenses, but usually refers only to the financing costs on bank loans, or dealer loans used to purchase the security or asset.

Cash-and-carry arbitrage: A theoretically riskless transaction of a long position in the spot asset and a short position in the futures contract that is desired to be held until the future expires. Such a transaction should earn the short-term riskless rate to eliminate any arbitrage profits.

Cash equitization: The strategy of using stock index futures to invest in the stock market while still retaining cash liquidity.

Cash yield: The yield-to-maturity on a cash instrument, typically a U.S. Treasury bill.

Central limit theorem: The proposition that the sum or average of independent random variables, which themselves may or may not be randomly distributed, will approach a normal distribution as the number of random variables grows.

Certainty equivalent: The amount of money that, if the individual were to receive it with certainty, would be regarded as equivalent to an uncertain sum.

Churn: Excessive turnover in a portfolio. Churning is sometimes used to simply demonstrate portfolio activity, or to generate unnecessary commission charges.

Cognitive bias: The tendency for investors to assign inappropriate (biased) estimates to probabilities and returns. The one example is a lottery with a chance in 10 million to win $5 million, which is perceived by many individuals as an attractive "investment."

Collar: The maximum and minimum rate of interest that will be paid on the par value of a floating-rate note.

Collateralized mortgage obligation: A security that is collateralized by a pool of mortgages.

Commission: The fee charged by a broker to trade on behalf of the customer.

Competitive risk: The unanticipated effect of competitors' actions (positive or negative) on a project's cash flows.

Complete market: Market in which investors can buy or sell combinations of securities that pay off in all desired states, i.e., in all desired circumstances.

Constant relative risk aversion: A description of risk aversion that holds that an investor allocates the same percentage of wealth to risky assets as his or her wealth changes.

Continuous return: The rate of return which, when compounded continuously, will cause an investment to grow by a factor equal to one plus the periodic return. For example, $1 invested for one year at an annualized continuous return of 9.53 percent will grow to $1.10. The continuous return is equal to the natural logarithm of the quantity, one plus the periodic return, minus one $[.0953 = \ln(1.10) - 1]$.

Contrarian: An investment approach which advocates purchasing assets which are currently unpopular or out of favor.

Convergence: The narrowing of the basis as a futures contract approaches expiration.

Conversion factor: An adjustment factor applied to the settlement price of the Chicago Board of Trade's Treasury bond and note contracts that give the holder of the short position a choice of several different bonds or notes to deliver.

Convertible debt: A debt agreement that gives the lender the option to convert the debt into stock.

Convexity: A measure of the change in the sensitivity of a bond's price to interest rates as interest rates change.

Correlation: A measure, ranging from −1 to +1, which demonstrates the tendency of two series to move together. A correlation of +1 indicates perfect positive correlation, so that the movements in the two series are always in the same direction (and same order of magnitude relative to volatility).

Correlation coefficient: A measure (ranging in value from −1 to 1) of the association between a dependent variable and one or more independent variables. A correlation coefficient is not necessarily a measure of causality but rather the strength of a relationship. A correlation coefficient of 1 implies that the variables move perfectly in lockstep; a correlation coefficient of −1 implies that the variables move inversely in lockstep; a correlation coefficient of 0 implies that the variables, as calibrated, are uncorrelated.

Coupon: The interest paid on a debt security.

Covariance: A measure of the extent to which a pair of variables moves together. It is computed as the average distance from the mean of one variable times the average distance from the mean of the other variable.

Covenant: A protective clause in a loan agreement to protect the lender's claim.

Covered call: A combination of a long position in an asset, futures contract, or currency and a short position in a call on the same.

Covered interest arbitrage: The purchasing of a money market instrument denominated in a foreign currency and hedging the resulting foreign exchange risk by selling the proceeds of the investment forward for dollars in the interbank market or going short in that currency in the futures market.

Cross-hedge: Exchanging exposure from one currency into another that is not the home currency of the investor.

Cumulative dollar return: Change in dollar wealth; total amount of dollars earned over a period of time.

Cumulative return: Percentage change in wealth, total percentage return earned over a period of time. Cumulative return is percentage change in wealth from starting wealth index to ending wealth index.

Daily settlement: The process in a futures market in which the daily price changes are paid by the parties incurring losses to the parties making profits.

Default-free: No possibility that promised payments will not be made.

Default risk: Risk associated with possible failure to live up to the terms of a contract.

Delivery: The tender and receipt of an actual financial instrument or cash in settlement of a futures contract, or the transfer of ownership or control of the underlying commodity or financial instrument under terms established by the exchange. The possibility that delivery can occur causes cash and futures prices to converge as the time for delivery approaches.

Delivery factor: See *Conversion factor.*

Delta: The ratio of the change in an option's price for a given change in the underlying asset or futures price.

Delta-neutral: A hedge position constructed using a combination of options, futures, and/or the underlying security that has a net delta of zero for the combined position.

Derivative asset: An asset whose payoff depends upon, i.e., is "derived from," the value of an underlying asset or variable.

Diminishing marginal utility: The notion that investors derive less and less satisfaction with each incremental unit of wealth. It follows, therefore, that investors suffer greater disutility from a decline in wealth than the utility that would accrue to an increase in wealth of equal magnitude.

Diversifiable risk: Risk that is specific to an asset. Also called *unsystematic* risk.

Diversification: The reduction in volatility which occurs by combining random variables which are not perfectly correlated. The volatility of the combined position will be less than the average volatility of the parts.

Dividend: Payment by a firm to its stockholders.

Dividend discount model: A model which estimates the value of a firm by calculating the present value of all expected future dividends, discounted at current interest rates.

Dividend yield: The ratio of a stock's dividends per share divided by the share's market price.

Duration: The effective maturity of a coupon bond, equal to the weighted average time at which cash income is received from the bond. Under special conditions, duration is also a valid measure of the sensitivity of a bond's price to changes in interest rates.

Dynamic hedge: An investment strategy, often associated with portfolio insurance, in which an asset is hedged by selling futures in such a manner that the position is adjusted frequently and simulates a protective put. Other option positions can also be created using dynamic hedging.

Early exercise: The exercise of an American option before its expiration date.

Earnings yield: The ratio of an equity's earnings per share (total company earnings/outstanding shares) to the share's market price.

Economic rent: Excess rate of return over the competitive rate of return from owning an asset or resource whose supply is fixed, or at least fixed in the short run.

Efficient frontier: Plotted in dimensions of expected return and standard deviation, a continuum of portfolios that have the highest expected returns for their given levels of standard deviation.

Efficient markets: The efficient markets hypothesis assumes that the prices of securities fully reflect all available public information. Investors buying securities in an efficient market should expect to obtain an equilibrium rate of return.

Efficient plane: Plotted in dimensions of expected return, standard deviation, and tracking error, a surface of portfolios that have the highest expected returns for their given levels of standard deviations and tracking error.

Efficient portfolio: A portfolio that yields the highest possible anticipated return for a given level of risk.

Empirical evidence: Evidence which can be measured and produced based on existing or historical data. Empirical evidence refers to identifiable historical data and events.

Endogenous: Determined within the model.

Equilibrium models: Academic or theoretical models that define equilibrium market conditions, conditions in which all assets are fairly valued relative to one another.

Equilibrium valuation: Valuation method that determines the value of an asset as that at which the model demand for the asset equals its supply.

European option: An option that can be exercised only on its expiration date.

Excess return: The return to an asset minus the return to the riskless asset.

Exercise: To invoke the right granted under the terms of the listed options contract to purchase or sell the underlying security. The holder is the one who can choose to exercise. Call holders exercise to buy the underlying security, while put holders exercise to sell the underlying security.

Exercise price: The price at which the holder of an option can force the seller to buy or sell the underlying asset.

Expected rate of return: The rate of return expected on an asset.

Expected shortfall: The probability of shortfall times the average shortfall when it does occur.

Expected value: The probability weighted sum of all possible values.

Expense ratio: A measure of all management expenses incurred against mutual fund values.

Expiration date: The date after which an option or futures contract is no longer effective.

Fair game: A game between two participants in which the expected outcome is equal for both participants.

Fair value: Normally, a term used to describe the worth of an option or futures contract as determined by a mathematical model or arbitrage relationship.

Fence: See *Collar.*

Fiduciary: Any person or institution who exercises discretionary control over the management of a plan or the management or disposition of its assets. A fiduciary is legally required to place client interests ahead of his or her own interests.

Fiscal policy: Government spending and taxation policy.

Forward contract: An agreement between two parties for the sale or purchase of an asset at a specified price on a specified date. Unlike a futures contract, forward contracts are not standardized and are not traded in a secondary market.

Frequency distribution: A summarization of data that shows the percentage of the observations that fall within specified ranges which collectively account for all of the data.

Fundamental analyst: Analyst who uses fundamental factors such as earnings, balance sheet variables, or management quality to gain insights about a company's or asset's value.

Futures: Financial instruments which derives their value from an underlying asset. A futures contract is a promise to buy (or sell) an asset at a set future date for a specific price. References to futures in this context are to stock or bond index futures, which are based on a underlying stock index, such as the S&P 500, or bond market, such as U.S. Treasury Bonds.

Futures contract: An agreement between two parties. One party agrees to sell an asset to the other party at a specified price on a specified date. Futures contracts are standardized and are actively traded on secondary markets.

Future value: The value of an asset or fund at a specified future date.

GAAP: Refers to generally accepted accounting practices.

Geometric average: A measure of return including that, controlling for contributions and disbursements, reflects the actual change in an asset's value. For example, if an asset increases 100 percent and then decreases 50 percent, its geometric average return equals 0 percent $[(1 + 1.00) \times (1 - .50) - 1]$. The arithmetic average return, however, is 25 percent $[(1.00 - .05)/2]$, which does not reflect the actual change in the asset's value.

Glamour stock: A stock that has performed well in the past and that the market expects to continue to perform well.

Growth rate: Often refers to the rate of growth of a company's earnings from year to year.

Hedge: A security transaction that reduces the risk of an existing position.

Hedge ratio: The ratio of options or futures to a spot position (or vice versa) that achieves an objective such as minimizing or eliminating risk.

Herd behavior: One person mimics the behavior of others.

Holding period: Holding period is the reciprocal of the turnover rate (e.g., a 5 percent turnover rate implies a twenty year holding period, a 20 percent turnover rate implies a five holding period).

Immunization: The construction of a portfolio of fixed-income securities whose return is protected against interest rate movements.

Implied forward rate: The forward interest rate implied by the yields of bonds with different maturities.

Implied repo rate: The cost of financing a cash-and-carry transaction that is implied by the relationship between the spot and futures price.

In the money: A call (put) option for which the price of the asset, future, or foreign exchange rate exceeds (is less than) the exercise price.

Indexed fund: A fund that keeps a portfolio of securities designed to match the performance of a market index.

Indexing spending rate: Annual withdrawals from a fund divided by the average assets. The term is most commonly used in connection with endowment funds, but the principle is applicable in other contexts.

Indifference curve: Plotted in dimensions of expected return and standard deviation, a curve connecting all combinations of expected return and standard deviation to which an investor is indifferent, because all these combinations convey the same amount of expected utility. This curve is typically positively sloped and convex (with expected return on the vertical axis), and its point of tangency with the efficient frontier represents the investor's optimal portfolio.

Industry-specific risk: An unanticipated effect on project cash flows of industry-wide shifts in technology, changes in laws, or changes in the price of a commodity.

Initial margin: The amount each participant in the futures market must deposit to the margin account at the time a buy or sell order is placed.

Insider trading: The trading of securities on the basis of private information.

International risk: The additional uncertainty created in cash flows of projects by unanticipated changes in exchange rates and by political events that affect foreign markets.

Intrinsic value: For a call (put) option, the greater of zero or the difference between the security (exercise) price and the exercise (security) price.

Leverage: For a company, this refers to the measure of debt to the total capitalization of a firm. For a portfolio it is the ratio of total market exposure relative to portfolio size.

Liquidity: Ease of converting an asset into cash.

Log wealth utility function: A function that maps wealth onto utility and assumes that utility is equal to the logarithm of wealth. This utility function, first proposed by Daniel Bernoulli, implies constant relative risk aversion and diminishing marginal utility.

Lognormal distribution: A distribution of returns that assumes the logarithms of the quantities, one plus the periodic returns, are normally distributed. A lognormal distribution is skewed to the right, which implies that the mean of the distribution exceeds the median. This skewness is caused by the compounding of random returns.

Lower partial moment: The expected value of the deviation of a random variable below a predetermined level raised to a power. The zero-order lower partial moment is equal to the probability of loss below the fixed point. The lower partial moment of the first order is referred to as expected shortfall while the second-order lower partial moment is referred to as the lower partial variance. If the fixed point is equal to the mean of the distribution, the lower partial variance is the semi-variance.

Margin: An amount of money deposited by both buyers and sellers of futures contracts to ensure performance of the terms of contract (the delivery or taking of delivery of the commodity or the cancellation in the position by a subsequent offsetting trade). Margin in commodities is not a payment of equity or down payment on the commodity itself but rather is a performance bond or security deposit or "good faith" deposit (also referred to as an initial or original margin).

Marginal utility: Within the context of portfolio optimization, the increase in a portfolio's expected utility associated with a small increase in exposure to one of its assets.

Mark to market: See *Daily settlement.*

Market down: A decrease in a security price because of changing market conditions.

Market index: An average (index) of the prices of a prespecified set of assets using a prespecified weighting scheme and computational method.

Market price: Price at which a security is traded in the market.

Market risk: The unanticipated changes in project cash flows created by changes in interest rates, inflation rates, and the economy. All firms are affected, but to differing degrees.

Market timing: Swapping between stocks and bonds (or groups thereof) on the basis of predictions that one group is over- or undervalued relative to the other.

Maturity: The date on which a contract expires.

Mean: The arithmetic average of a set of data. The mean is a measure of central tendency and is sometimes used to represent the entire distribution of data.

Mean return: The average return calculated by summing the product of a particular return and its probability of occurring across all possible outcomes.

Mean-variance analysis: An analytical framework in which assets are evaluated according to the mean or expected return and the variance or standard deviation of returns.

Median: The middle value of a set of data, where the data are ranked from smallest to largest. The median is a measure of central tendency and is sometimes used to represent the entire distribution of the data.

Merger: A combination of two or more firms in which the assets and liabilities of the selling firm(s) are absorbed by the buying firm.

Minimum-variance hedge ratio: The ratio of futures contracts for a given spot position that minimizes the variance of the profit from the hedge.

Monetary policy: Actions taken by the central bank to influence the availability and cost of money.

Mortgage: A conveyance of an interest in property as security for the repayment of debt.

Net cost of carry, or net carry: The net cost of financing, which is equal to the cost of financing (usually at the repo rate) minus the yield on the asset being carried.

Nominal rate of return: The rate of return of an investment where the purchase price and payoffs are measured in units of currency.

Normal distribution: The name given to a well-known probability distribution with particular bell-shaped curve. The normal distribution is symmetric around its mean and has zero skewness. About 2/3 of the probability lies within one standard around the mean, while approximately 95% of the probability lies within two standard deviations around the mean.

Operating cost: Cost incurred in transacting normal business operations.

Opportunity cost: The value given up from an action not taken.

Optimization: A mathematical procedure which maximizes expected return at any given level of portfolio risk or, alternatively, minimizes risk at any given level of expected return.

Option: A contract that gives the owner the right, but not the obligation, to do something. A common example is a European call option, which gives the owner the right to purchase an asset at a specified price on a specified date.

Out of the money: A call (put) option for which the price of the asset, currency, or futures contract is less (greater) than the exercise price.

Passive management: Buying a well-diversified portfolio to represent a broad-based market index. Passive management assumes that markets are "efficient" and that efforts to add value through active management will not add enough value to cover the trading costs.

P/E ratio: The ratio of a stock's price to its earnings per share.

Pension beneficiary: Refers to the eventual recipients of pension fund payments. It is the fiduciary's legal responsibility to ensure that all decisions about such portfolios are to the advantage of the pension beneficiary.

Portfolio: The proportions in which assets in some universe are held.

Portfolio insurance: An investment strategy using combinations of securities, options, or futures that is designed to provide a minimum or floor value of the portfolio at a future date. Equivalent to the payoff of a protective put on the portfolio.

Present value: The discounted value of future cash flows.

Price-earnings ratio: Price of a share divided by earnings per share.

Principal: The face value of a bond.

Probability distribution of returns: A schedule of all possible returns and the associated probability of occurring.

Probability of shortfall: The probability of a random variable falling below a predetermined point. The predefined point is often set at zero to reflect the probability of a negative value occurring.

Producer price index: A measure of the economy's underlying inflation rate. The producer price index measures the change in prices of a broad range of wholesale products (not consumer goods) against a base number from previous years.

Project risk: Risk that affects only the project under consideration and may arise from factors specific to that project or from estimation error.

Prospect theory: Prospect theory embodies the concept that investors value absolute gains and losses differently. As a result a gain does not offset a loss of equal magnitude and the investor will have a tendency to make decisions which takes this asymmetry into account.

Protective put: An investment strategy involving the use of a long position in an asset plus a put option to provide a minimum selling price for the asset.

Pure discount bond: A discount bond without coupon payments. Also called zero-coupon bond.

Put option: An option granting the holder the right to sell the underlying security or currency at a certain price within a specified period of time.

Put/call parity: The relationship between the prices of puts, calls and the underlying security, commodity, or currency.

Random variable: A variable that is not completely predictable.

Range forward: See *Collar.*

Real rate of interest: The interest rate measured in units of goods and services.

Rebalancing: Realigning the proportion of assets in a portfolio, typically to a fixed asset allocation.

Regression analysis: An analysis that describes the average relationship between a dependent variable (for example, stock market returns) and a set of predictive or explanatory variables.

Return: Price change plus dividend or coupon income on an asset. Return equals unity plus the Rate of Return on the asset, i.e., a return of $10 on a $100 investment equals a rate of return of 10 percent.

Risk adjusted returns: This can refer to any of a number of measures of returns per unit of risk. Typically it refers to the return that is earned above or below the return of a passive portfolio of equivalent risk.

Risk aversion: Investors' aversion to risk, where risk is measured in some given way.

Riskless asset: An asset for which the actual return is always equal to the expected return.

Risk premium: The expected rate of return in excess of the risk-free interest rate that an investor demands to compensate for the risks inherent in an investment.

Rollover: Reinvestment of money received from a maturing security into a similar security.

Semi-deviation: The square root of the semi-variance.

Semi-strong form efficiency: An expression of an efficient market theory that states that the present price reflects all the information contained in historical data as well as all publicly available information.

Semi-variance: The variance of a random variable calculated below its mean. For a symmetric distribution the semi-variance is equal to one half of the variance. If the semi-variance is calculated relative to a fixed point, it is referred to as the relative semi-variance.

Settlement date: See *Expiration date.*

Short sale: The sale of a security that one does not own and has to be borrowed to make delivery.

Signaling model: A model in which investors interpret others' actions and prices as credible signals about an asset's value or attributes when they are relatively uninformed.

Skewness: A measure of the lack of symmetry in a probability distribution around the mean return. A probability distribution with a longer right-hand tail is said to have positive skewness while a probability distribution with a longer left-hand tail is said to have negative skewness.

Spot: The characteristic of being available for immediate (or nearly immediate) delivery. An outgrowth of the phrase "on the spot," it usually refers to a cash market price for stocks or physical commodities available for immediate delivery. Spot is also sometimes used in reference to the futures contract of the current month, in which case trading is still "futures" trading but delivery is possible at any time.

Spot price: The price of an asset on the spot or cash market.

Standard deviation: In statistical terms, the square root of the variance. Standard deviation is used as a measure of volatility of a portfolio.

State-contingent claim: Also called an Arrow-Debreu contingent claim.

Stochastic: Random, probabilistic, nondeterministic (from the Greek word meaning "to aim at").

Stock: A piece of paper that certifies an ownership of a fraction in a firm.

Stock split: A proportionate increase in the number of shares outstanding without any monies received by the issuer.

Strike price: See *Exercise price.*

Strong-form efficiency: An expression of an efficient market theory that states that price reflects all information.

Swap: Exchange one asset for another.

Swaption: An option on a swap.

Synthetic security: A combination of securities that replicates the payoff of a different security or combination of securities.

Systematic risk: Also known as nondiversifiable risk. The risk caused by factors that affect the prices of all assets.

***t*-Statistic:** A *t*-statistic is a measure of how far a particular observation differs from an expected mean, measured in multiples of the standard deviation for the variable. A *t*-statistic larger than 2.0 is generally considered statistically significant, since there is less than a 5 percent likelihood that any random variable will stray this far from the mean.

Takeover: Activity to take control of a firm.

Tax swapping: Selling one security to realize a capital loss and buying another (typically similar) security. Because of the IRS "wash sales" rule, the purchase must not be "substantially identical."

Technical analyst: A person who studies the relationship among security variables such as the price, trading volume, and price movement to gain insights into the demand and supply for securities.

Term structure of interest rate: See *Yield curve*.

Time diversification: The notion that above average returns tend to offset below average returns over long time horizons. It does not necessarily follow, however, that time diversification reduces risk.

Time value: The difference between an option's price and its intrinsic value.

Total return transaction costs: All costs of purchasing or selling a security including brokerage commissions and the impact on the market price of the transactor's offer to buy or sell. For taxable investors, capital gains taxes are a major transaction cost.

Tracking error: The square root of the average value of the squared deviations between the returns of a portfolio and the returns of a benchmark. It is used as a measure of relative risk.

Tracking error (variance): The difference between a particular outcome of a random variable and a predefined point is referred to as the tracking error. The predefined point is often used as a benchmark. The variability of the tracking error is referred to as the tracking error variance or tracking error standard deviation. The term tracking error is often used as a shorthand phrase to refer to the tracking error standard deviation.

Trading cost: Cost associated with trading an asset on the market.

Trading volume: The amount of trading in a security during a given period.

Transaction cost: Cost associated with buying or selling assets.

Treasury bill: A short-term debt issued by the U.S. government that is sold in minimums of $10,000 and multiples of $5,000 above this minimum.

Turnover: Refers to the amount of trading in a portfolio divided by the total portfolio value, typically calculated on an annual basis.

Turnover rate: Turnover is the common measure of a fund's trading activity. It is usually defined as the lessor of annual purchase or sales divided by average assets.

Unanticipated inflation: The difference between actual inflation and expected inflation.

Underlying security: The security that an investor has the right to buy or sell via the terms of the listed option or futures contract.

Uniform distribution: A distribution in which there is an equal probability of experiencing each outcome.

Utility: A measure of satisfaction or happiness usually described as function of wealth or return. This concept was introduced by Daniel Bernoulli who argued that for the typical person utility increased with wealth but at a decreasing rate.

Utility theory: Utility theory provides a conceptual way of evaluating the utility or satisfaction derived from a given outcome. It can be used with prospect theory to indicate the asymmetry in comparing the relative value of a gain and loss of equal magnitude.

Value stock: The complement of glamour stock.

Variance: A measure of dispersion of a variable computed as the average squared deviation of that variable from its mean value.

Variance in returns: A measure of the squared difference between the actual returns and the expected returns on an investment.

Variation margin: Money added to or subtracted from a futures account that reflects profits or losses accruing from the daily settlement.

Volatility: Standard deviation of the return of a security.

Weak-form efficiency: An expression of an efficient market theory that states that the present price reflects all the information contained in historical price data.

Wealth relative: A value that is equal to one plus the periodic rate of return. This value is used to link returns in computing the geometric average, and its logarithm is equal to the periodic return's corresponding continuous return.

Window dressing: A practice where managers will non-systematically divest their portfolios of poorly performing assets to avoid the embarrassment of reporting assets that have lost value.

Yield: The percentage return of an investment.

Yield curve: The relation between bond yields and maturities. Also called term structure of interest rates.

Yield to maturity: The annual return on a bond held to maturity when interest payments and price appreciation are considered.

Zero-coupon bond: A discount bond without coupon payments. Also called pure discount bond if face value is unity.

INDEX